A Tribute to David N. Wilson

The World Council of Comparative Education Societies

The WCCES is an international organization of comparative education societies worldwide and is an NGO in Operational Relations with UNESCO. The WCCES was created in 1970 to advance the field of comparative education. Members usually meet every three years for a World Congress in which scholars, researchers and administrators interact with counterparts from around the globe on international issues of education.

The WCCES also promotes research programmes involving scholars in various countries. Currently, joint research programmes focus on: theory and methods in comparative education, gender discourses in education, teacher education, education for peace and justice, education in post-conflict countries, language of instruction issues, Education for All and other topics.

Besides organizing the World Congress, the WCCES issues a Bulletin in *Innovation*, the publication of the International Bureau of Education in Geneva, Switzerland, and in *CERCular* published by the Comparative Education Research Centre (University of Hong Kong), to keep individual societies and their members abreast of activities around the world. A web site is maintained, at http://www.wcces.net.

As a result of these efforts, comparativists have become better organized and identified, as well as more effective in viewing problems and applying skills from different perspectives. It is anticipated that we can advance education for international understanding in the interests of peace, intercultural cooperation, observance of human rights and mutual respect among peoples.

The WCCES Series

Series Editors: Suzanne Majhanovich and Allan Pitman

The WCCES Series is established to provide for the broader dissemination of discourses between its members. Representing as it does Societies and their members from all continents, the organization provides a special forum for the discussion of issues of interest and concern among comparativists and those working in international education.

This volume is the fifth of five, with their origins in the proceedings of the World Council of Comparative Education Societies XIII World Congress, which met in Sarajevo, Bosnia and Herzegovina, 3 – 7 September, 2007. The conference theme, *Living Together: Education and Intercultural Dialogue*, provides the frame linking the set. The books represent four major strands of the discussions at the congress, and a commemoration of the work of David N.Wilson, a major contributor to the field of comparative and international education and to the work of the World Council. Each chapter in this peer reviewed series has been developed from presentations at that meeting, as well as from contributions from former colleagues and students of David Wilson for that Tribute volume.

The books are: Tatto, M. and Mincu, M. (Eds.), *Reforming Teaching and Learning.* Geo JaJa, M. A. and Majhanovich, S. (Eds.), *Education, Language and Economics: Growing National and Global Dilemmas.*
Pampanini, G., Adly, F. & Napier, D. (Eds.), *Interculturalism, Society and Education*
Fox, C. & Pitman, A. (Ed.) *Comparative Education and Inter-Cultural Education*
and
Masemann, V., Majhanovich, S., Truong, N., and Janigan, K. (Eds.), *A Tribute to David N. Wilson:Clamouring for a Better World.*

A Tribute to David N. Wilson

Clamouring for a Better World

Edited by

Vandra Masemann
University of Toronto, Canada

Suzanne Majhanovich
University of Western Ontario, Canada

Nhung Truong
University of Toronto, Canada

Kara Janigan
University of Toronto, Canada

SENSE PUBLISHERS
ROTTERDAM/BOSTON/TAIPEI

A C.I.P. record for this book is available from the Library of Congress.

ISBN: 978-94-6091-260-3 (paperback)
ISBN: 978-94-6091-261-0 (hardback)
ISBN: 978-94-6091-262-7 (e-book)

Published by: Sense Publishers,
P.O. Box 21858,
3001 AW Rotterdam,
The Netherlands
http://www.sensepublishers.com

Printed on acid-free paper

TABLE OF CONTENTS

PREFACE

Remembering David Wilson

The circumstances of my meeting with David Wilson were slightly unusual. I met and came to know him in 1991 when he was the President of the Comparative and International Education Society (CIES). He and the society had chosen to hold the annual meeting of the society in Kingston, Jamaica in 1992. I was then a student at the State University of New York at Buffalo and was extremely keen to go. The only trouble was that I was (and indeed remain!) a South African. What was the trouble? South Africa at the time was governed by the *apartheid* government and a number of countries, like Jamaica, took extreme offence at its racist policies and refused to recognise it. My passport was, as a consequence, useless. Very interestingly the Jamaican government was prepared to issue a special travel document to me, as long as I could prove that my business in their country was legitimate. It was then that I turned to the President of CIES, David. David wrote a letter to the Jamaicans who then issued me with the papers that would make it possible for me to visit their country. And so began a special relationship between David and Southern Africa.

Southern Africans had been attending CIES meetings for many years prior to the nineties. Whether any had attended the Congresses of the WCCES is unclear. But it was with the establishment of the Southern African Comparative and History of Education Society (SACHES) that the possibility of the region becoming a member of the WCCES began to be formally discussed. The discussions in the WCCES were, predictably, difficult. South Africa remained outside of the United Nations and its structures, like UNESCO. Many questions were asked about South Africa and the role of "South African whites"—the beneficiaries of *apartheid*—in SACHES. What credibility did these people have and could they be trusted? It was during these discussions, first at Prague, then at Sydney, that David Wilson played an important leadership role in helping the WCCES come to understand the case of the Southern Africans.

Critical in David's participation in these discussions of the acceptability of the Southern African application was helping the WCCES work through the incredibly difficult politics of race. How these politics surfaced and were dealt with is not without significance for understanding David himself. The extraordinary issue of SACHES' members' colour, and by inference, their politics (were they really anti-apartheid people?), had arisen in the WCCES meetings. Whether it was *sotto voce* or direct is unclear, but the question, for instance, had come up of whether Harold Herman was white or not. What did it matter?, people like David had asked. And of course, few were to know that David had himself been subjected to a similar interrogation. In the course of doing a consultancy in Botswana during the 1980s, he had to pass through Johannesburg *en route* to Gaborone. He was stopped at the

Johannesburg airport by South African immigration police who questioned the validity of his Canadian travel documents. They thought that he was an "Indian" trying to sneak into South Africa on false pretences. This cemented David's friendship with a large number of South Africans and with SACHES. It was forged out of a real understanding and experience of how complex the South African situation was.

This relationship was to grow as SACHES made itself available to host the World Congress, initially in 1995 when it became impossible for the Chinese Comparative Education Society (CCES) to host the Congress. (It was then decided that the Australian and New Zealand Comparative and International Education Society [ANZCIES] would host the Congress in 1996). SACHES then offered again for 1998, when the Congress did take place.

David was enormously supportive of the SACHES bid to host the Congress. It took place in Cape Town during his presidency and allowed him to make a Presidential address which saw him expressing his full sense of internationalism. The Congress was a great success and yielded many fruits, both for SACHES and the WCCES. David successfully navigated a path forward for the two bodies to develop new approaches to hosting a large congress which have become standard features of how the WCCES currently operates.

In remembering David, I am personally grateful for his many acts of kindness, both large and small. I remember his thoughtfulness, his conscientiousness—remembering a simple gift—on the occasions of our gatherings. I see the twinkle in his eye behind his heavily framed glasses, a slight grin on his face as he quips about the state of the world. And so David brings you into his space.

But, organizationally, all of us in the WCCES ought to be even more grateful for the example he set for us all. In his personal demeanour, the way he carried himself, his bearing in meetings and in his interactions with all of us, not only was he unfailingly respectful but he showed us how to treat everybody equally. The WCCES is a complex organization. It has many venerable and truly important figures, many of whom are global leaders in their respective fields of scholarship, many of whom have made large contributions to the organizations they serve. It also has many young people who are making their way through the rules and idiosyncrasies of the comparative education community. In the midst of all of this social complexity David never lost his sense of correctness. He made sure that he would spend as much time with the young members of the WCCES as he would with his older colleagues. In so doing he was paying his respects to the "elders", but, as one himself, he was also taking seriously his role as a mentor for those younger than himself. In these ways he was committed to making the WCCES an inclusive organization. For this, all of us are thankful and remember him with gratitude and respect. It is largely for this reason that the Executive Committee of the WCCES took the decision at its meeting in Malaysia in January 2007, just after his death, to commission a book in his memory and to record its debt to him. I hope that this book will be read in the future as a fitting tribute to David Wilson's contributions.

Crain Soudien, WCCES President, November 2009

ACKNOWLEDGEMENTS

This book grew out of the deep sense of loss that his colleagues felt on the death of David N. Wilson on December 8, 2006. This sense was compounded by the fact that his final illness was diagnosed only a scant three months before his death. Because his family had set up a website in September under the auspices of *CaringBridge,* his many colleagues and former students from around the world were able to express their gratitude and sentiments to him in a public forum while his life was coming to its end. His website had nearly 4,000 hits in those final three months as family, friends, colleagues, former students and admirers expressed their thanks, respect and love. We owe his family our collective thanks for opening up a place where we could all say good-bye. This book is the scholarly extension of that feeling. His family has continued to support this effort, and we are very grateful for all of their cooperation and involvement. We also greatly appreciate the contribution to the introductory chapter of the written pieces by three of his children and their supplying us with David's bibliography.

The World Council of Comparative Education Societies (WCCES) met in Kuala Lumpur, Malaysia in January 2007, a few weeks after his death. At that meeting, they expressed their sorrow on the death of David who had been their Past President. Suzanne Majhanovich, Chair of the WCCES Publications Committee, suggested that the WCCES produce a *Festschrift* in his memory, and her motion was agreed upon. This book is the result of that decision. We owe our thanks to Mark Bray and then Crain Soudien as President of the WCCES, and to its Executive Committee, for their continuing support for this project. Panels were organized at the WCCES conference in Sarajevo in September 2007 and at the CIES meetings in New York in March 2008 where the preliminary versions of these chapters were presented. Three of David's children also attended the CIES panel in New York.

We also thank the Comparative, International and Development Education Centre at the Ontario Institute for Studies in Education, the University of Toronto, with Karen Mundy as Director, for their financial and administrative support. Two graduate assistants, Nhung Truong and Kara Janigan, were funded for a year each to assist with the very long editing job. They have also continued to work on this book after their assistantships were officially finished. We are very grateful to them for their untiring work.

We thank David's colleagues worldwide for their interest in and their support for this volume. In particular, we thank the colleagues who contributed so enthusiastically to this book and who did numerous revisions for us. Thanks are extended to all the external reviewers who were so punctilious in their work. We also thank the students and former students who submitted papers which, in some cases, they had originally written for David's classes or for dissertations supervised by him. We invited all of the contributors to mention briefly what was their connection with David Wilson and his life and work.

Suwanda Sugunasiri, whose poem opens this book, was a student of David Wilson's. He wrote his poem to express his admiration for the strength of David as he struggled back to life after his heart had stopped beating for 22 minutes—his heart which beat to the rhythms of many places and which "clamoured for a better world." Dr. Sugunasiri read this poem to David's family and friends during the shiva held at the Wilson residence in the days after his funeral.

Our appreciation also goes to Emily Mang at the Comparative Education Research Centre at the University of Hong Kong for her excellent Index for this volume. We also thank Peter DeLiefde and especially Michel Lokhorst at Sense Publishers for all of their assistance in the publishing of this book.

Lastly, our thanks go out to all of our colleagues in the Comparative and International Education Society of Canada, the Comparative and International Education Society (US), the World Council of Comparative Education Societies and on every continent who showed an interest in this tribute to David Wilson and who strongly supported this project. They were all of those who had met David at conferences, who had been advised, encouraged or interrogated by him, whose careers had been advanced by his support, who had chatted or argued with him, who had done research or consulting jobs with him, who had written or edited with him, who had dined with him in restaurants worldwide, or who had flown with him to or from the many countries he visited and worked in. This tribute is published here in the name of all of those who met David Wilson in his too brief but very full life's journey. May we too continue to "clamour for a better world".

The Unbeatable Beat

For Professor David Wilson

by Suwanda Sugunasiri

For 22 minutes
under the piercing glare
of the Emergency Room lights
you mocked
the Dragon
waiting
claws on the ready,
stopping your beat
giving your heart
a well-earned reprieve,
sucking in
the surround-energy
of a loving family.

A-plus
for valiant effort
though soon
in claw's grip
of the inevitable,
bloodying
your heart's resolve,

your beat zings
unallayed,
to varying rhythms
in distant Mozambique Botswana
tropical Sri Lanka
in neighbourly Latin America
in frigid Canada on the home-run,
your unbeatable beat
clamouring
through and through
for a better world.

SHARYN OUTTRIM, DIANNE WILSON, MICHAEL WILSON,
VANDRA MASEMANN, SUZANNE MAJHANOVICH,
NHUNG TRUONG AND KARA JANIGAN

INTRODUCTION

This introduction has come together through the efforts of David Wilson's children and the editors of this *Festschrift*. Each vignette pays tribute to a different facet of his dynamic life and work, dedicated to comparative, international and development education, and also illuminates his personal engagement and relationships with all those whose life he touched.

DAVID N. WILSON: EARLY INFLUENCES
BY SHARYN OUTTRIM

What is your favorite place in the world? This was the most asked question of our father, David Wilson, who would always respond quickly: "Favorite for what? Most historical? Best Asian food? Culture? Spiciest Indian curry? Best countryside views? Most delicious barbeque? Finest architecture?" and so on... Our Dad loved the world and saw the best of everything in places most people have never heard of. He would get a glint in his eyes as his mind traveled far away as he recollected the thousands of pleasures our planet and our people had to offer.

David believed that education should be experienced instead of just learned; he always felt that he did his best work, when he lived, worked and learned in the developing countries he sought so hard to improve.

How did an average boy born in Syracuse, New York in 1939 become the well-travelled Renaissance man so many came to know? We are often asked this question and after much discussion and retrospection, we realize the answer is as ordinary as David was not.

Esther, David's mother, came from an educated and accomplished family. Like many of the other women in her family, she was strong and determined. David's mother was the pivotal influence in his early years as she instilled the philosophy that anything is possible and that by figuring it out yourself as you go, you will excel. She was an unassuming, capable and calm person, whose deep wisdom and determination allowed her to outshine other women in her community. She was president of many educational, community and religious organizations over the years.

David's father Louis was a self-made man and the first in his family to get a university degree. He became a veterinarian by working to put himself through Cornell University. As a father, he challenged his boys to succeed educationally, and both of David's parents believed that a key part of learning was living. Thus was the beginning of David's adventurous life.

The oldest of three boys, David lived a typical middle class lifestyle, except for the annual adventures this family embarked on during the school year. His father would attend a veterinarian convention every year in different parts of the US and would pack up the family to drive the country for four to six weeks during the school year. Each boy was armed with his school work, but they learned history, geography and social studies by visiting all the places they read about in textbooks. Their parents brought their learning to life and thus created a hunger for exploration and adventure which was probably a key factor in David's keen interest in geography and history and desire to receive an undergraduate degree in Political Science and a Master's degree in Social Science and Education.

As a father, David carried on this untraditional family vacation with his own family. The big difference was that his horizon grew from North America to exotic places across the globe. He and Susan would pack up their growing family and often the dog to travel to his contracted jobs in Africa, Asia and Australia. They would take a month to get to each place and a month to go home. Yes, the children would be followed by Ontario correspondence courses no matter where they would end up.

So, the man that many came to know was molded in life early on by the richness of learning and living, by seeing and experiencing, by fulfilling the dream that anything is possible, not just for him but for all those that he touched.

DAD WILSON, A MAN BEFORE HIS TIME
BY DIANNE WILSON

David Wilson
A loyal member of the Audio Visual Club...a camper in the wide open spaces...photography fiend...fisher of the deep...a good word for all...true friend...conscientious worker...amiable
"Dave"

Yearbook, Nottingham High School, Class of 1956

To truly know and understand him was to love him. How poignant it is that I could not say I fully understood the many facets of Dad's personality and life works until it was too late to be able to discuss them with him. By the time my sister created the *Caringbridge* website and we were able to read the countless stories of David and his adventures, it was too late to discuss them with him. His memory had been stolen away from us by the cancer. The proud educator, although fluent in at least five languages, was having a hard time communicating his thoughts in his mother tongue.

He was a man connected to the real world, and well ahead of his time in many respects. It wasn't until my very "green" cousin came to visit me that I remembered how truly advanced a North American my Dad was. Eric, my cousin was showering in the guest bath. Upon thinking he was finished, I jumped into my master bath shower only to realize a minute later that Eric was merely shampooing his hair. My shower went ice cold as he turned the water back on to complete his morning routine. Bam, the memory came back to me about the time in the early 1980s, as I woke up early to obtain use of the shower in the number two slot instead of battling for hot water in fifth or sixth place in our family. In our comfortable North York home, we were fortunate enough to have two showers, so my competition was limited to the four "children". How many times was I steaming mad that I had prematurely jumped into the nice dry shower before any of my older and larger siblings only to have a few seconds to enjoy the hot shower. Dad, like Eric, was very conscious of preserving not only hot water, but all water. He would turn the shower on and off several times before he was finished bathing. When I would angrily announce to him later that morning at the breakfast table that I was once again frozen out of the shower, he calmly mentioned that he was being sensitive to our environment as well as the hot water tank. How many people did that in the 1980s? Yes, Dad was connected to the real world not only by caring about others but caring about our environment.

He saved everything for re-use. We even found old fuses in his workshop in 2009. Although they looked like foreign objects to me, Dad looked on them as possibly useful sometime or somewhere in the future. Moreover, he did not idle the car, and preferred the windows to air conditioning.

I came to realize how endearing my dear old Dad was to many of his longtime colleagues and students, and how many he angered by furiously sticking up for what he believed in. So many facets were revealed in the last months of his life and afterwards, so much knowledge that I am proud and amazed about.

Politically, he was ahead of his time. To grow up with the only home in the neighborhood who supported the New Democratic Party of Canada with a big huge yard sign on our corner lot, and realize he was not just eccentric but SO before his time was a huge revelation for me.

In matters of health, he was similarly progressive. I just saw him as silly ol' Dad who refused to be fitted for contact lenses twenty years after the first lenses damaged the eyes of early patients. Or the Dad who suffered through his slipped disk pain because years earlier the surgery had not always had the best success rates. Silly Dad even refused to consume pharmaceuticals to lower his high cholesterol. He set his mind to it and lowered his levels the "natural" way by cutting cheeses, shrimp and other beloved food items out of his diet. His doctor had never seen someone naturally reduce their bad cholesterol levels so quickly and effectively as Dad had. Too bad Dad was not so conscious of cigar and pipe smoking. Lung cancer would stake its claim on him at far too young an age.

Why is it that a man who dedicated his life to advancing our world was taken so prematurely from us? How many more nations, let alone families, could have been positively impacted by his passion for developing education systems in third world countries? How many people actually have this impact on "our" world? I am so very proud of my dear Dad!

DAVID N. WILSON, Ph.D., DAD
BY MICHAEL I. WILSON

It gives me great personal pride to be given the opportunity to say a few words about my father from a son's perspective. Most of my father's colleagues remember him as a fellow academic and scholar, while my siblings and I remember him simply as our father. The intersection of those two worlds came most often when he would travel for work and we would suddenly miss having him around. Growing up, I never understood exactly what he did for a living and even to this day, I'm not sure that I fully understand what he did. I am humbled to learn about the impact that he had on so many individual lives when it seems that the biggest impact he had was on our lives. He challenged us intellectually, pushed us to do beyond what we considered our best work in life and school, scolded and sometimes punished us for what seemed like arbitrary things. In hindsight, I think that he struggled to strike a balance between how he was raised and how he wanted to raise his own children and how things just turned out.

As I grew and as he saw me building my career and family, my relationship with him matured, and it's those memories and the stories of all the people's lives that he touched that I cherish the most. He stood by me and propped me up as I went through a long and troubling divorce and child custody battle; he drove by himself from Toronto to Baltimore over a half dozen times in as many years to stand by my side in court. Several years ago, I flew to Germany to spend a week with him while he was on sabbatical in Bonn and we toured the countryside together and had some wonderful experiences. I feel fortunate that he was by my side again as I remarried and later when my wife and I had another son. I thought that once he passed away, the image of my father would be set and wouldn't change; however, quite the opposite has happened. Memories and remembrances of my father have become enriched through opportunities to hear from his friends and colleagues and I find myself mixing and matching that new information in with my previous memories to create a new more complex image of my father.

He was not the perfect father, he was my father and I miss him and wish that I could share more of my life with him. Thank you for writing this book in his honour.

THE CAREER OF DAVID N. WILSON
BY VANDRA MASEMANN

David N. Wilson was born in and grew up in Syracuse New York, USA. He attended the University of Syracuse for his entire undergraduate and graduate education. He obtained his B.A. in Political Science in 1961, his M.Sc. in Social Science and Education in 1963, a Diploma in Eastern African Studies in 1968 and his Ph.D. from the Centre of Development Education in 1969. His thesis advisor was Professor Don Adams, and his thesis was entitled "The improvement of basic data used in educational planning: a case study-Malawi," available in the University of Syracuse Library. Professor Adams believes that David's experiences as a graduate student, the university's global commitment, and mostly, his international work and study and later international experiences all contributed to shaping his life's commitments. His interest in Africa and technical education was evident early in his career, and he served as Assistant Co-ordinator for the United States Peace Corps Training Programme in Technical Studies from 1964 to 1965. From 1965 to 1967 he was an Educational Planning Officer with the Ministry of Education of the Government of Malawi, under secondment from the Ford Foundation through the Overseas Professional Service Fellowship Programme, administered by the University of New Mexico, USA.

In 1968 he arrived in Toronto with his wife Susan and growing family that would eventually include Sharyn, Michael, James and Dianne. He joined the faculty at the Ontario Institute for Studies in Education (OISE) and the Graduate Department of Educational Theory at the University of Toronto as an assistant professor in the Department of Educational Planning, chaired by Professor Cicely Watson. Also arriving in Toronto just before him was Professor Joseph Farrell, his long-time colleague in what was to become the Comparative and International Development Education Centre. David worked at OISE until his (mandatory but unwilling) retirement in 2005, in the departments of Adult Education and Curriculum, depending on where the programme in Comparative, International and Development Education was located.

He taught courses in Comparative Education, Educational Planning, Development Education, Development Planning, Research Methodology, Evaluation, Occupational Training Programmes, and Technological Education, and others that reflected his special interests during his career.

He supervised and served on the thesis committees of many graduate students during this period at the Master's, Ph.D. and Ed.D. levels. Moreover, he met many students and junior colleagues from other universities at Canadian and international conferences and helped them establish themselves in their chosen areas of interest. Several of the authors in this book are among those students and colleagues.

He also undertook multiple overseas consulting assignments during various periods of leave and sabbaticals from OISE. In 1972, he served as a Specialist in the Administration, Planning and Financing of Education with UNESCO as Education and Manpower Planning Advisor to the Rivers and South-eastern (later Cross-Rivers) State Ministries of Education in Nigeria, under the United Nations Development Programme. Several of the papers here reflect his great interest and commitment to education in Africa. In 1976–77, he was a Project Officer in Technological-Vocational Education with the Asian Development Bank in Manila, Philippines. His missions that year took him to Nepal, Bangladesh and Burma; and he also evaluated projects in Thailand, Singapore and the Philippines.

In 1980–81, he was Honorary Visiting Professor at the Centre for Comparative and International Studies in Education at La Trobe University in Melbourne, Australia. That visit kindled a lifelong interest in Australian education. While in Australia, he conducted a research project on occupational training in Singapore and Malaysia. Then in 1986, he served as an Expert in Technical Education with the International Labour Organization of the United Nations to undertake a pre-investment study of the higher technical schools (industrial) in the Sudan for the World Bank. In 2000–2001, he was a Visiting Professor at the UNESCO International Centre for Technical and Vocational Education and Training in Bonn, Germany, and he continued working actively to develop that organization until his death. In the last ten years of his career, his interests focused increasingly on technical, vocational education and training, as well as on the use of technology in education. Several of the papers in this book reflect that interest.

These are all David's official projects during the period from 1970 to 2005. He also conducted a private consulting business which paralleled many of these interests. He conducted numerous evaluation studies of technical education and training programmes in Africa, North America, South America, Europe, and Asia, and feasibility studies for projected new educational institutions such as technical and community colleges. His published reports are too numerous to include here. His consulting demonstrated the strong link that he believed in between theory and practice.

He was very active in the professional societies in his field. In addition to his involvement in the field of comparative education (see the Suzanne Majhanovich section of this chapter), he was also active in the International Society for Educational Planning, of which he was President in 1999–2001 when he organized their annual conference in Toronto. During that same period, he was serving his second term as President of the World Council of Comparative Education Societies. He was also active on numerous other committees and boards during his career.

His publications are too numerous to list in their entirety. His publications were to be crowned by his editorship of the *International Handbook of Education for the Changing World of Work: Bridging Academic and Vocational Learning* which has now been co-edited by Rupert Maclean and published by Springer. It was published in 2009 after his death with him listed as co-editor and is dedicated to his memory. His colleagues at OISE, Karen Mundy, Kathy Bickmore, Ruth Hayhoe, Meggan Madden, and Katherine Madjidi likewise dedicated to him their volume on *Comparative and International Education: Issues in Teacher Education* (Toronto: Canadian Scholars' Press, and New York: Teachers College Press: 2008). The bibliography at the end of this chapter is a representative sample of his major academic works.

DAVID N. WILSON, CIESC, CIES AND WCCES PRESIDENT
BY SUZANNE MAJHANOVICH

When the news came that David Wilson had died, it did not seem possible. How could such a vibrant active person not be there any more? He had continued a full schedule of research and consulting after his retirement, and shortly before his death was close to completing an edited volume on technical and vocational education, one of his main interests. As former President of the Comparative and International Education Society of Canada (CIESC), of the Comparative and International Education Society of the US (CIES), as well as of the World Council of Comparative Education Societies (WCCES) he remained active as elder statesman, contributing his services and advice whenever asked.

He faithfully attended CIESC, CIES and WCCES conferences for many years from the First World Congress of Comparative Education Societies in 1970 in Ottawa (a fact he was very proud of) to the CIES meeting in Honolulu just a few months before his death in 2006. Moreover, he always came to his students' presentations to offer support and to start the discussion. In fact, it was at the CIESC conference in the early 1980s when I first met David Wilson. It was probably the first paper I had ever given at that conference, on immigrant women and their limited opportunities for jobs in Canada. The question David asked was a rather provocative one, and I was taken aback, even a bit offended. I wondered who this person was who was questioning my research. Later I realized that he was just being the consummate educator and challenging me to support my claims as any interested teacher would do.

Although David Wilson was never my professor, I learned a great deal from him about the many facets of comparative and international education from his presentations at conferences and his accounts of his experiences in the field. I greatly appreciate the concern David Wilson had for international graduate students in particular. Before our faculty had a doctoral programme, I often recommended promising students to David, hoping that he could find some way for them to continue their studies at the Ontario Institute for Studies in Education. More often than not, even in times of budgetary restraint, David did find a way to have these future comparativists admitted to OISE.

Because of his vast experience in consulting and research around the world, his interests related to comparative and international education were extensive. His *curriculum vitae* listed as areas of involvement technical and vocational education, as well as policy, globalization, multiculturalism, African education, aboriginal education and several other topics. After David Wilson's death, colleagues wanted to find a suitable way to honour his multitude of contributions to the field. As Chair of the Standing Committee for Publications of the World Council, I suggested that a collection of papers in his memory would be an appropriate way to commemorate David, and I asked his colleague and friend Vandra Masemann if she would consider editing such a collection with me. Fortunately Vandra accepted the challenge; and after securing approval from the WCCES Executive, we set out to publicize the project. We posted the list of areas in comparative and international education that David had been involved in and invited his colleagues and former students to submit abstracts of papers that might be included in the volume. The response was gratifying, with proposals for papers from many seasoned and esteemed academics and practitioners in the field around the world. Many former students also suggested papers. We were particularly pleased at the response from former students whose research and current careers had been influenced by David Wilson as their former professor and mentor or as someone they had met at academic conferences. Drafts of most papers were presented at sessions either of the 13th World Congress in Sarajevo, Bosnia and Herzegovina in 2007, or the 52nd annual Comparative and International Education Society (CIES) conference in New York in 2008. Authors received feedback and then submitted completed papers which were edited carefully by each member of our publication team consisting of Vandra Masemann, Nhung Truong and Kara Janigan, graduate research assistants kindly funded by the Ontario Institute for Studies in Education, and myself. Authors addressed our initial comments and resubmitted their chapters which were then sent out for blind review. Further revisions were made until the chapters as they now appear were ready.

We, the editors of this volume, believe the collection of articles honours David Wilson's longtime work in the comparative and international education field, and the areas to which he paid particular attention. We have enjoyed working on the project over the past three years, and I, for one, have learned a great deal about some of the many areas of endeavour that make up the field of Comparative and International Education that David Wilson was so actively engaged in over the many years of his estimable career. We hope he would be pleased with the outcome of the project and wish he could have been here to offer his informed commentary on these papers dedicated to him.

OVERVIEW OF THE CHAPTERS
BY NHUNG TRUONG

Every paper in this volume recalls an area of international and comparative education to which David Wilson contributed. The poem by Suwanda Sugunasiri, which opens this collection, refers to David Wilson's heart which beat to the "varying rhythms" of the places where he journeyed and which clamoured ceaselessly for a better world. From Africa to Asia to Latin America and throughout Canada, David Wilson left a mark, in resolve and dedication to making a difference in educational development.

We are pleased to include in the first two sections of the book many papers on African education and on technical and vocational education since David devoted so much of his career to those areas. In fact, his work has influenced many of the authors herein, one of whom spoke of a kind of epiphany he had after discussions with David on the importance of and need for vocational education in Africa, not just the usual post-colonial curriculum that did little to prepare people for the realities of their countries.

The first section is dedicated to his strong interest in Africa. The first chapter provides a broad overview of educational expansion and reform over fifty years since the end of colonialism in so many African countries. The authors note the parallel of this time period with David Wilson's "marathon professional career in comparative education", during which he also contributed to some of these reforms. Charl C. Wolhuter and M. Petronella Van Niekerk describe the shift from missionary and colonial education in the pre-independence period, to the impacts of the Addis Ababa declaration at the onset of independence as countries were seeking development, to the post-independence period with major efforts in expanding education across the continent. These reforms included the provision of education in conventional and unconventional ways including adult literacy programmes, distance education, Africanizing the curricula and emphasizing indigenous languages, and community-based initiatives. However, while some progress was made in the expansion of education over this period, many countries were also becoming indebted to donor countries and international funding agencies, with a resulting decline in public spending on education. Further, many issues of quality and equality in education remain. Despite progress, basic education is still beyond the reach of many, largely because of many social and economic problems, including the HIV/AIDS epidemic.

Looking more specifically at a country in Africa, Kingsley Banya reflects on polytechnic education in post-conflict Sierra Leone. In recent years, several African countries have emerged from conflicts which resulted in adverse effects on education, and have passed vocational and technical laws as part of the attempt to reconstruct and expand *Education for All* within the country. This chapter looks critically at recent laws in Sierra Leone, such as the Polytechnic Act and NCTVA of 2001, and the Education Act of 2004, to assess their implementation and impact on schooling in the country. The paper continues the tradition of

David Wilson's thinking that effective education should involve good planning and strong vocational/technical education for those students who pursue these types of careers.

The second section focuses on Technical and Vocational Education and Training (TVET), an issue that deeply interested David Wilson. He was specifically interested in how TVET could be developed appropriately in different contexts, particularly to promote development. David Wilson's contributions to the UNESCO International Centre for Technical and Vocational Education and Training (UNEVOC) were many. This set of chapters focuses on more in-depth issues in TVET in Nigeria, Poland and India.

Macleans A. Geo-JaJa looks at global factors and local trends affecting human resource development in the Niger Delta region of Nigeria in the 21st century. Education and training issues and challenges are discussed from the perspective of capacity building and poverty reduction, considering the poor education level and low skill level of the work force. The suggested solution is teaching and upgrading literacy and numeracy skills, in order to reach poorly educated citizens and those who have been excluded from primary and lower secondary school levels. The paper also notes the value of private-public partnerships to improve and expand continuing education and training in the region. It is considered, therefore, that reform should focus on content, delivery and resourcing. Further, the historical and political context should be taken into account, such as expanding technical, engineering and scientific manpower through promoting technical education and providing targeted scholarships.

The chapter by Ewa Kowalski describes reforms in the TVET system in the new political and economic climate of post-communist Poland. The post-1990 reform supported selectively-targeted training for graduates with a minimum secondary school education, while restricting such opportunities for graduates with basic vocational education. In consequence, the Polish labour market has failed to effectively utilize the skills of a considerable proportion of workers displaced from their jobs because of economic restructuring. The selectively-targeted training, compounded with the continued unemployment crisis and growing rate of migration of the Polish workforce to other European Union labour markets, demonstrates the critical need for a comprehensive, long-term approach to the planning and development of the Polish labour force, rather than one that fosters the use of short-term methods and solutions.

In the fifth chapter, Derek A. Uram paints a picture of TVET in India, highlighting major issues and developments since national independence in 1947. Various trends, especially related to globalization, have opened up new opportunities for employment, industry, communication, finance, and intellectual development in technology, innovation, and applied science. However, in spite of great economic gains in India, in which TVET has played a profound role, the constitutional goal of equality in India has not been met. Meeting this goal requires a comprehensive strategy and planning at all levels of education, also in conjunction with other public policy arenas, such as industrial, employment, commercial, and international policy. This chapter attempts to investigate the varying impacts of such developments on TVET in India, and relate them to the overall situation of development in the country.

The third section focuses on cross-cultural issues such as multiculturalism, teacher acculturation in international contexts, and aboriginal education policies. These issues are especially relevant today as people, ideas, and cultures continue to cross borders with increasing speed and magnitude, physically and virtually. David Wilson, who had studied anthropology, was always interested in the cultural context of institution building and educational development. Moreover, he was an inveterate crosser of borders.

Elizabeth Sherman Swing discusses the multicultural dilemma from the perspective of studies from Europe and the USA. In her chapter, she questions the concept of multiculturalism, which originally described the peaceful coexistence of groups with varying cultural, linguistic, intellectual, and religious norms. She looks at Ian Buruma's thesis that the murder of Theo van Gogh signaled a limit to the tolerance that previously characterized modern life in the Netherlands. Another topic raised is Ayaan Hirsi Ali's complaint that multiculturalism does not safeguard the rights of minorities, specifically Muslim women. Swing also examines Susan Okin's concern that the policies of Western governments aimed at preserving group cultures are actually in conflict with constitutional principles of individual freedom and equality between men and women. The chapter looks at the relationship between these developments to multicultural initiatives in Europe and the United States in the late twentieth century, as well as the Dutch sociological construct called the "Dutch pillars". Under consideration is the dichotomy between individual freedom and group rights, and the boundaries of protecting the group versus individuals within a group.

In chapter seven, Edward R. Howe analyses teacher acculturation through the lens of a comparative ethnographic narrative approach. He studies some cases of teacher acculturation in Japan, and sets these experiences alongside an auto-reflection on his own initial teaching experiences in Canada. This chapter is based on narratives of teachers encountered during the author's doctoral research, for which David Wilson was the supervisor. The "comparative ethnographic narrative lens" provides a potential framework for further comparative educational research, as an alternative to the more traditional nation-state unit of analysis. Through teacher-to-teacher cross-cultural conversations, stories were shared of experiences and challenges faced by beginning teachers, showing some transcultural commonalities. In Japan, the foundation for successful acculturation into the teaching profession is built on two pillars of education: kenshû (training or professional development) and shidô (guidance). His research showed that many novice teachers did not feel fully prepared for the transition from training to teaching on their own, and would have liked to have had stronger mentorship, although other more experienced teachers were helpful. Uram agrues that since many phenomena in education are culturally embedded and tacit in nature, they are better understood through micro-level ethnomethodological studies.

Kelly Crowley-Thorogood also takes an historical comparative approach in her chapter to look at indigenous education policies in Mexico and Canada. In state societies, formal education takes on a key role in the process of national incorporation and state formation, although this process could also result in national isolation.

In exploring Indian-state relations and education in the two countries, the paper compares such issues as the differing demographic statistics of the native population in each context, the importance of indigenous participation in large-scale political movements, and the presence or absence of the ideological element of *indigenismo*. During the first half of the twentieth century, governments in both countries used state institutions to mould the identity of their indigenous peoples to match their objectives. However, the chapter also discusses how the process was not unidirectional, as indigenous peoples could sometimes manipulate educational institutions to pursue their own objectives as well.

The chapter by Yaacov Iram, Nava Maslovaty and Eli Shitreet poses some serious questions about the acculturation of migrant minority youth in Israel. The paper looks at the attitudes of host populations, which can vary from rejection through passive tolerance, to support and even positive encouragement of variety, diversity and pluralism. Also discussed in depth are Berry's four possible acculturation strategies which immigrants can adopt: assimilation, integration, separation and marginalisation. Acculturation is a bidirectional process with interrelated changes occurring in both groups, although it could be argued that the attitudes of the host-majority members have the stronger impact on the acculturation preferences of the newcomer ethnic-minority groups. The authors propose a study in which the acculturation and adaptation processes of former Soviet Union and Ethiopian immigrants in Israel could be examined. The findings of such a study could assist in constructing varied acculturation models in diverse educational contexts to develop tolerance and social awareness by host and newcomer students. This chapter is also dedicated to one of its authors, Nava Maslovaty, who passed away before publication of this volume.

David Wilson was interested in questions of policy and aware of the potential of policy change for educational development. The next section focuses on policy concerns in various countries around the globe: Israel, Canada, Australia, Sweden, India and across the European Union nations.

In the tenth chapter, Norma Tarrow gives a historically comparative analysis of the impact and outcomes of policies and practices of education of the Bedouin of the Negev in two time periods thirty years apart. The review of socio-political factors, and realities and challenges identified in 1977 provide the background and basis of comparison for the 2007 field study, which included school observations, interviews with teachers, parents and administrators, and data from the Ministry of Education. The study examines such issues as attendance and drop-out rates, educational objectives, and budget and staffing, as well as the relationship of the "land issue" to the provision of education to children in government-planned, recognized and unrecognized sectors of the Bedouin society. The chapter concludes that there is now less danger of the Bedouin succumbing to government efforts to assimilate them into a totally western, urban lifestyle and more danger of an eruption of a formerly loyal society into active revolt against systemic discrimination in school and society.

The chapter by Rupert Maclean and John Fien suggests some lessons that can be learned from the private sector in the promotion of education for sustainable development. The topic is timely as we are now nearly at the end of the United

Nations Decade of Education for Sustainable Development. David Wilson had worked often with UNESCO and particularly its International Centre for Technical and Vocational Education and Training (UNEVOC), a hub for the network of organizations specializing in TVET worldwide. He had particular interest in TVET as contributing to sustainable social and economic development, and the role of public-private partnerships and the business sector in improving skills for employment. The authors examine cases of businesses and industry using education and training as part of Corporate Social Responsibility (CSR) policy and practice. Some examples include: corporate training programmes, partnering with local organizations and NGOs to provide community development and education programmes, and assisting education and training institutions with sustainability related teaching. This chapter is an invitation to learn from the private sector in recognizing motivations and overcoming barriers to take on the challenge of education and training for a sustainable future.

In the twelfth chapter, Melissa White, one of the final doctoral students of David Wilson, looks at issues of policy and practice in retraining initiatives for displaced workers in economically depressed areas. Specifically, the study looks at fisher workers in Atlantic Canada and Quebec who have been affected by the Canadian Federal Government moratorium on the Northern Cod industry. The Atlantic Groundfish Strategy was introduced by a government as a programme to restructure the fishery industry and provide re-training for those displaced by the closure. The chapter discusses why policy makers focused on education and training as a key ingredient for overcoming unemployment. The case study also illustrates why the problems of unemployment and goal of economic development cannot be achieved by focusing on a single policy issue. The problems that education and training are meant to overcome are far too complex for a single, short-term, often *ad hoc* approach.

The next chapter lends a critical perspective to higher education in Australia, another country of great interest to David Wilson as he took his family with him to work there, and his children attended school there. Anthony R. Welch looks at Australian education in an era of markets and managerialism, remarking on the increasing privatisation and commercialisation of higher education institutions, both old and new. Development plans include extending the numbers of private students, both national and international, and greater commercial exploitation of intellectual property. Universities contribute to this problem, making significant faculty redundancies, and over-enrolling students. In the face of this situation, student staff ratios have worsened appreciably over the past decade. The chapter examines such reforms, driven by an increasingly technicist, neo-liberal educational agenda, and assesses the extent to which marketisation has occurred. In addition, the use and abuse of performance indicators, and managerialist discourses and techniques of reform are assessed in arriving at an overall characterisation of contemporary educational reforms in Australia.

The chapter by Mina O'Dowd addresses another major policy issue today, the Bologna Process and its impacts on the re-structuring of higher education. The paper asks who will bear the brunt of unexpected outcomes of this re-structuring, looking at faculty, staff, students and other stakeholders in higher education. The author uses Torsten Husén's analysis of what constitutes the planning and implementation of successful educational reform, critically assessing the Bologna Process, in order to ascertain to what extent this Europe-wide initiative bears resemblance to the education reforms undertaken in Sweden over the last fifty years. The article concludes that none of the criteria posed by Husén as necessary for a successful education reform are found in the current Bologna Process. This conclusion gives rise to a number of vital questions, as to the nature of the Bologna Process and its consequences on universities and students in the future.

The issue of gender has been high on the international education agenda in recent years. In their chapter, Ratna Ghosh and Paromita Chakravarti look at implications of the National Knowledge Commission reports on women's education in India, from the perspective of equality, or rather, inequality, of educational and thus work and life opportunities. Although the rapid development of India can be remarked upon, its corresponding distribution of opportunities throughout its society has not been level, as was also noted in Uram's chapter. The National Knowledge Commission Reports cast the vision for education reform to bring the country further into the knowledge economy. The Structural Adjustment Programme in the country in the late 1980s led to cuts to educational expenditure at all levels of education. Changes in higher education included the growth in private colleges. Further, the National Commission Reports focus especially on science and technology, and English language skills. These priorities have serious negative implications for many female students, women and girls who are not largely represented in these fields of knowledge and who traditionally, and as argued by the authors, are still a most neglected segment in Indian society.

The three final papers are in a section designated simply as Comparative Education, and each one represents an area of particular importance to David Wilson. The effect of neo-liberal economic policies in a globalized world is an area that has consumed the interest of many comparative educators but none more so than David Wilson with his deep sense of equity and social justice. The development of the field of comparative education was always an abiding topic of interest to him.

In chapter sixteen, Carlos Alberto Torres writes about the crises and opportunities of neoliberal globalization and human rights. He identifies and addresses in particular five scenarios in modern society connected with more than 25 years of neoliberal globalization. Symptoms of a moral crisis include pervasive corruption in the public sector and lack of transparency in the business world. This conflict is also related to notions of tolerance in a diverse world, affecting how people of different backgrounds react to this conflict and to each other. The crisis of de-regulation sees the promotion of open markets and free trade on the one hand, and privatisation and decentralisation of education on the other. The resulting expansion of access to education does not necessarily guarantee an agenda of equity, equality and fairness in society, or the preservation of local languages and cultures, and in fact may be a mechanism that generates social exclusion. According to the author another crisis is that of human rights, immigration and multiculturalism as the bedrock of citizenship. How these notions are approached in education is a major issue of debate in educational policies and practice. The planetary crisis looks to environmental issues and idea of education for sustainable development. Finally, the epistemology crisis has arisen with the crisis of positivism as normal and hegemonic science, confronting more humanistic, social and cultural approaches to society and life. The author asserts that all of these crises can in fact be seen as opportunities in the field of education, to continue in the search for truth, as David Wilson did throughout his lifetime.

David Wilson was something of a linguist and had picked up bits of many languages through his work around the world. When in the presence of those of other linguistic backgrounds, he honoured them by inserting at least a few phrases of their language where possible. Thus Louise Gormley's paper on the role of foreign language fluency in the comparative education field recognizes his belief in the importance of knowing other languages when one works in international venues and contexts. Various comparative researchers are recalled, all of whom placed great importance on knowing multiple languages and living in other cultures. Isaac Kandel and William Brickman both emphasized the use of primary documents as sources of comparative research. George Bereday encouraged multilingualism in young scholars so that they could read about events or phenomena in different languages, and therefore understand different national perspectives. Harold Noah was also another notable polyglot comparative education researcher. Jürgen Schriewer compared Spanish, Russian and Chinese journals. Following the tradition of these scholars, the author relates experiences from her own field research in Mexico, where knowledge of the local language allowed deeper insight into the local realities of the people, and understanding of the nuances related to education in this context. She notes that having the comparison of Spanish with English also created interesting reflections on interpretations.

The final paper on the twin fields of comparative and international education addresses a long-standing debate within the field; namely, what comparative education is and does, and the role of international activities in the field. David Wilson, someone who was involved in both the theoretical and academic side of the field along with his hands-on activity in international situations, took up the challenge of the dichotomy in the field on the occasion of his presidential address to the CIES in 1994. In his judgment, the two facets were inextricably bound. In this last chapter, his longtime colleague on the World Council, David A. Turner revisits the question of whether the fields of comparative and international education could be conceptualized as Siamese or fraternal twins. The author notes the many developments in internationalisation and globalization since the year of David Wilson's speech, and argues that the comparative and international "twins" are now relatively amicably united and much more closely than before. The threat to the joint field now comes from the outside, rather than from any internal strife. This paper provides further philosophical musings on the topic and is, we think, a fitting concluding chapter to the book.

DAVID N. WILSON'S PUBLICATIONS, 1969–2009: A SELECTED BIBLIOGRAPHY
BY KARA JANIGAN

The following list of published articles, chapters, monographs, and books are a sample of David N. Wilson's scholarly works. David's most influential publications are noted below with asterisks. David also published numerous technical reports and papers which are not listed in this section.

REFERENCES

Africa

Wilson, D. N. (2002). Botswana: A different path towards development. *Educational Planning, 13*(2), 23–33.

Wilson, D. N. (1993). Foreword. In K. Banya, *Implementing educational innovation in the third world: A West Africa experience.* New York: Mellen Research University Press.

Wilson, D. N. (1984). Education and training implications of industrialisation models for Africa. In D. N. Wilson (Ed.), *Africa: A continent in crisis* (pp. 47–76). Toronto: Ontario Institute for Studies in Education.

*Wilson, D. N. (1978). Universal primary education in Nigeria: An appraisal of plan implementation. *Canadian and International Education, 7*(2), 28–52.

Wilson, D. N. (1976). National educational planning influenced by military government: Nigeria *Educational Planning, 2*(4), 64–83.

Rideout Jr., W. M., & Wilson, D. N. (1975). The politics of national planning: A case study of Zaire. *Educational Planning, 1*(3), 35–63.

Wilson, D. N. (1974). The interaction of urbanisation and education in three African states: Nigeria, Zaire and Malawi. *Canadian and International Education, 3*(2), 39–73.

Wilson, D. N. (1972). The role of rural, non-formal educational institutions in national development. In J. C. M. Shute (Ed.), *Issues in African development* (pp. 239–255). Waterloo: University of Waterloo.

Wilson, D. N. (1970). Education in Africa. *Canadian Journal of African Studies, 4*(3), 403–418.

Wilson, D. N. (1969). *The improvement of basic data used in educational planning: A case study - Malawi.* Syracuse, New York: University of Syracuse.

Technical and Vocational Education and Training

*Maclean, R., & Wilson, D. N. (Eds.). (2009). *International handbook of education for the changing world of work: Bridging academic and vocational learning.* Dordrecht: Springer.

Wilson, D. N. (2005). Promise and performance in vocationalising secondary education: Has the baby been thrown out with the bathwater? In J. Lauglo & R. Maclean (Eds.), *Vocationalisation of secondary education revisited* (pp. 71–90). Dordrecht: Springer.

Wilson, D. N. (2005). The education and training of knowledge workers. In J. Zaida (Ed.), *International handbook on globalisation, education and policy research* (pp. 49–64). Dordrecht: Springer.

Wilson, D. N. (2003). Workforce education. In J. P. Keeves & R. Watanabe (Eds.), *International handbook of educational research in the Asia-Pacific region (Part One)* (pp. 321–334). Dordrecht: Kluwer.

*Wilson, D. N. (2003). Planning technical and vocational education and training in Asia. In J. P. Keeves & R. Watanabe (Eds.), *International handbook of educational research in the Asia-Pacific region (Part Two)* (pp. 657–672). Dordrecht: Kluwer.

Wilson, D. N. (2002). Education, training and employment opportunities in the emerging knowledge-based economy. *Educational Practice and Theory, 23*(2), 5–27.

Wilson, D. N. (2001). Twenty-first century workers: Implications for technical and vocational education and training. *Sources (UNESCO)*, *13*(3), 10–12.

Wilson, D. N. (2001). Reform of technical and vocational education and training for the world of work. *Prospects*, *31*(1), 21–37.

Wilson, D. N. (2001). Technical-vocational adult education. In D. H. Poonwassie & A. Poonwassie (Eds.), *Fundamentals of adult education: Issues and practices for life-long learning*. Toronto: Thompson Educational Publishers.

Wilson, D. N. (1996). Reform of vocational and technical education in Latin America *Inter-American Dialogue, PREAL (Program to Promote Educational Reform in Latin America and the Caribbean)*. Occasional Paper No. 2.

Wilson, D. N. (1998). Reform of technological education curricula: A boundary-spanning approach. *Canadian and International Education*, *27*(2), 25–41.

Wilson, D. N. (1993). Reforming technical and technological education. *The vocational aspect of education*, *45*(3), 265–284.

Wilson, D. N. (1991). Reform of technical-vocational education in Indonesia and Malaysia. *Comparative Education*, *27*(2), 207–221.

Wilson, D. N. (1984). A comparative re-examination of the notion of institutional transfer as applied to technical-vocational education and training in developing nations. *ILO/Cinterfor Bulletin*, *1*(1), 5–30.

Cross-Cultural and Comparative Studies

*Wilson, D. N. (2004). A case study of PISA performance in Canada. In H. Döbert, E. Klieme & W. Sroka (Eds.), *Conditions of school performance in seven countries: A quest for understanding the international variation of PISA results* (pp. 15–64). Berlin: Waxmann Publishers.

Wilson, D. N. (2000). Development of the SENAI post-secondary sector in Brazil. *Higher Education Perspectives*, *2*(1), 82–95.

Wilson, D. N. (1994). What education and training for which future? A comparative perspective. *Canadian and International Education*, *23*(2), 27–60.

Wilson, D. N. (1997). The German dual system of vocational education and training: A comparative study of influence upon educational policy and practice in other countries. In C. Kodron, B. v. Kopp, U. Lauterbach, U. Schäfer & G. Schmidt (Eds.), *Vergleichende Erziehungswissenschaft: Heraus- forderung - Vermittlung - Praxis*. Köln: Böhlau Verlag.

Wilson, D. N. (1996). Comparative studies: Vocational education and training. In A. Tuijnman (Ed.), *International encyclopedia of adult education and training* (2nd ed., pp. 687–692). Oxford: Elsevier Science Ltd.

*Wilson, D. N. (1994). Comparative and international studies in technical-vocational education. In T. Husén & T. N. Postlethwaite (Eds.), International encyclopedia of education (2nd ed., Vol. 11, pp. 6261–6266). Oxford: Pergamon Press.

Wilson, D. N. (1992). Reform of technical-vocational education in the Eastern Caribbean. La Educación Revista Interamericana de Desarollo Educativo, 107(Ano XXXIV), 77–115.

*Wilson, D. N. (1992). A comparative study of the reform of technical-vocational education in Indonesia and Malaysia. In J. L. G. Garrido, J. M. M. Olmedilla, A. V. d. Santisteban & J. V. Ciordia (Eds.), Reformas e Innovaciones Educativas en el Umbral del Siglo XXI: Una Perspectiva Comparada [Educational reforms and innovations facing the 21st Century: A comparative approach] (pp. 363–385). Madrid: Universidad Nacional de Educación a Distancia.

Wilson, D. N. (1991). A comparative study of the transfer of the SENAI model of apprenticeship training to other Latin American nations. In C. d. M. Castro, J. B. Oliveira & D. N. Wilson (Eds.), *Innovations in educational and training technologies*. Turin: ILO Turin Centre.

Wilson, D. N. (1991). Innovations in educational technology for vocational training. In C. d. M. Castro, J. B. Oliveira & D. N. Wilson (Eds.), *Innovations in educational and training technologies*. Turin: ILO Turin Centre.

Wilson, D. N. (1991). Summary of lesson learned. In C. d. M. Castro, J. B. Oliveira & D. N. Wilson (Eds.), *Innovations in educational and training technologies.* Turin: ILO Turin Centre.

*Wilson, D. N. (1990). A comparative study of open universities in Indonesia and Thailand. *Canadian and International Education, 19*(2), 61–88.

Wilson, D. N. (1988). *Cognition in science and technology education: A barrier to third world development.* Paper published in the 13th Comparative Education Society in Europe Conference Proceedings, Budapest.

Wilson, D. N., & Rudnick, S. (1984). *A study of training needs of Indian bands in Ontario and the potential for Indian-specific training programs.* Toronto: Rudnick Research Associates.

Carnoy, M. M., Gorham, A. B., Morris, I. P., Teschner, W. P., & Wilson, D. N. (1988). *Education and development in Asia and the Pacific.* Manila: Asian Development Bank.

Wilson, D. N. (1981). *Education and occupational training in Singapore and Malaysia.* Toronto: Ontario Institute for Studies in Education (Sabbatical Monograph).

Wilson, D. N. (1981). Towards an anthropology of educational planning in developing nations. In S. Adesina (Ed.), *Introduction to educational planning.* Ibadan: University of Ibadan Press.

Wilson, D. N. (1974). A comparative analysis of four models in non-formal education: Denmark, Israel, Malawi and Côte d'Ivoire. *Canadian and International Education, 3*(1), 34–52.

Policy Issues

Wilson, D. N. (1997). Non-formal education: Policies and financing in the poorest countries. In J. Lynch, C. Modgil & S. Modgil (Eds.), *Education and development: Tradition and innovation.* London: Cassell PLC.

*Quazi, S., & Wilson, D. N. (1994). Macro level educational facilities policy and planning. In T. Husén & T. N. Postlethwaite (Eds.), *International encyclopedia of education* (2nd ed., Vol. 8, pp. 2225–2230). Oxford: Pergamon Press.

Wilson, D. N. (1991). Rates-of-return to LDC educational policy-formulation: Rejoinder to Walter W. McMahon's assertions. *Canadian and International Education, 20*(3), 76–83.

Wilson, D. N. (1990). *Exploratory study of technical-vocational education policy-making.* Jerusalem: Hebrew University Programme of Canadian Studies, Occasional Paper No. 10.

*Wilson, D. N. (1990). The deleterious impact of rate-of-return studies on LDC education policies: An Indonesian case. *Canadian and International Education, 19*(1), 32–49.

The Field of Comparative Education

Wilson, D. N. (2005). The World Council of Comparative Education Societies: A preliminary history. In D. Baker & A. Wiseman (Eds.), *Global trends in educational policy* (Vol. 6, pp. 289–308). London: Elsevier Ltd.

Wilson, D. N. (2003). To compare is human: Comparison as a research methodology. *Education and Society, 21*(3), 5–18.

Wilson, D. N. (2003). The future of comparative and international education in a globalised world. *International Review of Education, 49*(1–2), 15–33.

Wilson, D. N. (2000). The state of comparative and international education. In E. F. J. Lee (Ed.), *Education theory and practice in the new century* (pp. 113–135 in English and 127–153 in Chinese). Taipei: Li Wen Publishers.

Wilson, D. N. (2000, November 27). The prospects for comparative education in a globalised world. *Korean Universities Weekly.*

Wilson, D. N. (2000). *Methodologies in comparative education.* Dresden: Technische Universität Dresden, Gesellschaft für Vergleichende Pädagogik, Arbeitspapiere Internationale Beziehungen im Bildungswesen.

*Wilson, D. N. (2001). A prosopographic and institutional history of comparative education. In J. Schriewer (Ed.), *Discourse formation in comparative education.* Frankfurt: Peter Lang.

*Wilson, D. N. (1994). Comparative and international education: Fraternal or siamese twins? A preliminary genealogy of our twin fields (1994 CIES Presidential Address). *Comparative Education Review, 38*(4), 449–486.

Wilson, D. N. (1994). On teaching the methodology of comparative education: Why are there so few courses in Canada?" (1991 CIESC Presidential Address). *Canadian and International Education, 23*(1), 13–24.

Wilson, D. N. (1994). Comparative study of reforms in the post-compulsory education and training of young adults. *Comparative Education, 30*(1), 31–37.

SECTION I: AFRICA

CHARL C. WOLHUTER AND M. PETRONELLA VAN NIEKERK

1. 50 YEARS OF EDUCATIONAL EXPANSION AND REFORM IN POST-COLONIAL AFRICA

INTRODUCTION

David Wilson's marathon professional career in Comparative Education coincided with one of the biggest projects of educational expansion witnessed in world history, namely the expansion and reform of education in Africa over the past fifty years. The year 1957 may be pinpointed as the beginning of this reform, with the independence of Ghana, the first colony in Sub-Saharan Africa to become independent. David Wilson made a notable contribution to these reforms, having been active in education in various African countries over many years. He was also President of the World Council of Comparative Education Societies (WCCES) at the time of the Tenth World Congress of Comparative Education Societies, held in Cape Town, South Africa, during July 1998. As a tribute to David Wilson, this chapter presents a survey of the educational expansion and reform in Africa over the past fifty years—a project which also bears his mark.

THE PRE-INDEPENDENCE PERIOD

Missionary Education

With the exception of initiation schools, traditional education in Sub-Saharan Africa prior to Western contact was informal and took place spontaneously as a part of everyday life (Fafunwa & Aisiku, 1982; Moumoumi, 1968). Formal education was brought by missionaries from Europe who came to Sub-Saharan Africa during the nineteenth century. Since their primary objective was to convert the indigenous population of Africa to the Christian religion, education to promote literacy was very much a central part of their activities. The typical missionary station in Africa included a church, a hospital and a school. Generally, the missionaries offered elementary education only. Furthermore, this education was very academic. Only a very tiny fraction of the population was reached. Facilities were poor, as were standards.

Contemporary critical scholarly discourse harshly criticizes missionary education on two counts (Fafunwa & Aisiku, 1982). First, they condemn missionary education as being an agent of Westernization. Missionary education steered children away from their own culture into a new culture, and in that way taught them that African cultures were inferior. Second, missionary education has been accused of teaching

V. Masemann et al., (Eds.), A Tribute to David N. Wilson: Clamouring for a Better World, 3–15.

obedience (to God and to the church) and therefore promoting submissiveness to the prevailing socio-political disposition (colonialism) rather than equipping students with the tools necessary for free intellectual inquiry (Kallaway, 2007).

Colonial Education

During the last quarter of the nineteenth century, Africa was carved up and divided among England, France, Portugal and Germany as each staked their colonial claims in the "scramble for Africa" (Pakenham, 1991). Over the course of time, the colonial administrations also became involved in the provision of education. Originally, these colonial governments merely supported missionary education financially; later they established schools themselves. These schools served the indigenous population sparsely and were usually limited to elementary education. The essential aim of this education was to supply the subordinate personnel necessary for the effective functioning of the colonial administration, such as clerks and interpreters, employees in commerce, nurses and veterinary assistants, elementary and secondary school teachers, assistants to doctors, and workers in various fields (Moumoumi, 1968). In colonies with a substantial segment of the population of European descent (generally in Southern, Central and Eastern Africa), racially segregated school systems came into being. In contrast to the inferior schools provided for the indigenous population, those catering to the Whites were very good—on a par with schools found in Europe.

Surging Expectations

During the decades immediately following the Second World War, there was pressure in the international climate for weakened European powers to prepare their colonies for independence. In contrast to the motivations that the colonial powers may have had for education (as previously outlined), national leaders in the colonies as well as international aid providers and social scientists had other views on education. After the advent of theories such as human capital theory and development theory, education came to be seen not only as one (or the main) instrument for effecting economic growth and development, but as a panacea for every societal problem. In the context of newly independent African states, with borders arbitrarily drawn during the colonial era by European powers, education came to be seen as an instrument of moulding national unity, of producing a nascent civil service and of educating the populace to participate in the political process (Cowan, O'Connell & Scalon, 1965; Idenburg, 1975; Thompson, 1981). In 1960, on the eve of Africa's independence, with an adult literacy rate of nine per cent and primary, secondary and tertiary enrolment ratios of 44 per cent, five per cent and one per cent respectively, the stage was set for a massive expansion of education.

THE EDUCATION DECLARATION OF ADDIS ABABA AND BEYOND

The majority of African countries gained independence circa 1960. Losing little time, the Ministers of Education of the 36 newly independent African countries met in Addis Ababa, Ethiopia, from 15 to 25 May 1961, and drafted an *Outline of a Plan for Educational Development in Africa* (UNESCO, 1961). They stated the economic rationale for the immediate expansion of education in chapter two (dealing with economics and education), namely, that educational expansion would produce economic growth. Ambitious quantitative targets were set for the expansion of education: specifically, to achieve universal primary education, a 23 per cent secondary school enrolment ratio, and a two per cent tertiary education enrolment ratio, all by 1980 (UNESCO, 1961). A plea was also made that education be relevant to the current needs and situation in Africa. Curricula and textbooks were to be reformed to reflect the African environment and cultural heritage, and education had to be aligned to the economic needs of African countries. The objective was to provide more technical, vocational and agricultural education, and less academic content in education programmes. Attention was drawn to the fact that half of the teachers in Africa were unqualified, and therefore the expansion of teacher training had to be a priority.

The Addis Ababa conference was followed by conferences of the Ministers of Education of African States (MINEDAF) at regular intervals:
- MINEDAF II: Abidjan, Côte d'Ivoire, 17–24 March 1964;
- MINEDAF III: Nairobi, Kenya, 16–27 July 1968;
- MINEDAF IV: Lagos, Nigeria, 27 January - 4 February 1976;
- MINEDAF V: Harare, Zimbabwe, 28 June - 3 July 1982;
- MINEDAF VI: Dakar, Senegal, 2–6 July 1991;
- MINEDAF VII: Durban, South Africa, 20–24 April 1998;
- and MINEDAF VIII: Dar es Salaam, Tanzania: 2–6 December 2002.

The main themes of the Addis Ababa conference were repeated at the subsequent meetings: the expansion of education provision and enrolments, adult literacy, Africanization of curricula, increasing teacher training capacity, and linking education with the economy and job market. Other themes were added in the course of time. At the Nairobi conference (Anonymous, 1969) and thereafter, the need to replace ex-colonial languages with indigenous languages as the medium of instruction was mooted. At the Lagos conference, colonial examination systems were criticized (UNESCO, 1977). The objection was that the inherited examination systems tended to test whether or not students were ready to proceed to the next level of education, rather than assessing the abilities of students to use their abilities to serve their communities. From the 1991 Dakar conference onwards, the deterioration of educational quality attracted attention. The economic decline of Africa in the 1980s and eventual cuts in governmental spending, forced by structural adjustment agreements signed with the International Monetary Fund and the World Bank by the late 1980s, necessarily led to drastic curtailments in educational spending. Coupled with a persistent enrolment explosion, a decline in educational quality materialized. Addressing this decline in relation to the amount of public funds available for education, calls were made to enlist community participation in the building of schools.

In the wake of the worldwide surge of the concept and promotion of lifelong learning, and in particular the Hamburg Declaration and the Agenda for the Future adopted by the Fifth Conference on Adult Education held in Hamburg in 1997, lifelong education entered into discussions at the Durban and Dar es Salaam conferences.

5

THE POST-INDEPENDENCE PERIOD

The Addis Ababa Declaration was followed by massive efforts in educational expansion. Education became the single biggest item on the public budgets of African countries, regularly claiming a quarter of the national budget (Hawes & Coombe, 1984) and sometimes more. For example, 45.8 per cent of Côte d'Ivoire's 1988 national budget was allocated to education. Between 1960 and 1968, educational expenditure in Africa doubled (Kareklas, 1980). Throughout Africa, many kinds of strategies and endeavours were undertaken to raise the educational standard of the people and to adapt education to the African reality. A detailed account of these efforts follows.

Linear Expansion

The first strategy followed by independent African countries was the linear expansion of existing, inherited education systems, in a process that Coombs (1985) called "more of the same" (p. 3). The resulting enrolment growth during the first two post-independence decades is presented in Table 1.

Table 1. Enrolment growth in Africa, 1960–1980 (numbers of students in thousands)

Year Level	1960	1970	1980
Primary	19 312	33 372	61 284
Secondary	1 885	5 353	13 738

From Coombs, 1985, p. 74; UNESCO, 1997, p. 2–9.

Expanding the Provision of Education in Unconventional Ways

Multiple-shift schooling was introduced in areas of high population density as a way to overcome the shortage of school buildings and of qualified teachers. On the other end of the spectrum, multi-grade schools (that is, one teacher responsible for teaching several grades in one classroom) were introduced in the low population density areas of the Sahel countries (such as Burkina Faso, Guinea, Mali, Togo and Mauritania). In efforts to supply education to nomadic communities, Somalia tried a short-lived experiment with mobile teaching units in the 1960s.

Eradicating Adult Illiteracy

Most African countries at the time of independence attempted to reduce the high levels of adult illiteracy prevalent in their countries by various means. Bhola (1990) describes three literacy approaches used by African governments: the project approach, the programme approach, and the campaign approach. The literacy project approach is the most conservative of the three. These projects are small in scale—for example, the integrated literacy project in Mali since the 1960s (Turritin, 1989).

The literacy programme is a nationwide approach under bureaucratic control; an example is the Botswana National Literacy Program launched by the Ministry of Non-Formal Education in 1980. The campaign approach is big in scale and involves high political fervour and popular mobilization. Examples of the campaign approach are the Somali urban and rural literacy campaigns (1973 and 1974, respectively). The most comprehensive adult literacy campaign in Africa was that of Tanzania in the 1970s (Nyerere, 1985). According to Arnove (1982), in the worldwide history of literacy campaigns, there are three that stand out as the most remarkable: Cuba in 1961, Nicaragua in 1980, and Tanzania in the 1970s.

Distance Education

Faced with a dearth of school buildings and qualified teachers, many African countries have looked to distance education projects to increase participation in education. The financial constraints since the 1980s have given further reason to expand distance education.

Africanization of Curricula

Post-independence education reform in Africa has been characterized by attempts to change curricular content to reflect the natural and cultural heritage, cultures, world-views, ideals, attitudes and values of the erstwhile colonial powers to those of Africa (Merryfield & Tlou, 1995). Despite these efforts, schools in Sub-Saharan Africa still quite visibly carry the mark of their European origins as far as organization, curricula, textbooks, language of instruction and examinations are concerned. Rayfield (1994) writes of a case in Francophone West Africa, where a 1940s textbook, with few changes, was still being used in the 1980s. In Côte d'Ivoire since independence, three major attempts failed to dismantle the French-modelled education system (Assié-Lumumba & Lumumba-Kasongo, 1991). When a South African author writing on education in Côte d'Ivoire approached the cultural attaché of Côte d'Ivoire in Pretoria for information, the author was met with the answer, "notre système éducatif est exactement comme celui de la France" ["our education system is exactly like that of France"] (Wolhuter, 2000, p. 163).

Developing Indigenous African Languages as the Media of Teaching

At the 1964 Abidjan conference, the sentiment was still in favour of retaining the ex-colonial languages as the media of instruction in schools. However, in an about-turn at the 1968 Nairobi conference, calls were made for the replacement of ex-colonial languages with indigenous African languages (Anonymous, 1969). At the 1976 Lagos conference, these calls rose to passionate pleas. Apart from a few limited cases, the situation in Sub-Saharan Africa has remained unchanged: at some level in the primary school cycle, vernaculars are replaced by the ex-colonial language as the medium of instruction. In Anglophone Africa, 20–25 per cent of the adult population are proficient in English. Similarly, 10–15 per cent of the

7

adult population of Francophone Africa are proficient in French, and five per cent of adults in Lusophone Africa are proficient in Portuguese. On the other hand, it is accepted that a primary school pupil requires a vocabulary of at least 3,000 words in a given language to benefit from education offered through the medium of that language. Considering these factors together, the damaging effect of a continual employment of the ex-colonial language as a medium of instruction in schools can be appreciated (see Rubagumya, 1991, in the case of Tanzania).

Examination Reforms

At the Lagos conference examination systems were criticized as testing readiness for subsequent levels of schooling, rather than assessing the ability of the student to use his/her qualities in the service of the community to which he/she belonged. A related frequent criticism is that examinations tend to measure the ability of students to recall facts, with little attention given to higher order cognitive skills (Bray, Clarke & Stephens, 1986; Kellaghan & Greaney, 1992; Roy-Campbell, 1992). This process encourages rote memorization, rather than comprehension, information gathering and discovery learning (Frencken, 1988; Welle-Strand, 1996). Two countries in Africa that undertook reform initiatives to address these problems were Kenya and South Africa. Kenya reformed its primary school termination examinations in the mid-1970s. The examinations were revised to include a much broader spectrum of cognitive skills, as well as skills that could be applied in a wider range of contexts in and out of school (Kellaghan & Greaney, 1992; World Bank, 1988). The post-1994 South African government addressed this issue by changing its education system from a content-based system to an outcomes-based education system (Wolhuter, 1999).

Aligning Education with the World of Work

Most African states have attempted to link the world of school with the world of work. Four major strategies have been used. First, most states introduced vocational subjects into the curriculum. Second, another type of initiative was the introduction of polytechnical education (whereby pupils spent part of the school day on farms or in workshops), as exemplified in Mali in 1962 or, on a more limited scale, the Business Education Partnership Agency in Zimbabwe (BEPAZ) project. Third, a more extreme form was the transforming of schools into production units, such as in Benin in 1971, the Education for Self-Reliance of Tanzania in 1967 (Roy-Campbell, 1992), or the Brigades, a private initiative in Botswana. Fourth, National Youth Community Service Schemes were introduced in countries such as Botswana, Ethiopia, Ghana, Malawi, and Nigeria. It should be added that these initiatives generally were not very successful and that the governments found many of them impossible to implement (for reasons, see Durt, 1992). A notable exception is the Brigades in Botswana, which has been hailed an unqualified success.

Teacher Training

Throughout this period of expansion, conventional teacher training institutions could not supply the quantity of trained teachers required by swelling enrolments fast enough, nor could they accommodate the training of the huge percentage of unqualified teachers inherited at independence. In order to address these problems, some ingenious methods of teacher training have been devised, two of which have attracted much attention and praise from comparative educationists. The first initiative was that of Tanzania which, in 1974, set for itself the aim of universal primary school enrolment within three years (Coombs, 1985; Nyerere, 1985; World Bank, 1988). The biggest obstacle to reaching this goal was the shortage of trained teachers. The conventional mode of training (a three-year full-time teacher training college course for secondary school graduates) would have been too time-consuming. It was then decided to train primary school graduates as primary school teachers, using an initial six week residential course followed by a combination of supervised (by qualified teachers) primary school teaching, a correspondence-cum-radio course, and a final examination after three years. Zimbabwe's Integrated National Teacher Education (ZINTEC) scheme, a slight variation on the Tanzanian model (Dzvimbo, 1992) likewise was widely lauded by comparativists (Bray Clarke, & Stephens, 1986; Lockheed et al., 1991). Other countries that use modes of distance education for teacher training include Kenya, Lesotho, Nigeria, Swaziland and Zambia. Nigeria has established a Mobile Teachers Training Unit.

Community Initiatives

A community school is a community based, owned, financed, and managed learning institution that meets the basic/primary education needs of students who, for various reasons, cannot enter government schools (Muyeba, 2007). An early example of community schools in Africa was the Harambee school movement in Kenya. Following a call by Kenyatta shortly after independence, community members built hundreds of Harambee or self-help schools. These schools serve more than half of Kenya's secondary school population (Mwiria, 1990). At the 1964 Abidjan conference, delegates from Rwanda and Sudan reported that self-help schemes for setting up schools functioned in their countries. Community initiatives have contributed significantly to the expansion of education in other countries, such as Botswana, Ghana, Guinea-Bissau, Malawi, Mali, Nigeria, Swaziland, Tanzania, Zambia, and Zimbabwe.

Lifelong Education

Lifelong education was discussed at the MINEDAF conferences held in Durban (UNESCO, 1998) and Dar es Salaam (UNESCO, 2002); however, no significant initiatives have been taken up to now.

Desegregation of School

In African countries with significant numbers of inhabitants of European descent, such as Kenya, Namibia, South Africa, Tanzania, and Zimbabwe, pre-independence racially segregated school systems were desegregated after independence in the interest of equity considerations (the "White schools" were invariably better endowed, equipped and staffed than the "Black schools") (Atkinson, 1982; Wolhuter, 2005).

ANALYSIS AND EVALUATION OF PROGRESS

Quantitative Progress

Adult literacy. In 1960, the adult literacy rate in Africa was nine per cent. Likewise, this figure for Sub-Saharan Africa was nine per cent. Aggregate figures on Africa's progress with the alphabetization of its adult population are not readily available, especially for the period since 1980. As far as Sub-Saharan Africa is concerned, while the percentage of illiterate adults is constantly declining, projections indicate that, even by 2015, universal adult literacy will still be a distant ideal. In 2000, adult literacy rates varied from 85.2 per cent in the case of South Africa to 16.0 per cent in Niger (UNESCO, 2003, p. 310). In six Sub-Saharan countries, adult literacy rates are below 40 per cent (UNESCO, 2002).

School enrolments. During the 1970s and 1980s, Sub-Saharan Africa was hit by a series of economic crises: the first oil crisis of 1973, the ensuing global recession, and the second oil crisis of 1979. Africa's total (foreign) debt rose from US$ 14 billion in 1973 to US$ 125 billion in 1987 (Kennedy, 1993). By the mid-1980s, payments on loans consumed about half of Africa's export earnings. The causes of Africa's economic decline since the 1970s, besides those enumerated above, were as follows: rising foreign debt, poor governance (e.g. political instability and governments being hostile to the business community), the population explosion, environmental degradation and the consequential deterioration of agriculture (Africa South of the Sahara 1997, 1997, p. 15).

With the Third World becoming increasingly more indebted, the International Monetary Fund (IMF) and the World Bank gradually evolved as the lenders of last resort for the Third World, arranging to reschedule debts and make structural adjustment loans conditional upon the adoption of a standardized range of policies. These policies encompassed the reduction of governmental expenditure, the privatization of state corporations, the liberalization of the economy, the encouragement of the private sector, the controlling of the money supply to contain inflation, and currency devaluation. The latter redresses the balance of payments to make imports more expensive and exports cheaper, thus at the same time stimulating exports and domestic industry for import substitution. On the basis of the belief that the growth of state bureaucracy has led to corruption, waste and inefficiency, the IMF and World Bank require debtor countries to reduce the role and staffing of the state. By 1988, over 28 African countries had embarked upon such structural adjustment programmes.

The above depicted economic predicament meant less money for education as debt in Sub-Saharan Africa rose. In Sub-Saharan Africa, public spending on education (in 1983 US$ terms) rose from US$ 3.8 billion in 1970 to US$ 10 billion in 1980, only to decrease to US$ 8.9 billion in 1983 (World Bank, 1988). Under these circumstances, the enrolment boom in the early years of independence could not be sustained. As stated above, at independence in 1960, the gross primary education enrolment ratio in Africa stood at 44 per cent. For Sub-Saharan Africa, the figure came to a paltry 36 per cent. The gross primary education enrolment ratio surged from 36 per cent in 1960, to 53 per cent in 1970, to a peak of 80 per cent in 1980, whence it declined year after year to a low of 73 per cent in 1982. After 1993, it rose year after year, to reach 82 per cent in 2000. The 2000 gross enrolment ratio was below 50 per cent in two countries: 36 per cent in Niger and 44 per cent in Burkina Faso. In Equatorial Guinea, it was less than 60 per cent.

As previously stated, Africa's gross secondary school enrolment ratio stood at 5 per cent in 1960. In 1970, the aggregate gross secondary school enrolment ratio for Sub-Saharan Africa grew to 7 per cent, whence it more than doubled in the next decade, reaching 18 per cent in 1970 (UNESCO, 1999, pp. 11–19). In the 1980s, amidst the economic decline, the rate of increase decelerated, and in 1990 the figure was 22 per cent (UNESCO, 2003).

Tertiary enrolments have also grown miraculously. From 1960 to 1970 to 1980, higher education enrolment numbers in Africa increased from 22 million to 39 million to 76 million, respectively (Coombs, 1985).

Quality and Equity

"Quality" of education is a concept that defies a short and simple definition. A more meaningful exercise is to enumerate the components of quality. Bergmann (1996) identifies four components of quality in education: (a) input quality (human resources, material resources), (b) time-process quality (teaching-learning interactions in classrooms), (c) curricula-output quality (student achievement) and (d) value quality (the degree to which the objectives and output of an education system correspond to the value system of society).

Given the poverty in most African societies, it is not surprising that all indicators point to an alarmingly low and probably declining quality of education in Africa. These materially poor governments find themselves in the vice between the economic squeeze since the early 1970s on the one hand and, on the other, rapid population growth and pressures of educational expansion.

The picture still does not look good for input quality, such as human resources, in spite of the tremendous efforts made to increase teacher training, as discussed above. Training levels required of teachers are low. Only Namibia, South Africa and Zimbabwe require teachers to have university degrees (Smith & Motivans, 2007)—a common requirement not only in developed countries, but also in many developing countries in other parts of the world. Moreover, large percentages of teachers do not meet the already low minimum training levels. For example, Congo and Mozambique require a training level equal to lower secondary school completion for primary school teachers, yet only 57 per cent and 60 per cent respectively of primary school teachers in these two countries meet those requirements (Smith & Motivans, 2007).

The universal dimensions of educational inequality—gender, socio-economic origin, rural-urban and regional (especially the core-periphery gradient) (Wolhuter, 1993)—are all present in Africa, and steeply so. Surveying university enrolments in Sub-Saharan Africa, Teferra (2006) writes that "major enrolment disparities by gender, economic status, regional setting (rural-urban), ethnicity and race abound" (p. 558). In studying the results of grade six reading tests from 14 Southern and Eastern African countries, Zhang (2007) found that on a standardized score scale (mean = 500; standard deviation = 100), the average difference in the 14 countries between rural and urban students was 50 points.

External Objectives

Published research on the attainment of nation building and other political goals by post-independent African education does not exist. It is, however, cause for concern that the first 50 years of independent Africa was characterized by severe socio-political turmoil (Meredith, 2005).

Likewise, research measuring the relation between education and economic growth in Africa does not exist. However, one glaring inconsistency is evident. During periods of the biggest educational expansion such as in the 1970s, the economies of most African countries faltered. In times when policies of economic austerity dictated the curtailment of educational expansion such as since the early 1990s, the economies of most African countries registered some of their most spectacular growth figures. In the 1990s, the average annual growth of the gross domestic product of Sub-Saharan Africa was 2.5 per cent, while for the period 2000–2003 the average annual growth of gross domestic product was 3.9 per cent (World Bank, 2006).

PROGRESS, PROBLEMS AND PROSPECTS

During the past fifty years, progress in the expansion of education in Africa was phenomenal. Nonetheless, great as the strides were, even basic education is still beyond the reach of many. Quality-wise, progress has not been as impressive; indeed there is cause for concern about low and declining quality.

Four obvious problems hamper educational progress in Africa: population growth, the economic crisis, socio-economic deprivation, and the AIDS pandemic. Despite a heartening decrease in recent years, the average population growth in Africa is still high. In Sub-Saharan Africa, the aggregate annual population growth rate stands at 2.5 per cent—the highest of all world regions (World Bank, 2004). The effect of the economic crisis–structural adjustment agreements translated into less state expenditure and therefore less money for education—has been explained above. Africa is a poverty-stricken continent. Many children live in conditions of extreme socio-economic deprivation, which negatively affects their ability to perform well in schools, and which in many cases may even prevent them from enrolling in educational institutions. Africa is also the continent with the highest incidence of HIV/AIDS in the world. In Botswana, the country with the highest infection rate in the world, 38.8 per cent of adults are infected with AIDS (UNESCO, 2003).

The present decline in population growth rates, combined with impressive economic growth rates in recent years, creates a context wherein ever more available resources can be allocated to improve education systems which in turn will be better able to accommodate swelling population numbers.

Such efforts to improve education in Africa will come to their best fruition when guided and underpinned by research. The excellent pockets of indigenous research on education in Africa should be supported, strengthened and expanded. Then the work of David Wilson in Africa which culminated in strengthening the Comparative Education research capacity in Africa—the incorporation of the Southern African Comparative and History of Education Society (SACHES) into the World Council of Comparative Education Societies (WCCES) in 1994, and the hosting of the Tenth World Congress of Comparative Education Societies in Cape Town, South Africa, in 1998, when Wilson was WCCES president—would form an enduring basis for the continual advancement of education in Africa.

REFERENCES

Africa South of the Sahara 1997 (26th ed.). (1997). London: Europa Publishers.

Anonymous. (1969). Educational progress in developing countries. *School and Society, 93*, 120–129.

Arnove, R. F. (1982). The Nicaraguan national literacy crusade of 1980. In P. G. Altbach, R. F. Arnove, & G. P. Kelly (Eds.), *Comparative education* (pp. 433–450). New York: Macmillan.

Assié-Lumumba, N., & Lumumba-Kasongo, T. (1991). The state, economic crisis and educational reform in Côte d'Ivoire. In M. B. Ginsburg (Ed.), *Understanding educational reform in global context: Economy, ideology and the state* (pp. 257–284). New York: Garland.

Atkinson, N. D. (1982). Racial integration in Zimbabwean schools, 1979–1980. *Comparative Education, 18*(1), 5–25.

Bergmann, H. (1996). Quality of education and the demand for education: Evidence from developing countries. *International Review of Education, 42*(6), 581–604.

Bhola, H. S. (1990). Adult literacy for development in Zimbabwe: The third phase of the revolution examined. In S. H. Arnold & A. Niteki (Eds.), *Culture and development in Africa*. Trenton, NJ: Africa World Press.

Bray, M., Clarke, P. B., & Stephens, D. (1986). *Education and society in Africa*. London: Edward Arnold.

Coombs, P. H. (1985). *The world crisis in education: The view from the eighties*. New York: Oxford University Press.

Cowan, L. G., O'Connell, J., & Scanlon, D. J. (1965). *Education and nation-building in Africa*. London: Fredrick Prayer.

Durt, M. (1992). *Bildungspolitik in Zimbabwe: vom "Industrial Training" zu "Education with Production": Erfahrungen mit einem praxis-orientierten Bildungskonzept*. Frankfurt: Iko.

Dzvimbo, P. (1992). *Formulation and implementation of teacher education reforms in Zimbabwe*. Paper presented at the conference of the Southern African Comparative and History of Education Society, Wilderness, South Africa.

Fafunwa, A. B., & Aisiku, J. U. (Eds.). (1982). *Education in Africa: A comparative survey*. London: George Allan & Unwin.

Frencken, H. (1988). *Voor de klas in Zimbabwe*. Amsterdam: VU-Uitgewerij.

Hawes, H. W. R., & Coombe, T. (1986). *Education priorities and aid responses in sub-Saharan Africa: Report of a conference at Cumberland Lodge, Windsor, 4–7 December 1984*. London: Overseas Development Administration.

Idenburg, P. (1975). *Theorie van het Onderwijsbeleid*. Groningen, the Netherlands: Tjeenck Willinck.

Kallaway, P. (2007). *The targets and goals of missionary education in nineteenth century Southern Africa: A reconsideration*. Paper presented at the conference of the Southern African Comparative and History of Education Society, Wilderness, South Africa.

Kareklas, P. M. (1980). *The education dilemma: Policy issues for developing countries in the 1980s*. Oxford: Pergamon Press.

Kellaghan, T., & Greaney, V. (1992). *Using examination to improve education: A study of fourteen African countries*. Washington, DC: World Bank.

Kennedy, P. (1993). *Preparing for the twenty-first century*. London: Fontana Press.

Lockheed, M. E., Verspoor, A. M., Bloch, D., Englebert, P., Fuller, B., King, E., et al. (1991). *Improving primary education in developing countries*. Washington, DC: World Bank.

Meredith, M. (2005). *The state of independence: A history of fifty years of independence*. Johannesburg: Jonathan Ball.

Merryfield, M. M., & Tlou, J. (1995). The process of Africanizing the social studies: Perspectives from post-independence curricular reform in Botswana, Kenya, Malawi, Nigeria and Zimbabwe. *Social Studies, 86*(6), 260–269.

Moumoumi, A. (1968). *Education in Africa*. London: Andre Deutsch.

Mwiria, K. (1990). Kenya's Harambee secondary school movement: The contradictions of public policy. *Comparative Education Review, 34*(4), 350–368.

Muyeba, K. C. (2007). *New comparative perspectives in Zambian education: The rise and impact of community schools*. Paper presented at the conference of the Southern African Comparative and History of Education Society, Wilderness, South Africa.

Nyerere, J. K. (1985). Education in Tanzania. *Harvard Educational Review, 55*(1), 45–52.

Pakenham, T. (1991). *The scramble for Africa*. Johannesburg: Jonathan Ball.

Rayfield, J. R. (1994). Neo-neocolonialism in West African education. *Africana Journal, 16*, 255–268.

Roy-Campbell, Z. M. (1992). The politics of education in Tanzania: From colonial to liberalization. In H. Campbell & H. Stein (Eds.), *Tanzania and the IMF: The dynamics of liberalization* (pp. 147–170). Boulder, CO: Westview Press.

Rubagumya, C. M. (1991). Language promotion for educational purposes: The example of Tanzania. *International Review of Education, 37*(1), 67–85.

Smith, T. M., & Motivans, A. (2007). Teacher quality and Education for All in Sub-Saharan Africa. In D. P. Baker & A. W. Wiseman (Eds.), *Education for all: Global promises, national challenges* (pp. 363–394). Amsterdam: Elsevier.

Teferra, D. (2007). Higher Education in Sub-Saharan Africa. In J. F. Forest & P. G. Altbach (Eds.), *International handbook of higher education* (pp. 557–569). Dordrecht: Springer.

Thompson, A. R. (1981). *Education and development in Africa*. New York: St. Martin.

Turrittin, J. (1989). Integrated literacy in Mali. *Comparative Education Review, 33*(1), 59–76.

UNESCO [United Nations Educational, Scientific and Cultural Organization]. (1961). *Outline of a plan for educational development in Africa*. Paris: UNESCO.

UNESCO. (1977). *Education in Africa in the light of the Lagos conference*. Paris: UNESCO.

UNESCO. (1997). *UNESCO statistical yearbook 1997*. Paris: UNESCO.

UNESCO. (1998). *Seventh conference of ministers of education of African member states (MINEDAF VI)*. Paris: UNESCO.

UNESCO. (1999). *UNESCO statistical yearbook 1999*. Paris: UNESCO.

UNESCO. (2002). *Promoting adult education in the context of life long learning*. Retrieved February 10, 2006, from http://portal.unesco.org/education/en/ev.php-URL_ID=5926&URL_DODO_TOPIC&URL_SECTION=201.html

UNESCO. (2003). *Gender and education for all: The leap to equality*. Paris: UNESCO.

Welle-Strand, A. (1996). *Policy evaluation and leadership: The context of educational change in Zimbabwe*. Stockholm: Institute of International Education, Stockholm University.

Wolhuter, C. C. (1993). *Gelyke onderwysgeleenthede met spesiale verwysing na die implikasies daarvan vir onderwysvoorsiening in die RSA*. Unpublished Doctor of Education dissertation. University of Stellenbosch.

Wolhuter, C. C. (2000). Education in Côte D'Ivoire: Africa's showpiece also lodestar for the continent's gearing for the 21st century. In H. J. Steyn & C. C. Wolhuter (Eds.), *Education systems of emerging countries: Challenges of the 21st century* (pp. 107–149). Noordbrug: Keurkopie.

Wolhuter, C. C. (2005). Progress in the desegregation of schools in South Africa: Experiences of school principals. *Education as Change, 9*(1), 108–126.

Wolhuter, C. C. (1999). Sociaal-wetenscappelijke literatuur over onderwijs in Zuid-Afrika: Van verzuiling tot eensgezindeid vanuit verscheideneid. *Pedagogische Studiën, 76*, 361–370.

World Bank. (1988). *Education in Sub-Saharan Africa: Policies for adjustment, revitalization and expansion*. Washington, DC: World Bank.

World Bank. (2004). *World development report 2005*. New York: World Bank and Oxford University Press.

World Bank. (2006). *2006 World development indicators*. Washington, DC: World Bank.

Zhang, Y. (2007). Urban-rural literacy gaps in Sub-Saharan Africa. *Comparative Education Review, 50*(4), 581–682.

Prof. C. C. Wolhuter
North-West University
Potchefstroom Campus

Dr. M. Petronella Van Niekerk
School of Education
University of South Africa

15

KINGSLEY BANYA

2. REFLECTING ON POLYTECHNICS IN POST-CONFLICT SIERRA LEONE

David Wilson spent most of his early professional career promoting educational planning and vocational education in several countries in sub-Saharan Africa. It is thus appropriate, as a tribute to David's foresight in this area, to analyze a recent decision by the post-conflict government of Sierra Leone to upgrade teacher training institutions to polytechnics. During the 1990s, Sierra Leone experienced a vicious rebel war that practically destroyed most social structures, including education. Throughout this time, with an economy on "life support" from donor agencies and governments and with millions of internally displaced citizens, as well as thousands who fled to every part of the world, the country barely functioned as a nation. The advent of sustainable peace in 2001 brought in a stable, elected civilian government that sought to rehabilitate and change all social sectors of the country. This paper examines the government's efforts to improve the education system with particular reference to polytechnic education.

This discussion is divided into four parts: a brief history of vocational education in Africa; an account of the establishment of polytechnics in Sierra Leone; an assessment of the current situation; and recommendations for the future of these polytechnics.

HISTORY OF VOCATIONAL EDUCATION IN AFRICA

Various commissions on the establishment of higher education in the twelve states which were formerly British colonies in Africa have made attempts to include vocational education as part of the curricula. While both the Elliot and the Asquith commissions, formed in 1943 with reports completed in 1945, were concerned with creating universities overseas, the Elliot Commission also recommended that three technical institutions be set up in West Africa (Ashby, 1996; Banya & Elu, 1997; Sherman, 1990). The Elliot Commission's report included a passage succinctly introducing the issues of vocational education on the continent.

> Each institution should at least be partly residential, since many of the students will come from a distance; and library and recreational facilities should be provided. Technical, commercial, and perhaps art courses should be as broad as possible. It is essential for the educational basis of the institutions that close contact should be established and maintained with the subsequent employers of the students, and that representatives of the technical department of the government and of private enterprise in commerce and industry, and of workers' organizations, should be closely associated with the management of the institutions. (Pedler, 1992, p. 266)

V. Masemann et al., (Eds.), A Tribute to David N. Wilson: Clamouring for a Better World, 17–29.
© 2010 Sense Publishers. All rights reserved.

Despite such recommendations, there have been numerous expressions of regret that the universities have been insufficiently integrated into the life of the communities in which they are situated (P'Bitek, 1973). The problem was that vocational education was always considered inferior to a university degree, and the reward system was skewed against its graduates. The link between the vocational schools and the universities in these countries was never strong. For example, for several years the doyen of the African university, Fourah Bay College in Sierra Leone, emphasized theology and the classical languages. It was much later that the university prepared students for the Durham Bachelor of Arts (Economics) degree. Like other universities of that time, Fourah Bay was affiliated with an English university, the University of Durham. The history and evolution of Fourah Bay College as the first British university on the continent has been widely written about (Banya & Elu, 1997; Harris & Sawyerr, 1968; Sumner, 1960). Except for those specifically established to train vocational experts (for example, Achimota in the Gold Coast-Ghana, 1931; The University College at Makerere in Uganda, 1939; Yaba in Nigeria, 1930; and the Nigerian College of Arts, Science and Technology, 1949), universities provided degree courses in the arts subjects: language, literature, music, history, economics, and sociology. These were subjects often unrelated to the lives of the bulk of the population in the country. It should be noted that secondary school education was a prerequisite for technical and commercial courses. At that time, there were very few people so qualified as secondary schools were scarce. Thus, recruitment for vocational education came from the same secondary school source as the universities, a circumstance that had a profound effect on the future development of technical education.

In English-speaking Africa between 1955 and 1962 all colleges of arts, science, and technology started to offer courses leading to university degrees. The colleges concentrated on degree courses to the exclusion, or near exclusion, of the teaching of technical skills which had been envisaged as their main business, directed towards the ancillary skills, such as plumbing, electrical skills, and the like. In some instances, there was not enough space to simultaneously teach university level courses and technical skills at the same institution, nor enough qualified staff (Senior Lecturer at Freetown Teachers College, personal communication, December 7, 2005). Moreover, there were never enough students with the educational prerequisites to fill courses of both kinds. For reasons of prestige, career opportunities, as well as salary considerations, most students wanted to get a university degree. The fact that technical schools were considered "second tier"/periphery institutions, and that on the eve of independence no influential political leader had such a background, rapidly led to their demise.

The issue was whether a university is the best place to teach students ancillary skills. While it was generally agreed that there had been over-investment in university development while technical-professional training had been neglected comparatively to other fields, there was no agreement on the best remedy. Some believed that training technicians within the university environment would increase their prestige and might in consequence increase the flow of trainees at a level vital to the economy (Harris & Sawyerr, 1968). Others considered that the best university contribution might be the encouragement of, and cooperation with, existing technical institutions, to work collaboratively on mutual issues such as staff training and student qualifications (Head of Technical Education at the Ministry of Education, Science and Technology, personal communication, December 20, 2005). In the end, a binary system of tertiary education became the norm in sub-Saharan Africa as all the technical institutions became the nuclei of new universities.

THE ESTABLISHMENT OF POLYTECHNICS IN SIERRA LEONE

The term polytechnic comes from the Greek *polú* or *polý*, meaning "many", and *tekhnikós* meaning "arts". Prior to 1989–2001, and more so after the rebel war, the government of Sierra Leone realized that the education system inherited from past administrations was extremely inadequate to meet the needs of an emerging self-governing state requiring rapid economic expansion. A need was felt for an education system that would adapt and respond to the changing economic, scientific and technological environment. The changes brought about by globalization and by the liberalization of economies have also brought change in workplace dynamics. Accordingly, the needs of industry and employers are also changing. Like other parts of Africa, Sierra Leone hopes that these changes will improve its standard of living and enable much needed development. The government maintains that globalization and liberalization of markets and economies should benefit the poor as well as the rich. These forces should be better harnessed to help the poor and improve living standards of the less developed countries, with help from the more developed countries.

The new millennium is characterized by rapid technological and other changes that aim to improve the welfare of humanity. Technology all over the world has progressively become part of everyday life, being integrated in all areas of human activity, in homes, offices, and industry, urban as well as rural areas; for example, cell phones and money transfers are used in all parts of the developing world. Technical education unquestionably makes a contribution towards socio-economic development in developed and developing countries. It is recognized that sustainable development and economic growth cannot be achieved without mastery of technology.

However, the imbalances between the developed and developing world are still many. According to the United Nations Development Programme Report (2002), 20 per cent of poor countries worldwide, the majority of which are in Africa, share a miserable fraction of 1.1 per cent of the global income, which is inadequate to stimulate meaningful development. According to the same index, Sierra Leone was listed as second to last in terms of development (UNDP, 2006). The country's gross domestic product (GDP) per capita was US$ 121. One of the many reasons given for the conflict in the country was the high level of poverty, with implications for rural-urban drift and youth unemployment. After the war (2001), the government understood education to be a major means to alleviate poverty. According to the Deputy Minister of the Ministry of Education, Science and Technology (Ministry Official II, personal communication, December 18, 2005),

Professional and technical institutions can play an important role, direct and indirectly, in formulating and implementing viable poverty reduction strategies, and should become more closely involved. Vocational education should take on this strategy through acting as entrepreneurs in skills development helping to supplement the skills acquired by vocational education graduates in areas of specialization, empowering them to take on developmental projects, create jobs, and contribute to economic growth and development. The unemployment rate is already high and on the increase. The only sure way to be employed is through self-employment, a route adopted by many vocational education graduates with entrepreneurial skills.

According to the Deputy Chair at Bunumbu Polytechnic (personal communication, December 20, 2005),

One among many strategies which should be undertaken to contribute to sustainable development by some polytechnic institutions is to extend some of the technical students' practical experience beyond workshops and industrial attachments to rural communities, where poverty levels are at the highest. This will provide help in the setting up of appropriate technologies to assist with such community services as sanitation, safe drinking water. In addition value is added to their agricultural products. It will also help to harness cheap sources of energy, set up cottage industries and small-scale enterprises, and construct low cost houses.

A persistent problem in Africa is that the rural poor, despite promises by governments to reverse the pro-urban migration, continue to bear major costs associated with poverty. The main economic activity of most African countries is agriculture. It is very difficult for a country to raise living standards and significantly reduce poverty on the basis of agricultural production alone, especially when it is predominantly for subsistence as it is in most of Africa. Due to the poor conditions of service and working conditions in schools for teachers, young qualified and trained teachers are always leaving the profession. There has been a low turnout of high quality primary and secondary school teachers. Currently, it is estimated that 65 per cent of teachers are untrained and unqualified. A gap exists in the teaching expertise in key subjects and skills needed to be taught in the 6-3-3-4 system; six years of primary, three years of junior secondary, three years of senior secondary, and four years of tertiary education. Consequently, there is an acute shortage of teachers of Sierra Leonean languages, French, and most of the technical and vocational subjects. Moreover, the infrastructure and equipment required to make the technical and vocational subjects practically oriented are not readily available (Deputy Minister of the Ministry of Education, Science and Technology, personal communication, December 17, 2005).

Meanwhile, the effect of the rebel war continues to affect the education system because of the decade-long destruction and vandalism of several educational institutions. In addition, pressure continues to be put on "safe regions" such that the double shift continues to operate especially in western area schools.

Nevertheless, there is a growing awareness that education holds the key to overall national, social, economic, cultural and technological development. Sierra Leoneans are now more concerned about what happens in education. Almost all of the development sectors, including the political system, depend on the efficacy of the educational instruments for their effective growth and development. The Education Act of 2004 has made ample provisions for educational improvement which, if realized, will ensure a just, united and prosperous Sierra Leone.

As part of the educational reform movement, the Polytechnic Reform Act of 2001 called for the establishment of five polytechnic institutions to be located throughout the country with corresponding Polytechnic Councils to make provisions for the management and supervision of each institution. At present, three polytechnics have been established and are operational, integrating existing technical-vocational institutions for wider course options. The three institutions are The Milton Margai College of Education and Technology (MMCE), Eastern Polytechnic (EP), and Northern Polytechnic (NP). It should be noted that Freetown Teachers' College and Port Loko Teachers' College have not yet received polytechnic status. Their offerings are limited to Teacher Elementary Certificate (TEC) and Higher Teacher Certificate (HTC). According to the Polytechnics Act (Ministry of Education Science and Technology, 2001), the aims of the new institutions are

to develop self-reliance and self-actualization in individuals as well as the progressive development of society and the economy of the country through technical and vocational training in all areas of urgent need especially the agricultural, industrial and commercial sectors. (p. 12)

The objectives of the Act (Ministry of Education Science and Technology, 2001) are

i. To fill the gap in technical and vocational manpower needs of Sierra Leone by substantially increasing the number of indigenous skilled lower middle level "blue collar" workers;
ii. To produce a more literate, numerate and enterprising lower middle level technical and vocational workforce and thus speed up national development;
iii. To encourage women and girls to participate in national development through the acquisition of technical and vocational skills;
iv. To correct the present geographical imbalance in distribution of technical and vocational resources;
v. To develop appreciation and understanding of the increasing complexity of science and technology;
vi. To create an enabling environment for the development of appropriate indigenous technology;
vii. To provide training for technical and vocational instructors, teachers, and lecturers;
viii. To develop an appreciation of cultural and aesthetic values in productive work. (p. 13)

A provision was made for the establishment of polytechnic councils which have control and supervision of the general policy and property of the polytechnic institutions. Each council consists of a chairperson and ten others appointed from various parts of society, including the local area in which each institution is established. The objective of the council is "to administer the polytechnic institution as a teaching, learning and research institution" (Ministry of Education Science and Technology, 2001, p. 14). Responsibilities of the council are to

a) provide instruction in such branches of learning as it may think fit and make provision for research and for advancement and documentation of knowledge;

b) grant diplomas and certificates through the National Council of Technical, Vocational and other Academic Awards;

c) preserve academic freedom and prevent discrimination in teaching and research, in the admission of students and the appointment of staff;

d) preserve, enrich and contribute to the development of the cultural heritage, economy and welfare of the Republic of Sierra Leone in particular and humanity in general, holding out the benefits to all persons without discrimination;

e) establish principal lectureship, senior lectureship and any other such posts as it may approve;

f) establish administrative offices and posts as may be required by the polytechnic institution and appoint persons thereto;

g) cooperate with other polytechnic institutions or educational authorities on such matters and for such purposes as may be determined from time to time by the Council;

h) admit students for courses of study in the polytechnic institution;

i) provide for the printing and publication of research and other works which may be used by the students for courses of study in the polytechnic institution; and

j) act as trustee of any property, endowment or gift for the purposes of education or research or otherwise in the furtherance of the work or welfare of the polytechnic institution and invest any funds representing the same in accordance with the terms of this Act. (Ministry of Education Science and Technology, 2001, p. 18)

Provision was also made to establish an academic board with, among other responsibilities, the functions to

a) determine the minimum matriculation requirements for admission of students into various courses in the polytechnic institution;

b) present candidates for awards to the National Council for Technical, Vocational and other Academic Awards;

c) discuss any matter relating to the objects and powers of the council and to report its findings on the academic implications of such matters to the council;

d) determine what facilities and courses of study should be instituted and where they are to be located and make recommendations thereon to the council (p. 21).

A campus management committee was instituted with the following membership:

a) the Principal who shall be chairman,

b) the Dean of Campus,
c) the Registrar who shall be secretary,
d) the estate officer,
e) academic heads,
f) Deans of Faculties,
g) One student representative, and
h) One senior staff representative. (Ministry of Education Science and Technology, 2001, p. 22)

Funding for polytechnics was to come from

a) monies appropriated by parliament for the purposes of the polytechnic institution;
b) fees charged for the services of the polytechnic institution, including tuition and examination fees;
c) gifts or donations from any person or organization, whether local or external; and
d) any monies otherwise accruing to the polytechnic institution in the course of its activities. (p. 22)

In summary, the main focus of the 2001 Polytechnics Act was to advance and promote the teaching of vocational skills by specifically addressing issues pertaining to the quality and improvement of technical education, equity, promotion of appropriate technology development and transfer, good governance through institutional leadership and management, capacity building including research and development, and sharing of information, experiences and views.

The next section reviews the successes and drawbacks to this "new" orientation.

PROGRESS ON THE IMPLEMENTATION OF THE POLYTECHNICS

A word of caution is necessary. The reorganization and change of nomenclature of vocational institutions is only eight years old, too early to make a definite judgment on the polytechnics. However, a base-line has been established that requires assessment in order to further strengthen the polytechnics.

Polytechnics are seen as a source of national development and engines of economic growth. As noted by the Senior Education Officer, "the most developed nations of the world were those that used their human resources most efficiently and gave most financial support to vocationally oriented education" (personal communication, January 14, 2006). Such an education would adapt and respond to the changing economic, scientific, and technological environment.

To implement the various changes envisaged in the Vocational Education Act of 2001 and adapt to other educational changes, the government has progressively increased financial allocation to the education sector. Currently, 23 per cent of the national budget is allocated to the education sector, up from 18 per cent in 1996/1997. In the 1996/1997 academic year, the government grant to tertiary education was approximately USD$ 1.6 million. Of this, the University of Sierra Leone (USL) received 60 per cent; Milton Margai College of Education (MMCE) received nine per cent, while the other five teachers colleges (Bo Teacher's College, Freetown Teachers' College, Makeni Teachers' College, Bunumbu Teachers' College and Port Loko Teachers' College) received about six per cent each. Salaries and emoluments accounted for 66 per cent of that year's actual expenditure on education (Ministry of Education, 2000).

More than 90 per cent of the funds for tertiary education come from the government. The rest comes from school fees and donations from donor agencies. The government also provides grants-in-aid and study leave with pay to students and teachers in tertiary level institutions. About 45 per cent of students in these institutions benefit from either the grants-in-aid or study leave or both. Teachers and other lecturers are also supported for further post-graduate studies to service the local polytechnic institutions (The polytechnic institutions are: Milton Margai College of Education (MMCE), Northern Polytechnic (NP), and Eastern Polytechnic (EP). Two Teachers' Colleges—Freetown Teachers' College (FTC) and Port Loko Teachers' College (PLTC)—have not yet received polytechnic status.

Table 1 below shows government support for students over a period of eight years at various higher education institutions before the full implementation of the Polytechnics Act.

Table 1. Number of tertiary level award of government grants-in-aid per institution, 1997/98 to 2004/05

Institution*	1997/ 1998	1998/ 1999	1999/ 2000**	2000/ 2001	2001/ 2002	2002/ 2003	2003/ 2004	2004/ 2005
MMCE	110	114	-	168	175	183	183	557
FTC	110	120	-	120	140	150	150	310
PLTC	110	120	-	156	162	168	168	389
MTC	110	120	-	125	136	139	139	392
BuTC	110	120	-	150	158	162	162	294
BoTC	110	106	-	120	149	156	156	306
FBC	80	224	-	357	370	397	397	594
NUC	80	170	-	185	200	254	254	502
COMAHS	9	16	-	21	22	32	32	42
IPAM	-	30	-	77	79	89	89	112
Law School	-	7	-	7	7	7	7	11
Total	829	1267	0	1,486	1,598	1,736	1,736	3,509

* MMCE = Milton Margai College of Education; FTC = Freetown Teachers' College; PLTC = Port Loko Teachers' College; MTC = Makeni Teachers' College; BuTC = Bunumbu Teachers' College; BoTC = Bo Teachers' College; FBC = Fourah Bay College; NUC = Njala University College; COMAHS = College of Medicine and Applied Health Sciences; IPAM = Institute of Public Administration and Management.
Makeni Teachers' College is now Northern Polytechnic; Bunumbu Teachers' College is now Eastern Polytechnic.
** During the year 2000 the rebels entered Freetown, the capital, and the government went into exile.

Source: Ministry of Education Report, Government of Sierra Leone, (2006)

As a result of generous government financial support, 3,003 students are enrolled at the University of Sierra Leone, and an estimated 10,000 students are currently enrolled at the ten technical and vocational institutions. These numbers are, however, low for a country with a population of 5.4 million (Sierra Leone Higher Education Profile, UNESCO 2007).

The government has solicited external resources and expatriate services for the education sector. For example, in 2002, the government allocated US $9 million to be expended on various programmes and activities by the Ministry of Education, Science and Technology. This amount was 25 per cent of the total Highly Indebted Poor Countries (HIPC) funds available to Sierra Leone. This funding was used to rehabilitate/reconstruct 83 institutions from primary, secondary and technical-vocational, two teachers' colleges, and five district inspectorate offices. A total of 5,500 sets of school furniture and beds were supplied to schools. The Ministry, in collaboration with UNICEF, Plan Sierra Leone, the Norwegian Refugee Council, and a host of other organizations undertakes various programmes in the development of education in Sierra Leone. For example, the African Development Bank assisted in procuring science equipment, materials and chemicals and technical/vocation subject equipment for schools and in rehabilitating school laboratories. UNICEF is implementing the three-year Non-Formal Primary Education Program (NFPEP) and the Complementary Rapid Education Programme Schemes (CREPS). UNESCO supported the development of a national science and technology policy in Sierra Leone, while the United Kingdom-based NGO project known as Knowledge Aid Sierra Leone has introduced Internet service to schools and colleges in the country (Ministry of Education, Government of Sierra Leone, Annual Science and Technology Report, 2003, p. 53).

Despite the above mentioned financial and organizational efforts, there are serious drawbacks to the full implementation of the Polytechnics Act of 2001. Some of the difficulties are highlighted below.

Lack of Fundamental Changes

The 2001 Act is simply a result of efforts to upgrade vocational education from the original and historical role as intermediate technical education and teacher training institutions to polytechnics. It seems that the polytechnics have emerged solely through an administrative change of statutes, including a name change; for example, Bunumbu Teachers' College has become Eastern Polytechnic, and Makeni Teacher's College is now Northern Polytechnic. The cachet of a degree in technical studies does not necessarily make them quality academic studies. There is still a lack of specialized intermediate technical professionals which results in the shortage of skilled workers in many fields. Evidence has also shown a decline in the general quality of teaching and graduates' preparation for the workplace because of the fast-paced conversion of technical institutions to more advanced higher level institutions (Senior Education Officer, Ministry of Education, Science and Technology, personal communication, January 14, 2006). The upgrading of the teaching staff has been slow and spasmodic. Many of the lecturers have only bachelor degrees and only a handful have Master's or doctoral degrees. The teaching staff must endure poor working conditions and earn lower salaries than their university counterparts. Furthermore, although the polytechnics are set up to attract students into vocational careers, student demand and lack of appropriate equipment have pushed the polytechnics toward teaching the social sciences and humanities, resulting in graduates who still seek government employment. Few graduates of the polytechnics have established businesses of their own. The vast majority have become teachers who depend on the government for employment.

Funding

After 11 years of a particularly vicious war, the economic difficulties currently experienced by Sierra Leone inevitably lead to inadequate funding for polytechnics. Polytechnics are seriously and constantly under-funded when compared with the University of Sierra Leone. Operational costs of Polytechnics are expensive, especially considering the type of equipment and trained staff needed. Although the government secured initial funding to equip some of the institutions, providing funding for the continuous maintenance of the equipment is a real challenge. With a GDP of only US$ 121 million, the country depends heavily on outside donor agencies. This can sometimes lead to outsider priorities dictating educational policies, especially in the case of the polytechnics, where government efforts in the past were minimal at best. It should be pointed out that forces both within and outside the country undermine government efforts. For example, until 2007, the debt burden of the country amounted to five times the value of its annual exports (Ministry of Finance, 2005). The country was spending more on paying interest on its debts than on health, education and other social services combined. In addition, there is the problem of poor governance, sometimes associated with corruption which contributes to nepotism in appointments. Hence, there is poor implementtation of well-intended ideas. Added to this mix are diseases that have become endemic, such as HIV/AIDS, malaria, and tuberculosis which negatively affect development efforts and worsen poverty. The total collapse of the country's infrastructure during the war has added to the difficulties of implementing any radical changes in education.

Collaboration with Industries

Despite the provision of a governing council that allows for the membership of some industries, there is a general lack of active participation of industries. A high degree of employer participation is essential to the healthy functioning of a polytechnic. A substantial proportion of the governing body should be drawn from trade associations, nationalized corporations, and private companies. Such cooperation frequently leads to the provision of courses that are custom-built by the polytechnic for local industries and services, both private and public. The most successful polytechnics and technical institutes are those which completely integrate with local industry. Rather than a student who attends full-time on a student grant, the ideal student would be one who comes on day-release or block-release, or for sandwich courses, and who is supported by wages paid by an employer on standard rates. Thus, job insecurity would be eliminated. Sadly, there are hardly any private sector industries or enterprises that can employ many of the graduates of polytechnic institutions. Unemployment, especially among the youth, continues to skyrocket.

RECOMMENDATIONS FOR THE FUTURE

Emphasis on Rural Enterprise

It is generally recognized that for development to occur, the country's higher education institutions should devote more effective attention to the problems of rural areas. Although the University of Sierra Leone constituent College at Njala has developed facilities for agriculture and veterinary science which provide for students to learn skills relevant for the countryside, there is little complementary development in the polytechnics. The five polytechnics are situated in "urban" areas that have little or no connection with the rural areas where the bulk of the population resides. For example, Bunumbu Teachers' College used to be in a rural part of eastern Sierra Leone; today, because of the war, it is still in Kenema, the regional center of the east, away from its rural setting.

Close Collaboration between Schools and Polytechnics

There is a need for a high degree of cooperation between the polytechnics and secondary schools. Polytechnics should provide technical teaching staff for secondary schools. The incorporation of technical subjects in the secondary curriculum is desirable even though it may be an expensive undertaking. Although technical subjects are much more expensive to equip and staff than traditional school subjects, in a technological age this may be a worthy expenditure. Similarly, it is reasonable to suggest that polytechnics collaborate with the university, in a process where the polytechnics provide subject-content courses for teachers while the university provides pedagogical courses (World Bank, 2000).

Funding

The government should provide sufficient funding for the polytechnics with the objective of ensuring educational quality. It should also ensure that any cost-saving income generated by the institutions is retained as a supplement, not a substitute, to public spending. In this regard, both local and international funding agencies must be encouraged to play an important role in the revitalization of the polytechnics and bring dynamism in technological initiatives and innovations. Their involvement may lead to replacing obsolete equipment and technology and venturing into new lines of creativity which rapidly enhance technology, productivity and prosperity. The previous experience of constant government intervention must be curtailed.

The government's role should be strictly limited to oversight responsibilities. Polytechnic councils must be given the power and authority to be autonomous in management and in taking initiatives. The councils must be continuously encouraged to set annual performance goals that are measurable and to publicly report their achievements and maintain transparency.

Staffing

As noted, the bulk of the faculty and staff at the polytechnics were originally employed because of their pedagogical skills and training. With a new disposition, there is a need to upgrade their knowledge base in order to effectively carry out their new mandate. Unfortunately, the knowledge and skills that are needed are not locally available, as the University of Sierra Leone is not equipped to undertake such an enterprise. The only alternative is an overseas training course provided by an institution situated either in another African country or outside of the continent. Whatever the case, it is an expensive proposition and one for which the government does not have funds. By necessity, the government will have to rely on donor agencies or other governments to train the staff. This dependence on outside agencies makes it extremely difficult to predict whether such training will ever occur, given the size of both the teaching and administrative staff.

CONCLUSION

Despite the terrible upheaval that Sierra Leone experienced for over ten years, the government has embarked on an ambitious programme to rehabilitate the education system, hence the economy. To bring the country into the technological age and help speed up development, the 2001 Polytechnics Act was passed. The implementation of the Act has been fraught with difficulties, partly because of the poor state of the economy and partly because of the lack of skilled human resources to teach many of the necessary technical skills. While the government should be commended for its forward thinking, the realities are that many of the ambitious programmes cannot be implemented in the current economic situation. Heavy dependence on donor agencies will not be enough to sustain the long-term development of the country. A reorientation by the polytechnics toward rural development should help in sustainable growth. Unfortunately, the current efforts as seen by the implementation of the Polytechnics Act of 2001 are rather inadequate due to various reasons outlined above. However, innovation and change in tertiary education in Sierra Leone are inevitable for institutional renewal and transformation, as well as nation building. There is a great awareness in the country that all the development sectors, including the social, economic, cultural and technological sectors, as well as the political system depend on the efficacy of the education system. The polytechnics are one such instrument for effective growth and development, an idea that David espoused throughout his life's work in developing countries.

REFERENCES

Ashby, E. (1966). *Universities: British, Indian, African: A study in the ecology of higher education.* London: Weidenfeld & Nicolson.

Banya, K., & Elu, J. (1997). The crisis of higher education in Sub-Saharan Africa: The continuing search for relevance. *Journal of Higher Education Policy and Management, 19*(2), 151–166.

Harris, W. T., & Sawyerr, H. (1968). *The springs of Mende belief and conduct: A discussion of the influence of the belief in the supernatural among the Mende.* Freetown: University of Sierra Leone Press.

Ministry of Education Science and Technology, Government of Sierra Leone. (2000). *Annual Report.* Freetown: Government Press.

Ministry of Education Science and Technology, Government of Sierra Leone. (2001). *Polytechnics Act.* Freetown: Government Printer.

Ministry of Education Science and Technology, Government of Sierra Leone. (2003). *Annual Report.* Freetown: Government Printer.

Ministry of Education Science and Technology, Government of Sierra Leone. (2006). *Annual Report.* Freetown: Government Printer.

Ministry of Finanace, Government of Sierra Leone. (2005). *Annual Report.* Freetown: Government Printer.

P'Bitek, O. (1973). *Africa's cultural revolution.* Nairobi: East Africa Publishing House.

Pedler, F. (1972). Universities and polytechnics in Africa. The twelfth Lugard memorial lecture. *Africa: Journal of the International African Institute, 42*(4), 263–274.

Sherman, M. (1990). The university in modern Africa: Toward the twenty-first century. *Journal of Higher Education, 61*(4), 363–385.

Sumner, D. (1960). *History of education in Sierra Leone.* Freetown: University of Sierra Leone.

United Nations Development Programme. (2002). *Human Development Report 2002.* Oxford: Oxford University Press.

United Nations Development Programme. (2006). *Human Development Report 2006.* New York: Palgrave Macmillan.

United Nations Educational, Scientific and Cultural Organization. (2007). *Sierra Leone higher education profile.* Paris: UNESCO.

World Bank. (2000). *Higher education in developing countries: Peril and promise.* The Taskforce on Higher Education and Society. Washington, DC: The International Bank for Reconstruction and Development/World Bank.

Kingsley Banya
College of Education
Florida International University

SECTION II: TECHNICAL AND VOCATIONAL EDUCATION AND TRAINING

MACLEANS A. GEO-JAJA

3. TVET IN NIGERIA

Issues, Concerns and New Directions in the 21ˢᵗ Century

"Education should be inclusive, responding to the diverse needs and circumstances of learners and giving appropriate weight to the abilities, skills, and
knowledge they bring to the teaching and learning process" (UNESCO, 2004a).

INTRODUCTION

Governments worldwide are designing strategies to increase the accessibility and
efficiency of national education systems. Akin to many sub-Saharan African nations,
one great concern in Nigeria today is cultivating education and training to satisfy
human resources needs and to meet undiminished social demand for more and
better schools. In order for governments to address these concerns effectively, human
resources and education must be carefully designed from within and simultaneously
be participatory and linked to national development plans. Otherwise, stakeholders
may not be willing to invest any resources (ranging from money to unremunerated
time use and other inputs from disadvantaged people) in development planning.
According to this rationale, Harbison and Hanushek (1992) contended that a
country which is unable to develop the skills and knowledge of its people and
utilize them effectively in the national economy will be unable to develop anything
else. Further, according to Harbison (1973), "human resources constitute the
ultimate basis for the wealth of nations" (p. 3). The implied suggestion here is that,
in educational planning, the limited resources of a country should be allocated to
develop its human resources. The framework of carefully and deliberately matching
educational output with social and economic needs results in the most effective
human resources development. To this end, this chapter will explore the forces that
shape and drive the new economy in Nigeria, so as to address the challenges that
globalization, competitiveness and the knowledge economy present to the workforce of the 21ˢᵗ century.

   Most studies indicate that successful development of human resources coincides
with careful and efficient planning of the education system. The author of this paper
will argue that in most instances in Nigeria, as in most developing countries, plans
for developing education and technical training differ significantly from the desired
and intended social and economic development needs. Presently, it appears that
education which is viewed as a human right and directed to the full development of
the human personality cannot vindicate its deeper objectives of articulating a concrete

V. Masemann et al., (Eds.), A Tribute to David N. Wilson: Clamouring for a Better World, 33–49.
© *2010 Sense Publishers. All rights reserved.*

relevance to the socio-cultural and politico-economic opportunities within the communities it aspires to serve. The underlying rationale for schooling design therefore is rendered more complex by external political-economic influences and methods that are not linked directly with training in the labour market, including the inculcation of shared socio-cultural values and attitude development for nation-building (Carnoy, 1986; Cummings & McGinn, 1997; Lewin, 1998; Tikly, 2004). Subsequently, to be competitive in the global economy, Nigeria must design appropriate and workable methods to educate and train the bulk of its citizens up to a significant educational level and for employment across a range of rapidly emerging sub-sectors—biotechnology, nanotechnology, engineering, and exotic processes. It is therefore imperative for Nigeria to provide appropriate technological and vocational education and training in order to have a workforce that is highly skilled at all levels.

This paper's primary theme is Technical and Vocational Education and Training (TVET) intervention that can result in human resource development closely linked to the world of work. This is illustrated on the industrial staircase (see Figure 1). As a response to emerging social, economic, and technological needs, a broad range of issues will be discussed that relate to TVET under the main theme, "The Strategy for Skills Development in an Emerging Economy". This discussion has been motivated from conversations with the late Professor David Wilson at the Comparative and International Education Society (CIES) Annual Meeting at Stanford University in 2005 that led to my revisiting my doctoral study on "Education and Training and Occupational Skills Development in Nigeria" (see Geo-JaJa, 1986). This topic has become central to the current debate concerning poverty reduction and promoting sustainable development in developing countries. The significant contribution of that previous study is that the vast skills needs of Nigeria mean that the federal government must pursue the development of skills at all levels of the spectrum: basic, secondary and tertiary levels, with emphasis on the skills levels that correspond best to the stage of economic development and the needs of the local labour market. It was then argued that the compulsory implementation of such an effective TVET system in strategic fields such as nanotechnologies, computer literacy, construction and maintenance, and particularly in agriculture, will significantly contribute towards the challenges of remedying poverty and providing valuable employment. Today, as then, I still believe that the broader and high-end pathway for skill development of an under-prepared workforce must include public health, information technologies, community infrastructures, and quality assistance to trade related occupations, and the provision of agriculture extension officers. These I argue will ensure growth out of poverty and into prosperity. Suggested is that in defining what TVET truly is (high level cognitive and practical skills), it must be conceptualized/understood in the context of the shifts that nations have passed through over time from the agrarian age, to the industrial/manufacturing age, and to the information age.

Note that even in the agrarian age on the industrial staircase, where Nigeria has been until recent time, extension officers are essential to developing equipment and technology for agriculture, forestry etc. and to teach others to use it. More recently

34

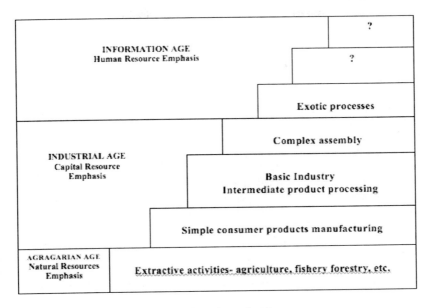

Figure 1. The industrial staircase.

Source: Mangum, 2005, p. 541

it has been essential to train technicians such as machinists and mechanics for oil well drilling and pipeline development. Those numbers are multiplied as the industrial/ manufacturing age becomes the emphasis, and the need does not disappear as the information age dawns. Even though higher levels of academic education becomes more important in the latter stages, the needs established in the agrarian and industrial ages still exist, and technical education and vocational training remain essential.

BACKGROUND

The 21st Century is dominated by information and communication technology with labour market demands constantly in flux. Providing relevant TVET programmes or schooling with diversified curriculum is deemed central to the effort to foster sustainable development, as a step to eradicating extreme poverty and promoting employability. To borrow the definition provided by the United Nations Educa-tional, Scientific and Cultural Organization (UNESCO) and the International Labour Organization (ILO) (2002) TVET refers to "aspects of the educational process involving, in addition to general education, the study of technologies and related sciences, and the acquisition of practical skills, attitudes, understanding and know-ledge relating to occupations in various sectors of economic and social life" (p. 7). Consequently with this definition, the understanding that TVET as limited to just simple, manual demonstrations of skill or competence is not correct. Any revision of TVET must ensure that high-level cognitive skills are combined with quasi-specific practical training skills.

In this author's view, TVET is an organized, intentional and explicit effort to promote learning and to enhance the quality of life. As a demand driven system it must be: Relevant, Effective, Efficient, Flexible, Sustainable, Accessible, and contribute to nation-building and sustainable development. Compared with schooling, TVET has the following main characteristics: learner-centeredness, community and employment-oriented content, use of local resources, and age-inclusiveness for learners. Therefore, it is no accident that TVET and conventional schooling systems are at variance in both means and ends as TVET makes a diverse but useful and more pervasive contribution to the workforce, livelihoods, and sustainable development than does ordinary schooling. In most instances, TVET can be obtained in school, at the work place, or even at home. In the typical school population, TVET, being an integral part of the total education system and being a basic right according to Article 26 of the United Nations Universal Declaration of Human Rights, contributes to bridging the gap between education and the world of work and, through quality skills development, contributes to economically viable sustainable societies. TVET can also serve disadvantaged social groups in great need including unemployed youths, graduates of the compulsory conventional education system, school drop-outs, adults in employment (training and retraining) and deskilled workers, who can take up technological and vocational education as a contribution to the country's socioeconomic development. In order to reach the trained, untrained, and those in need of retraining, TVET can be offered in both formal and non-formal settings in a flexible manner. New information and communication technology offers the means to make TVET flexible and possible. Flexibility is obtained through modularization of the system, as modules can easily be changed as well as abolished or developed in accordance with perceived industry and society needs.

More pointedly, TVET could grant all segments of society access to life-long learning resources and enable participants to acquire practical skills and knowledge that will enable them to function as members of their communities. Aderemi (1997) and Olaitan (1996) tied the wider contribution of technical and vocational education to nurturing skills necessary for agricultural, trade and industrial occupations, and informal enterprise commercial development. These methods, pedagogy or content of TVET, borrowed or not borrowed, weigh heavily on investments to upgrade facilities, to attract, develop, and retain good teachers, and to develop new curricula and materials.

Despite favourable arguments for TVET, international evidence shows that TVET has been a neglected component of most national development plans (Johanson & Van Adams 2004; Tan & Savchenko 2005; Valerio & Prawda, 2005). In the case of Nigeria, it is a run-down system of TVET designed to train low skill workers. Another inadequacy is that it is a system that is teaching according to curricula that are at least 30 years old and based on teachers who have received little training in vocational skills. Unfortunately, unlike in many developed countries, education and training in Nigeria is largely decentralized and financed from private resources.

However, power and authority for regulation and curriculum is the purview of the federal government, and to a lesser extent rest at the lower tiers of government. This system has limited the possibility to link education systems more closely to the world of work and to promote the expansion and improvement of technical and vocational education in the light of changing employment needs. These variants— strengthening the general education component of TVET, funding and budget allocation, or ensuring that TVET is not a dead end——are consistent with historic legacies which influenced the form, content and methods of education, bottlenecking the effective development of human resources and limiting the number of entrants to the technical and vocational schooling track. One reason for this failure is found in ambitious, yet unrealistic, policies of many developing countries to invest in non-diversified secondary and tertiary institutions as the means to catch up with developed countries (Carnoy, 1986; Torres, 2002).

Unfortunately current national educational choices have had a dampening effect on providing solutions to the fragility of the demand among the disadvantaged groups in society and economic needs of Nigeria. National problems include a great need for qualified human resources and high youth and graduate unemployment rates coupled with the high poverty rate that has become a sizeable social and economic issue. Another issue of concern is parental disillusionment with the present education systems and expressed support for more relevant curricula and providing practical skills for students. A solution requires rethinking the educational strategy that is now under siege. Should Nigeria not attempt to learn from and adapt good practices derived from the successful models of TVET from Taiwan, Japan, Germany, Korea, and elsewhere (Boyd & Lee, 1995; Woo, 1991; Yamamoto, 1995)?

SCHOOLING AND TVET IN NIGERIA

In Nigeria, the TVET curriculum is competency-based and employment led. Technical training of the agrarian stage of the industrial staircase pre-dates modern education in Nigeria. The apprenticeship system has long trained youths in marketable levels of competencies and skills specifically related to occupations like weaving, pottery, metal working, wood-carving and working, leather, farming and a multiplicity of other local occupations. The Yaba College of Technology, established in 1932, was Nigeria's earliest formal technical and vocational education and training (TVET) institution at the tertiary level. Other institutions that delivered these respective skills are Kaduna and Enugu Polytechnics, established in the 1950s, and Ibadan and Auchi Polytechnics, established in the 1970s. Many other institutions have since been haphazardly established on the basis of federal government stipulated mandates. At the time of Nigeria's independence in 1960, TVET was accorded high priority as a conscious effort of formulating a national TVET programme was put in place. The system consisted of an education and training programme that strived for balanced development of the students, releasing their potential as community developers. The system was labour market relevant, equitable, and of high quality. Most features of this comprehensive education and training system that served the nation, communities and individuals well are no longer prominent in the contemporary education system. Longe (1992) and Geo-JaJa (1987) stated that the current education system which takes place almost exclusively in schools but excludes periods of practical instructions in other locations concentrates on the production of high level manpower to the detriment of the production of skilled manpower. Again the standards at different education levels are not based or dependent on the stage of development of the economy and society. Therefore education construction is not reflective of the stage on the industrial staircase.

The contemporary system of education is organized by the levels: primary, secondary and tertiary. The duration of the primary level is six years. Secondary education is divided into junior and senior levels with a total of six years. Both junior and senior secondary educations are three years in length. The duration of tertiary education level and training varies depending on academic need. For instance, the intermediate level (Polytechnic) is usually part of a degree college that takes students up to diploma level and is two years beyond senior secondary level. Universities offer post degree and research programmes. The position occupied by TVET within each level varies from region to region, reflecting its assigned level of importance.

Much has been achieved in relation to increasing primary enrolment levels towards Universal Primary Education. However, a devastating picture emerges when comparing the performance of the education and training system in Nigeria with that of other emerging economies. Studies have suggested low internal efficiency indicators as well as skill-employment mismatch (see Geo-JaJa 1986, 2006; Hinchliffe, 1989). It is also evident from these and other studies that the dominant system has a prescribed curriculum and teachers are trained to implement a predetermined set of educational tasks. Curriculum is implicitly not organized around work nor designed for a transition economy. Schooling neglected adult education and training as workers were expected to be in one job throughout their working life.

The System of Education and Training

Despite many increases in quantitative and educational facilities after independence, the lack of political will to institute the necessary reforms has nullified the possible advances and gains that might have been attained by the 6-3-3-4 school system. For instance, participation rates at all levels are low and progress towards universal primary education and post-primary education has been slow, with educational quality continuing to deteriorate; curricula remain outdated and irrelevant to the needs of society. Vocational education that served society well in the past has not been successful in recent years. Education as a conceptualization of the colonial West has not ensured equitable access to opportunities nor has it been able to empower workers with required skills. The above negatives have had a dampening effect on relevance to local needs and adaptability to local culture and on sustainable development. Data indicate a secondary school and university graduate unemployment rate of 60 per cent coupled with a "broken" education system that annually produces millions of graduates who do not have the skill sets required by the private or public sector (Gboyega, 2007).

Further assessment of the external efficiency of schools indicates that graduates have qualifications but lack the required human capital and proper values and attitudes to act and work competently in an occupational environment. Graduates lack what it takes to gain employment in multinational oil companies, banks, and biotechnology and nanotechnology conglomerates. A survey, conducted in 2007 by the Lacuna After School Graduate Development Centre, reported that only about 10 per cent of graduates gained employment after graduation every year (Gboyega, 2007). However, there were marked differences in employment patterns according to levels and area of training. The national unemployment rate has continued to escalate unabatedly in comparison with earlier 2007 data. This situation has brought into sharp focus the mismatch between what students learn and what the labour market and national development plans require. A reason for this underutilization and ineffective resource application and high graduate unemployment is the absence of private sector involvement in school curricula design and the standardization of learning over the dual-system. This policy has resulted in the disappearance of traditional apprenticeship practices, rather than the academic system and industry working together to provide the student education as well as apprenticeship. However, the dual-system has several prerequisites that are not currently in place in Nigeria, so its application as a solution is a collective responsibility that requires more thought and resources.

Unemployment has increased from 4.3 per cent in 1985 to a staggering 60 per cent by 1997 (Ajao, 2004). Of those unemployed in 2003, 14.7 per cent were primary school graduates, 53.6 per cent were secondary school graduates while 12.4 per cent were tertiary graduates (Ajao, 2004). These percentages indicate the need for a sweeping radical reform that would require significant commitment on the part of policy makers and buy-in from the private sector. Their participation in decision-making should be not only at the national and state-levels but also at the inter-national level. What this analysis illustrates is that providing more schooling cannot, by itself, be enough; quality and labour market relevance are crucial.

TVET Institutions and Sectoral Manpower Needs

Technical and Vocational Education and Training has been considered crucial in developing manpower for labour markets and national development. But Nigeria in the last two decades has suffered from an acute shortage of manpower in new high technology areas, a shortage which will become more intensified in the immediate future. Post-secondary institutions (polytechnics) which were originally designed to supply such quality human resources for the industrial sector have suffered tremendous setbacks over the years. These setbacks are due to a lack of curriculum responsiveness to the changing needs of the labour market, a shortfall in resources for the maintenance of facilities, and a lack of meaningful dialogue with employers. Newly established institutes such as the Petroleum Training Institutions (PTI) and the Army Command and Staff Colleges have contributed only minimally to skills development. Even when considered cost-effective to prepare new entrants to the labour force, or upgrade or retrain deskilled workers with quality skills ideally suited for the promotion of sustainable practices in society, the impact of informal TVET institutions on mid-level manpower is deemed inadequate or has been minimal. It is most significant to note that the efforts made by the private sector that consumes most of this manpower have remained at best inconsequential, as no private sector engineering or technological universities exist. Thus, re-orienting TVET towards sustainability requires significant reform or what Cuban (1988) calls "second-order change" (p. 341). In this context, formal and informal TVET institutions include new curriculum development and structures.

A different picture might have been expected of TVET. However, the score card reflects problems and missed opportunities in developing competencies, employment skills and knowledge and attitudes when compared to previous decades. These could be attributed to scarce resources, the effectiveness of the system, or to lack of continuous teacher training and curricula development. The pursuit of current reforms does not go beyond internal colonialization as it is not an integral part of human and sustainable development plans which would transform graduates into local or globally competent workers. Beyond its implication for TVET, contemporary education strategy affects the functioning of education output and negatively impacts nonmarket outcomes, including income distribution, human rights, social cohesion and human capabilities. Any benchmark indicators will show that Nigeria lags behind similar oil-producing countries in providing current skills for up- and down-stream oil industry requirements (Azaiki, 2007). It is anticipated that this trend will predictably hurt Nigeria's long-term chances for skills development, poverty reduction, and sustainable development. This is further affirmed by the United Nations Development Programme (UNDP) Human Development Report (2006) as it contends that this process has adverse effects on locals benefiting directly from employment from the oil exploration that has also destroyed natural resources central to their livelihoods. It is on the basis of this understanding that the following contentions are made. Not only is the contextual framework of TVET delivery system in Nigeria a rundown system, the place of TVET in the education system is marginal both in terms of enrolment and number of institutions.

TVET: ESSENTIAL BUT UNSUPPORTED

TVET remains a sector that is insufficiently resourced, relatively fragmented, and lacking firm government steering. Furthermore, uncoordinated training institutions and fragmentation means duplication in development of curricula and a non-transparent system, resulting in an inefficient and costly TVET. Other critical challenges for TVET in Nigeria are private sector participation and decentralization, as it can no longer be the monopoly of the State. In this rationalization, the participation of the private sector and other stakeholders can no longer be nominal. Improving relevance requires diversifying the sources of funding. The broad connection of different actors also indicates the significance of collaboration and synergy amongst stakeholders, necessary to motivate quality-driven education and training reforms in tandem with skills development in an increasingly competitive globalized information and knowledge-based economy. TVET focal points need to be tied to policy support and linked with industry, employer and worker representatives who are able to feel the pulse of labour market needs.

Financing TVET

Since the 1980s, while schooling enrolment has been increasing in Nigeria, TVET enrolment and funding have either remained static or systematically declined (Geo-JaJa, 1990). Coupled with a lack of federal government support, technical and vocational education and training has been unable to supply the skill needs of the private sector. Public investment in education has been somewhat significant but it has not been a major benefit in the TVET sector. Small amounts of federal government funds combined with state and private sector funds for the expansion of existing TVET programmes would have a significantly favourable effect on the shortage of skilled workers, the revitalization of industry, and the contemplated expansion of the agriculture and oil sector of the economy. For these reasons, it is considered of utmost importance to establish a sustainable mode of financing for the system of TVET.

Currently in Nigeria, as in the rest of sub-Saharan African countries, TVET is financed almost independently of public funds, but a small proportion of state and federal government budget provide the rationale for a disproportional amount of public direction and control. In contrast, at independence in 1960, when the government goal was to bring the education sector in line with the dynamics of the labour market, TVET funding was an integral part of public funding of the education sector.

The author suggests that it is imperative that all tiers of government show direction and commitment to the development of human resources and human capabilities by raising the level of resources to this sector of education. Other stakeholders including employers and beneficiary trainees are also encouraged to contribute to the funding of TVET. The participation of employers and beneficiaries in financing of the system is important, as this stresses industry and worker ownership and interest, and thus strengthens the link between them and the training system. Clearly, the above suggestions espouse the need to establish a unified funding mechanism to avoid conflict of interest. The inference here is that even under Structural Adjustment Regimes (SAR) or in economic meltdown levels of funding, TVET should not be cut, as it is indeed central to the success of human resources and of national development plans.

Given the importance of TVET in the 21st century, the fragmented, isolated, uneven funding situation, present state of facilities and the huge investment required to rehabilitate and establish additional TVET institutions, it is generally seen as a necessity to seek external funding to supplement public investment. This must be viewed as a short-term external bridge-funding measure that requires proper coordination through a commonly agreed agency and judicious use for effectiveness and positive impact. In sum, gazing into the educational future and skills development of the 21st century, one considers it of utmost importance to establish a sustainable mode of adequate and stable long-term financing of TVET. Government has a crucial role in providing this stability, in order to develop and increase the capacity of TVET systems. It is recognized that this need for financing will increase vastly under globalization, as the system is in great need of reengineering and development. Justification for stable public funding of this unique skill development education and training system is based on a number of assumptions: it promotes competiveness in the global economy, it promotes industrial growth and development, and it promotes valuable employment as well as essentials for sustained livelihoods and the competitiveness of rural economy.

TVET for Quality of Life and Sustainable Society

We affirm that skills development leading to age-appropriate TVET should be integral to education at all levels, and can no longer be regarded as optional or marginal. In order for this to happen, it requires not only a revision of the central institutional organization and the way of financing, but would also necessitate a renovation of the established mode of operation. (UNESCO, 2004b, p. 1)

The above statement by UNESCO raises several issues of concern for the future in Nigeria, and in most developing countries. First, TVET in Nigeria continues to be marginalized in education design and thrust. Clearly, from an educational planning perspective, the continued and growing ineptness of schooling to meet the demand for workers with technical/vocational skills has complex implications. Second, the challenges posed by a fast-changing, technologically-oriented and knowledge-driven economy require a new generation of skilled workers (see Figure 1). These workers have the potential to engender equity by sharing the wealth created by globalization, and contributed by revitalizing Nigerian business. However reforms and funding continue to favour generalized education. In addition to these reforms associated with globalization, the commodification of education opposes the expansion of TVET, resulting in mitigating the match of education output with labour market need. The outcome tends to be a shortage of technical/vocational skilled manpower, and decline in the rate of returns of investment to TVET.

In recent years, a desire has surfaced to recognize anew the role of TVET in promoting poverty reduction, developing life skills, and human security, as outlined in the Millennium Development Goals, as well as in sustainable development, through technical innovations spurred by the advance of globalization. It seems clear that priorities should focus on improvements in access and quality that are now demonstrably unsatisfactory. The evidence for this convincing position was confirmed in 2004 during the UNESCO meeting on "Learning for Work, Citizenship and Sustainability", hosted in Bonn, Germany. International experts on technical and vocational education and training at this meeting added weight as they agreed that technical and vocational education and training (TVET) must be the master key that can alleviate poverty, promote peace, conserve the environment, improve the quality of life for all, and help achieve sustainable development. Furthermore, recognizing that the vast majority of the worldwide labour force, including knowledge workers, requires technical and vocational knowledge and skills throughout life, they affirmed that skills development leading to age-appropriate TVET should be integral to education at all levels, and that it can no longer be regarded as optional or marginal. These experts affirmed that it is especially important to integrate skills development in Education for All (EFA) programmes, and to satisfy TVET demand created by learners completing basic education (UNESCO, 2004b).

The Bonn meeting further affirmed that TVET has to reorient its agenda for action, so as to continually provide scientific and technical skills within relevant and responsive programmes, and consequently develop a new generation of human resources. This is the import of flexibility. It seems clear that priorities should focus on TVET's integration into all levels of education, as preparation for work includes equipping people with the knowledge, competencies, skills, values and attitudes to become productive and responsible citizens who appreciate the dignity of work, and contribute to sustainable societies (UNESCO, 2004b).

In regard to labour market dynamism, this author and a colleague, in a study on Nigeria, argued for a specific model of education—outcomes-based education with a localized curriculum (Geo-JaJa & Mangum, 2002). Enthusiasm for a new view of education was not forthcoming, as reforms are primarily the means of changing who is in control, rather than changing the specifics and substance of education (Geo-JaJa, 2004, 2006). Generally speaking, non-comprehensive reforms have only resulted in technical and vocational education occupying a low status position in the education sector, thereby only reaching a particularly small segment of the population. In this connection, an education system (training, re-training, and knowledge acquisition) that is demand-driven (developed in cooperation with the private sector) can prepare individuals to benefit from the evolving employment environment, as well as to meet equity and economic development needs. In sum, the soundness of a TVET programme will depend on the degree and extent to which it is responsive to definition as distinguished and defined by UNESCO in this paper.

The application of sustainable development principles is best accompanied in a comprehensive approach through their inclusion in TVET curricula. The internationalization of the workforce through globalization and labour migration is also a cogent argument of the importance of developing respect for cultural sensitivity in TVET. Other tenable needs to consider in TVET are the expected shortage of skilled manpower and unskilled youth workers; the intensification of graduate unemployment; the influx of unskilled graduates to the labour market; the oil sector manpower challenge and the need for revitalization of Nigeria's industry. All of these require rationalizing the utilization of technical and vocational education and training facilities, upgrading curricula, and strengthening and integrating TVET into education.

There is a strong case for rethinking public investment in education, removing obstacles to the access of people into TVET and equalizing their access to opportunities, and for shifting policy to maintain consistency of educational purposes and skills development. These are the most important factors in adjusting to labour market changes and to adverse social and economic conditions. On the other hand, lack of, inappropriate or outdated skills could lead to trapping individuals in a kind of employment "no man's land". The risk involved is creating a social ghetto of people dependent on social safety nets and deprived of positive social inclusion (Clarke, 2005). From these assertions, TVET becomes a passport for poverty reduction over the conventional school model whose objective is to produce loyal citizens and a large number of graduates whose learning and values are mismatched to the labour market.

New Thrust from UNESCO and Other Multinationals

As far back as 1974, there has been a debate for provision of technical and vocational education and training as "an integral part of general education," (UNESCO, 1995, p. 29; World Bank, 1974). The World Bank, like UNESCO, criticized schooling curricula as exceptionally theoretical and abstract in content. Indeed, other international agencies are returning to the expanded vision of EFA that extend beyond the walls of general schooling (UNESCO-IIEP, 2004; UNESCO, 2002, WCEFA, 1990). Though there has been resistance to such sweeping reform from certain quarters, there has also been an increasing effort to include formal and informal education, private formal/informal enterprise-based training, school-based TVET at primary and post-primary levels, and tertiary education in skills development (UNESCO, 2004b). Also, in response to the disproportionately growing poverty rate and high unemployment rates among youth who have completed basic education in comparison to the general population, the World Bank, ILO, UNESCO, and other organizations have recently recognized anew the role of TVET in empowering such youths.

In summary, it seems that under enabling environments, which may differ from region to region and country to country, investment in diversified schooling or TVET does contribute to employability and may also be linked to externalities that can contribute to sustainable development (Lewin, 1998; Woo, 1991). The position of McGrath and King (1999a) and Honig (1993) is more circumspect in regard to these possibilities. They remain skeptical to the effectiveness of diversified curricula even though the ideas are widely supported by empirical evidence. Recently, however, McGrath and King (1999b); King and Palmer (2005), and McGrath (2005) make the case for the contribution of skills and higher-level skills to poverty alleviation, rural development, and economic growth. These authors also further supported the policy of using TVET as a way to meet "different needs for different communities". Other criticisms concerning the ineffectiveness and high cost of TVET to meet the varied requirements of the productive sector and needs of society might have led to cuts in the amount of training provided in different institutions and to shifting more of the responsibility for providing initial skill training to individuals and private institutions. These are reasons for the focus of this discussion on sweeping radical reform in design and funding for TVET.

TVET'S ROLE IN EMPLOYMENT AND UNIQUE EMPLOYABILITY

As Keith Lewin (1993) reminds us, there is much that we need to know about the cost-effectiveness of TVET interventions that go beyond statements of hope.

As has been stated in previous sections, TVET among other things is considered by its advocates and this author to be a great equalizer and expander of opportunities: as it contributes to poverty alleviation and empowerment, as it addresses issues of human capabilities and entitlement, and as it plays an important role in economic and social change.

Leading scholars have lent strong support to technical and vocational education and training. For instance, Van Rensburg (2001) emphatically argued that the practical orientation of TVET is of cardinal importance to the productivity and welfare of nations. He had no doubt that its important advantage is its orientation towards the world of work and the emphasis of its curriculum on the acquisition of employable skills (UNESCO & ILO, 2002). Thomas Balogh (1969) was similarly emphatic: "As a purposive factor for rural socio-economic prosperity and progress, education must be technical, vocational and democratic." In fact, he suggested that even "elementary education must impart technical knowledge to rural youths in an eminently practical way" (p. 265). Grubb (1985) also states that TVET is an answer to the enrolment problem for lower class and disadvantaged students who have the tendency to drop-out of school without occupational skills or for the high opportunity costs of schooling rather than work at home, a problem that TVET resolves by providing a more functional and job-relevant curriculum.

More recent studies report positive rates of return on vocational secondary education. A study in Turkey shows that male graduates of technical and vocational high schools not only have a higher probability of wage employment but also significantly higher wages and rates of return than general high school graduates (Ziderman, 1997). Even Psacharopoulos (1994), who has been a strong opponent of vocational secondary schooling, in an 11-country Latin American study found "that the [social] rates of return for vocational secondary education is higher than that for secondary general education and that the private rates of return to secondary education does not differ between general and vocational education (p. 7). Hansen (2000) opined that today's schools are designed to create good citizens in an industrial era dominated by physical capabilities, by bureaucratic command, and by entrepreneurship and skill centres/organizations which leave little room for creative education. These authors feel that real-world challenges should be brought into classrooms as the starting points for learning, around which curricula and subject content can be integrated. Chung (1995) also reported 12 studies showing higher rates of return to vocational education than to general secondary education.

Some economists indicate that the content of general school curricula and syllabi does not contribute towards the industrial and economic growth of a country, just as the non-integration of TVET models into mainstream education at all levels has also affected the viability of specific fields of study such as "learning for work, citizenship, and skills development leading to age-appropriate TVET (see DFID, 2001; UNESCO 2004b). However, these arguments ignore factors such as the relevance of subject content, employable skills, and values and attitudes of learners and teachers. Common sense tells us that if a learner is taught specific technical and vocational skills, that learner will be better equipped to function productively and

45

effectively in the national economy. This means that higher productivity, greater competence to do work, and better quality workmanship are all real contributing factors to economic growth.

Lillis and Hogan (1983) observe, as would Geo-JaJa (2006), that negative indicators of educational internal efficiency could be resolved or MDGs met by diversifying the curriculum of post-primary schooling. I therefore agree with Ziderman (1997) that in order for TVET to be successful in developing countries, Nigeria included, it must be comprehensive in nature and be more responsive to the skill needs of industry and societies.

CONCLUSIONS AND RECOMMENDATIONS

This paper highlights the short-term nature of the current academic education and TVET system, which is geared to meeting the immediate needs of the global market, and lacking in a long-term strategic vision of how to combat povertization and intensify graduate unemployment among those with low productivity, as well as the disempowerment of people and communities. It is clear that the education and training system needs to be redefined and made consistent with producing appropriate and adequate human resources for sustainable development. As there is no doubt of the contribution of TVET to human capital and human development, poverty alleviation, community enablement, as well as to national-building and sustainable development, the commitment to a sweeping radical rethink to promote TVET as an integral part of the wider education system and not a separate entity is a necessary and sufficient condition for success and progress.

The soundness of an education system depends on the degree and extent to which it responds to human resource development and national development plans. Consequently, the critical elements for an effective technical and vocational education and training are its match or mismatch to industrial growth, teaching methods and materials, and methods and content. Finally, the author affirms that the future success of Nigeria, and also that of individuals, industry and businesses and communities, increasingly depends on the starting of enterprise skills education from basic education and on expanding and improving the quality of TVET systems. The effort will be such that the target group can reinforce and build on its own development capacities and consequently overcome their economic poverty. Also crucial is the recognition of the important role TVET plays in inculcating in individuals the relevant skills and knowledge, and attitudes and values necessary for citizens to participate in social, economic and technological innovation processes. Thus, examination in higher education (college of technologies) and TVET should not be stressed so as to allow innovation, creativity and excellence in education.

In sum, the prospect for skills development and effective TVET requires dynamic interaction among all stake holders, academia, industry, business, research and development, chambers of commerce, student bodies, parent organizations, civil society and NGO's. Governments who represent the interests of society, employers and business, must lead from the front. Furthermore, adequate funding, as well as embedding TVET into national development plans is also imperative. Surely it must be seen as an integral part of a comprehensive education system. To conclude, as Nigeria is endowed with traditional arts and crafts at the village-level, these should be encouraged as many of them are of great value in terms of economic empowerment of rural Nigeria. Indeed, they could be magnified considerably if some of these existing arts and crafts could be integrated into the schools in the respective local areas and modernized using the latest TVET courses which use modern materials, tools, implements and techniques to make products faster, better and at lower cost. Consequently the only starting point to reversing povertization and low skills and competencies of the work force is through the provision of high quality technical and vocational education and training and by complementing the school curriculum with Enterprise Education. This would help school children, when they leave school, to seek options of alternative economic income generating activities.

Along with the urgent need to reduce poverty and unemployment in the short-term, Nigeria posting any significant progress in TVET requires an enormous effort within all tiers of government and industry-business, including a fiscal pact to ensure the efficient use of public resources, transparency, accountability, and clear rules and greater availability of resources so that the government can meet development priorities. Observations about the end result of the existing education system and TVET practices that are partly analyzed in this work is that which informed these recommendations.

REFERENCES

Aderemi, A. A. (1997). Role of women in vocational education for economic development. *Bichi Journal of Education, 1*(2), 73–75.

Ajao, W. (2004, December 23). Neglect of technical vocational education increases youth unemployment. *The Vanguard.*

Azaiki, S. (2007). *Oil, democracy and the promise of true federalism in Nigeria.* Port Harcourt: Treasure Books.

Balogh, T. (1969). Education and agrarian progress in developing countries. In K. Hufne & J. Naumann (Eds.), *Economics of education in transition* (pp. 259–268). Stuttgart: Ernst Klett.

Boyd, T. F., & Lee, C. (1995). Educational need and economic advancement: The role of vocational education in the Republic of China. In A. H. Yee (Ed.), *East Asian higher education: Traditions and transformations* (pp. 193–210). Issues in Higher Education.

Carnoy, M. (1986). Educational reform and planning in the current economic crisis. *Prospects, 16*(2), 204–214.

Clarke, P. (2005). *Technical and vocational education systems in Australia and India: An experiment in cross cultural learning.* Washington, DC: World Bank Working Paper.

Chung, Y.-P. (1995). Returns to vocational education in developing nations. In M. Carnoy (Ed.), *International encyclopedia of economics of education* (pp. 175–181). Oxford: Pergamon.

Cuban, L. (1988). A fundamental puzzle of school reform. *Phi Delta Kappan, 70*(5), 341–344.

Cummings, W. K., & McGinn, N. (1997). Introduction. In K. W. Cummings & N. McGinn (Eds.), *International handbook of education and development: Preparing schools, students and nations in the twenty-first century* (pp. 3–43). New York: Elsevier Science, Inc.

Department for International Development (DFID). (2001). *Learning to compete: Education, training and enterprise in Ghana.* DFID.

Gboyega, A. (2007, December 24). Unemployment: Why some may not get jobs. *This Day, 12*(4629), 27.

Geo-JaJa, M. A. (1986). *Education and training and occupational skills development in Nigeria: An empirical analysis.* Invited paper presentation at the World Bank, Education Sector, Washington, DC.

Geo-JaJa, M. A. (1987). Manpower planning with occupational choice: A Nigeria example of mismatch. *Social and Economic Studies Journal, 39*(3), 127147.

Geo-JaJa, M. A. (1990). Non-formal education: A proposed solution to graduate unemployment in Nigeria. *Education and Training Journal, 32*(6), 23–26.

Geo-JaJa, M. A. (2004). Decentralization and privatization of education in Africa: Which option for Nigeria? *International Review of Education, 50*(3–4), 309–326.

Geo-JaJa, M. A., & Mangum, G. (2002). Outcome-based education and structural adjustment policies: Nigerian case study. *World Studies in Education, 3*(2), 81–102.

Geo-JaJa, M. A. (2006). Educational decentralization, public spending, and social justice in Nigeria. *International Review of Education, 52*(1–2), 129–153.

Grubb, W. N. (1985). The convergence of educational system and the role of vocationalism. *Comparative Education Review, 29*(4), 526–548.

Hansen, R. (2000). The role of experience learning: Giving meaning and authenticity to the learning process. *Journal of Technology Education, 11*(2), 23–32.

Harbison, F. H. (1973). *Human resources as the wealth of nations.* Oxford: Oxford University Press.

Harbison, R., & Hanushek, E. (1992). *Education performance of the Poor: Lessons from Northwest Brazil.* New York: Oxford University Press.

Hinchliffe, K. (2002). *Public expenditures on education in Nigeria: Issues, estimates and some implications.* Washington, DC: The World Bank.

Honig, B. (1993). *Research perspectives on African education and the informal sector.* Paper presented at the Annual Meeting of the American Educational Research Association (April), Atlanta, GA.

Johanson, R., & Van Adams, A. (2004). *Skills development in Sub-Saharan Africa.* A World Bank Publication.

King, K., & Palmer, R. (2005). *Education, training and their enabling environments.* Post-basic Education and Training Working Paper Series No. 7, Centre of African Studies, University of Edinburgh, Edinburgh.

Lewin, K. (1993). Investing in technical and vocational education: Review of the evidence. *Journal of Vocational Education and Training, 45*(3), 217–227.

Lewin, K. (1998). Education in emerging Asia: Patterns, policies and futures into the 21st Century. *International Journal of Educational Development, 18*(2), 81–118.

Lillis, K., & Hogan, D. (1983). Dilemmas of diversification: Problems associated with vocational education in developing countries. *Comparative Education, 19*(1), 89–107.

Longe, G. (1992). *Higher education in the nineties and beyond. Report of the Commission on the Review of Higher Education in Nigeria, Ministry of Education.* Federal Republic of Nigeria.

Mangum, G. (2005). The interaction of human development, economic development and nation-building on the industrial staircase. In J. Zajda (Ed.), *International handbook on globalization, education and policy research.* Amsterdam: Kluwer Academic Publishers.

McGrath, S. (2005). *The challenge of rural skills development.* Debates in Skills Development, Paper 10, Working Group for International Cooperation in Skills Development. Geneva: ILO/NORRAG/SDC.

McGrath, S., & King, K. (1999a). Enterprise in Africa: New contexts, renewed challenges. In K. King & S. McGrath (Eds.), *Enterprise in Africa: Between poverty and growth.* London: Intermediate Technology Publications, Ltd.

McGrath, S., & King, K. (1999b). Learning to grow? The importance of education and training for small and micro-enterprise development. In K. King & S. McGrath (Eds.), *Enterprise in Africa: Between poverty and growth.* London: Intermediate Technology Publications, Ltd.

Olaitan, S. O. (1996). *Agricultural education in the tropics.* London: Macmillan Publisher Ltd.

Psacharopoulos, G. (1994). Earnings and education in Latin America. *Education Economics, 2*(2), 1–29.

Tan, H., & Savchenko, Y. (2005). *In-Service Training in India: Evidence from the India firm-level investment climate survey.* World Bank Working Paper.

Tikly, L. (2004). Education and the new imperialism. *Comparative Education, 40*(2), 173–198.

Torres, C. A. (2002). The state, privatization and educational policy: A critique of Neoliberalism in Latin America and some ethical and political implications. *Comparative Education, 36*(4), 365–385.

United Nations Development Program. (2006). *Niger Delta Human Development Report.* New York: Oxford University Press.

UNESCO. (1995). *Education strategies for the 1990s: Orientations and achievements.* Report on the State of Education in Africa 1995. Paris: UNESCO.

UNESCO. (2004a). *EFA global monitoring report.* Paris: UNESCO.

UNESCO. (2004b, October). *Learning for work, citizenship and sustainability.* A UNESCO International Meeting of Technical and Vocational Education and Training Experts, Bonn, Germany.

UNESCO – IIEP. (2004, January). *Promoting skills development.* Report of an international seminar on assisting the design and implementation of education for all skills development plans: Skills development to meet the learning needs of the excluded. Paris: UNESCO and IIEP.

UNESCO and ILO. (2002). *Technical and vocational training for the twenty-first century.* Paris.

Valerio, A., & Prawda, J. (2005). *Competency-based training, technical and vocational education and lifelong learning programs.* Australia and New Zealand study tour report.

Van Rensburg, P. (2001). *Making education work. The what, why and how of education with production.* Johannesburg: Foundation for Education with Production International.

Woo, J. H. (1991). Education and economic growth: A case of successful planning. *World Development, 19*(8), 1029–1044.

World Conference on Education For All [WCEFA]. (1990, March). *Meeting basic learning needs: A vision for the 1990s.* Background document for the WCEFA in Jomtien, Thailand. WCEFA: New York.

World Bank. (1974). *Education.* Sector paper. Washington, DC: World Bank.

Yamamoto, S. (1995). Traditionalism versus research and development at Japanese universities. In Yee (Ed.), *East Asian higher education: Traditions and transformations* (pp. 25–35, 1st ed.). Issues in Higher Education Series. New York: Elsevier Science.

Ziderman, A. (1997). National programmes in technical and vocational education: Economic and education relationships. *Journal of vocational education and training, 49*(3), 351–366.

Macleans A. Geo-JaJa
David O. Mckay School of Education
Brigham Young University

EWA KOWALSKI

4. TECHNICAL AND VOCATIONAL EDUCATION AND TRAINING REFORM IN POLAND'S NEW POLITICAL AND ECONOMIC CLIMATE

INTRODUCTION

As I revisit some of the many papers that David Wilson wrote on Technical and Vocational Education and Training (TVET), I am struck by the diverse range of countries and regions that his work and research spanned over the years. Wilson has written papers focusing on education and training in North America (Canada, the United States), Europe (Germany, Switzerland), Latin America (Brazil), Asia (Indonesia, Japan, Malaysia, Sri Lanka), the Middle East (Israel), Africa (Kenya, Tanzania), and Oceania (Australia, New Zealand). However, except for occasional references to the Czech, Slovak and former East German TVET systems, one geographical area notably absent from this body of research is Eastern and Central Europe.

Little attention is given in Wilson's work to the former Eastern Bloc countries, either before or after their transition from centrally-planned, communist economies to more democratic, market-oriented systems in the early 1990s. Perhaps the TVET sector in these countries during communism drew sparse research interest because of its limited relevance and viability for countries with market-based systems. Moreover, for more than four decades, the uncompetitive nature of the nationalized and centrally-planned economic infrastructures in the region provided no stimulus for constructive change and development of these countries' TVET sectors, until the collapse of the Soviet system in the early 1990s. The ensuing political and economic transformation that took place across numerous former Eastern Bloc countries, as well as their entry into the European Union (EU) in 2004[1] and 2007[2], and their inclusion into the globalizing world economy created the impetus and necessity for educational reform, including TVET.

These reform efforts and experiences were topics of the Vietnam Study Tours, the last teaching project David Wilson undertook in the summer of 2006, in which I participated as a presenter. Designed for senior policy makers and ministry officials from Vietnam, the Programme had two main objectives. The first was to provide participants with the context and key issues in the design, development and implementation of TVET policy primarily in Canada as well as selected transition economies relevant to Vietnam. The second objective was to provide participants the opportunity to learn first-hand about Ontario's TVET system by visiting colleges and institutions in Toronto, including the Ontario Ministry of Training, Colleges and Universities, and by meeting and establishing contact with the institutions' senior officials.

V. Masemann et al., (Eds.), A Tribute to David N. Wilson: Clamouring for a Better World, 51–66.

This paper, presented as part of the Vietnam Study Tours, focuses on TVET reform in Poland which has one of the largest and fastest-growing transition economies in Eastern Europe after 1989. It examines changes that occurred in the Polish TVET sector both pre- and post-1989, analyzes the successes and failures of recent reform efforts and explores some of the lessons learned in the process. To better understand the effect of these developments, the discussion is placed within the broader context of the Polish education system before and after 1989. Designed as a single country case study, the presentation set the scene for Professor Wilson's subsequent programme sessions, which included a cross-country comparison of policy transition in Poland and Vietnam. Expanded further to include comparisons with TVET policies and policy-making approaches in Canada, the presentation also examined the relevance of the different approaches to Vietnam, thus enabling a better understanding of the challenges and opportunities faced by Vietnamese policy makers.

Making the comparison with Poland's decade-long experience with educational reform as part of the Vietnam Study Tours was relevant for two reasons. First, learning from the experiences of other countries was an important aspect of Professor Wilson's teaching and research methodology (Wilson, 1994). Second, it was relevant because, despite Vietnam's limited experience with education reform, some contextual similarities exist between these two countries. Although geographically distant, both Poland and Vietnam are countries that share the experience of socialism and that have recently undergone a transition from command to global market-based economies. However, the patterns of transition of these two countries differ quite significantly. While Poland took a more radical approach toward economic as well as political reorientation by simultaneously adopting democracy, Vietnam chose a more gradual and partial approach in economic reform while continuing on the socialist path (Guo, 2004). Despite divergent transition patterns, both countries now face the challenge of reforming outdated and ineffective TVET sectors that exist as part of the socialist legacy as well as ensuring that this change occurs in concert with the new social, economic and educational goals within a broader European and global context. This paper will now turn to Polish education reform efforts.

THE POLISH EDUCATION SYSTEM UNDER SOCIALIST RULE

The Polish education system underwent a number of profound changes following the establishment of the communist regime in 1947. One change involved aligning the new system with the Soviet model of education by nationalizing all educational infrastructures and adopting the doctrine of Marxism-Leninism. Numerous structural changes were then introduced to reflect these ideological and educational principles and to prepare the workforce for the specific demands of Poland's centrally-planned economy and its newly nationalized industrial sector. These changes in turn resulted in a substantial vocationalization of Polish post-primary, secondary and tertiary education. The restructured system consisted of an eight-year primary school followed by four tracks: a four year general-academic track secondary school, a four to five year technical-vocational secondary school (*technikum, liceum zawodowe*), a two to three year basic vocational school, or a one year on-the-job apprenticeship in various occupation-specific tracks (see Figure 1) (BUWiWM, 2000). The tertiary level comprised one to three year technical-vocational postsecondary schools and various kinds of higher education (HE) institutions aligned along vocational lines. Following the Soviet model, numerous faculties were removed from universities and re-established in specialized university-type institutions, comprising academies (*akademie*), higher vocational schools (*wyższe szkoły zawodowe*), polytechnics (*politechniki*) and institutes (*instytuty*), and placed under the supervision of related governmental ministries to reinforce the specialized aspects of their training (Jung-Miklaszewska, 2003; Sorensen, 1997).

THE EDUCATION SYSTEM IN POLAND

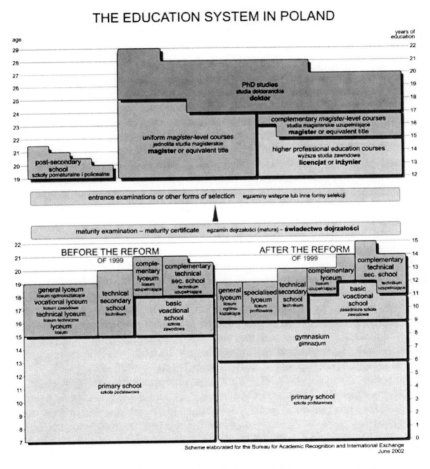

Figure 1. Polish system of education before and after the reform of 1999.

Source: Jung-Miklaszewska (2003).

The impact of the technical-vocational orientation of the Polish education system becomes evident when examining post-primary school enrolment data prior to 1989. Available data show that secondary schools, in both the academic and technical-vocational tracks, accommodated only about 35 per cent of every age cohort. The remaining 65 per cent, which included many academically able and ambitious students, were streamed into basic vocational schools (Jung-Miklaszewska, 2003). As suggested by GUS (2005a), access to the general-academic track was limited to only about 15 per cent of secondary school entrants, a process which resulted in a low number of academically-oriented graduates. The remaining 20 per cent of secondary school entrants proceeded to technical-vocational tracks. While both of these secondary school tracks led to tertiary education upon successful completion of the secondary school exam (*matura*), admittance to HE institutions in Poland was restricted with only about 8 to 10 per cent of every age cohort graduating from their programmes (Organisation for Economic Co-operation and Development [OECD], 2006).

In contrast, graduates of basic vocational schools, which were based on a terminal curriculum that prevented further enrolment in regular secondary education, were required to proceed directly into the workforce upon graduation. Students who wanted to pursue secondary education could do so only by enrolling in evening and extramural programmes, while maintaining their daytime employment (BUWiWM, 2000; GUS, 2005a). The limited data that are available suggest an adverse impact of these highly inflexible and constraining education policies on the school completion and participation of vocational graduates in secondary education, leading consequently to a high percentage of the workforce with less than a secondary school diploma. For example, the GUS (2007) data suggest a drop-out rate of about 27 per cent of the entire vocational student cohort during the period 1990/1991, with only 0.5 per cent of this group re-entering basic vocational education in the following years.

The same data further suggest low graduation rates from evening/extramural secondary education programmes in the early 1990s, with only 13,000 (general-academic) and 40,000 (technical) graduates out of approximately 49,000 and 147,000 students, respectively, who entered these programmes in the late 1980s. The number of secondary school graduates for each of the two groups, which includes both basic vocational graduates and secondary school drop-outs, appears to be relatively low given the total of approximately 236,000 students who graduated from basic vocational schools in, and possibly before, 1990/1991.

The policy of expansion of TVET during socialism was consistent with Poland's rapid industrialization initiated in the 1950s and its emphasis on the expansion of the extraction and productive sectors. In response to the growing demand for workers in these sectors, many technical and, primarily, vocational schools were established to provide the necessary occupation-specific training (e.g. in coal mining, ship-building, metallurgy, textiles). However, this narrow vocationalism, which inherently encouraged the marginalization of the academic curriculum in Polish schools, proved to have adverse implications for several generations of Polish students. One problem was the failure of the TVET system to enable students to acquire a solid academic foundation (e.g. in mathematics, science) needed to successfully prepare workers for lifelong learning, skills upgrading and retraining in response to changing skills demands.

From a sociological standpoint, the extreme vocationalization of Polish education contributed to the differentiation and hierarchy in social status based on education lines, leading to the perceived social elitism shared by individuals with higher education levels (i.e. the "intelligentsia") and to, what Wilson (1993b) describes as the "blue-collar" stigma associated with basic vocational education and members of the working class. An additional, if not critical, factor was that by the late 1980s, after more than four decades of policies excessively emphasising narrow occupational training, the Polish labour market faced a severe crisis resulting from the over-production of employees with vocational skills, coupled with an equally severe shortage of highly skilled professionals. While unemployment was avoided during socialism because state-owned enterprises were required to hire more workers than needed and that they could profitably employ, the collapse of communism brought with it a new reality, new challenges and new opportunities (Tracy, 2004; BUWiWM, 2000).

POLISH EDUCATION REFORM AFTER 1990

As in other former Eastern bloc countries, the transition from socialism to political democracy and market economy has created a need to address the changing economic, social and educational needs. The first decade of the transition was marked by considerable efforts to make Poland's economic system and institutions more structurally responsive to these needs, and to reorient its sphere of interest from the east toward integration with the European Union (EU) and other western structures (NATO, OECD, IMF). As part of the process, constitutional changes were introduced to restore democratic political structures and Poland's centrally planned economic infrastructure has been dismantled, leading to the privatization or elimination of state-owned enterprises (Tracy, 2004). The ensuing shift from resource extraction to services, occurring within the broader context of change from the industrial society to the knowledge society, and the growing Europeanization and globalization of economic activities have dramatically altered the structure of the Polish labour market. With demand for workers with vocational skills sharply declining in the 1990s and demand for skilled professionals rapidly increasing, a comprehensive reform of the Polish education system became a necessity.

The New Structure of Polish Education

New education legislation introduced in Poland after 1989 focused primarily on addressing reform at the tertiary level, seen by authorities as critical to the production of a professional workforce and the production of knowledge for the country's economic growth and development. The substantial reform of Poland's primary and secondary education was introduced almost a decade later, due primarily to the high cost of its implementation.

Tertiary education. A new law[3] on higher education, passed in Poland between the period 1990–1991 and amended in 2005, marked the beginning of a broad range of reforms aimed at the transformation of higher education and the creation of a new HE landscape. The reforms re-introduced institutional autonomy and academic freedom, and introduced changes that affected the content of education and the system of administering it, thus allowing for greater democratization, de-politicization and de-ideologization of teaching and academic activity (Dąbrowa-Szefler & Jabłecka-Prysłopska, 2006). Other significant changes included diversification of Poland's HE landscape, evident in the emergence of a private (non-state) higher education system alongside the public (state) sector; and differentiation of a once uniform degree structure, replaced in the 1990s with a three-cycle degree system of bachelor (*licencjat/inżynier*), master (*magister)* and doctoral (*doktorat*) level courses. These changes resulted in a rapid demand for and expansion of a once highly elitist Polish HE system. In addition to free public higher education for full-time students (based on Article 70 of the Constitution), numerous tuition-bearing courses have been created by both public (part-time) and private (full-/part-time) institutions, with student enrolments increasing about five times from 400 thousand in 1990 to 2 million in 2004 (Kwiek, 2005).

On the one hand, this expansion and massification of higher education signified a democratization of educational opportunities and a response to the aspirations for the economic and social advancement of a large portion of the Polish society who were denied access to higher education during the socialist period. It also allowed for greater professional diversification and preparation of graduates in relation to the different fields and levels of the job market. On the other hand, however, the expansion of higher education, combined with the limited capacity of the state budget to finance its provision, led to a substantial underfunding of HE institutions and the subsequent adoption of the market rhetoric in relation to their functioning (Kwiek, 2005). Impacted further by the worldwide trends towards marketization and vocationalization of higher education in the 1990s, the rationale of Poland's HE institutions became increasingly viewed by authorities and some academics as a type of "market" and "enterprise" that yields economic benefits and is a vehicle for economic development (Szapiro, 2007, Kwiek, 2005; Kwiek, 2003). This pragmatic rationale, also driven by Poland's high unemployment and a growing economic emigration of a large portion of its population to the EU countries in the 1990s and 2000s, has closely linked HE institutions to the demands of the labour market and the goals of economic development.

Similar to the reform efforts at the national level where the social development has been largely subsumed by the economic development, the law on higher education, passed since the mid-1990s, strongly reflects this approach by giving high priority to the professional preparation of students over the social and civic preparation (see Act on Professional Higher Education Institutions, 1997; Law on Higher Education, 2005). According to the law, both the undergraduate and graduate study cycles are deigned to prepare students for work in a specific profession, which, to some extent, is reminiscent of the educational goals pursued during the socialist period (Article 2, Law on Higher Education, 2005). Within the public sector, the institutional structure of higher education, which was fragmented along vocational lines during the socialist period, has been further expanded to include newly created higher professional institutions. This change has made the higher education system even better placed to respond to the economic goals and needs, and the growing demand among students for practical training that brings immediate rewards in the marketplace.

Today, the Polish HE system comprises over 94 public (59 university-type and 35 higher professional) institutions, 250 private institutions, the church-run Catholic University of Lublin, and a broad range of colleges (e.g. teacher training colleges), operating in partnership with Poland's universities and fulfilling a role of a basic professional education institution (Ministry of Science & Higher Education, 2009). As part of the Bologna Process, Poland has also adopted the ECTS framework (European Credit Transfer and Accumulation System) and is implementing quality assurance procedures in the move to encourage greater mobility of students and faculty within the EU higher education institutions. As noted by a number of scholars (O'Dowd chapter in this book; Tomusk, 2007), the implementation of these outcome-based procedures raises serious questions of the extent to which they will result in the standardization of higher education and reduce it to skills and competency development, thus driving it toward even greater vocationalization.

Primary/secondary education. Similar to the higher education reform, the reform of Poland's primary and secondary education was implemented in several phases. The legislation, passed in 1991, focused primarily on greater democratization of Poland's education structure, content of education, and instruction. Thus the first phase of the reform was marked by the breaking down of the State monopoly in education, evident in de-politicization and de-ideologization of school curricula, decentralization of the management and administration of the education system, and increased diversity of school choice (e.g. public, private, denominational schools). These changes allowed more autonomous practices within the education system, reorientation of school curricula and instruction, as well as afforded students the right to choose their educational path (Sorensen, 1997). The provisions which were passed during the second phase (in 1999 and 2001) of the reform altered the structure of the pre-1989 education system, and were part of the EU accession mandate requiring Poland to increase the number of secondary school graduates able to proceed to higher education closer to EU norms and standards. More recent efforts, which include the 2008 curriculum reform, have focused, among others, on the inclusion of a European dimension in the National Curriculum and the development of related curriculum materials and school textbooks for various subjects across the primary and secondary curricula.

As part of the above initiatives, a new 6-3-3 model was adopted in 1999–2000 to replace the "old" model (8-4) by 2007, thus extending compulsory schooling from 8 to 9 years. This new model, which can be viewed as a hybrid of the pre- and post-1989 educational structures, consists of six years of primary school, three years of lower secondary school (*gimnazjum*), three years of upper secondary school differentiated into an academic- (*liceum*) and vocational-track lyceum (*liceum profilowane/liceum zawodowe*), and a four year technical-track school (*technikum*).

The various upper secondary school streams lead to the secondary school completion exam (*matura*) (*see Figure 1*). Lower secondary school graduates who do not wish to proceed to an upper secondary institution may enrol in a two to three-year basic vocational school. This school differs significantly from its predecessor because it offers a non-terminal and more flexible curriculum, which allows students to continue their education in a two to three year compensatory secondary school (e.g. lyceum/technical school) and proceed to a higher vocational school upon graduation, as well as to re-enter the system after several years in the workforce (Jung-Miklaszewska, 2003; GUS, 2007; Dąbrowa-Szefler & Jabłecka-Prysłopska, 2006). These structural and curricular changes enable students to pursue career-oriented education and engage in life-long learning, which will result in a better-educated and adaptable workforce. They are also likely to have a positive influence on changing the negative public image of TVET which has prevailed in Poland in recent decades.

Changing Enrolment Patterns

The impact of the recent restructuring becomes even more evident when examining the proportion of students across general-academic and technical-vocational schools. The data provided by GUS (2003, 2004, 2005b, 2007) suggest a gradual reversal of the schooling patterns that existed during socialism, leading to the expansion of student participation in the upper secondary system and a decline in the number of basic vocational schools (e.g. in coal mining, metallurgy) and their student enrolments after 1999. For example, the number of students entering basic vocational schools dropped from 65 per cent of every age cohort before 1990 to 16 per cent in 2002/03 and 10 per cent in 2003/04 (see Table 1).

Table 1. Percentage of Students Enrolled in Post-Primary and Upper Secondary School Levels in Poland Before and After the Reform of 1999.

School Type and Level / School Year	Basic Vocational	Upper Secondary		
		General Academic (Lyceum/ Liceum)	Technical (Technikum)	Vocational (Lyceum/ Liceum)
Before/Early 1990s	65	15	20	
2002/03	16	38	23	13
2003/04	10	41	23	13
2004/05	14	47	26	13
2006/07	14	47	31	8

Source: GUS 2003, 2004, 2005b, 2007; Vulcan, 2006.

Concurrently, the proportion of students in the rapidly expanding secondary school system increased in the period between the early 1990s and 2003/04 from 15 per cent to 41 per cent in general-academic track lyceums and from 20 to 36 per cent in technical-vocational schools, with 23 per cent enrolled in technical schools (*technikum*) and 13 per cent in vocational lyceums.

These changes point to several issues. On the one hand, the shift in the proportion of students across upper secondary and basic vocational schools suggests a change toward a better-educated occupationally diverse workforce, and away from specializations based on narrow vocational skills. On the other hand, however, the data also demonstrate that the shift started to occur after 1999, following the restructuring of the Polish education system. The failure to introduce the necessary reforms at the secondary level in a timely manner deepened the crisis of overproduction of graduates with basic vocational skills, many of whom were trained throughout the 1990s for obsolete or low-skilled jobs for which there was no or little demand. As a result, these graduates further added to an already substantial pool of unemployed workers that the Polish labour market was unable to absorb. The economic migration primarily to the "old" EU labour markets, reminiscent of the socialist period, once again became a reality.

The Resurgence of Technical and Vocational Education and Training

The above data further point to the changing professional preferences of Polish students in response to the labour market needs, following Poland's entry into the EU in 2004. The drop in the number of enrolments in vocational lyceums (from 13 to 8 per cent between 2004/05 and 2006/07), combined with a simultaneous increase in the number of enrolments in basic vocational schools (from 10 to over 14 per cent) and technical schools (from 23 to 31 per cent), may be indicative of a renewed interest in TVET programmes (GUS, 2004, 2005b, 2007; Vulcan, 2006). Given Poland's persistent high unemployment (10.5 per cent in 2008) and the demand for a skilled workforce in the "old" EU job markets, students increasingly tend to opt for professional preparation programmes that they believe will ensure their economic security, if not mobility (Ministry of Foreign Affairs, 2009). Greater flexibility in the Polish education system that allows students to re-enter its programmes at any point in their career as well as access to the EU labour markets have also played an important role in an increased interest in skill-specific education as a means of enhancing employment opportunities and higher income potential outside Poland (Finanse, 2007; Kurier Szczeciński, 2007). Programmes that have been especially popular among students have typically been in areas that offer well-paid jobs in "old" EU markets, such as hospitality, car mechanics, carpentry, nursing, hairdressing, and electrical technology. The migration of skilled workers and, more recently, professionals to those markets has become, as noted by Whewell (2006), a solution to Poland's national unemployment problem. The adverse effects of this trend, which are already beginning to have a noticeable impact on the supply of skilled local manpower, underscore Poland's inability to deal with this persistent problem and to effectively utilize the skills of its own workforce.

Emergence of the Private Education Sector

A key aspect of the Polish education reform is the establishment of the private education sector alongside the public system. The impact of this change is most evident at the tertiary level where the early enactment of new legislation in 1990–1991 resulted in a rapid expansion of private education, for about one-third of all tertiary students in Poland (Kwiek 2005; Jung-Miklaszewska, 2003; BUWiWM, 2000). The timing of this change was significant given the combination of demographic and economic forces throughout the 1990s, which created a substantial demand for postsecondary education and a need for a more diversified higher education landscape. Not only did the existing tertiary system lack the sufficient capacity to accommodate this increased demand, but also to finance the provision of education in its expanding public institutions (Szapiro, 2007). The economic recession and the financial crisis that erupted in Poland in the 1990s led to a substantial under-funding of public higher education, limiting its post-1989 transformation. These circumstances in turn created a favourable environment for the development of private fee-paying tertiary education (Dąbrowa-Szefler & Jabłecka-Prysłopska, 2006; Kwiek, 2005; Polityka, 2001).

The establishment of the private postsecondary sector has had differing effects on higher education, local and social development, and labour market experiences of students. Established and managed by the local academic community, private institutions were initially created in a hope of becoming centres for innovative education programmes, designed to complement and extend beyond the range of programmes offered at the public institutions. In reality, however, the goals and roles envisaged for private institutions have often become intermingled with short-term profit-driven motivations as teaching in the private sector has increasingly become a source of part-time employment for the local academic community, and education reduced to job preparation with a focus on skills and competency development (Axer, 2002; Kwiek, 2003). With the focus on teaching-oriented activities, the research function has become glaringly absent from private institutions. Little attention has also been paid to ensuring greater diversification and complementarity of study programmes between the private and public sectors. Among over 250 private higher education institutions that exist in Poland today, the majority have tended to follow workforce trends and respond to market demands, offering training primarily in areas such as economics, banking, computer technology, business, and management, and sparingly in the humanities, social sciences, and the liberal arts that were neglected during the socialist period.

The private education sector also had a positive impact, evident in several other areas. For example, data suggest that since the early 1990s, many of the 250 private HE institutions have been established outside the big cities where the level of competition with public institutions was lower compared to urban areas. Further, the demand for postsecondary education has been high as a result of staggering unemployment caused by the dismantling or restructuring of the socialist industrial infrastructure. Given these circumstances, the private sector has played an important role in providing local populations, especially in rural and small-town areas, with access to postsecondary education and retraining opportunities, which they may not otherwise have been able to afford or access (Dąbrowa-Szefler & Jabłecka-Prysłopska, 2006; Jung-Miklaszewska, 2003). On the one hand, it can be concluded that private institutions have contributed significantly to altering the occupational composition of workforce, especially in non-urban areas, and thus to the economic development of the region constrained by the socialist legacy. On the other hand, however, the question arises as to the extent to which private, as well as public, postsecondary institutions prepare students for future unemployment, given the low level of study program, and thus professional, diversification they provide (e.g. marketing, banking) and the narrow and local focus of specializations in which they train students. This is not to undermine the contributions of private institutions in Poland's tertiary education, but rather emphasize the need for a greater diversification of study programmes and a broader preparation of their graduates that extends beyond skills development toward more academic social and civic goals, and thus prepares students more effectively for life and work in a variety of contexts (local, national, European, global).

While the positive impact of some private institutions in transforming higher education is evident, an issue that still requires continued attention is assuring quality education in other, both private and public, fee-paying schools (Polityka, 2001). With the creation of the State Accreditation Committee in 2001, the legal framework for the establishment and operation of both public and private postsecondary institutions has become much more restrictive and requires institutions to undergo periodic mandatory accreditation. As explained by Dąbrowa-Szefler & Jabłecka-Prysłopska (2006), the creation of the Committee was a necessity given the lack of any administrative controls before 2001, especially in the area of private postsecondary education. As they further note, the efforts of the Committee since the beginning of its operation in 2002 have focused primarily on weeding out "diploma mills" and other institutions that have used the favourable demographic and economic conditions primarily for the purpose of generating a profit, while failing to maintain high academic standards.

The Issue of Quality in Technical and Vocational Education and Training (TVET Curriculum)

According to Wilson (1993a), the integration of academic and vocational skills, knowledge and positive work-related attitudes, primarily toward life-long learning, is crucial to students' ability to retrain, perform and compete effectively in today's knowledge-based and technology-driven world. Addressing these issues in relation to TVET programmes became a necessity as well as a challenge following Poland's political and economic transformation. Given the narrow nature of job-specific training of these programmes during the socialist period, the much needed reform could not be effective without Poland re-defining the purpose and values of technical and vocational education in relation to the new social and economic goals and needs. The re-definition of the concept of TVET programmes occurred within the context of the conflicting pressures for such change. On the one hand, the purpose of TVET was viewed by supporters of vocational training (e.g. state authorities) as providing "practical" knowledge and skills that prepare students for employment. On the other hand, however, as part of the EU membership mandate, Poland was required to move away from the concept of TVET as narrow-skill job training toward a broader education that integrates academic and vocational learning and is concerned with questions of social, ethical and moral values, which were disregarded during the socialist period. This approach further meant moving beyond the mere removal of political and ideological influences from the TVET curriculum, toward reshaping its content so as to enable students to develop, in addition to vocational skills, the academic skills that students in other types of schools acquire and practice (Dąbrowa-Szefler & Jabłecka-Prysłopska, 2006).

An examination of the vocational curriculum, revised in the early 2000s and subsequently in 2008, reveals an increasing emphasis on the academic and a more well-rounded preparation of students in TVET programmes. Theoretical and practical vocational preparation constitutes 30 per cent of the study load in the first year, 50 per cent in the second year and 70 per cent in the third year. The academic component, which constitutes the remainder of the curriculum, offers a variety of basic general subjects such as Polish language and literature, one foreign language, history, mathematics, natural sciences, social sciences, economics foundations, the choice of religious education or ethics, preparation for national defence and physical education (Jung-Miklaszewska, 2003). In accordance with the provisions of the new National Curriculum, passed in 2008, students in vocational schools also have an option to take a (ethnic) minority language (Ministry of Education, 2009). When comparing study loads, the study load of secondary technical-vocational schools is greater in technical schools with 35–36 study periods than in vocational lyceums with 32–33 study periods. Compared to vocational schools, secondary technical-vocational schools also include additional general subjects such as business/entrepreneurship foundations, informatics, cultural studies, philosophy, two foreign languages (in technical schools only), and an option to take a minority language (Ministry of Education, 2009). These academic subjects constitute about 66 per cent of the core programme in technical schools and only 22 per cent in vocational lyceums, with the remaining 34 per cent and 78 per cent of their programmes, respectively, comprising occupation-specific theoretical preparation (Jung-Miklaszewska, 2003). Practical on-the-job training is also offered, the extent of which varies for different occupational specializations.

These findings suggest that, when compared to vocational lyceums where the academic component remains relatively limited, the revised curriculum in technical and basic vocational schools appears to be broader and is oriented to produce more well-rounded graduates. Vocational lyceums, which are a combination of basic academic and vocational courses, appear to lack a clear mission as to the profile of graduates they aim to produce. Though the TVET curriculum has undergone major revisions twice since 1999, an issue that is problematic is the discrepancy between the desired skills and the learning objectives. While the curriculum emphasizes the importance of developing the skills of critical thinking and problem solving in

TVET programmes, the learning objectives for various subjects fail to reflect it. This is especially evident in the prevalent use of more passive verbs such as "describe", "characterize", "give examples" and "identify" as opposed to more active verbs such as "formulate", "use", "demonstrate" or "construct" (Ministry of Education, 2009). This tendency is especially evident in the case of the vocational school curriculum.

Lack of Retraining Opportunities in the 1990s

Data presented in this paper thus far suggest that the adjustment to the new economic reality in the 1990s was substantially easier for young people with a minimum secondary level of general education than for graduates of basic vocational schools who lacked such education. With the growing need for skilled professionals, priority was given to retraining workforce at the postsecondary level, the move that benefited the former group, while disadvantaging the latter group. Especially vulnerable among the latter group were middle-aged and older workers who entered the workforce during the socialist period and who were often seen by employers as lacking the adequate occupational knowledge, skills, work habits and attitudes needed in the post-1989 job market (OECD, 2006). According to OECD (2004) data, the unemployment rates in Poland increased sharply from 6 per cent in 1990, to 16 per cent in 1994, and to 20 per cent in 2003. The same data show that 84 per cent of the unemployed in 1998 and 71 per cent in 2002 were graduates of basic vocational schools residing in rural and small town areas, as compared to 58 per cent of the unemployed workers in urban regions in 1998 and 44 per cent in 2002. In contrast, the unemployment rate for secondary school graduates in rural areas was 13 per cent in 1998 and 22 per cent in 2002, and only 2 per cent in 1998 and 4 per cent in 2002 for university graduates. In urban regions, the unemployment rate for secondary school graduates was 31 per cent in 1998 and 38 per cent in 2002, with 9 per cent in 1998 and 13 per cent in 2002 for university graduates.

These high unemployment rates for graduates of basic vocational schools in urban and non-urban regions may be attributed to several factors. One of them was the limited demand for skilled manual labour, following the elimination or privati-zation of a large number of state-owned enterprises, which, during socialism, were the main source of employment for local populations in non-urban areas. In addition, it may also be linked to a limited job mobility of people in non-urban areas due to higher costs of living and a growing unemployment in cities. Most importantly, however, Poland lacked the relevant infrastructure for or model of continuing education that would provide meaningful retraining to workers. As a result, retraining opportunities available to graduates of basic vocational schools were extremely scarce, despite the catastrophic proportions of unemployment that affected this group in the 1990s. Many of these workers left the workforce during that time (e.g. early retirement, welfare) and some entered a black labour market in Poland or "old" EU member states (Tracy, 2004; OECD, 2006). The situation of these redundant and often jobless workers (e.g. coal miners, steel workers), largely abandoned by the post-1990 governments and market economy, seemed para-doxical given the critical role that these workers played in bringing down the socialist regime. The selectively targeted training in the 1990s and fragmented reform efforts that resulted in the inability of the Polish authorities and the market to utilize the skills of workers for economic restructuring can be characterized as being underlain by, primarily what Wilson (1993a) calls a sense of "greater expediency than foresight."

LESSONS LEARNED (CONCLUSIONS)

The case study of Poland presented in this paper offers a number of key findings regarding the successes and failures of its recent education reform. One finding indicates that TVET reform has been less a long-term planned action, and more a spontaneous and rather an ad hoc reaction to changes that have resulted from: the economic restructuring and changing labour market demands in the local, European and global contexts; worldwide shifts toward vocationalization in higher education; or Poland's accession to the EU. The lack of a clear vision of transfor-mation and a long-term approach to its facilitation has resulted in addressing immediate needs that bring short-term gains. An important lesson to be drawn from this experience is that with all the attention that has been given to the economic restructuring and development, the social development and the human factor have been lost in Poland's post-1989 transformation. Similar tendencies can be identified in relation to Poland's post-secondary education. Although post-secondary education structures and curricula, both public and private, have been modified to meet the new social needs, the purpose of education and its role in preparing students for participation in democracy have been subsumed by the purpose of professional preparation. While the economic and political circumstances have changed drama-tically since the beginning of Poland's transformation in 1989, the national and societal priorities have not been re-defined or altered substantially, and continue to be heavily influenced by economic goals.

The findings further show that the post-1989 reform of the Polish TVET sector has been fragmented in its purpose and direction. On one hand, initiatives such as the establishment of the private education sector and non-terminal vocational system have resulted in better-educated and more vocationally diverse workforce at the post-secondary level. On the other hand, factors such as selectively targeted (re-)training, marginalization of graduates of basic vocational schools, and late implementation of the TVET reform have affected the effectiveness of broader reform efforts, both in the economic and social spheres. The development in the early 2000s of continuing education, based on the concept of lifelong learning for all employees regardless of their educational and professional background, has laid a foundation for a culture of professional development, retraining and learning in the future. However, given its late implementation and the lack of a tradition of participation in continuing education for professional growth, it will take years before continuing education becomes an integral aspect of Poland's professional landscape, a change that is much needed and urgent.

NOTES

[1] The Czech Republic, Estonia, Hungary, Latvia, Lithuania, Poland, Slovakia and Slovenia formally joined the EU on May 1, 2004.

[2] Bulgaria and Romania joined the EU on January 1, 2007.

[3] The most notable legal acts include the 1990 *Act on Schools of Higher Education (Ustawa o Szkolnictwie Wyższym)* with further amendments added in 2005, conferring major legal and financial autonomy to HE institutions and their representative bodies, the 1990 *Act on Academic Title and Academic Degrees (Ustawa o Tytule Naukowym i Stopniach Naukowych)*, providing criteria for academic degree/title conferral, and the 1991 *Act Establishing the Committee for Scientific Research (Ustawa o Utworzeniu Komitetu Badań Naukowych)*, introducing the procedures for awarding research funds. These documents were followed by the 1997 *Act on Professional Higher Education Institutions (Ustawa o Wyższych Szkolach Zawodowych)*, providing a legal framework for professional higher education.

REFERENCES

Axer, J. (2002). Liberal arts – Liberated from what? *Polish Market, 6,* 36–37.

Biuro Uznawalności Wykształcenia i Wymiany Międzynarodowej (BUWiWM)/Bureau for Academic Recognition and International Exchange. (2000). *Szkolnictwo Wyższe w Polsce – 2000 Przewodnik.* Retrieved February 24, 2009, from http://www.buwiwm.edu.pl/publ/przew/index.htm

Dąbrowa-Szefler, M., & Jabłecka-Prysłopska, J. (2006). *OECD thematic review of tertiary education: Country background report for Poland.* Retrieved February 24, 2009, from http://www.eng.nauka.gov.pl/_gAllery/30/69/3069/OECD_Tertiary_Review_CBR_Poland.pdf

Finanse. (2007). *Zawodówki Powróciły do Łask.* Retrieved January 9, 2008, from www.finanse.wp.pl/wid.8863941,wiadomosc.html

Główny Urząd Statystyczy (GUS)/Central Statistical Office. (2003). *Oświata i Wychowanie w Roku Szkolnym 2002/2003.* Warszawa.

Główny Urząd Statystyczy (GUS)/Central Statistical Office. (2004). *Oświata i Wychowanie w Roku Szkolnym 2003/2004.* Warszawa.

Główny Urząd Statystyczy (GUS)/Central Statistical Office. (2005a). *Ścieżki Edukacyjne Polaków.* Warszawa.

Główny Urząd Statystyczy (GUS)/Central Statistical Office. (2005b). *Oświata i Wychowanie w Roku Szkolnym 2004/2005.* Warszawa.

Główny Urząd Statystyczy (GUS)/ Central Statistical Office. (2007). *Oświata i Wychowanie w Roku Szkolnym 2006/2007.* Warszawa. Retrieved January 9, 2008, from http://www.stat.gov.pl/cps/rde/xbcr/gus/PUBL_oswiata_wychowanie_2006-2007.pdf

Guo, S. (2004). Economic transition in China and Vietnam: A comparative perspective. *The Journal of Asian Law, 32*(5), 393–410.

Jung-Miklaszewska, J. (2003). *The education system in Poland. Biuro Uznawalności Wykształcenia i Wymiany Międzynarodowej (BUWiWM)/ Bureau for Academic Recognition and International Exchange.* Retrieved January 9, 2008, from [English Version] http://www.buwiwm.edu.pl/publ/edu/System.pdf [Polish Version] http://www.buwiwm.edu.pl/publ/system/index.htm

Kurier Szczeciński (2007). *Zawodówki Wracają do Łask.*

Kwiek, M. (2005, February 11–12). *Poland: A higher education policy review.* Turku Workshop Papers. Retrieved July 13, 2009, from http://www.policy.hu/kwiek/PDFs/HE_policy_Poland.doc

Kwiek, M. (2003). Academe in transition: Transformations in the Polish academic profession. *Higher Education, 45*(4), 455–476.

Law on Higher Education, Act of 27 July 2005. Retrieved July 13, 2009, from http://www.cepes.ro/hed/policy/legislation/pdf/Poland.pdf

Ministry of Education. (2009). Retrieved July 13, 2009, from http://www.reformaprogramowa.men.gov.pl/dla-nauczycieli/rozporzadzenie-o-podstawie-programowej-w-calosci

Ministry of Foreign Affairs. (2009). Retrieved July 13, 2009, from http://www.poland.gov.pl/

Ministry of Science and Higher Education. (2009). *Higher education*. Retrieved July 13, 2009, from http://www.eng.nauka.gov.pl/ms/index.jsp?place=Menu06&news_cat_id=28&layout=2

O'Dowd, M. (2010). Project Europe, the Bologna Process and the re-structuring of higher education: Who will bear the brunt of unexpected outcomes? In *A tribute to David N. Wilson: Clamouring for a better world* (pp. 235–250). Rotterdam: Sense Publishers.

OECD. (2004). *Thematic review on adult learning – Poland: Background report*. Ministry of Economy and Labour, Poland.

OECD. (2006). *Economic survey of Poland 2006: Education and training: Boosting and adapting human capital*. Retrieved February 24, 2009, from http://www.oecd.org/document/51/0,3343,en_33873108_33873739_36979955_1_1_1_1,00.html

Polityka. (2001). Ranking Wyższych Uczelni 2001.

Sorensen, K. (1997). *Polish higher education en route to the market: Institutional change and autonomy at two economics academies*. Stockholm: Institute of International Education.

Szapiro, T. (2007). Autonomia Uczelni i Jej Relacje z Biznesem. Uczelnia Zaczarowana. [The Autonomy of the University and its Relation to the World of Business. The University under a Spell (Summary)] *Autonomia Uniwerystetu: Jej Przyjaciele i Wrogowie*. Warszawa: Fundacja "Instytut Artes Liberales."

Tomusk, V. (2007). Bologna process – for the men of integrity, for the women of letters. *Autonomia Uniwerystetu: Jej Przyjaciele i Wrogowie*. Warszawa: Fundacja "Instytut Artes Liberales."

Tracy, P. (2004). *Five ways to profit from exploding growth in Eastern Europe*. Market Advisor. Retrieved February 24, 2009, from http://web.streetauthority.com/cmnts/pt/2004/07-26.asp

Vulcan (2006). *Wspòlczynniki Skolaryzacji*. Retrieved February 24, 2009, from http://vulcan.edu.pl/badania/szkoly/skolaryzacja.html

Whewell, T. (2006, July 2). Polish concern as workers migrate. *BBC*. Retrieved February 24, 2009, from http://news.bbc.co.uk/2/hi/programmes/crossing_continents/5129224.stm

Wilson, D. N. (1993a). *Training discussion papers: The effectiveness of national training boards* (No. 110). Geneva: International Labour Office.

Wilson, D. N. (1993b). Reforming technical and technological education. *The Vocational Aspect of Education, 45*(3), 265–284.

Wilson, D. N. (1994). On teaching the methodology of comparative education: Why are there so few courses in Canada? *Canadian and International Education, 23*(1), 13–24.

Ewa Kowalski
Ontario Institute for Studies in Education of the University of Toronto

DEREK A. URAM

5. ISSUES AND DEVELOPMENTS IN TECHNICAL AND VOCATIONAL EDUCATION AND TRAINING (TVET) IN INDIA

Since independence in 1947, India has achieved phenomenal growth in education including development in technical and vocational education and training, or TVET. Rapid advances in technology and education have had major impacts on the Indian experience. Various innovations, reforms, trends, and decisions have all affected TVET in India to some degree, most importantly those related to globalization, or more specifically, the reduction in power and influence of certain national governments in economic affairs, and the escalating power and influence of the international corporate sector. How does this affect the lives of ordinary citizens in India, and what is the potential for TVET in the future development of India's economy? This paper investigates the varying impacts of such developments on TVET in India, and relates them to the overall Indian situation. It appears that technology has created great avenues of opportunity and wealth for millions, while at the same time reinforcing existing inequalities in Indian society. In many ways, the proliferation of high technology in India is inextricably linked to these inequalities.

Technical (or technological) and vocational education is a topic discussed in academic and public policy circles worldwide. It is a form of education which offers a great deal of potential but unfortunately also tends, in some cases, to lead to unrealistic expectations for industrial and national development. India has experienced a variety of outcomes related to educational policy initiatives in this area. In each case, it is hoped that technical education will lead to positive returns. With the passage of time, this form of education only grows in importance. David N. Wilson described his personal affinity for technological education when he related how his own children not only grew up with technical literacy and computer skills, but also ended up working in high-tech areas of employment. When his eldest son took a job with the Goddard Space Center analyzing satellite data, David stated "the old expression, 'The sky is the limit,' seems to me to have been significantly altered by technological change and technological education" (Wilson, 1992, p. 37).

The first section of this chapter defines TVET, stating the specific framework of analysis. The second section provides a historical overview of TVET in India, detailing how the current situation came to exist as it does. The third section presents a description and analysis of current trends and practices relating to TVET in India,

V. Masemann et al., (Eds.), A Tribute to David N. Wilson: Clamouring for a Better World, 67–83.

and describes the impact some of these changes have had on Indian society. The fourth section analyzes various implications on inequality in India, with respect to high technology and TVET. Finally, some brief conclusions are presented. Above all it must be remembered that TVET is not a magical cure-all for developing nations. There exists no "one-size-fits-all" policy or programme for economic and industrial development, which may or may not involve elements of TVET. Different forms of TVET are useful at different times in history, in different phases of national development. TVET does indeed have a great deal to offer, but only when it is implemented and maintained at an appropriate and sustainable level, in any country.

DEFINING TECHNICAL AND VOCATIONAL EDUCATION AND TRAINING

Prior to any analysis of technical and vocational education and training, the term itself must be concisely defined. TVET includes education and/or training at predominantly secondary and post-secondary levels, offered at diverse institutions (public, private, or mixed), in a multitude of technical and vocational subject areas. *Technical* refers to the practical application of science and technology, whereas *vocational* refers to programmes geared towards immediate employment, such as in the skilled trades. Depending on the context, these two terms may be mutually exclusive or overlapping. This definition also includes formal education (within schools, colleges, universities, and institutes) and non-formal (private technical and vocational institutes where formal credit for courses may or may not be given). Although TVET does normally include informal learning such as on-the-job training, this will not be a major element in this paper.

HISTORICAL OVERVIEW OF TVET IN INDIA

India is a nation unlike any other in the world. Its population exceeds one billion people, most of whom cannot be considered privileged or even middle class. Millions continue to live in poverty. It is a nation of historical inequalities coexisting with modern, constitutional, and democratic principles of equality. Its extremes in wealth, education, and access to amenities are substantial. As with other public policy issues, TVET has benefited India to a great degree, but this benefit has not been equally shared, with enormous implications.

In India, as in other developing countries, support for TVET was often, and continues to be, a response to the growing problem of increasing unemployment, particularly unemployment of educated individuals. Many who have attained higher levels of education usually do not desire paid employment that is outside of or considered below the level of their chosen field of study. Unfortunately, employment opportunities for such individuals are often quite limited, resulting in an ever-growing number of educated unemployed. This situation is relatively recent (i.e. late 20th century) and has not always been a serious problem.

India's past colonial experience shares characteristics with other countries. In much (but not all) of the developing world which was under European domination throughout the 19th century, particularly in Asia and Africa, the number of local people who were able to attain higher levels of education were relatively few (if at all). The academic, Euro-centric curriculum of secondary and higher level educational institutions favoured by the ruling foreign powers was originally set up to provide a literate and relatively well-educated class of bureaucrats to staff the offices of the imperial administration. Thus it was generally a higher social class which staffed the colonial government offices. This was certainly the case in India, where high caste English-speaking Brahmins dominated the British civil service throughout the colonial era.

Although technical and vocational education was initially established in India in the 19th century, most development in this area took place in the late 20th century. Colonial India under British rule remained primarily agrarian, undiversified, and underdeveloped. The colonial rulers did very little (some would argue, nothing) to promote economic development or industrialization in India. For the most part, British-led industrial development in India served British interests. Nehru (1946) and Anstey (1946) both describe the predicament of India under British rule in the 19th century, how India's economic and industrial situation was comparable to that of any other nation of the world at that time until British policy and trade practices effectively wiped out many of India's domestic industries, such as the textile industry, forcing masses of skilled workers back to the land. At the same time, British policy was to promote India as a producer of agricultural commodities, such as cotton, to be shipped to Britain and used as raw materials in British industry. Not surprisingly, technical education in 19th century India was itself underdeveloped.

India's first three universities were established by the British in 1857 in Bombay, Madras, and Calcutta. Some engineering colleges were also set up throughout India around this time. However, there was essentially no real technical education in India outside the fields of law, medicine, and engineering prior to the First World War (Crane, 1965).

It was not until the end of the Second World War and the independence of India in 1947 that special emphasis was placed on the development of domestic industry. In many former colonies in the newly named "Third World", including India, significant numbers of individuals within the expanding middle classes attempted to further their opportunities through traditional academic avenues. Formal academic education was not just a luxury for those who could afford it, but a practical means to quality employment.

In the 1950s, 1960s, and 1970s, this phenomenon was not obvious to policymakers in many Third World nations who saw TVET as a logical means of addressing the problem of educated unemployment, supposedly gearing education directly to job market requirements. Governments during this time actively promoted the establishment of various TVET institutions at secondary and post-secondary levels, including fundamentally changing the existing secondary curricula to include TVET courses and programmes. However, many important factors were simply not considered, one being the severe lack of job opportunities in technical fields. An increase in the number of technical graduates does not necessarily lead to an increase in the number of job opportunities in those same technical fields, but instead, may simply increase the number of educated unemployed.

Many nations introduced TVET as a solution to employment market deficiencies without having an industrialized economy, or even a strategy for industrial development or expansion. TVET may or may not be ideal for any nation at any given point in time, depending on the existing level of development and plans for future development in that nation.

Educated unemployment is a problem in all nations, whether fully industrialized or in earlier stages of development. The work of David N. Wilson illustrates an important factor in a nation's industrialization and the utilization of TVET—i.e. the temporal element. As a nation and its economy changes over time, so do job market requirements. In the early stages of industrialization, a nation may produce an excess of technically educated graduates who are unable to find work in their respective fields. Ghana in the 1960s fell into this category, as there were very few employment opportunities for graduates of TVET programmes at that time (Foster, 1965). By the 1970s, however, David N. Wilson's own research shed light on a new situation in Ghana. He reported that graduates of the Accra Technical Training Centre were finding employment in the new economy, and that unemployed secondary school graduates were returning to school to undertake technical training to make themselves more employable (Wilson, 1977). The temporal element is especially important in India today, as technological progress is rapid and any educational policy that attempts to address these changes can barely keep pace. In short, TVET has a positive and future-oriented role to play.

Any choice in support of TVET is an important one, in terms of financial costs and societal attitudes towards this type of education. Quality TVET requires four key elements: (1) complex machinery or apparatus which must be maintained on a regular basis and constantly upgraded to avoid obsolescence; (2) elaborate and current textbooks and other teaching aids; (3) up-to-date curriculum and teaching methods; and (4) a fairly well paid and highly qualified (and often difficult to acquire) teaching staff. All these elements must complement an existing educational foundation of very basic elements, i.e. blackboards or whiteboards, chalk/markers, tables or desks, textbooks, and sufficiently qualified teaching staff. Traditional academic education, on the other hand, only requires these basic elements. Developing countries often lack the financial resources to adequately deliver quality TVET at all levels, but again, this situation varies through place and time, and by the specific types of TVET delivered.

Traditional academic education does not suffer from the social stigma often associated with TVET. In much of the developing world, particularly Asia and Africa, these traditions have not died out. This is especially the case in India, where ancient caste-based identities still prevail, particularly in rural areas.

Despite all of the above, TVET has played a significant role in the industrial development of India. Industrialization in India went through a variety of phases, some of which saw a surplus of TVET graduates, others a deficit. Rapid industrialization was a national goal for India after independence, and, unlike many other developing nations, India promoted TVET along with simultaneously promoting industrial expansion. Initially, there was great demand for technical graduates. In 1947 the Indian government-appointed Scientific Man Power Committee recommended that in the first five to ten years post-independence, at least 54,000 engineers and 27,000 technologists would be required. The resources available for education and training, however, were insufficient to meet even 50 per cent of these requirements (Kaur, 1985).

The greatest emphasis in TVET was in the area of higher education, and a significant expansion occurred during the post-war era. At the time of independence in 1947, India had 28 engineering colleges and 41 polytechnics which could produce 2,520 and 3,150 graduates, respectively. By 1956, the number of engineering colleges increased to 47 with 4,900 students while the number of polytechnics providing technical education more than doubled to 88 with 9,400 students (Mukherjee, 1967). Total enrolment in higher education increased dramatically from 416,000 in 1951 to 3,100,000 in 1971, with operating expenditures increasing from 171 million Rs. (rupees) in 1951 to 1,195 million Rs. in 1968 (Dhar, 1974). This rapid expansion, however necessary, placed excessive stress on the amount of resources available at that time. By 1964, the engineering colleges and polytechnics faced many shortages including a 35 per cent shortage in instructors, 53 per cent in equipment, 51 per cent in instructional buildings, and 55 per cent in hostel accommodation (Rawat, 1970). As a result, higher technical education was not always of the quality desired.

In response to this problem, the Indian Institutes of Technology (IITs) were established to meet India's demand for high calibre scientific and technical higher education which could compete at international standards. These institutes were modelled after the Massachusetts Institute of Technology (MIT) in the United States. The first five IITs were set up, commencing in the 1950s, in Kharagpur, Bombay, Madras, Kanpur, and Delhi, with assistance from the United Kingdom, Soviet Union, West Germany, and the United States in the form of technical and educational experts as well as millions of dollars worth of equipment (Sebaly, 1972). Several other IITs have been established since these original five.

Technical education expanded in other areas. The few IITs in India should not be confused with the roughly 5,000 Industrial Training Institutes (ITIs). ITIs offer occupational training in 64 specific trades (38 classified as engineering trades) to 327,000 students (National Office of Overseas Skills Recognition [NOOSR], 1996). Whereas the IITs offer four-year bachelor degrees and Master's and doctoral level graduate degrees, the ITIs offer practical one- and two-year certificate and trade programmes. In addition, there are numerous other types of educational institutions in India, both public and private, which teach technical and vocational skills, some of which are specific to certain fields and occupations.

Given this rapid expansion in technical education since the end of the Second World War, many problems have arisen. To a great extent, uncontrolled output in the universities has produced too many engineering graduates, without serious regard for opportunities for their employment in their given fields. The problem of educated unemployed, common to many developing countries of the time, became a reality in India. Educational output was not tied in any way to economic output, which is often the case in any nation. Sethi (1983) points out that the Indian government for many years had a science policy but lacked any sort of realistic technology policy. As a result, planning was done *ad hoc* with decisions being made on political rather than technical grounds. Many students in India, as elsewhere in the developing world, chose their studies based on employment status, rather than on trends in the overall labour market (United Nations Educational, Scientific and Cultural Organization [UNESCO], 1983).

Much of this has to do with lack of guidance resources in secondary schools as well as with traditional societal attitudes towards different types of work. The caste system was based on occupational specialization, and the lowest castes performed manual labour. Although discrimination based on caste has been illegal in India since Independence, Indian society remains greatly influenced by the division of labour and tends to look down at what is considered an extension of manual work. Not surprisingly, TVET programmes leading to a graduate's status as a professional engineer were more greatly sought after than those leading to technologist or technician status.

By the late 1960s and 1970s there were noticeably fewer employment opportunities for highly educated technical professionals in the Indian economy. The excessive number of institutes of technical education had produced an over-abundance of senior level technical professionals such as engineers, without enough middle and junior level technicians and technologists. As a result, many engineers were employed in positions requiring only lower level skills. In India, as in other developing countries overburdened with educated unemployed, there existed a significant waiting period or time lag between when an individual graduated and their being hired for their first (and perhaps only) job.

Migration of the technically educated from India also became an issue. Many graduates from the prestigious IITs went overseas for employment, often at a higher rate than graduates from other institutions (Chowdhury & Nandy, 1974). As recently as the late 1990s this was still the case, when the software industry had an attrition rate of 30 per cent of professionals migrating to the United States, and a higher rate among the more experienced ranks (Roy, 1998). More recently, however, this has not been as great a problem in India's growing economy. In fact, the International Monetary Fund (IMF) reports an economic growth rate in India of 9.4 per cent for 2007, 7.3 per cent for 2008, as well as a projected 5.4 per cent and 6.5 per cent for 2009 and 2010 respectively (International Monetary Fund, 2009). Even during the current global recession, India, as in many other developing economies, has economic growth opportunities, many of which are enhanced through TVET.

Geographical inequalities also existed in India, and continue to this day. The age-old problem of urban/rural imbalances in many areas included employment, as there was often a surplus of educated unemployed in the cities but shortages in the villages. Such imbalances are usually ignored in planning methods (Sanyal, 1987).

In addition, the rapid expansion in education was not accompanied by an equivalent expansion in the type of academic and professional culture required to sustain it. Specifically, there was a lack of academic and professional journals, scientific agencies, and academic associations, which are quite common in Western countries (Crane, 1965). Such a culture is necessary to promote and sustain research, development, and innovation in science and technology, or any field. Although this problem was severe in the early years of independence, India has since become a major producer of academic, technical, and professional knowledge through the proliferation of research journals and other publications.

Economic reforms in the 1990s, along with rapid technological change and new patterns of trade and competition, have created the need for skilled people for a globalized economy. In 1991, India changed its entire economic orientation and outlook from inward and socialistic to outward and capitalistic, when then finance minister Manmohan Singh initiated a series of reforms. The results were sharp cutbacks in government spending, the devaluation of the rupee, increases in foreign investment, and a reformation of Indian government bureaucracy simplifying the business investment process (Wolpert, 1997). India's once protected markets were opened to the globalized world economy.

Although many in the ever-growing Indian urban middle-class benefited greatly from these reforms, the mostly rural masses generally did not. Consequently the gap between the haves and the have-nots widened significantly. Traditionally, many in India, particularly the educated, sought employment within the government sector because of the relatively high job security and the social status associated with these positions. At one point, up to 80 per cent of post-high school qualifiers in India were employed in the public sector (Indiresan & Nigam, 1993, p. 356). In the near future, this is likely to decrease if the international trend towards downsizing of governments and emphasis on private investment continues, although to what extent remains unclear. The trend in recent years has been one of increasing employment in the private sector, and decreasing employment in the public sector, along with a growing overall population and labour force. Between 2001 and 2004, for example, the total number of employees in the public sector in India decreased steadily from 19,138,000 to 18,197,000 (Naukrihub, 2007). Given that Manmohan Singh, the architect of India's liberalization policy of the early 1990s, is now prime minister, current trends are unlikely to change significantly. Nevertheless, the potential for TVET has increased greatly since 1991 when the reforms were initiated.

CURRENT TRENDS AND PRACTICES OF TVET IN INDIA

India has not been immune to international trends in TVET. Some trends have established themselves in India as new and intricate parts of India's economic and education systems, such as the relatively recent development of the information technology (IT) industry, while others have not. The most significant trends appear to be those relating to current events in the economy and the increasing influence of the international private sector in technological and educational concerns. The following discussion will reveal some of these trends, particularly those which have had the most profound impact upon the Indian condition.

One of the most noteworthy trends in TVET has been the development of the computer and IT industries. The changing economic climate of India has helped the IT industry expand since the early 1990s. The computer sector was established in the early 1980s in urban centres such as Bangalore, Chennai (Madras), Hyderabad, and New Delhi. At the dawn of the new millennium India had only 3.7 million personal computers (Pentium I or superior), yet was home to the largest number of software specialists outside California (Sood, 2001). Since then, the number of computers has been growing rapidly. By 2005 India was home to 15 million computers, while some projected this figure to reach 75 million by 2010 (Jagadheesan, 2005). It is also important to note that small-scale private enterprise has entered this business with great enthusiasm, as small computer kiosks and internet cafes exist for public use in most cities and semi-urban areas. This indicates that the computer is available at relatively inexpensive rates to a large percentage of the population which does not own personal computers (at least for urban and semi-urban dwellers).

The international IT trend has also hit the education sector. Many private and independent educational institutions teaching IT courses have sprung up all over India in addition to the many institutions which already exist. Such schools often promote themselves as a means to highly rewarding employment opportunities, just as they do in the West. While degree granting institutions, such as IITs, are governed by the All India Council for Technical Education (AICTE), these other private and independent educational institutions are not regulated and lack accountability. As a result, they are often of poor quality (Roy, 1998). As a whole, they range tremen-dously, and they appear to be popular choices for those who can afford them. The high cost of attending such institutions, however, is prohibitive to most classes of people in India. In fact, the vast majority of individuals in rural India do not, and will not in any time soon, own or have access to a computer, giving rise to the phenomenon "digital divide", a term which describes the gap that separates the haves from the have-nots *vis-à-vis* computers, high technology, and education.

This digital divide is most obvious in India's traditional urban/rural imbalance. The cities possess the infrastructure necessary for internet connections, whereas many villages continue to lack essential services such as piped water and electricity (not to mention telephone hook-ups) as well as trained personnel and institutions of TVET. The telecommunications sector in India underwent a process of deregulation yet the country's teledensity (i.e. number of telephone connections per 100 persons) rose from 0.06 in 1990, to only 3.0 in 2001 (for comparative purposes, China's teledensity at that time was under 10) (Sood, 2001). India's teledensity rose from 4.63 in 2003 (International Telecommunication Union, 2004) to 20.52 by July 2007 (Telecom Regulatory Authority of India, 2007). In 2008, the number of telephone subscribers per 100 persons was 32.44 (International Telecommunication Union, 2009a).

Despite an increasing number of connections, the disparity between urban and rural teledensity (40 urban, 2 rural) remains an important issue (Singh, 2006). India's telecommunications system is not always the most modern, efficient, or inexpensive, but the major urban centres usually receive the greatest benefit, given what is available.

It is also important to consider cell phone usage in India, as cell phone connections are also included within teledensity statistics. In mid-2000 over 50,000 villages were connected and more than a million people had bought into the system.

Mobile phones are relatively inexpensive when compared to their cost in Europe and North America. People living in both urban and rural areas are not waiting to install landlines in their homes but are using cell phones instead. Even those with lower paid jobs are using mobile phones. The importance of cell phones cannot be understated, as in 2008 some 90 per cent of telephone subscribers used cell phones (International Telecommunication Union, 2009b). Despite this relatively recent proliferation of cell phones throughout India, millions of individuals do not possess telephones of any kind, particularly those in rural areas.

India's urban/rural imbalance is accompanied by other, more traditional forms of inequality, such as caste and class barriers, as well as language affiliations. IT education has a natural, elitist tendency to favour those with the following characteristics: (1) individuals who are urban and have access to institutions of IT education; (2) individuals who are of higher caste and class, and can afford computers and education; (3) individuals who already possess an excellent working knowledge of the English language and have the accompanying literacy skills necessary for computer literacy; and (4) individuals who have the vital urban and kinship/caste connections necessary to attain meaningful and remunerative employment in the modern workforce.

Given these imbalances and inequalities, what then is the possibility for reform of TVET in effectively improving the situation? There have been some recent technological innovations in India. One such innovation has been the installation of free-access computer kiosks in slum areas (Hindustan Times, 2000; India Express, 2000). Launched on November 18, 2000 in the Ambedkar Nagar area of Delhi, computers with free internet access were installed in various small kiosks which were quite literally holes in local walls. This initiative was known as the "hole in the wall" experiment and was funded by the Delhi government. It demonstrated that local slum children, uneducated, underprivileged, and illiterate, were fully capable of teaching themselves how to access websites and use the computer for basic functions, without any form of outside instruction whatsoever. This strategy, known as minimally invasive education (MIE), demonstrates that there is more to IT than initially meets the eye, in terms of accessibility and potential, and India's government has already expanded this project to other parts of India.

Another innovation from India is the *simputer* (simple computer, or simple, inexpensive, multilingual people's computer). Developed by four professors from the Indian Institute of Science (IISc), the simputer is an easy-to-use, hand-sized alternative to personal computers, priced at around US$200 (IPS News, 2001). Although most rural villagers still cannot afford the simputer at this price, it is a device which can easily be loaned or rented out at a low cost by village authorities and used by both literates and illiterates alike. In such cases, villagers only need to purchase an individual smart card while the actual simputer is owned by the village. The Simputer Trust has been formed collaboratively between academia and technologists in the private sector within a perspective of addressing the greater problems facing India. According to the Simputer Trust website (2009), the central ideas behind the simputer are to bridge the digital divide, eliminate illiteracy as a barrier to the effective use of technology, and bring the benefits of information technology to the average person. This is yet another example of the kind of overlapping of trends in technology, education, and private sector involvement that have taken a rather unique form in India. Whether or not such initiatives are adopted by other developing countries is another matter that only time will tell.

A similar Indian invention is the *iStation*, which is also a hand-held device, and is used for sending and receiving e-mail without the use of a personal computer (Deccan Herald News Service, 2000). Like the simputer, the iStation also provides low-priced access to the conveniences of the modern world. The iStation however, requires literacy skills, but is eventually to be targeted towards speakers of several of India's regional languages. There is even speculation on a proposed $100 computer from Indian entrepreneurs (Kanellos, 2005), although producing one has proved more difficult than simply proposing the idea.

IMPLICATIONS FOR INEQUALITY

The trends discussed above describe a society in transition. From the proliferation of computers and technology schools, to the developments in high-tech gadgets, one sees the many advances made through computer technology. Upon close examination, however, one also detects numerous inequalities within these recent developments. Age-old inequalities in India such as urban/rural imbalances and caste/class differences continue to thrive despite advances in technology.

A more realistic approach towards addressing India's problems utilizing technology and education may involve the kinds of approaches taken by some non-governmental organizations (NGOs). Such organizations have taken initiatives and implement projects, particularly in education and rural development, that governments and the private sector reject, refuse to consider, or are unable to fund. One example is the All India Society for Electronics and Computer Technology (AISECT). Founded in 1984, AISECT's mission is to disseminate knowledge of electronics, computers, and new technology via education and training, throughout India, particularly in the rural and less developed regions (AISECT, 2001). AISECT aims to spread technical and vocational education, predominantly in IT-related areas, as well as in electronics, in an easily accessible manner, and has concentrated great efforts on the exceptionally underdeveloped rural and tribal areas of India.

While AISECT's activities emanate from within India, there has also been international attention. In 2000 the World Bank granted the government of India US$64.9 million to be spent on a 7-year project promoting access to polytechnic education in the more remote and underdeveloped regions, including emphasis on women and tribal groups. The emphasis here is on meeting the requirements of specific industrial sectors, namely qualified graduates in certain growth sectors of the economy, such as IT, automobile engineering, and the garment industry (World Bank, 2000). Often, little or nothing is mentioned about the perspective of those who are labeled "underdeveloped". Do these people define their major problem as a lack of up-to-date polytechnic education? Do they see their solutions as further integration in modern industry? It is interesting to note the following comments made by Shashi Shrivastava, the task leader and Senior Education Specialist for this project:

> Liberalization of India's economy and its gradual integration into the world economy have increased the demand for a well-trained workforce...We are happy to support the Government's improvements to polytechnic education and specific efforts to increase participation from disadvantaged segments of society. (Shashi Shrivastava, quoted in World Bank, 2000)

Perhaps those who are considered to be the "disadvantaged segments" of society have no other apparent choice but to be integrated into the new world economic order as mid-level technicians or skilled labourers. These plans for expansion in TVET may sound similar to those advocated by AISECT described above, but they differ in philosophical motivation. More specifically it could be asked, why are these different groups doing what they are doing? The purpose of many NGOs in the developing world is to promote the welfare and well-being of the marginalised masses, the poor and rural masses who have been left out of the economic and social benefits enjoyed by the more fortunate. The purpose of the World Bank and the government of India here may or may not be different. Reading between the lines may suggest that the real goals of this project might not be to promote improvements in the lives of those who are most in need, but to utilize the relatively lower wage labour of those in the underdeveloped regions to fill the employment gaps for the kind of industrial growth desired by those in New Delhi. The promotion of TVET has traditionally been very politically charged and controversial in nature. It seems that current arguments promoting TVET are similar to those made forty years ago. However, the trend today involves a rationale which includes terms like globalization, liberalization, competitiveness, and integration into the world economy.

Whether or not such a project is ultimately desirable depends on one's perspective. Do the individuals involved in this initiative genuinely want to be involved? If so, are they aware of the alternatives? Were they given a choice? There are, after all, many other ways to spend US$64.9 million. This particular World Bank initiative, known as the Third Technician Education Project, achieved a variety of results that were classified primarily as satisfactory, with some results also rated as moderate and highly satisfactory (World Bank, 2007). What is really important about this project, though, are the lessons learned from this experience. Among these lessons were the "[q]uality and relevance of education," the "importance of industry involvement in technical education," and the lesson that the perceived poor "prestige of technician education can be overcome" (World Bank, 2007, p. 24–25).

The increasing influence of the technology sector in India is a major impetus for the rapidly expanding promotion of TVET. As in any economy with a shortage of skilled workers, wages for workers with skills in high demand within the labour market will rise. If, on the other hand, an excessive number of TVET graduates enter the job market without a corresponding increase in job opportunities, then wages will drop. It is in the private sector's best interests to promote the vast expansion of TVET, especially at public expense, to ensure that the employment market is saturated with skilled technicians and technical professionals. This, in turn, will keep a private firm's salary and wage expenses down. Large numbers of educated and unemployed workers in the Indian economy, particularly those educated in IT, may not be socially desirable, but the private sector gains some benefit from such a situation. Any increase in TVET programmes and institutions specifically geared towards contemporary job requirements will result in employers being able to employ people with the kinds of skills they need while paying lower wages.

India's massive and increasing population has provided multi-national corporations (MNCs) with relatively cheap labour of all kinds, from unskilled agricultural workers to IT specialists. The trend today is for India's low-wage tradition to extend into the more highly skilled areas (at least as seen through the eyes of many MNCs), not necessarily as a matter of explicit public policy but as a consequence of international circumstances and unspoken government agenda. Although highly skilled jobs are relatively well paid by Indian standards, such workers are still paid less than most of their Western counterparts, hence this foreign corporate interest in India. Unfortunately, access to educational opportunities in high quality TVET, just as with traditional academic education in earlier times, is dominated by a relatively privileged few. The trend in Western countries of a polarization between high-skill, high-wage employment and low-skill, low-wage employment continues to persist in India.

The effects of current trends on higher education have been mixed. That is, some institutions have received important funding, while others have not. Developments and investments that have been put into some of India's more elite institutions of higher learning, for example, have paid off considerably. The IITs, the IIMs (Indian Institutes of Management), and the IISc (Indian Institute of Science) in Bangalore are all world renowned centres of education and research. India has traditionally been a "research superpower" within the Third World. In the early 1990s India accounted for approximately 8 per cent of the Third World's research and development funding, and produced a much larger proportion of the Third World's scientific output in the form of books and articles (Altbach, 1993). Today, India is still a major player although it has been lagging behind China in scientific output among developing nations (Sen, 2007). Much of the investment in the elite institutions (IITs, IIMs, and IISc) has come at the expense of India's universities, many of which have been left behind in the race for quality and funding. This over-emphasis on high quality research institutions such as the IITs has resulted in an educational stratification: "One observes a new hierarchy in which [the elite research institutions] stand apart from universities in aristocratic seclusion while universities slip further and further into mediocrity" (Chitnis, 1993, p. 25). This still appears to be the case, most notably with "the cash-strapped state-funded ones [universities and colleges] that shoulder the lion's share of the country's educational burden" (Yarnell, 2006, p. 19–20).

Although the number of degree granting institutions has increased in India, so have other institutions. The expansion in the less elitist forms of TVET, such as the ITIs and the polytechnics, illustrates this trend. The number of polytechnics, for example, increased by 64 per cent between 1991 and 1996, while the population of India increased by 10 per cent in this same period (Government of Punjab, 2002). For years India was over-burdened with engineering professionals while lacking sufficient numbers of technicians and technologists. The ancient caste-based perceptions of "lower" status forms of work were partly to blame for this, but the industrial sector is heavily influenced by the modern world, and caste identities are not as relevant or as obvious in the urban and more technologically advanced parts of India. There now appears to be significant interest in technician and technologist level educational programmes in various institutions which impart TVET, as evidenced by the enrolment numbers in India's polytechnics and ITIs. The number of ITIs, for example, grew from 56 to 5,000 between 1959 and 2006 (Indian Institute of Technology, Delhi, 2007). Like many of India's universities, many of these institutions remain inadequately funded.

The increasing influence of the private sector on educational matters is one of the most significant and noticeable trends in recent years, a trend also experienced in the West. Foreign-owned MNCs have exhibited great interest in India because of the availability of skilled labour and relatively lower wages. MNCs have set up business operations in India and have also begun their own educational operations. These may take a variety of forms. Companies may undertake educational program- mes independently, promoting their products and their applications in private institutes or through distance education. Many companies also ally themselves with more established institutions of learning. For example, by the late 1990s, Texas Instruments had educational linkages with 12 universities in India; Intel Corporation had five multimedia facilities in various IITs and IIMs, and had also reorganized engineering curricula in certain colleges; Philips had influence in training at the IIT in Delhi; Microsoft had five technology laboratories on various campuses including IITs and IIMs; and IBM had set up a Solution Research Centre at the IIT in Delhi (Roy, 1998). This trend continues. For late 2007, Intel planned to establish its technology entrepreneurship programme in 45 different institutions of higher learning in India (Krishnadas, 2006). Intel's Higher Education Programme is currently being implemented in 300 institutions, with more than 20,000 students participating in the program. The programme includes research and development of university curricula in collaboration with Indian government bodies including the Ministry of Communication and IT, the Department of Science and Technology, and the Department of Technical Education (Intel, 2009).

Other MNCs are also beginning educational operations in India. IBM has recently made an agreement with several universities in India for the promotion of its own curriculum in "service science," specifically designed for the expanding technical support industry (McCloskey, 2007). Microsoft also has plans to establish its own high-tech university in Bangalore (Tejaswi, 2007).

As in other nations, this trend is controversial. It has the potential to promote the corporate sector and its interests over other aspects of education, thus compromising the impartiality and independence of academic research. The trend towards "India, Inc." gears course curricula to the requirements of business and industry rather than societal needs. The role of national and state governments also becomes compromised with the increasing influence of the corporate sector, especially since many of these corporations are foreign owned and thus have no inherent interest in India's national development. A certain degree of national integrity is absolutely necessary for the successful promotion of national development, especially through education. India's democratically elected national and state governments at least possess some measure of public accountability which the international corporate sector fundamentally lacks.

CONCLUSION

Much has changed in India over the decades. TVET has opened up new opportunities for employment, industry, communication, finance, and intellectual development in technology, innovation, and applied science. India's current economy owes much to the technological sector, and to TVET policy which has helped to open India to the rest of the world. India's constitutional goal of equality, however, has not been met, and in many ways the problem of inequality continues to worsen despite the obvious economic gains. Widespread poverty remains an important issue, while those who already possess wealth, access, and opportunity are able to gain even more. This should not force one to view TVET negatively, as TVET does indeed have a profound role to play in the development of the Indian economy.

This role requires attention and participation from many actors in the public policy process in addition to government officials. The non-profit sector, as well as the domestic and international corporate sectors, all have definite roles to play, although no single sector should dominate TVET policy in India. National TVET policy that is dominated by the international corporate sector, for example, rarely serves the masses of have-nots at the bottom of society. Such policy may serve existing interests in the Indian high-tech industry as well as promote national economic growth, but it almost guarantees the continuance of existing inequalities at many levels. Promoting TVET in remote and economically underdeveloped regions may or may not be the best solution available. TVET may, in such cases, be best supported through the promotion of other policy areas that improve the quality of life, such as infrastructure improvements, basic primary education, and adult literacy campaigns. Universal internet access, for example, might be more effective if it is accompanied by access to food, water, shelter, basic literacy education, and employment opportunities.

Effective TVET policy requires a comprehensive strategy rather than a reliance on *ad hoc* initiatives. Over-reliance on electronic gadgets does very little to address the genuine problem of the digital divide in India. In certain cases it may even exacerbate it. Any public or private spending of funds may involve high-tech solutions, or conversely, medium or low-tech solutions. The concept of appropriate technology should be given consideration prior to the implementation of policy initiatives. It is often assumed that high-tech solutions are the best (and indeed, only) solutions available, especially by those who profit from the proliferation and sales of high-tech solutions. Those on the receiving end of public policy programmes and projects must be given a say as well—sometimes this is already the case, and sometimes it is not. Rural villagers in remote regions, for example, may or may not agree that their most pressing requirement is bridging the digital divide, when bridging the education divide, the employment opportunities divide, or the overall standard of living divide may, in fact, be more important.

The age-old problem of massive urban/rural imbalance in Indian society must certainly be addressed if significant improvements are to be made. Given that approximately 70 per cent of India's population is rural, this topic is of no small concern. Equality in India does not have to have a geographical component, although at this moment it does. One of the greatest selling features of technology—such as the internet—is its purported ability to negate geographical boundaries. This has already occurred at the international level, as India is now home to many global corporations dealing in telecommunications and internet-related commerce. As a result, millions of new employment opportunities have been created. Yet urban India has been the prime recipient of these developments. Can rural India benefit to the same degree? New technologies in this area are very promising, and offer a great deal to a country such as India (and many others), although not without significant changes in existing infrastructure, investment, and public policy.

Effective TVET policy requires planning at all levels of education, and in conjunction with other public policy arenas, such as industrial, employment, commercial, social, and international policy. Perhaps only when this is recognized will the greater situation in India be widely addressed and properly managed.

REFERENCES

All India Society for Electronics and Computer Technology [AISECT]. (2001). *AISECT: Leading IT training and services network of India*. Retrieved July 17, 2009, from http://www.aisect.org

Altbach, P. G. (1993). The dilemma of change in Indian higher education. *Higher Education, 26*(1), 3–20.

Anstey, V. (1946). *The economic development of India*. London: Longmans, Green and Co.

Chitnis, S. (1993). Gearing a colonial system of education to take independent India towards development. *Higher Education, 26*(3), 21–41.

Chowdhury, P. N., & Nandy, R. K. (1974). Scientific and technical personnel. In A. Singh & P. G. Altbach (Eds.), *The higher learning in India* (pp. 103–118). Delhi, India: Vikas Publishing House Pvt. Ltd.

Crane, R. I. (1965). Technical education and economic development in India before World War I. In C. A. Anderson & M. J. Bowman (Eds.), *Education and economic development* (pp. 167–201). Chicago: Aldine Publishing Company.

Deccan Herald News Service. (2000). *E-mail without PC to be launched in B'lore in December*. Retrieved December 29, 2001, from http://www.inablers.net/dherald.htm

Dhar, T. N. (1974). *The politics of manpower planning: Graduate unemployment and the planning of higher education in India*. Calcutta: Minerva Associates, Publications, Pvt. Ltd.

Foster, P. (1965). The vocational school fallacy in development planning. In C. A. Anderson & M. J. Bowman (Eds.), *Education and economic development*. Chicago: Aldine Publishing Company.

Government of Punjab. (2002). *Manpower not easily available*. Retrieved January 4, 2002, from http://www.nic.in/dte_punjab/infra10.htm

Hindustan Times. (2000). *Delhi govt to take internet to city slums*. Retrieved December 16, 2001, from http://www.hindustantimes.com/nonfram/181100/detCIT04.asp

India Express. (2000). *Slum children surf the net in internet kiosks*. Retrieved December 16, 2001, from http://www.ananova.com/news/story/sm_120337.html?nav_src=newsIndexHeadline

Indian Institute of Technology Delhi. (2007). *Equity assurance plan for the disadvantaged groups in vocational education and training in India.* Retrieved November 15, 2007, from http://www. dget.nic.in/WorldBank/1Contents-Summary.pdf

Indiresan, P. V., & Nigam, N. C. (1993). The Indian institutes of technology: Excellence in peril. In S. Chitnis & P. G. Altbach (Eds.), *Higher education reform in India: Experience and perspectives* (pp. 334–364). New Delhi, India: Sage Publications.

Intel. (2009). *Transformation through innovation: Intel higher education in India.* Retrieved July 16, 2009, from http://www.intel.com/cd/corporate/education/apac/eng/in/highered/241528.htm

International Monetary Fund. (2009, July 8). *World economic outlook update: Contractionary forces receding but weak recovery ahead* (p. 2). Retrieved July 15, 2009, from http://www.imf.org/external/pubs/ft/weo/2009/update/02/pdf/0709.pdf

International Telecommunication Union. (2004). *Teledensity of countries/territories.* Retrieved November 14, 2007, from http://www.itu.int/itudoc/itu-t/com3/focus/72404.html

International Telecommunication Union. (2009a). *Basic indicators.* Retrieved July 16, 2009, from http://www.itu.int/ITU-D/icteye/Reporting/ShowReportFrame.aspx?ReportName=/WTI/BasicIndicators Public&RP_intYear=2008&RP_intLanguageID=1

International Telecommunication Union. (2009b). *Mobile cellular subscriptions.* Retrieved July 16, 2009, from http://www.itu.int/ITU-D/icteye/Reporting/howReportFrame.aspx?ReportName=/TI/CellularSubscribersPublic&RP_intYear=2008&RP_intLanguageID=1

IPS News. (2001). *Simputer brings basic education to the children of Bastar.* Retrieved December 16, 2001, from http://www.infochangeindia.org/Itanddltop.jsp?recordno=296&section_idv=9#296

Jagadheesan, L. R. (2005, August 1). India launches its first cheap PC. *BBC.* Retrieved December 4, 2007, from http://news.bbc.co.uk/1/hi/world/south_asia/4735927.stm

Kanellos, M. (2005, June 25). *India's tech renaissance: The $100 computer is key to India's tech fortunes.* Retrieved August 11, 2009, from http://news.cnet.com/Indias-renaissance-The-100-computer/2009-1041_3-5752054.html

Kaur, K. (1985). *Education in India (1781–1985): Policies, planning and implementation.* Chandigarh: Centre for Research in Rural and Industrial Development.

Krishnadas, K. C. (2006). Intel to help promote innovation at Indian universities. *Electronic Engineering Times Asia.* Retrieved December 11, 2007, from http://www.eetasia.com/ART_8800433156_499489_NT_73daec22.HTM

McCloskey, P. (2007). *IBM, Indian Universities Develop Curriculum for 'Service Scientists'.* Retrieved December 10, 2007, from http://campustechnology.com/articles/49021/

Mukherjee, K. C. (1967). *Underdevelopment, educational policy and planning.* New York: Asia Publishing House.

National Office of Overseas Skills Recognition [NOOSR]. (1996). *India: A comparative study* (2nd ed.). Canberra, Australia: Department of Employment, Education, Training and Youth Affairs, Government of Australia.

Naukrihub. (2007). *Industrial relations – Naukrihub.com: Employment in India.* Retrieved August 11, 2009, from http://industrialrelations.naukrihub.com/employment-in-india.html

Nehru, J. (1946). *The Discovery of India.* New Delhi: Oxford University Press. (16th Impression, 1996)

Rawat, P. L. (1970). *History of Indian education.* Agra, India: Ram Prasad and Sons.

Roy, A. (1998). Tingle in the training mill. *Computers Today.* Retrieved January 3, 2002, from http://www.india-today.com/ctoday/051998/cover.html

Sanyal, B. C. (1987). *Higher education and employment: An international comparative analysis.* London: Falmer Press.

Sebaly, K. P. (1972). *The assistance of four nations in the establishment of the Indian Institutes of Technology, 1945–1970.* Ann Arbor, MI: The University of Michigan School of Education.

Sen, B. K. (2007, January 25). Whither science in India. *Current Science, 92*(2), 171–173.

Sethi, J. D. (1983). *The crisis and collapse of higher education in India.* New Delhi, India: Vikas Publishing House Pvt. Ltd.

Simputer Trust. (2009). *Simputer: Radical simplicity for universal access*. Retrieved July 31, 2009, from http://www.simputer.org

Singh, P. (2006). Ringtone reality check: India cellphone story long way to go. *Indian Express*. Retrieved November 14, 2007, from http://www.indianexpress.com/story/13001.html

Sood, A. D. (2001). *Background and perspective*. Retrieved December 2, 2001, from http://www.Info changeindia.org/Itanddlbp.jsp

Tejaswi, M. J. (2007). Microsoft to set up university in city. *Times of India*. Retrieved December 10, 2007, from http://timesofindia.indiatimes.com/Bangalore/Microsoft_to_set_up_university_in_city/articleshow/ 2196363.cms

Telecom Regulatory Authority of India. (2007). *Latest statistics on teledensity and wireless connectivity in India -by TRAI*. Retrieved November 14, 2007, from http://www.mgovworld.org/resources/latest-statistics-on-teledensity-and-wireless-connectivity-in-india-by-trai

United Nations Educational Scientific and Cultural Organization. (1983). *The transition from technical and vocational schools to work*. Paris: United Nations.

Wilson, D. N. (1977). Evaluation as a component of the educational planning process: Evaluation of a transferred Canadian technical institution, the Accra Technical Training Centre. *Educational Planning*, *3*(3), 20–33.

Wilson, D. N. (1992). *Technological education in Canada*. Washington, DC: Organization of American States, Regional Program for Educational Development.

Wolpert, S. (1997). *A new history of India* (5th ed.) New York: Oxford University Press.

World Bank. (2000). *India receives World Bank financing to improve technical education in under-developed states*. Retrieved November 12, 2007, from http://web.worldbank.org/WBSITE/ EXTERNAL/PROJECTS/0,,contentMDK:20013033~menuPK:64282138~pagePK:41367~piPK:279 616~theSitePK:40941,00.html

World Bank. (2007). *Implementation completion and results report (IDA-34130) on a credit in the amount of SDR 48.9 million (US$ 64.9 million equivalent) to India for a Third Technician Education Project*. World Bank: Education Sector, Human Development Unit, South Asia Region. Retrieved August 1, 2009, from http://www-wds.worldbank.org/external/default/WDSContentServer/WDSP/ IB/2008/04/11/000333038_20080411013038/Rendered/PDF/ICR5700ICR0P0506580Box327353B0 1public1.pdf

Yarnell, A. (2006, March 20). A funding evolution: Some of India's scientists find research dollars easier than ever to obtain, but inequities remain. *Chemical and Engineering News*, *84*(12), 19–20. Retrieved December 4, 2007, from http://pubs.acs.org/cen/coverstory/84/8412India5.html

Derek A. Uram
Institute of Higher Education
University of Toronto

SECTION III: CROSS-CULTURAL ISSUES

ELIZABETH SHERMAN SWING

6. THE MULTICULTURAL DILEMMA

Studies from Europe and the USA

For David Wilson, multiculturalism was the defining focus. His sojourn in 110 countries set the pragmatic parameters, with a scholarly exploration of the multi-cultural dimensions of 20th and 21st century life, his legacy. This essay extends David's focus by probing what could be called a *multicultural dilemma*—the rejection by some within Western democratic countries of peaceful coexistence with those whose cultures differ from their own. The essay begins with reference to an emblematic murder on the streets of Amsterdam and its relationship to Enlight-enment values and to multiculturalism. Thereafter, it examines a continuum of school programmes designed for a multicultural population. It ends with an examination of some challenges to multiculturalism and a plea for a multicultural resolution.

The murder which is the starting point for this essay took place early in the morning of November 2nd, 2004 (Buruma, 2006), when Mohammed Bouyeri, a dis-affected Moroccan-Netherlander, rode his bicycle through the streets of Amsterdam to find Theo van Gogh, a film maker and distant relative of the painter, Vincent van Gogh. He then shot van Gogh in the stomach several times, cut his throat with a machete, and pinned a letter to van Gogh's body. The letter, which called for a holy war against all unbelievers, was addressed to Ayaan Hirsi Ali (2006, 2007), a Somalia-born political activist and writer, whose film *Submission* van Gogh had produced— a film that predictably offended members of the large Muslim population living in the Netherlands with its images of naked women on whom quotations from the Koran were projected. That Mohammed Bouyeri knew what he was doing there can be no doubt. The only regret he expressed after being shot by a policeman was that he had not died a martyr.

The Netherlands is a small country that for centuries set out to find a *modus vivendi* for heterogeneous religious beliefs, a country that pioneered in the acceptance of Enlightenment tolerance within a milieu of pluralist intellectual and religious traditions. Within this frame of reference, such an act of violence is particularly shocking. As Ian Buruma (2006) phrased it, the murder in Amsterdam challenged the "limits of tolerance". It did so during an era of disorientation, when churches had lost their power, when icons were broken, when national identity appeared to be subsumed in the European Union, an era characterized by a culture of undiffer-entiated relativity. The tolerance that Buruma refers to implies a willingness to pursue rational discourse within a disparate multicultural environment. It implies a willingness to coexist with values and customs one does not share. It implies, to quote

V. Masemann et al., (Eds.), A Tribute to David N. Wilson: Clamouring for a Better World, 87–98.

Samuel Taylor Coleridge, a "willing suspension of disbelief" It is this "suspension of disbelief" that was so abruptly rejected by the murder of Theo van Gogh. Is a multicultural society possible under such a circumstance?

WHAT IS MULTICULTURALISM?

Multiculturalism as a social ideal is based on the assumption that seemingly incompatible customs, religions, languages, or ethnicities are able to coexist. Such coexistence may take place within an individual. For example, Bill Richardson, formerly a Democratic candidate for President of the United States has a Hispanic mother and an Anglophone father and is completely at home in Spanish-language and American-Anglophone worlds. Coexistence may also exist, either peacefully or otherwise, within communities or nations——Canada with its French- and English-speaking citizens, or Belgium with its Flemings and Francophones, although coexistence there is now near breaking point, or Bosnia and Herzegovina, the venue of the 2007 World Council of Comparative Education Societies Congress, a region that has known catastrophic ethnic warfare. We may wonder, however, at what point acrimonious coexistence is evidence of multiculturalism.

Disparate groups within multicultural societies may be native or *autochthonous* to the area in which they now live; i.e., they may have migrated to this area sufficiently long ago to consider themselves its rightful inhabitants, a claim not always uncontested. Or they may be, to use a word frequently found in discussions of this topic, *allochthonous*, people who came from elsewhere more recently—guest workers or refugees, for example. During the last five decades, large numbers of *allochthonous* people have migrated to and within North America, South America, Africa, Asia, Australia, and parts of Europe, including migration to countries which were in the past not considered *immigrant* nations. These people then form allochthonous populations, which literally means "formed elsewhere." Much, but not all, of the present concern over *multiculturalism* in Europe and North America relates to these populations.

As a way of organizing society, the ideal of *multiculturalism* has recently been in difficulty. In the United States it has been mired in debates over immigration policy, bilingual education, human rights, and feminism (Okin, 1999). In Europe, educators have begun to document the retreat of what, with some irony, they refer to as a "multicultural orthodoxy" (Shadid, 2006, p. 10)—by which is meant a retreat from school programmes designed to facilitate coexistence in countries with a significant population of guest workers and refugees. Initially such programmes represented a partial response to the European Economic Community Directive of 1977 (European Economic Community, 1977) calling for the education of migrant workers' children in their mother tongue and the language of the receiving country, a directive premised on the assumption that workers would return to their country of origin. Today, however, there is tacit recognition that reverse migration is not likely to happen. Of great concern are acts of violence—destruction of the World Trade Center in New York City, bombings on London public transportation—and the emergence of radical right-wing groups such as *Vlaams Blok* in Belgium. Whereas before, multicultural ideals provided a fragile balance, now balance is less possible.

Two very modern post-Enlightenment values are connoted by the concept of *multiculturalism:* 1) that there should be quiet, possibly unexamined, acceptance of the relativity of "incompatible" beliefs and customs; 2) that all cultures will have parity of esteem with the culture of the dominant group and with one another. In the next section of this paper, these assumptions are examined as they relate to a continuum of school practices designed for a multicultural population: *verzuiling*, segmented pluralism in the past in the Netherlands; education for separatism in Belgium; early 20th century assimilation in the American melting pot; recent ambiguous pluralism in France, England, and Germany; and several bilingual, bicultural, and intercultural European Pilot Projects of the 1990s that represent attempts to cope with multiculturalism. Under consideration throughout is the familiar dichotomy—individual freedom versus group rights—and an unanswered question: How do we teach for peaceful multicultural coexistence when active rejection of the values of others is part of a particular minority group's beliefs?

A CONTINUUM OF SCHOOL PRACTICES

Segmented Pluralism, Verzuiling in the Netherlands

Zuil is a Dutch word meaning *pillar. Verzuiling*—"pillarization," segmentation, compartmentalization, or separation—is a description of educational structures (*zuil*), and by analogy social structures throughout the Netherlands, as they existed for much of the 20th century (De Kwaasteniet, 1990). *Verzuiling*, which might be described as segmented pluralism, became educational policy as a result of a compromise over government support of religious schools whereby a subsidy was given to each of the major Christian religions (pillars) for support of their own schools, an implicit agreement by religious factions to cooperate in protecting one another. The unintended consequence of this compromise was the evolution of coexistent religious "pillars" into networks of social, cultural, political, and educational organizations based on ideological and denominational identity. These networks came to dominate every aspect of Dutch life. The choice of friends, of a political party, of a newspaper, of which neighbourhood store to patronize, and of course the choice of a school for one's child, all took place within one or another *zuil*. We should note, however, that the reverse process, *ontzuiling*, literally depillarization, has been underway since the 1960s in what has become one of the most open societies in Europe.

Verzuiling as a way of organizing a multicultural society came close to fulfilling post-Enlightenment values. Under *verzuiling*, "incompatible" beliefs and customs did exist peacefully side by side, but within self-contained *zuils*. There was official parity of esteem between and among the *zuils*, although it was the Christian churches, the Dutch Reformed Church and its several branches, that were at the beginning selected to coexist with Roman Catholicism. The *zuils*, moreover, did not communicate with one another. *Verzuiling* produced a multicultural society, but it did not produce a multicultural community.

Education for Separatism in Belgium

After centuries of conflict between French-speaking Belgians and Dutch-speaking Flemings, Belgium has become a federation of unilingual territories that now threaten to form their own separate nation-state. In the clearly demarcated geographical territories—Flemish in the north, Francophone in the south, plus bilingual Brussels, a capital city area with separate networks of French and Flemish institutions—each linguistic community controls its own institutions: schools, libraries, athletic teams, newspapers, TV channels, radio stations, even symphony orchestras. The all-too-painful reality in the past was that Flemings who adopted the French language for social and economic advancement were likely to become part of a three generation language shift in which bilingual education seemed to be a step toward cultural annihilation (Swing, 1980). In the words of the Final Report of the Harmel Centre, the research group that formulated assumptions on which the Language Law of 1963 was based, "Le bilinguisme dans l'enseignement doit être condamné. [Bilingualism in education must be condemned.]" (Centre de recherche, ca. 1950, p. 6). In the not-too-distant past, there was one national Ministry of Education; after 1969, there were two national Ministries of Education—one for Dutch-language schools and the other for French-language schools. Currently there is no national Ministry of Education in a federalized Belgium (Constitution 1994, Art. 127); communities formulate and carry out school policy. In Parliament, members of each group are likely to give speeches in their own language—a Constitutional right that represents a dramatic change from past practice when all speeches were given in French.

How close does Belgium come to fulfilling post-Enlightenment multicultural values? Flemings and Francophones do coexist in close proximity to one another, but each in a separate linguistic domain. Within this frame of reference, Flemings and Francophones have achieved a multicultural, if separate and not always peaceful, coexistence. They do not, however, seek to achieve an integrated multicultural community.

Americanization, Melting Pot Assimilation in the United States

In the first half of the 20th century, public schools in the United States were the foremost agents of a process of assimilation sometimes called "Americanization". Israel Zangwill's play *The Melting Pot* (first produced in Washington, D.C. in 1908) provides a handy metaphor. The play follows the fortunes of a group of immigrants to the United States: Russian Jews escaping pogroms and upper-class Russian Christians, some of whom had conducted the pogroms. In the play, the protagonist, David, a composer, refers to the United States as "God's crucible...where all the races of Europe are melting and reforming." The assumption is that in America, individuals in a multicultural population will meld into New Americans more like one another than like their former selves, or like the countrymen they left behind. These New Americans would produce their own new identity from their very heterogeneous origins. In a postscript to his play, Zangwell lists the nationalities of the 1,417,227 "aliens" admitted to the United States in 1913—a list that includes Africans, Armenians, Bosnians, Chinese, Dutch, English, French, Italians, Serbians, Russians, and many more. The transformation of this multicultural mix was assumed to be possible. New Americans would emerge from the melting pot with a *tabula rasa,* minds like a blank slate, the experience in the pot having wiped clean their emotional and intellectual identity and history.

In terms of post-Enlightenment multicultural values, assimilation within a melting pot poses a particular challenge. It is assumed that incompatible beliefs and customs are transformed within the melting pot. Within this transformation, however, parity of esteem between and among the many cultures brought to the United States is not an issue. All are assumed to be equal, although the issue of parity of esteem between "New Americans" and "Old Americans" is unresolved. We know now that such a transformation, were it even possible, might not have been an unmitigated source of joy, however much many immigrants wanted to leave behind the pain they had experienced in the Old World. At the least, this transformation would burden them with the need to cope with the difficulty of learning to live in a foreign, linguistically challenging, world. Nevertheless, the melting pot metaphor remained powerful in the United States until the social upheavals of the 1960s. For those who come from families that eagerly sought to assimilate, it is still very, very powerful.

Ambiguous Assimilation in France

A somewhat less stringent variety of assimilation has existed in several European countries. One third of the French population, for example, has an immigrant grandparent; but the French are not likely to view themselves as descendants of immigrants. As in the United States, schools play a major role in socializing newcomers (Boyzon-Fradet, 1992). Foreign children under the age of 16 must enroll in school, regardless of the legal status of their parents. Although there are private Catholic schools, most "foreigners" enroll in public schools that are secular and offer uniform treatment, i.e., equal opportunity. At first glance, there appear to be big differences between the academic performance of foreign children and those of French origin. Immigrant children in some elementary schools have indeed produced inferior results on mathematics and French tests (Vallet et Caille, 1996). By secondary school, differences between foreign children and children of French origin from similar social and economic backgrounds are no longer significant in mathematics but are significant in French, particularly for newcomers. What was found to be critical was the time the students had spent in French schools, the degree of the students' ambition, and the educational level of the family, particularly the educational level of the mother (Vallet, 1996). Compared to French children from equivalent socioeconomic backgrounds, "foreign" children are actually doing better in school. They have higher aspirations than do the children of working class French families. Despite the many clashes between native born and immigrants, an ambivalent assimilation of a multicultural population is in the process of taking place, even though immigrants still retain the identity of "outsiders." Unknown at this time

91

is the impact that the November 2007 riots in the "suburbs" of Paris will have on the Algerian students who participated. In terms of the post-Enlightenment values we have been examining, foreign children still carry the burden of a lack of acceptance from those who categorize them as "outsiders."

A Christian Humanist Curriculum in England

A somewhat different process characterizes education in England where the curriculum has the democratic intent of providing equal access to materials and testing procedures to every student in every Local Education Authority (Lawton, 1989). All students are expected to master the same core subjects: English, mathematics, and science, and all are expected to study history, geography, physical education, music, art, a modern language, plus technology. All, with few exceptions, are also expected to participate in some form of religious education, although some Muslim minority groups have successfully demanded waivers to set up their own schools. Nevertheless, the exposure of all students to a common set of cultural referents and values—even minority students from India, Pakistan, or Africa whose indigenous cultures do not carry such a Eurocentric worldview—could be interpreted as a form of educational colonialism. Whether such students will "benefit" from a Western curriculum is a separate issue. Not everyone within the large multi-cultural population now living in England accepts the assumptions on which such a curriculum is grounded. For some, a Christian humanist curriculum implies the necessity of acculturating to the values and worldview of the dominant culture. From this vantage point the curriculum looks like an instrument for assimilation that does not assume a parity of esteem of the cultures of newcomers with the culture of the dominant group.

The Education of "Others" in Germany

In Germany the existence of many who are perceived to be "others" poses a problem when juxtaposed with the ideology of one nation, one language, and one people. People of German origin can claim German citizenship (*jus sanguinis*) even if they do not know the German language and have never lived in Germany. This preferential status is widely resented by some immigrants without such status. Moreover, immigrant indigenous Danes, Frisians, and Serbs are protected by special legislation which guarantees mother tongue education for those who desire it. More germane to this study are those categorized as *Ausländer*, a group who are not of German origin. In the 1990s eight per cent of the population of Germany, 6.5 million people, were *Ausländer* (Council of Europe, 1994, p. 121), a term which means literally "away from the land" and conveys a wide range of connotations—outsiders, foreign, different, strange, unknown and ultimately unknowable (Schäffter, 1991). The word *immigrant,* however, is not frequently used because Germany is understood not to be an immigration country, but one that initially accepted guest workers on a temporary basis. The largest group of *Ausländer*, Turks, appears both to have been denied the chance to assimilate and to have rejected assimilation—in response perhaps to recognition that the concept of a Turkish-German does not appear to exist, not even with German citizenship. Meanwhile, at the same time German industry seeks workers who know English, not Turkish, many Turks in the largest minority community continue to have self-identifying markers, whether they be head scarves or their own language. Multiculturalism has not been a goal. The reality is a somewhat uneasy truce in spite of evidence of mistreatment of Turks, including the presence of educational barriers such as tracking into lower sections, and religious and class issues.

Multicultural Initiatives, A Bilingual-Bicultural Pilot Project

For many years, supranational agencies such as the Council of Europe and the European Union subsidized pilot projects for children of migrant workers in a series of programmes based on what might be considered a "multicultural orthodoxy" (Shadid, 2006). The programme that began in 1979 at *Rijksmiddenschool Borgerhout*, a lower secondary school in Antwerp, for example, was designed for a student population that was 84 per cent of foreign origin. Many students came directly from their native country: 77 per cent from Morocco; six per cent from other nations such as Chile, Turkey, Spain, Egypt, Portugal, Laos, and mainland China. Many were illiterate when they arrived in Belgium. The pilot project had an ambitious goal: to prepare minority students for the economic realities of their present environment while protecting and reinforcing their ethnic and cultural identity (Baert, personal communication, June 14 1985; Corijn, 1982). For the first year, the minority students, mostly Moroccans, followed a flexible timetable (1B Variant): eight periods a week of Dutch, two of French (a mandatory second language), two of Arabic as a modern language, five of mathematics, four of environmental studies, two of plastic arts, three of gymnastics, four of technical activities. They also participated in the required two periods each week of religion—a choice among Catholicism, Judaism, Protestantism, secular humanism ("morals"), and, since 1978, the Islamic religion. Islam provided a rubric under which Arabic, a formal language of religion, could be taught in a country of strict language laws (Corijn, Leemans, Verhult & Xhoffer, personal communication, June 27, 1985). A curious paradox is the fact that the ethnolinguistic center of this project was not a mother tongue, for the mother tongue would have been one of the several competing Moroccan dialects. Most students learned Arabic as a foreign language. After following this curriculum, Moroccan students were assigned to the same courses as their Belgian counterparts but continued to reinforce their cultural identity through contact with Moroccan teachers, a group recruited by the Flemish Cultural Community and the Moroccan government.

The school's model curriculum was based on a series of assumptions about the role of schools in fostering multiculturalism. A programme which stresses environmental arts, plastic arts, and technical studies would not expose minority students to Eurocentric humanist values explicit in traditional history and geography programmes. Nevertheless, despite the stringency of Belgian language laws, the programme provided continual reinforcement of cultural and linguistic identity.

At the same time, it also prescribed instruction in the language of Flemish Belgium; and after the first year, minority students followed the same common core curriculum as their (Flemish) Belgian peers, a programme that does communicate the reality of a Flemish cultural environment.

The implicit assumption of the bilingual-bicultural project was that each minority student would come to identify with two disparate cultures: one based on a Flemish-Belgian worldview, the other on a Moroccan worldview. However, only the minority students were expected to achieve this dual frame of reference, not the Flemish Belgians. The design implied a belief in the existence of both a Flemish worldview grounded on ethnic absolutes and a Moroccan worldview grounded on its own absolutes. It was implicitly assumed that Moroccan immigrants in Flemish Belgium might have difficulty acquiring a Flemish identity, and, paradoxically, that it is possible to transform a group of minority students into bicultural adults ready to integrate into a Belgian (Flemish) world. Questions unasked include whether these mutually contradictory cultural referents can coexist within a single multicultural person. In terms of our post-Enlightenment values, the programme starts with the assumption that incompatible beliefs and customs can coexist and that parity of esteem is desired but not always achieved.

An Intercultural Curriculum

Other pilot projects have focused on mutual exploration of cultures (ECCE, 1990) and on "medium-term integration strategies which take account of the cultural pluralisation of society" (ECCE, 1990, p. 7) while rejecting "a crude distinction between 'foreigners' and 'natives' " (p. 5). The intercultural project under discussion in selected Francophone Brussels schools reflects this set of assumptions. Unlike the pilot project at the Rijksmiddenschool Borgerhout with its bicultural goals directed just at minority students, this project had intercultural goals for Francophone-Belgian and minority students. The intercultural curriculum, similar to intercultural projects found throughout Europe at that time, diverged from the dominant curriculum pattern of many other Belgian Francophone schools. It began with recognition of the need for better integration of immigrant students and their families into the Belgian social fabric, the need for better scholastic success for students of immigrant origin, the need for better access to the teaching of the language and culture of origin ("Un projet pédagogique multiculturel,"1990). It was a curriculum that sought richness rather than liability in multicultural diversity (Leunda & Deprez, 1988). It was also a multicultural curriculum that viewed schools as agencies for diffusing cross-national perspectives (Jones & Kimberley, 1986), a curriculum based on the assumption that ideals and values from one culture can be of interest and value to members of another culture.

Recognition of non-European languages was therefore part of the agenda. A first year French-language text, for example, made allusions to Arabic and Turkish literature in its instructional sequence (*Institut des Arts et Métiers* [IAM], 1989a). Although Belgian language laws regulate the language of instruction, which in this case must be French, Arabic as a formal language of worship could be used in the Muslim religion class. In addition, schools could use professionals recruited from the immigrants' countries of origin as teacher aides. These "embassy teachers", however, encountered difficulty in defining the culture of immigrant students who have never lived in their parents' country of origin (Leunda & Deprez, 1988). Given its setting in Francophone schools, success in this project was as likely to be equated with French language competence as with mother tongue competency. As a publicity brochure prepared by one of the participating schools (IAM, ca. 1990) pointed out, it was considered essential that a student of immigrant background acquire full knowledge of the structure of French in order to succeed in Belgian (Francophone) society.

This was a curriculum based on relativist assumptions. The study of secondary school history and geography at the *Institut des Arts et Métiers, Ville de Bruxelles* had the overt intent of introducing all students, Belgian as well as minority, to a world beyond Belgium and Europe. The first year history course stressed Roman roots in Africa and the Near East (IAM, 1989c). The following year it emphasized intercultural evolution in contacts with the Orient, formation of the Arab world, the civilization of the Arabs in Spain, the expulsion of Jews from Spain, and the implications for Morocco of the reconquest of Spain (IAM 1989d). The birth of the city of Fès in Morocco—its geography, history, historical monuments, cultural life, its arts and artisans, and origins of its bourgeoisie and nobility—paralleled a history of the city of Brussels during the Burgundian period (IAM, 1989d). Geography lessons emphasized, in addition to Belgium and Europe, the countries of origin of immigrant students—Morocco, Italy and Turkey (IAM, 1989b).

Unlike the relativism of the bicultural curriculum model in Antwerp, based on the coexistence of different truths within minority students, this intercultural model was based on multiple worldviews, on a diffused, reciprocal relativism in which both majority and minority students were expected to adapt to the world view of one another. Students were invited to construct their own patterns of truth, pragmatically adapting what worked best from each culture. Which was the geographic center of these students? Brussels? Fès? How do Muslims adapt to Catholic schools while remaining Muslim? How do Catholic schools remain Catholic while teaching a Muslim population? Nevertheless, this was a one-sided interculturalism. The program's success was linked to the acquisition of French by minority community members, yet the Francophone majority was not expected to enroll in Arabic classes. The dominant culture still controlled the curriculum—a symbol, perhaps, of the difficulty of achieving balance in any multicultural, pluralist design.

Interculturalism becomes even more complicated within the framework of religion. There is consensus within the Office of Catholic Education in Belgium that schools with different cultures invite an intercultural pedagogy, a concept which means situating children within their own culture, recognizing the diversity of student cultures, and opposing assimilationist strategies (Conseil General, 1990). The problem is not whether school officials can agree on intercultural goals. The problem is how to provide respect for the religion of Muslim children while providing young Catholics with the education that caused their parents to enroll them in a Catholic school in the first place. The relativist premises of intercultural education and the absolute premises of Catholicism have managed to coexist, but with some sense of strain. There is coexistence of "incompatible" beliefs and customs. There is an attempt at parity of esteem. But there is nevertheless no real multicultural resolution.

A MULTICULTURAL RESOLUTION?

Is it possible that programmes like the pilot projects described above will lead to conflict resolution in a larger society? Can we hope to see peaceful multiculturalism lead to an end of ethnic warfare? In all the programmes we have examined, multicultural coexistence has difficulty. At one extreme, coexistence requires the segmented pluralism of *verzuiling* or the separatism of Belgium's competing linguistic groups that threaten to rip the nation-state apart. At the other extreme, a melting pot assimilation that destroys an individual's history makes coexistence impossible; and the ambiguous pluralist worlds of France, England, and Germany still see minorities as "others". Do the multicultural pilot projects which we examined really represent a multicultural "orthodoxy"? Their existence did not prevent the outrage that led to the murder in Amsterdam.

Given our cherished post-Enlightenment values, should we assume parity of esteem for all cultures? The feminist Susan Moller Okin does not think so. Okin (1979, 1999) rejects protecting minority cultures in which are embedded practices such as polygamy, honour killings, forced marriage, child marriage, genital mutilation of women, and exoneration of rapists who marry their victim. Okin also rejects cultural preservation as a value in instances where a religion is willing to accept violations of human rights. For Okin, cultures that flout the rights of individuals cannot peacefully coexist with those cultures that do not, and should not be given special protection, even if lack of such protection endangers the minority culture's continued existence. Within her worldview a "willing suspension of disbelief" can mean violation of basic human rights. Within her worldview, multiculturalism does not always benefit individuals. Is Okin's analysis an adequate reason for rejecting post-Enlightenment multicultural values?

What new values do we need for the organization of 21st century life in communities that will continue to be more, not less, multicultural? Is a "willing suspension of disbelief" still needed? If not, what is? Did multiculturalism die on the streets of Amsterdam with Theo van Gogh? The author of this article sincerely hopes that it did not. And all of us know that David Wilson, if he were still with us, would share this hope.

REFERENCES

Baert, G. (1985, June 24). *Personal communication*. Brussels: Belgium.

Boyzon-Fradet, D. (1992). The French education system: Springboard or obstacle to integration. In D. L. Horowitz & G. Noiriel (Eds.), *Immigrants in two democracies: French and American experience*. New York: New York University Press.

Buruma, I. (2006). *Murder in Amsterdam: The death of Theo van Gogh and the limits of tolerance*. New York: Penguin.

Centre de recherche pour la solution nationale des problèmes sociaux, politiques, et juridiques en regions wallonnes et flamandes [Harmel Centre]. (ca. 1950). Xeroxed typescript, p. 6.

Council of Europe. (1994). *Recent demographic developments in Europe.* Strasbourg: Council of Europe Press.

Conseil Général de l'Enseignement Catholique. (1990, May). *École et immigration: Pistes de reflexion et proposition d'action.* Typescript.Brussels.

Constitution 1994. Art. 127, 129. (Belgium)

Corijn, H., Leemans, R., Verhult, J., & Xhoffer, J. (1985, June 27). *Personal communication.* Antwerp, Belgium: H.M.S. Borgerhout.

Corijn, H. (1982). *Pilootexperiment: Rijksonderwijs, 1979-1982. Pedagogische Opvangvormen voor Migrantenkinderen in het Secondair Oderwijs.* Borgerhout: R.M.S. Borgerhout.

De Kwaasteniet, M. (1990). *Denomination and primary education in the Netherlands, 1870-1984.* Amsterdam: Koninklijk Nederlands Aadrijkskundig Genootschap.

ECCE Interkulturell. (1990). The European Communities Comparative Evaluation Project, "Pilot Project Programme of the European Communities, 'The Education of the Children of Migrant Workers.' Results and Recommendations from the Comparative Evaluation." Landau. EWH. Im Froty, D-6840, West Germany.

European Economic Community. (1977). *Council Directive of 25 July 1977 on the education of the children of migrant workers* (77/486/EEC). Retrieved January 7, 2009, from http://eur-lex.europa.eu/LexUriServ/LexUriServ.do?uri=CELEX:31977L0486:EN:NOT

Hirsi Ali, A. (2006). *The caged virgin: An emancipation proclamation for women and Islam.* New York: Free Press.

Hirsi Ali, A. (2007). *Infidel.* New York: Free Press.

Institut des Arts et Métiers (IAM). (1989a). *Français Textes 1ère. Degré d'observation.* Établissement désigné comme École Pilote pour l'intégration des Cultures sous l'égide de la Communauté Economique Européenne. Ville de Bruxelles: Institut des Arts et Métiers.

IAM. (1989b). *Géographie. 1ère observation. Degré d'observation.* Établissement désigné comme École Pilote pour l'intégration des Cultures sous l'égide de la Communauté Economique Européenne. Ville de Bruxelles: Institut des Arts et Métiers.

IAM. (1989c). *Histoire 1ère Obs. Degré d'observation.* Établissement désigné comme École Pilote pour l'intégration des Cultures sous l'égide de la Communauté Economique Européenné. Ville de Bruxelles: Institut des Arts et Métiers.

IAM. (1989d). *Histoire 2ème Obs. Degré d'observation.* Établissement désigné comme École Pilote pour l'intégration des Cultures sous l'égide de la Communauté Economique Européenné. Ville de Bruxelles: Institut des Arts et Métiers.

IAM (ca. 1990). *L'école du futur... ta future école. 3 Implantations.* Etablissement désigné comme Ecole Pilote pour l'intégration des Cultures sous l'égide de la Communauté Economique Européenne. Ville de Bruxelles: Institut des Arts et Métiers.

Jones, C., & Kimberley, K. (1986). *CDCC's Project No. 7: The education and cultural development of migrants.* Strasbourg, France: Council for Cultural Cooperation.

Lawton, D. (1989). The national curriculum. In D. Lawton (Ed.), *The Education Reform Act: Choice and control* (pp. 27–43). London: Hodder & Stoughton.

Leunda, J., & Deprez, P. (1988). *Rapport d'Evaluation de l'expérience-pilote d'enseignement multiculturel (1984–1987).* Bruxelles: Commission des Communautés Européennes.

Okin, S. M. (1979). *Women in Western political thought.* Princeton, NJ: Princeton University Press.

Okin, S. M. (1999). *Is multiculturalism bad for women?* Princeton, NJ: Princeton University Press.

Schäffter, O. (1991). Modi des Fremderlebens. Deutungsmuster im Umgang mit Fremdheit. In O. Schäffter (Ed.), *Das Fremde: Erfahrungsmöglichkeiten zwischen Faszination und Bedrohung* (pp. 11–42). Wiesbaden, Germany: VS Verlag für Sozialwissenschaften.

Shadid, W. A. (2006). Public debates over Islam and the awareness of Muslim identity in the Netherlands. *European Education, 38*(2), 10–22.

Swing, E. S. (1997). Education and separatism in multicultural Belgium: An American perspective. In K. de Clerck & F. Simon (Eds.), *Studies in comparative international and peace education* (pp. 235–252).Ghent, Belgium: C.S.H.P.

Un projet pédagogique multiculturel [A multicultural educational project]. (11 Novembre 1990). *Le Soir*. Belgium: Brussels.

Vallet, L. A., & Caille, J. P. (1996). *Les élèves étrangers ou issus de l'immigration dans l'école et le collège français*. Paris: Dossiers d'Éducation et Formations.

Zangwill, I. [1909/1915]. *The melting pot drama in four acts*. New York: Macmillan.

Elizabeth Sherman Swing
Professor Emerita
St. Joseph's University

EDWARD R. HOWE

7. A COMPARATIVE ETHNOGRAPHIC NARRATIVE APPROACH TO STUDYING TEACHER ACCULTURATION

This book chapter evolved from my doctoral research; however, the genesis is a paper that I wrote in 2001 for Professor David Wilson, my thesis supervisor, mentor and friend. David actively encouraged me to pursue my doctoral studies and supported my research approach. When I was unable to find a suitable course to jump-start my search for the most appropriate research methodology, David offered an ethnographic reading course to meet my needs. The purpose of this chapter is to highlight my research methodology through the narratives of teachers encountered during my doctoral research conducted from August 2002 through March 2003 in Tochigi, Japan. While the focus of this paper is mainly on methodology, the study is situated within the broader contexts of comparative education and teacher education. Although these narratives are a partial account of the diverse challenges facing teachers in Canada and Japan, there are significant commonalities for all teachers. Nevertheless, care must be taken in generalizing the findings of this study. Thus, what follows is a brief introduction to my conceptual framework, a description of comparative ethnographic narrative (CEN), my narrative juxtaposed with those of Japanese teachers, and a discussion of teacher acculturation.

BACKGROUND TO THE STUDY

In my doctoral research, of which this study is a part, teacher acculturation in Canada and Japan were compared and evaluated (Howe, 2005a, 2005b, 2008). As a detailed comparative analysis is beyond the scope of this chapter, what follows is a highly condensed summary of the findings. Essentially, Canada's strengths lie in well-developed preservice teaching programmes. However, graduates are left to "sink or swim" in their critical first year of teaching. In contrast, Japan's comprehensive yearlong internship offers an effective apprenticeship induction model with an emphasis on assistance rather than assessment.

While reforms to Japanese teacher education in the early 1990s have resulted in an exemplary model of teacher induction (Howe, 2006), there were significant shortcomings uncovered as a result of my research, including underdeveloped preservice education programmes, poor articulation between universities and schools, inadequate training of mentors and a rigid hierarchical system stifling innovation. Furthermore, the comprehensive induction for full time new teachers and gradual acculturation into the profession of teaching is not possible for the vast majority

V. Masemann et al., (Eds.), A Tribute to David N. Wilson: Clamouring for a Better World, 99–113.

of neophytes who begin their careers as temporary or assistant teachers. Finally, a most salient point is that these findings would not have been discovered or understood properly without the CEN methodology described in the next section.

COMPARATIVE ETHNOGRAPHIC NARRATIVE: A PERSONAL EXPERIENCE

Educational research presents a myriad of methodological choices. Researchers must select culturally appropriate approaches while also trying to balance practical concerns. Often this results in the use of surveys. However, micro-level ethnomethodological studies involving the researcher as co-participant provide a deeper understanding, in-depth analysis and thick description. Narrative inquiry (Clandinin & Connelly, 2000), reflexive ethnography (Brewer, 2000) and other interpretive ethnographic research methods show great promise in this area.[1] When researchers compare their own experiences with those of others, insights can be gained that would otherwise be lost in surveys or structured interviews. The CEN methodology used in this study blends reflexive ethnography and narrative inquiry to compare my own teacher acculturation with that of other teachers. Rather than focusing on the macro-level of nation-states or schools as the units of analysis, this research looks at the micro-level of individual teachers. Through participant observation, journal writing, email exchanges, and extended conversations with novice and veteran teachers, I have uncovered significant stories regarding teacher induction practices[2]—issues that would have remained hidden or at the periphery if I had used traditional survey research (Howe, 2005a, 2005b).

For ethnographic research, engagement in the field is the single most potent strategy ethnographers have to enhance veracity, yet the trends lean towards more efficient and rapid approaches, for example, "rapid appraisal", "focused ethnography" and "microethnography" (Stewart, 1998). However, more time spent in the field can help overcome challenges such as dispersion, size, and informants' stories, and also allow the researcher to develop deeper contextual understandings of local histories, relationships and culture (Stewart, 1998). In fieldwork that is genuine, a researcher stays long enough to learn something about people's lives and thinking, while developing relationships and sense of involvement.

Education, language and culture are all firmly embedded in the larger structure of society. They cannot be studied in isolation but rather must be investigated as a whole in order to be understood and related to a living context (Beattie, 1964). Indeed, the first comprehensive studies of Japanese education incorporating ethnomethodology were conducted by anthropologists (see Rohlen, 1983; Singleton, 1967). More recently, reflexive anthropological approaches demonstrate how ethnographic fieldwork provides significantly deeper understanding of linguistic and cultural differences (see Hendry, 1999).

In addition to time in the field, ethnographers have a variety of observational techniques and different "lenses" to guide their descriptive narratives. Capturing words alone is not sufficient, as ethnographies should also reflect tacit knowledge and experiences. Fetterman (1989) speaks of using the "big net approach" to ensure a wide-angle view of events before the microscopic study of specific interactions begins" (p. 43). Reflexive ethnography is a dynamic cyclical process—wide angle, zooming in, and then back to wide angle, with commensurately varying depths of field. In my study I used a CEN lens, including reflections through journal writing to capture the essence of teacher acculturation.

I had conversations with 57 teachers from rural and urban areas of Tochigi, Gunma and Tokyo in the Kanto region of Japan. Included were 30 first-year, 2 second-year, 8 mid-career, 13 veteran, and 4 retired teachers, with careers spanning five decades. Through CEN, I learned about teachers' daily routines; their interactions with students, teachers, administrators, and parents; and their professional development. Field notes, email exchanges and a personal journal were used to document my experiences and the narratives of the teachers. At the end of each day of participant observation, I de-briefed with my spouse before documenting reflections in my journal. This process continued for eight months in conjunction with email contributions from teachers. I met with teachers on a number of occasions for feedback and clarification, and to ensure that their voices were adequately represented.

Initial semi-structured interviews and a survey of over 130 teachers were inconclusive as the questions elicited limited responses. The survey data seemed to add voices to back up the interview data, but provided little new information. However, significantly more was learned in subsequent "teacher to teacher conversations" (Yonemura, 1982) focusing on the same questions. These informal discussions are better described as *conversations* rather than *interviews* as my spouse and newborn child were present in addition to the Japanese teachers.[3] The conversations took place over lunch, dinner or a cup of tea in a relaxed and familiar atmosphere, which contributed to putting the teachers at ease. The few conversations I had at schools tended to be much more stifled and rigid experiences. Teachers indicated that they couldn't open up to me in the same way they could in their own homes away from the prying eyes and ears of their administrators and curious colleagues.

Critical elements to obtain reliable data from teachers were making initial contact, then establishing trust and developing rapport. This was a time-consuming and difficult process that was only made possible through personal introductions from mutual friends or acquaintances. While interview and survey data was obtained from over 180 teachers, here I will focus on one novice teacher juxtaposed with my own narrative of teacher induction.[4]

As teaching is largely a cultural activity, learning to teach cannot be explained merely by the formal mechanisms of teacher induction programmes, or through document review alone. Informal, "behind the scenes" glimpses of teaching provide a more comprehensive view of teacher acculturation. Thus, I use the term acculturation rather than induction. Acculturation seems to better capture the personal and serendipitous journey of becoming a teacher, rather than the conventional sociological and anthropological terms socialization or enculturation. In my view, teachers are not socialized into the profession, nor are they moulded into professionals through the efforts of other members of the teaching community. Learning to teach is a far more personal endeavour.

NARRATIVES OF LEARNING TO TEACH

CEN provides a window into the situation of novice teachers. While the challenges faced depend on the socio-cultural context and other considerations, there are many commonalities and lessons in teacher induction that may be shared. This process is illustrated through juxtaposing my narrative of first-year teaching in Canada with that of Miss Sakaguchi from Japan. I first give an account of my own teacher acculturation.

My Narrative of First Year Teaching

I was born and raised in Victoria, British Columbia (BC), Canada. I did not plan to be a teacher but fell into the profession when my Bachelor of Science degree in Physics failed to prove the "meal ticket" I hoped for. After graduation, I entered the secondary teacher education programme at the University of British Columbia. Twelve months later I was a certified teacher. I went straight from student to teacher, with little time for second thoughts. I taught secondary school science for one year in BC, before moving to Japan, where I was an assistant language teacher from 1990–1992 in Tokyo public schools. I then moved back to Canada, where I returned to teaching secondary school for ten years.

While it was not my dream to become a teacher, I was predisposed to the profession. I had positive experiences as a student and a tutor, so I felt inclined to give it a try. Thus, almost on a whim, directly after completing my first degree, I chose to enter teaching. In the spring of 1990, I had my 13-week practicum at a local secondary school in Surrey, BC. I taught grade 8 and 9 Science as well as grade 11 and 12 Physics. My practicum could be perceived as having progressed rather well, as I taught in basically the same manner as that of my secondary school science teachers, while trying to incorporate what I had learned in teacher training. However, I was given very little guidance from my sponsor teacher and I rarely saw my faculty advisor. Somehow I was expected to know how to plan and implement original lessons, to effectively manage classes and to carry out the daily routines of teaching. I was not given any feedback until the end of the practicum, when I was told "what I had been doing wrong" and which areas needed further improvement as I began my teaching career. This practicum experience gave to me a whole new meaning to the well-known "sink or swim" cliché of teacher induction. My pre-service teacher education had not adequately prepared me for the challenges of teaching high school students. While I learned a great deal, there was an emphasis on theory with little practical advice.

I passed the practicum and upon graduation was immediately hired as a *teacher on call* (T.O.C.) for the same school district where I had carried out my practicum. This is the usual way for beginning teachers to "get their foot in the door" in Canada, as many school districts hire directly only from their T.O.C. lists. I received a phone call on the first day of school, as a teacher had taken a sudden indeterminate leave of absence. I taught classes as if I would be there the entire year but I fully expected the other teacher to return at any time. As days turned into months, it became clear that he was not returning. My temporary position eventually became a continuing permanent contract at 70 per cent full time equivalency. I was assigned three blocks of grade 11 Physics and two blocks of grade 11 Biology. Although well prepared to teach physics, I had no training in biology.

I began to rely on the help of seasoned veteran biology teachers to show me everything from dissecting a crayfish to operating a film projector. The mentorship of these teachers was essential to my survival that first year. As a part-time teacher, I had no homeroom, only two classes to prepare for, and three spare blocks instead of the usual one block and, still, I was swamped with work! Most first year teachers have to teach seven out of eight blocks a day, with up to seven different classes to prepare for, in addition to managing a homeroom, coaching and other expected duties. I consider myself fortunate as a first year teacher to have had sufficient time to plan as well as the expert guidance of experienced teachers; however, it took me several years before I felt I was an effective teacher.

Narrative of Miss Sakaguchi, English/Band teacher, Sakura High School

At the time of this ethnographic study, Miss Sakaguchi was in her second year of teaching English and her first year teaching Band at Sakura High School in Tochigi. She is a highly competent and dedicated professional who spends long hours at school, devoting most of her energy and free time to her work. Miss Sakaguchi is an outstanding example of young teachers in Japan. Her story, while unique, captures the atmosphere of Japan's teacher acculturation.

Miss Sakaguchi was born in Yokohama city in October 1978 but is a long-time resident of Tochigi. She moved to Tochigi at age seven where she grew up in a mid-sized city of about 83,000 people, living just 15 meters away from the local elementary school. From an early age, Miss Sakaguchi showed an interest in English. At five, she began to play the piano. It was obvious that Miss Sakaguchi had a gift in the area of music as she excelled in her piano lessons. Later, she learned that she had perfect pitch and could easily imitate sounds and melodies she heard. This talent carried over to her ability to speak and comprehend English.

In elementary school, Miss Sakaguchi had many friends, most of whom were boys. This is unusual in Japan where gender differentiation is common from early ages. For a short time, the other girls bullied her. This was likely out of jealousy, as she was one of the top students. While this experience was unpleasant, she perceives that it made her a stronger person and gave her more self-confidence, as she was able to transcend the immature behaviour of her peers. This experience also gave her empathy for others, which later would prove invaluable in her teaching. While Miss Sakaguchi does not recall any specific teachers or moments of inspiration, she indicated that as a young girl she wanted to be an elementary school teacher. In grade four she joined the school band and learned to play the flute.

In junior high school, Miss Sakaguchi continued to excel and was again one of the top students. She was good at all her subjects but enjoyed English and Band most. She continued to play the flute, eventually becoming a club leader of the junior and senior high school orchestra. This was quite an honour and distinction as club leaders are nominated by student members and elected by popular consensus. Miss Sakaguchi enjoyed listening to English pop music and this motivated her to learn more English informally on her own. Pivotal to her academic life at this time was her participation in Tochigi's speech contest, for which she was chosen to be the sole representative of her school in two years of both junior and senior high school. The intense preparation for these competitions, with the support and guidance of her English teacher, helped to further hone her English communication and natural pronunciation skills. In high school she continued to develop her English to a much higher level. She credits her success to hard work and natural ability combined with the support from teachers. These characteristics carry over to her teaching philosophy.

Miss Sakaguchi believes that an effective teacher must have a good understanding of students while providing feedback and positive reinforcement to facilitate learning. She sees teaching as a continuous learning process but also that it is a talent or gift that some will have and others will not. However, she indicated that if someone has the essential qualities, effective teaching could be developed through further study and practice. Miss Sakaguchi believes that her interest and ability in music, in particular her good ear and time spent listening to English pop music as a teenager, helped her to develop her English skills. The intense preparation and daily practice for the speech contests was seminal to her future career as an English teacher. She noted that teaching "seemed like an easy job" and something she thought she was familiar with as a student.

An important life event for Miss Sakaguchi was her experience as a participant in an exchange programme with the USA. In both junior high and high school she spent two weeks abroad. Her home-stay experiences in Pennsylvania and Indiana as well as her travel around the USA put her English language skills to the test. She quickly learned that her English skills would have to improve considerably for her to communicate effectively with native speakers. Miss Sakaguchi still keeps in touch with the host family from her visit as a 17-year old high school student. As a result of these experiences abroad, she decided that she would like to live in a foreign country.

After graduation from a prestigious girls' public high school in Tochigi, Miss Sakaguchi attended Sophia University, an elite private institution in Tokyo specializing in English and international affairs with more than half the courses taught in English and with faculty from all over the world. This experience prompted her to travel to San Francisco where she studied for nine months earning credits towards her Bachelor of Arts from Sophia University. However, she became more interested in sociology, psychology and general education rather than teaching English grammar. Her experience as an exchange student in the USA provided her with an opportunity to pursue greater diversity in courses. This liberal arts education appealed to her since it allowed greater flexibility in course selection than was available in her Japanese university. By age 20 she had decided to become a teacher as she had thoroughly enjoyed her experience teaching at a *juku*[5] in Tokyo and tutoring Japanese to foreign students while in San Francisco.

According to Miss Sakaguchi, most of what she learned about effective teaching was through *zatsudan* (informal discussions with colleagues). Nevertheless, her brief two-week practicum experience in June of her fourth year of university studies was the most significant formal education event along her teaching journey. Her sponsor teacher proved to be highly enthusiastic and full of creativity. While Miss Sakaguchi had to work extremely hard during these two weeks, she ascribes her sponsor teacher for providing her with inspiration to use a variety of teaching strategies. He was most influential in her teacher induction—significantly more so than her designated mentor teacher in her first year of teaching or any other teacher in her experience as a first year teacher. However, Miss Sakaguchi indicated that while she had significant latitude during her practicum and first year of teaching, her colleagues at Sakura high school encouraged her to follow their lead in subsequent years. In having to conform to Sakura's way of doing things, Miss Sakaguchi lamented she did not have the same freedom she previously enjoyed.

Miss Sakaguchi cares a great deal about her teaching, placing her job as English and Band teacher at Sakura high above all else. This became evident in conversations with colleagues but the most significant indicator was her recent choice of career over marriage. Miss Sakaguchi was to be married in December of her second year of teaching but broke off the engagement one month prior in order to pursue her teaching. Her fiancé, also a Tochigi teacher ten years her senior, had insisted she become a traditional wife (bear children, give up her position at Sakura, move to a school closer to his home in order to take care of the family and household) but she could not bear the thought of leaving her teaching job at Sakura. In her first year of teaching, this seemed a reasonable prospect, but in her second year she came to really appreciate her role as a teacher and gained a great deal of personal satisfaction from her job. In particular, Miss Sakaguchi is proud that she has been credited for bringing the school band back into the spotlight, since it earned the first gold medal in recent years in the annual Tochigi competition. Sakura has a long-standing tradition of excellence in music that had waned in recent years due to her predecessor's lack of interest in instructing the band. If she were to leave Sakura, she wonders what would happen to the band program. Finally, Miss Sakaguchi also enjoys helping the students with the speech contest and those who wish to go on exchanges abroad. Through her teaching, she has the chance to help students succeed in the same way her teachers helped her. Perhaps this is the most powerful lesson of all for her and her students.

Transcultural Commonalities in Teacher Acculturation

Just like Miss Sakaguchi, I get a great deal of personal satisfaction facilitating my students' growth and helping them to reach their full potential. Why do people become teachers? The love of learning is a common response. But learning to teach is a difficult and complicated process. It is a personal journey, fraught with roadblocks, detours and accidents along the way, as illustrated in these narratives of teacher acculturation. Individual differences are overshadowed by significant commonalities. Whether the socio-cultural context is that of a first year science teacher in Surrey, BC, Canada in the 1990s or of a beginning English and Band teacher in Tochigi, Japan, a decade later, teachers share similar concerns and challenges. Clearly, issues pertaining to teacher induction transcend culture. Thus, to better understand teacher acculturation, in the following section, I supplement Miss Sakaguchi's narrative with other Japanese teachers from novices to veterans.

TEACHER TO TEACHER CONVERSATIONS

As teacher stories emerged, I was able to check for understanding and completeness. Teachers could enjoy telling their stories, opening up and becoming engaged in the informal conversations much more than they had through semi-structured interviews with open-ended questions.

Pertinent teacher issues with implications for teacher induction were discovered through CEN as shown in vignettes from conversations, email exchanges, as well as my field and electronic journals. These partial texts serve to illustrate some of the significant findings, such as the importance of *sempai/kohai* teacher relationships and effective mentoring, while highlighting the shortcomings of the teacher induction programmes, an integral part of teacher training for all newly appointed teachers in Japan.[6]

Novice Teachers

I had the chance to speak with a group of junior high school teachers from Gunma over dinner, on their way home after an overnight retreat. What follows is a vignette from my electronic journal, December 28, 2002:

> We sat around the Korean BBQ table and had the chance to speak over a leisurely two-hour dinner. This was a great environment—much better than the teachers' room. I spoke mostly with Keiko while Emmy talked with two other women. Some survey questions were asked to the group such as what are the challenges you face and so on. As they were fresh from their overnight retreat they had lots of insights to share with us. Perhaps the most important thing is that they enjoy these professional development activities because it is a means for them to get together with friends, share teacher stories and experiences and to learn from one another. All 182 of Gunma's first year teachers (elementary, junior high and high school as well as special education) participated. This includes 23 English teachers! The focus was on human rights and classroom management (giving discipline and praise for example). The two-day sojourn to a youth facility consisted of a lecture followed by seminars in groups of eight or nine teachers.
>
> All these teachers are about the same age (23). Two of them didn't pass the prefectural exam for teacher certification the first time round. All agreed that informal conversations between teachers is the best form of teacher education but they like the formal induction programme as it gives them a chance to do

just that with other new teachers. Most have someone to cover their classes (often their mentor) when they are away. Everyone made it clear that other teachers are the most helpful element of teacher induction.

Keiko said that her two-week practicum was inadequate for her to learn how to be an effective teacher. She said "it helped me learn how to teach English, but not how to be a teacher." To manage all the various roles and duties of a teacher requires much more time and can only be learned on the job. Her views of the job changed during her first year of teaching. As a student teacher she thought of her role in a one dimensional way as simply "English teacher." But now she sees the role of teacher as a complex hybrid of subject teacher, councillor, coach and more.

Extended conversations with other groups of first year teachers over lunch at the Tochigi Education Centre during training sessions and through email exchanges allowed me to probe for deeper understanding and to keep in touch with the teachers, despite their busy teacher schedules.

We spoke with a group of eight first year elementary and junior high school teachers at the education centre over lunch. Most indicated their mentors were not very effective. Only one individual described his mentor as an exemplary teacher—the others had more criticism than compliments for their mentors. In one case, an elementary teacher said his mentor was more a "minus than a plus". When we probed him for an example, he indicated that his mentor observed a lesson, then proceeded to publicly criticize trivial things such as how he wrote on the blackboard and so on, right in front of his students. A junior high school teacher indicated he had only received three meetings with his mentor over the last eight months. There was a consensus that generally mentors were chosen out of convenience rather than leadership or outstanding teaching. According to these young teachers, mentors tended to be senior teachers who were picked to minimize their negative impact on students or to provide an outlet for them to provide service to the school that would free them from other duties.

The other significant finding that emerged from our conversation was the lack of support and assistance for beginning teachers in their acculturation through substitute teaching. Most of these teachers had subbed [substituted] for one or more years before landing their contracted positions and going through this induction programme for "first year teachers". They complained of only receiving a half-day of training before taking on their duties as substitute or temporary teachers. This training session covered administrative items like how to apply for a job and so on rather than the nuts and bolts of teaching and classroom management. [Electronic journal, 12/11/02]

Looking back on the year, I see the children's progress in different areas. This makes me happy. For example, one student had difficulty speaking up in class when he started but now he is much more confident. I have grown as a teacher too. At first if there was extra time at the end of a class period I was at a loss as to what to do. Today I have lots of ways to cope... it is all routine now. [Ai is a grade 5 teacher. This excerpt is from a translated taped conversation with five first year teachers at Tochigi Education Centre on 01/23/03]

In summary, by the end of their teacher induction year, individuals have grown from neophyte student teachers to competent and confident novice professionals. They have made the important transition from "student" to "teacher". However, it takes several years or more of experience before novice teachers can become fully acculturated into the teaching profession. Therefore, it is necessary to talk with veteran teachers to gain a more comprehensive view of teacher acculturation.

Mid-Career and Veteran Teachers

Teachers with experience beyond the first year of teaching offer different perspectives of teacher acculturation, as shown in the narratives of Kimura-sensei and Shimazaki-sensei, colleagues at Sakura High School.

During her first year and beyond, Shimazaki-sensei received much help from Kimura-sensei who became a sort of surrogate mentor. Her designated mentor teacher was of little help. He seemed too busy. Kimura helped with everything, but Shimazaki also relied on the other teachers that sat close by in the teachers' room.

Kimura-sensei has 14 years of experience at two different high schools in Tochigi. He also mentioned the importance of *sempai* teachers to his own teacher induction. We talked mostly about the nature of *sempai/kohai* and teacher relationships. He feels that teachers are fundamentally colleagues who must function within the framework of *sempai/kohai* relationships. He indicated that in his department these Japanese social structures were rather superficial things, like just the way they spoke and their behaviour to one another. However, he said that this could lead to problems in some departments and schools where junior teachers would hesitate to offer their opinions to senior teachers or speak their minds clearly to others. Nevertheless, Shimazaki and Kimura share lessons and ideas freely despite their differences in age and experience. Kimura said that the energy and enthusiasm of younger teachers helps rejuvenate the veterans. [This excerpt is taken from our conversation, recorded in my field journal, 2/4/03]

It is interesting to compare Kimura and Shimazaki's collegial narrative with other Tochigi teachers with different perspectives.

Yumiko's husband who teaches grade 5, graduated in 1986, before the teacher induction reforms took place. He indicated he received little or no formal in-service (training) and things are much better now. Yumiko's husband was adamant that he learned how to be an effective teacher through personal experience rather than formal training or collaboration with others (both pre-service and in-service). [Electronic journal, 8/16/02; 1/7/03]

Kojima-sensei, a veteran teacher in his mid-sixties, spoke at length about his teaching philosophy. He felt that learning alongside the students was critical to developing his teaching. Kojima focused on his involvement in the judo club and one exemplary student who motivated him to improve his teaching. [Electronic journal, 1/7/03]

Summary of Results

In Japan, the foundation for successful acculturation into the teaching profession is built on two pillars of education: *kenshû* (training or professional development) and *shidô* (guidance). Time after time these two terms came up in teacher conversations, the survey results, emails and document review. Teacher induction in Japan facilitates collegiality. First-year teachers receive substantial assistance and guidance under the tutelage of senior teachers. All newly appointed full-time teachers also receive 20 to 30 days of intensive *kenshû* and *shidô* from specially trained master teachers at prefectural education centers and overnight retreats. These programmes give new teachers opportunities to form life-long friendships and significant collegial bonds with their peers. Prefectural education centers provide additional professional development at 5, 10 and 20 years of service to further enhance ongoing inservice training. The notion of teacher as "life-long learner" is an integral part of Japanese educational philosophy.

However, there are a number of failings in Japanese teacher education. First, preservice training of teachers is not well connected to the first-year of teaching. Preservice teacher education programmes are not well developed, nor are they respected and supported by the teaching community. The teaching practicum is limited to 4 weeks or less, and is usually restricted to observation, with few teaching opportunities. Learning to teach is characterized by one-way pedagogical exchanges, with little offered from the neophyte to the veteran sponsor teacher. Therefore it is difficult for new teaching strategies to be disseminated from universities through student teachers, and eventually to become accepted by the mainstream, since it is assumed the more experienced teachers must pass down all the lessons to be learned.

Second, many teachers begin their careers as temporary or part-time workers and are thus ineligible for the induction training of full-time employees. If they later become hired as full-time teachers, they are required to take the induction training alongside the fresh graduates, and this undermines their significant practical knowledge of teaching gained in the field. Subsequently, these teachers tend to dismiss much of the induction programme as an unnecessary extra burden. There is a widespread belief among all teachers that the *kenshû* received during the first-year as a full-time employee is simply too much, too late.

Third, school-based mentors assigned by administrators receive no special training for their role and are primarily selected based on seniority and convenience rather than their ability to assist, guide and lead others. The quality of mentorship varies widely and much of the designated time for mentoring is not used effectively or as intended, due to the busy schedules of teachers. There is no monitoring by the Ministry of Education of the arrangements made between mentors and mentees. As a result, most teachers do not adhere to the 60 days of school-based mentoring mandated.

In Japan, formal preservice and inservice teacher education programmes tend to ignore the personal practical knowledge of novice teachers. Nevertheless, Japan's teacher acculturation, successfully integrates time to think and reflect, a shared culture of the craft of teaching, and an apprenticeship model of teacher development. Rather than working in isolation, Japan's teachers recognize the power of colla-boration.

In summary, the most significant features of teacher acculturation in this study of Japanese teachers were found to include the following:

1. Provision for time to reflect and for collaboration.
2. Flexible organization of timetable, physical layout and other structural features to facilitate teacher talk and collegiality.
3. Gradual acculturation into the profession.
4. Professional development as a continuous and ongoing process.
5. In-service training as a job requirement.
6. An apprenticeship model of teacher development.
7. Assistance of veteran colleagues in teacher induction.

DEVELOPING A FRAMEWORK FOR EDUCATIONAL RESEARCH METHODOLOGY

The intricacies of Japan's teacher acculturation are not well known amongst educators outside the country. Further ethnographic studies are needed to better understand the nature of teacher acculturation and to advance theories of teacher socialization within the cultural context of Japan and elsewhere. Ethnographic fieldwork and participant observation in particular are ideally suited to the study of culture; therefore, a socio-cultural framework may be most aptly chosen (Wolcott, 1999). Culture is distributed differentially across participants as well as researchers, each of whom confers individual meaning (Stewart, 1998). Hence, it is not sufficient to interview in order to understand culture. One needs to experience culture personally. To go beyond surveys and interviews, researchers should investigate "speech-in-action" first-hand, listen carefully to what people say, and observe what they do.

The ethnographer's text is, by nature, a partial, select and personal account of events. Moreover, the increasing processes of globalization, cultural hybridity, and creolization demand research methods that accommodate a fusion of global and local perspectives (see Willis, 2001). Thus, care must be taken in attempts to generalize findings. But through CEN and other reflexive approaches, we can learn how cultures or subcultures of people interpret the world, while coming to terms with our own cultural biases. In taking an insider's view of society, researchers can better understand other people's worldview. Accordingly, I came to better understand this group of teachers and also my own teaching and learning. Nevertheless, my account of the "Japanese" teacher culture is in no way absolute but is inevitably partial. It is constructed through a juxtaposition of my own experience and theirs.

Had I been a Chinese researcher for instance, I probably would have gained a different understanding and description of "Japanese" teacher acculturation. What might be described as "uniquely Japanese" is often defined in terms of its difference from what one is accustomed to—in my case, the "Canadian" ways of doing things. This highly partial nature of this study must be taken into account. That perspective is central to the notion of "reflexivity".

Generally, the majority of cross-cultural comparative studies have been highly quantitative and based entirely on Western survey research. The strengths of large-scale surveys have traditionally been greater external reliability and validity. However, many of the finer points and considerable depth of analysis have been compromised, and voices may have been lost in the process. Other means must be sought in order to properly understand the complex nature of teaching and learning. In this regard, comparative ethnographic studies show great promise. "Anthropological studies of education in every country and setting can help bear witness to the rich diversity of modes of cultural transmission and the great variety of experiences that can be called educational" (Masemann, 1999, p. 130). Ethnographic case studies have the potential to go well beyond the typical surface treatments of survey research to uncover deeper meaning. In particular, "more space devoted to comparative, ethnographic work would go a long way toward changing the current dialog about comparisons with Japan and perhaps inhibit the recurrent use of stereotypes and reasoning based on stereotypes that has afflicted so much of the current debate" (LeTendre, 1999, p. 43).

Perhaps the best window into the thinking of educators is through their own narratives (see Clandinin & Connelly, 2000; Farrell, 1986). As Hayhoe (2000) indiated in her Comparative and International Education Society Presidential Address:

> My six months in Japan helped me to see, in ways that are hard to capture through the grid of Western social science, some of the strengths of Japanese cultural resources...Patterns of thought emerged that seemed to be deeply connected to the varied regional cultures...Indigenous Japanese forms of expression—visual images or metaphors, expressed in the language of ordinary people, rather than abstract concepts from social science literature—seemed to go to the heart of Japanese culture (p. 438).

Comparative educators should not be too eager to embrace the multiple perspectives of postmodernism without giving further thought to meta-narratives of practitioners from different cultures. There are culturally specific, different ways of perceiving, knowing, understanding and interpreting events (see Masemann, 1999). Hayhoe (2000) characterized two such meta-narratives as "humanizing modernity" in the case of China and "harmonizing modernity" in the case of Japan in contrast to her Western notion of redeeming modernity.

CONCLUSIONS

The research reported here evolved from personal and professional cross-cultural learning and teaching experiences in Canada and Japan. Drawing mainly from reflexive ethnography and narrative inquiry, I have used a comparative ethnographic narrative method to investigate the nature of teacher acculturation. The research methodology parallels the serendipitous and personal nature of teacher induction. My educational journey as a learner, teacher and researcher is linked to these teachers' stories based on lived experiences. We are connected through the common thread of learning to teach. The narratives of these teachers are thus forever linked to my own personal narrative, through my research and connections to the teachers. In this study, my deeply held beliefs and tacit personal knowledge of curriculum, teaching and learning have been brought to the surface and I have come to terms with my own theory of learning. This has helped me in turn to better understand teacher acculturation in Japan and elsewhere.

CEN could be an effective research tool for further cross-cultural studies. As the predominant unit of analysis in comparative education continues to be nation-states, the problems inherent in various methodologies will continue to plague comparative and international education research (Wilson, 1994). Until these limitations are confronted, researchers will be unable to adequately understand the intricacies of education and culture. Theoretical frameworks should make sense to practitioners and should be easily understood within different socio-cultural contexts. These issues were of great importance to the late Professor David N. Wilson, to whom I dedicate this chapter.

NOTES

[1] Narrative is a kind of life story comprised of many short stories. Narrative inquiry is a qualitative method used for unearthing teachers' personal practical knowledge. It involves making meaning of experience through stories that both refigure the past and create purpose for the future.

[2] As Bestor, Steinoff and Bestor (2003) point out, this ethnographic technique might be better labeled "inquisitive observation" since the "participation" by any foreign researcher in Japan is rather limited in this context.

[3] I remain truly indebted to my spouse, Fumie Emmy Howe, who should be credited as co-researcher. As she is a Japanese native speaker and a former secondary school teacher in Canada, her participation in each conversation was indispensable. I believe that her presence with our baby proved a natural icebreaker to connect with many teachers, especially elementary teachers, many of whom are young women.

[4] Pseudonyms are used for people and place names to protect privacy and anonymity of individuals.

[5] *Juku* are cram schools offering extra help in preparing students for examinations.

[6] *Sempai/kohai* (senior/junior) relationships are a major part of Japanese schooling and Japanese society in general.

REFERENCES

Beattie, J. (1964). *Other cultures*. London: Cohen & West.

Bestor, T., Steinhoff, P. G., & Bestor, V. L. (Eds.). (2003). *Doing fieldwork in Japan*. Honolulu, HI: University of Hawai'i Press.

Brewer, J. D. (2000). *Ethnography*. Philadelphia: Open University Press.

Clandinin, D. J., & Connelly, F. M. (2000). *Narrative inquiry: Experience and story in qualitative research*. San Francisco: Jossey-Bass.

Farrell, J. P. (1986). *The National Unified School in Allende's Chile. The role of education in the destruction of a revolution*. Vancouver: University of British Columbia Press.

Fetterman, D. M. (1989). *Ethnography: Step by step* (Vol. 17). Newbury Park, CA: Sage.

Hayhoe, R. (2000). Redeeming modernity. *Comparative Education Review, 44*(2), 423–488.

Hendry, J. (1999). *An anthropologist in Japan: Glimpses of life in the field.* New York: Routledge.

Howe, E. R. (2008). Teacher induction across the Pacific: A comparative study of Canada and Japan. *Journal of Education for Teaching: International Research and Pedagogy, 34*(4), 333–346.

Howe, E. R. (2006). Effective teacher induction: An international review. *Educational Philosophy and Theory, 38*(3), 287–297.

Howe, E. R. (2005a). *Japan's teacher acculturation: A comparative ethnographic narrative of teacher induction.* Unpublished doctoral dissertation, University of Toronto.

Howe, E. R. (2005b). Japan's teacher acculturation: Critical analysis through comparative ethnographic narrative. *Journal of Education for Teaching, 31*(2), 121–131.

LeTendre, G. K. (1999). The problem of Japan: Qualitative studies and international educational comparisons. *Educational Researcher, 28*(2), 38–46.

Masemann, V. L. (1999). Culture and education. In R. F. Arnove & C. A. Torres (Eds.), *Comparative education: The dialectic of the global and the local* (pp. 115–134). Oxford, UK: Rowman & Littlefield Publishers.

Rohlen, T. P. (1983). *Japan's high schools.* Berkeley, CA: University of California Press.

Singleton, J. (1967). *Nichu: A Japanese school.* New York: Holt, Rinehart and Winston.

Stewart, A. (1998). *The ethnographer's method* (Vol. 46). Thousand Oaks, CA: Sage.

Willis, D. B. (2001). Pacific Creoles: The power of hybridity in Japanese-American relations, in the age of creolization in the Pacific: In search of emerging cultures and shared values in the Japan-America borderlands. In T. Matsuda (Ed.), *The age of creolization in the Pacific: In search of emerging cultures and shared values in the Japan-America borderlands.* Hiroshima, Japan: Keisuisha.

Wilson, D. N. (1994). Comparative and international education: Fraternal or Siamese twins? A preliminary genealogy of our twin fields. *Comparative Education Review, 38*(4), 449–486.

Wolcott, H. F. (1999). *Ethnography: A way of seeing.* Walnut Creek, CA: AltaMira Press.

Yonemura, M. (1982). Teacher conversations: A potential source for their own professional growth. *Curriculum Inquiry, 12*(3), 239–256.

Edward R. Howe
Faculty of Education
Utsunomiya University

KELLY CROWLEY-THOROGOOD

8. NATIONAL INCORPORATION VS. NATIONAL ISOLATION

An Historical Comparison of Indigenous Education Policies in Mexico and Canada

INTRODUCTION

This paper presents an historical comparative analysis of state education policies toward indigenous people in Mexico and Canada at the turn of the twentieth century. In state societies such as these, formal education plays an important role in the process of national integration or isolation and state formation. This paper was greatly influenced by the work of David Wilson, particularly his strong commitment to education of indigenous people in Latin America and Canada. His work has provided invaluable insights into this topic.

Several theoretical approaches are used in this paper, in particular the concept of hegemony as introduced by Gramsci (1971) in *The Prison Notebooks*. The term *indigenismo* is also referred to, as it relates to the legacy of the historic school systems in Mexico and Canada. State formation and cultural revolution are also important theoretical discourses in the context of indigenous education. According to Corrigan and Sayer (1985), state formation involves a cultural revolution: for a state to fully integrate its citizens; the activities and institutions of the "State" must stimulate cultural change which allows for the acceptance of state dominance. Education is one of the principal means of effecting cultural change. In state societies, education becomes formalized in official institutions in which,

> certain forms of activity are given the official seal of approval; others are situated beyond the pale. This has cumulative, and enormous cultural consequences; consequences for how people identify (in many cases, have to identify) themselves and their place in the world. (Corrigan & Sayer, 1985, p. 4)

INDIGENOUS PEOPLE OF MEXICO AND THEIR RELATIONSHIP TO NATIONAL EDUCATION POLICIES

During four major time periods—the colonial period, the nineteenth century, the revolutionary decade (1910–1917), and the post-revolutionary era—indigenous peoples' active participation in external and internal conflicts and resistance to imposed state policy forced various Mexican regimes to acknowledge and support Indian demands for social change. Rather than being a passive group subject to the whims

V. Masemann et al., (Eds.), A Tribute to David N. Wilson: Clamouring for a Better World, 115–128.

of elite interests, the indigenous people of Mexico took an active political role and were participants in the development of the Mexican state. As a result, the "Indian" became integrated into Mexican state policy and ideology, although only at the lowest levels. However, they were invited into state negotiations and policy making because of their potentiality to create disruptive social uprisings.

As a whole, indigenous people in Mexico were a large demographic group whose subversive activities were not easily ignored by the governments. Rather than isolation, the regimes in Mexico chose a policy of integration to deal with the indigenous populations. One of the key methods of integration was education, something that Indians had been demanding for some time. This was a demand the governments, particularly the post-revolutionary regimes, were willing to meet.

Education: The Means for a Cultural Revolution

Cultural revolution is a hegemonic process. Hegemony, according to Gramsci (1971), is a balance between force and consent:

> The 'normal' exercise of hegemony on the now classical terrain of the parliamentary regime is characterized by the combination of force and consent, which balance each other reciprocally, without force predominating excessively over consent. Indeed, the attempt is always made to ensure that force will appear to be based on the consent of the majority. (p. 80–81)

The early revolutionary governments of Madero, Huerta and Carranza never achieved hegemony because they were unable to secure the consent of the majority. Therefore their regimes were characterized by a continual use of force to maintain power. However, later governments, starting with Obregón's in 1921, initiated reforms that were more in line with the desires of the people. They were better able to reduce their use of force as their policies earned the consent of more Mexican groups. For example, Obregón increased the distribution of land to rural ejidos; by the end of his term three hundred million acres had been distributed to communal ejidos. He was also able to negotiate with the indigenous communities to allow more than three hundred million acres to remain in private hands, specifically with the hacendados (Suchlicki, 2001). In this way, "Obregón's policies introduced the foundation for a growing alliance between rural groups and the government" (Suchlicki, 2001, p. 121). The reforms gave rural people an investment in the state. They were integrated into state policy and became active participants in state formation. Obregón's government was also the first post-revolution government to tackle the problem of education in Mexico. In the education arena, the consent that was gradually being built could be solidified.

According to Gramsci (1971), once a group gained dominance within the state, hegemony became a more powerful tool than force. He also asserted that "political hegemony" could and should be procured by the dominant class, even before the attainment of government power (Gramsci, 1971).

Again, through his policies Obregón allowed for greater input from rural and industrial workers. For example, Obregón openly encouraged industrial workers to form unions. He granted favour to one union, CROM, which eventually gained control over the whole labour movement in Mexico (Suchlicki, 2001). Although he encouraged labour unions, Obregón was also careful to maintain control over those unions. For peasants, Indians and industrial workers, Obregón's reforms allowed them to have direct dialogue with the government in Mexico City. At the same time, they could participate in that dialogue only as far as Obregón and his ministers saw fit. They were in no way allowed to hold senior government positions and thus were not a threat to Obregón's hold on power. The state stayed firmly in the control of Obregón's elite party.

Florencia Mallon (1995) builds on Gramsci's original concept in her works on Mexico and Peru. Hegemony can be seen as a continuous process, always changing and adapting to current social realities. This was particularly true in a place like Mexico, where the many changes in politics and economics contribute "to the emergence of a common social and moral project that includes popular as well as elite notions of political culture" (Mallon, 1995, p. 6). Through the use of this concept, it is possible to see how the project of the cultural transformation of Mexican Indians into Mexican citizens was a hegemonic process. The policies of land reform and the introduction of a new education system served to reduce the state's reliance on force through the generation of consent among the lower classes.

Land reform and education were very important parts of the government's hegemonic project. An ideological component of these reforms was *indigenismo*, which became one of the bases of the national education system. Schools played an essential role in disseminating the state's notion of appropriate citizenship, particularly in rural schools and through indigenous education. Local teachers played a central role as state agents. They became the face of the state in many indigenous communities, and their actions were critical in determining the local success of state policy. Discussing teachers, Derek Sayer (1994) argues that the state exists only through the performance of its actors. Sayer (1994) states that, "individuals live the lie that is 'the state', and it lives through their performances. Their beliefs are neither here nor there. What is demanded of them is only - but precisely - performances" (p. 374). It does not matter what teachers believe in, as long as they are willing to play the role given to them by the state agencies. This willingness comes from the exercise of power and authority (Sayer, 1994). If people refuse to play their assigned role, the state itself (the power structure of domination) cannot exist. People resist by changing the way they perform their part.

Schools of the Mexican Revolution (1910–1917)

The post-revolutionary governments in Mexico during the 1920s saw political and economic stability as a key to turning around the fortunes of many Mexicans after close to a hundred years of instability. They saw a positive notion of citizenship as a way to unite the diverse groups of the country. Several presidents, starting with Alvaro Obregón and his Minister of Education José Vasconcelos, would use a national education programme to promote their views of proper citizenship (Vaughan, 1982). *Indigenismo* was one of the currents underlying any type of educational reform. There were also many splintered groups with differing agendas. Obregón's ministers saw a new nationwide education system as a tool for their hegemonic project of creating Mexican citizens. The education system would be so effective because it could reach out to all these groups in the name of progress rather than politics.

President Diaz's (1876–1910) educational policies had continued to isolate indigenous groups from the state. By failing to include indigenous groups in educational opportunities, the pre-revolutionary regimes had always been unable to have them be active participants in the construction of the Mexican nation (de la Peña, 2002). Any schools that had existed were locally created and managed; in fact, the schools would often be staffed by private teachers hired by villagers or hacienda owners (Rockwell, 1994). Prior to the revolution, indigenous people often sought out educational opportunities with suitable teachers for their children. If the teachers failed to meet community expectations, community members would pull their children from school or burn down the school in their village in protest. Because of limited state resources in many rural areas, government officials had no choice but to submit to indigenous demands. Without the support of the local community, the life of an appointed teacher would have been exceedingly difficult (Vaughan, 1997). This was potentially dangerous for the state, but an advantage for the local communities. As a result, there was no nationalist agenda being promoted, only local concerns.

Throughout the decade of the revolution, the popular movement put considerable support behind calls for educational reforms. However, the liberal elites were slow in determining how they could best use the education system to advance their own interests. In addition there was still a great deal of political instability throughout the 1910s. As a result, educational reform did not occur until 1921, while President Alvaro Obregón was still dealing with a splintered nation (Vaughan, 1982). He needed an instrument through which he could consolidate his power over the many regions of Mexico. To do this, his government, directed by Education Minister Vasconcelos, would have to carry out a cultural revolution. This process started in 1921 with a new national education programme (Vaughan, 1997). The new schools would promote a nationalist programme influenced by indigenismo, and play a major role in shaping Mexican nationalism over the next few decades.

The education system of the revolution really started to develop under the guidance of Obregón and his ministers. In 1921 the first Secretariat of Public Education (SEP) was created (Morales-Gómez & Torres, 1990). The Secretariat would be responsible for implementing the fundamental principles that were laid out in the third article of the 1917 Constitution: education would be free; education would be secular in nature; and new schools could only be created with the approval of the State and under direct official supervision (Morales-Gómez & Torres, 1990).

Schooling was organized under a centralized federal system that was expected to control the resources, the administration, and the curriculum. This new system permitted only limited freedom to municipal and state governments in the implementation of their local systems of education. However, it provided the State with a strong mechanism of control over the delivery, the content and the management of education. (Morales-Gómez & Torres, 1990, p. 63)

Obregón's Secretary of Education, José Vasconcelos, ordered a survey of national schools in 1921. He found the state of education to be very disturbing. The survey showed that 40.3 per cent of children aged 4–14 could not read or write. For those who were deemed to be literate, over 72 per cent of them went to private, not public, schools (Morales-Gómez & Torres, 1990). Vaughan (1982) states the reason why private schools continued after the Revolution: "The growth in the private school system can be explained in terms of its importance to the middle and upper sectors of society and the impetus provided to private schools by the Church-state struggle" (p. 152).

Seeing the problem of illiteracy, Vasconcelos decided to immediately embark on a literacy campaign and to establish a series of public libraries (Morales-Gómez & Torres, 1990). Between 1922 and 1923, 285 new libraries were established throughout Mexico (Schoenhals, 1964). However, demographics and geography were not on Vasconcelos' side. Over 71 per cent of the population lived dispersed in rural areas, and the location of the libraries became an issue (Morales-Gómez & Torres, 1990). Despite the challenges involved, Vasconcelos forged ahead with his literacy and education plan in general. Federal funds for education became readily available. By 1922, education funding reached 8.9 per cent of Mexico's budget (Vaughan, 1982). This percentage remained constant throughout the 1920s. Given the greater amount of resources allocated, government officials were sent into rural areas to consult with villagers about the type of school that would be acceptability to their communities (Morales-Gómez & Torres, 1990).

This was the first time that the government had sought local input before establishing the schools. Throughout the post-revolutionary period, federal officials and teachers provided concessions to local communities. Between 1921 and 1940, the SEP oversaw 12,561 primary schools with an enrolment of 720,647 students. The SEP took over state and municipal schools and established new schools in remote areas where there had previously been none. By 1940, the SEP had success-fully enrolled 70 per cent of Mexican children between the ages of 6 and 10, a great increase from the 30 per cent enrolled in 1910 (Vaughan, 1997). Early curriculum focused on "integrating rural communities into the market economy by introducing new skills and behaviours, product diversification, and cooperatives" (Vaughan, 1997, p. 29). The massive expansion of rural indigenous schooling is evident as the number of schools in rural, indigenous communities grew from 1,023 in 1923 to 6,132 schools by 1930 with an increase in students from 50,000 to 324,798 (Schoenhals, 1964).

By the end of the 1920s, the SEP's focus seemed to shift more into the articulation of a national popular culture. This culture emphasised citizenship rather than religion and was promoted in the textbooks permitted by the SEP. The textbooks moved from highlighting solely middle-class urban families to discussing rural issues. They also promoted the concept of Mexican citizenship as inclusive and group-oriented (Vaughan, 1997). For example, a 1920s textbook, entitled "Adelante", focused on a modest urban middle class, where women were restricted to the home, children were always obedient and there was never any social conflict. Unions were discouraged and social mobility was only possible through conformity. In contrast, a late 1930s textbook, entitled "Fermín", focused on a peasant child and his family and their struggles against class hierarchy and poverty. The textbook showed conflict and talked about the benefits of communal life (Vaughan, 1997). Throughout the 1930s and 1940s the Mexico promoted by the SEP was inclusive and proud of the artistic achievements of the past and its rural heritage. These were the notions of citizenship promoted by the government.

Schools had existed in Mexico before the revolution. So what was it that made the new schools a successful part of the post-revolutionary process? Earlier schools had been isolated local entities. Oftentimes in indigenous communities the schools were merely a formality to comply with the public obligation to educate children (Rockwell, 1994). Post-revolutionary governments realized that schools were effective ways to pass on ideology and to monitor a disparate population. The indigenous population was spread all across Mexico, up in the hills and far from Mexico City. Because of the high degree of illiteracy and a greatly varied language base in indigenous communities, simple surveys of the population were not possible. Thus, the government needed to find a way to track the Indian populations that were spread around the countryside.

State schools were used by the governments in their attempt to simplify complex social realities. This demographic knowledge was important because the Indians had proven their ability and willingness to fight, and the government wanted to keep track of the Indian populations and locations. The establishment of schools in rural areas gave the state eyes in terms of the placement of state employees (teachers). Also, by instructing local school directors to go out and find students in rural communities, the governments gained insight into the community structure, learning where there might be stronger resistance. Education was an especially useful tool in garnering local information since almost everyone was involved in community activities, particularly parents and community elders (Dawson, 2001).

The Mexican Revolution, which started as an armed uprising in 1910, turned into a cultural revolution within a decade. This cultural revolution was generated through a state-driven hegemonic project to create a single, unified Mexican culture, or at least a politically and economically stable one. To do this, the state had to create the notion of an ideal citizen to act as the symbol of the future of the nation. This image would be an amalgamation of the various groups within Mexico since the majority of the population was either Indian or Mestizo. The regimes of the 1920s would attempt to integrate the indigenous groups of rural Mexico. Previous regimes had failed to realize the potential of the indigenous groups to mobilize and bring about social change. To prevent any future indigenous uprisings, the governments realized they had to find a way to integrate the indigenous groups into the nationalist ideology. In order to do this, the government utilized the notions of the liberal indigenismo movement. Indigenismo became ingrained in institutions like the SEP and later the Instituto Nacional Indigenista (INI). This discourse became a language of contention, where the issues of power and domination could be played out, and was articulated within the new national education system. As a result, the teachers and schools of the revolution became essential parts of the state hegemonic project to create Mexican citizens. This process would give previously isolated groups an investment in the state in terms of the advantages they could expect to receive as citizens of Mexico. These advantages, whether real or perceived, were articulated within the federal schools. It is through this process that the education system became an integral part in transforming the armed Mexican revolution into a cultural revolution.

The indigenous people of Mexico played an active role in the development of the education system in their communities and nationally. In Mexico, from 1867 to the mid-1930s, there was a concerted effort by the state to wrest control of the education system from the church. There was an emphasis on a secular and free education system. However, the logistics and cost of a nation-wide education system forced the state to seek out partnerships within local communities to maintain a viable learning system that was not dependent on church sponsorship. Thus, local indigenous groups were better able to maintain a level of control over the education that was provided to their members. This was made possible by the ideals concerning indigenous identity within the Mexican state. Since Indian was principally a socio-economic or class-based identity, rather than a biologically-based one, Indians were deemed to be capable of learning with proper guidance. This was reflected in the local-state relationship that developed within the education system. As shall be seen in the following section, a differing sense of Indian identity and other varied social processes led to a very different situation for indigenous education in Canada.

STATE EDUCATION FOR INDIGENOUS PEOPLE IN CANADA: CONVERSION TO ISOLATION

This section will contrast the development of the education system in relation to indigenous people in Canada with that in Mexico. These differences once again relate to perceptions and ideals surrounding the definition of whom and what was an "Indian" in both places. Also, the development of the education policies cannot be seen apart from the larger historical processes occurring in both places.

The Residential School System: 1867–1986

When Canada became a nation in 1867, the government was faced with many key decisions, including how to address the "Indian Question". The Constitution Act of 1867 left the constitutional responsibility for Indians and their lands squarely in the hands of the federal government (Royal Commission on Aboriginal Peoples [RCAP], 1996, p. 333). The governments of the late nineteenth century chose a policy of assimilation to deal with their Indian "responsibilities" (RCAP, 1996). This policy did not just emerge but rather was rooted in the colonial experience of relationships between whites and indigenous peoples. Education would be a key element of the assimilationist policy of Canada.

In 1879, the Prime Minister, Sir John A. MacDonald, commissioned Nicholas Flood Davin to study the American Industrial Schools for Indians and report back to the House of Commons on the viability of implementing such schools on Canadian reserves, which were tracts of Crown land set aside for use by indigenous communities (RCAP, 1996). The industrial schools in the United States were set up with the idea that, "Indian children were best prepared for assimilation into the dominant society if they were removed from the influences of home, family and community" (Barman, Hébert & McCaskill, 1986, p. 6). While conducting his research, Davin met with the American Commissioner of Indian Affairs and toured several of the industrial schools (RCAP, 1996). He was very keen on the system's ability to "decrease the influence of the wigwam", and his report fully endorsed the establishment of similar schools in Canada (Barman, Hébert & McCaskill, 1986). Davin (1879) reported back that:

> It was found that the day-school did not work, because the influence of the wigwam was stronger than the influence of the school…The experience of the United States is the same as our own as far as the adult Indian is concerned. Little can be done with him. He can be taught to do a little at farming, and at stock-raising, and to dress in a more civilized manner, but that is all. The child, again, who goes to a day school learns little, and what little he learns is soon forgotten, while his tastes are fashioned at home, and his inherited aversion to toil is no way combated. (p. 1–2)

Therefore, he recommended that children must be separated from their homes and families as these were understood to be the sources of the "Indian malaise".

Davin's (1879) report contained 12 principal objectives for the new industrial school system of Canada. First, the schools were to be built outside of the reserves. They had to be far enough away that families and other community members could not easily make contact with the students. This idea was partly based on the experience of earlier missionaries who had been critical of the influence parents could exert over the learning of their children. Second, the curriculum would include arts, crafts and industrial skills needed in a modern economy (RCAP, 1996). There would be no study of indigenous culture, and all instruction would be in the English language. Davin's report also left the running of the schools in the hands of the churches, since they had already demonstrated a passion for "civilizing" the Indians (Barman, Hébert & McCaskill, 1986). He listed the following as appropriate organizations for running a school: "The Friends, the Orthodox Friends, the Methodists, the Roman Catholics, the Baptists, the Presbyterians, the United Presbyterians, the Congregationalists, the Protestant Episcopalians, the Reformed Episcopalians, the Unitarians, the Christian Union, and the Evangelical Lutherans" (Davin, 1879, p. 3). A contract would be signed between the government and the religious organization for the running of the schools. The government would pay the school $125 a year for each student boarder, up to a maximum of 30 students. Any school with more than 30 students would receive $100 per student. The overall cost of the structure was to be no more than $1000, and preferably around $800 (Davin, 1879).

When submitted to the government in 1879, the Davin Report was accepted wholeheartedly by state and church officials. The Department of the Interior started doling out funding to various religious denominations for the construction of new industrial residential schools. It also provided funds to upgrade and maintain existing schools (Barman, Hébert & McCaskill, 1986). The residential schools would be administered by a partnership of church and state, for the Canadian government was becoming acutely aware of the economics involved with taking care of the Indian problem. In fact, Sir John A. MacDonald's Deputy Superintendent General of Indian Affairs, L. Vankoughnet, espoused the economic benefit of the residential school system in 1879 when he assured MacDonald that the schools were a good investment because education would allow Indians to contribute to the revenue of the country, rather than just taking from it (RCAP, 1996). Davin (1879) had also promised that each new school would cost less than $1000 and only 400 schools would be required.

So under the new system the church and the government would have equal financial responsibility for the running of the schools, but each would have clear roles in the education of indigenous children. According to Kirkness (1992), "the church's duty was to manage the school, contribute part of the operating cost, and, most important, to provide Christian guidance to the children. The government was responsible for inspection, special rules and regulations, as well as for financial grants" (p. 10).

Many churches had already established day schools on the reserves, so they would be able to build on this experience. Day schools were usually built on reserves by the local church group and were located on the outskirts of the reserves. In these schools students were to receive "a useful education (manual and industrial skills, basic literacy and teaching in hygiene, manners and Christian morality)" (Coates, 1992, p. 134). Because they were on reserves and out of the public eye, many day schools fell into disrepair (Coates, 1992). Day schools were an important part of the education system, and the churches and communities were often hesitant to replace them with distant industrial schools. As a result, day schools continued to operate in many areas. Day schools were much cheaper to run than the residential/ industrial schools and thus were favoured by the government especially by the turn of the twentieth century when the high cost of national administration was becoming abundantly clear to the Canadian federal and provincial governments. Barman, Hébert and McCaskill (1986) report that by 1900, there were 61 industrial/residential schools operating in Canada.

For their part, indigenous communities were eager for an increase in educational opportunities for their children. Many saw education as essential for survival in the white world (Archibald, 1993). However, indigenous communities were not prepared for the direct cultural assault proposed by the Canadian government's new education system. During the residential and industrial school era, indigenous children were openly, and often brutally, punished for speaking their native languages and practicing traditional activities (Archibald, 1993). As Archibald (1993) states,

the children's lives were rigidly timetabled and filled with religious instruction, basic academic subjects and homework, and industrial trades and school maintenance work. They lived in a strict formal institutionalized manner for ten or more months of every year from the ages of 7 to 16: a lifestyle antithetical to that of their cultural community. (p. 99)

Many parents were also critical of the physical treatment their children were receiving. There was an extremely high mortality rate among children at the residential schools. Kirkness (1992) reports that at the turn of the twentieth century, 50 per cent of all indigenous children sent to the schools died prematurely. A major blight in the schools was tuberculosis, which flourished in their crowded, dirty and malnourished environments. Tuberculosis became so bad in some schools that on average 24 per cent of the students in 15 prairie schools succumbed to the disease (Fournier & Crey, 1997). Once community members and parents became aware of abuses, they reacted quickly. As early as 1900, community leaders petitioned the government to have their children removed from the residential schools. They wanted day schools established on their reserves so that their children could attend school during the day and be with their families and communities at night (Archibald, 1993). The closer proximity to school would allow parents to better monitor their children's educational experiences. Some communities were fortunate enough to have day schools set up on their reserves; however most requests fell on deaf ears. Local efforts were hampered by a bureaucracy that was not eager to see successful Indians, just segregated Indians. The lack of a healthy environment in indigenous schools would remain an issue throughout the residential period and present day (Wilson, 1991).

The federal government was unable to fully understand the needs of indigenous communities and had a general lack of interest in doing so. What developed was a relationship filled with misunderstandings and frustrations. All of this would come to a head as of 1910 and would lead to a new direction in the education system.

By the turn of the century, only half of the eligible indigenous children were attending school. Those attending school were not abandoning their cultures the way government officials had hoped with their initial policy of assimilation (Barman, Hébert & McCaskill, 1986). One former residential school student reported that the Indian students were "using the best that the white man had to teach and were endeavouring to work out their own plans and their own self determination" (Barman, Hébert & McCaskill, 1986, p. 7).

Officials were further disturbed by the fact that some students were trying to enter the paid labour market with their new skills. This was particularly a concern when the overall economy of the country was suffering. Politically, politicians would not promote the education of Indians when people in their districts were already struggling to find employment. One Indian Affairs official summed up the situation by saying, "we are educating these Indians to compete industrially with our own people, which seems to me a very undesirable use of public money" (Barman, Hébert & McCaskill, 1986, p. 8). This sentiment grew among many government officials.

The proportion of funding for indigenous education was a source of contention. By 1911 only 1.5 per cent of the Canadian population was Indian and since most lived on reserves, an "out-of-sight, out-of-mind" syndrome developed. What frugal resources had been expended were scaled back and a policy of assimilation was transformed into a policy of isolation and segregation. No longer would students receive an education to prepare them for life in the wider Canadian society. Instead, education would be used to prepare them for life on the reserve (Barman, Hébert &

McCaskill, 1986). This change in policy was reflected in a 1910 revision to the Indian Act, with the goal "to fit the Indian for civilized life in his own environment" (Wilson, 1986, p. 83). This environment was to be the reserve. The new policy ensured that Indian education would be minimal at best (Wilson, 1986). A system already considered by some as negligible was about to lose more of its funding.

The resistance and dissatisfaction of many indigenous communities continued unabated until 1951 when the Indian Act was revised. A new provision in the Act allowed the "federal government to make financial agreements with provincial and other authorities for Indian children to attend public and private schools educating non-Indians" (Barman, Hébert & McCaskill, 1986, p. 13). The result was that by 1960, a quarter of Indian students were in provincially-controlled institutions and the proportion of Indian students beyond grade 6 doubled between 1960 and 1969 to almost 20 per cent (Barman, Hébert & McCaskill, 1986). However when compared to the wider society, this number appears woefully inadequate.

CONCLUSION: SIMILARITIES AND DIFFERENCES

Indigenous education systems in Canada and Mexico were reflective of the social reality facing indigenous peoples within each nation. In this comparison of the schools established by and for indigenous people, larger social processes can be observed.

As mentioned, hegemony exists when a government establishes and maintains its authority by balancing the use of force and the generation of consent. In both Mexico and Canada at the turn of the twentieth century, the governments were seeking ways to maintain authority and social balance. Each country set about trying to encourage consensus without being dependent on the use of force. Each state's level of success varied across both time and space. In general, the hegemonic projects of the post-revolutionary Mexican governments were more successful than those of their Canadian counterparts. The Mexican policies, which often took local concerns into account, did more to build up indigenous consent than did Canada policies, which were developed and applied in a top-down manner.

Education policies also reflected the social reality that being Indian in Mexico was very different from being Indian in Canada. In Mexico, Indian-ness became symbolic of a class position, while in Canada, Indian was very much a racial label. The reasons for this distinction are many: varying demographics, geography, economics and the historical experiences of colonialism. All of these factors were combined within the educational experiences of the indigenous people in Canada and Mexico. Adams (2005) states that,

> at the turn of the twentieth century, *race* referred to populations that shared common cultural and biological origins and that were usually allocated within a hierarchical ordering of the larger society. It was widely but not universally held that behaviour was in some manner hinged to biological inheritance. (p. 132)

This definition seemed to hold true in both Mexico and Canada in the late years of the nineteenth century and the early twentieth century. In both nations, indigenous people were considered lowest within the hierarchical order of society, with their low status based on biological and cultural rationales. In Mexico, during the Diaz dictatorship and the early revolutionary regimes, Indians were seen as a hindrance to progress because of their group-oriented mentality and the belief they had a biological tendency toward "laziness". In Canada, during the early years of nation-hood, Indians were also seen as obstacles to progress due to their continued reliance on subsistence hunting and claims on potentially productive lands.

However, it was in the early years of the twentieth century that the treatment and perception of indigenous people in both areas diverged. It was after the revolution in Mexico and after the isolationist shift in Canadian federal policy that being Indian came to mean something very different in both places. As has been outlined earlier, indigenous groups in Mexico historically comprised a large portion of the population; thus, their physical isolation was impossible both for the colonial and post-colonial regimes. As a result, there were many connections made between indigenous villages and the Spanish society. This led to the emergence of a "mixed blood" group who came to be known as Mestizos. In contrast, in Canada the indigenous population was much smaller and the physical isolation of Indians became possible because of the vast amount of available land in what would become Canada. In the early twentieth century, most indigenous people lived on reserves and had very little contact with people outside of their own community. Therefore, the pockets of mixed blood groups such as the Métis that emerged in Canada, were very small percentages of the population compared to the percentages of Mexico's Mestizos.

In Canada, government officials knew they could isolate the remaining indigenous people, and this idea was manifested in the establishment of residential and industrial schools. Indian children were forced by state policy to go to these schools. This led to a process of "alienation and de-culturation" (Wilson, 1972). In contrast, the Mexican governments had little opportunity to establish isolated schools intended only for indigenous children. Not only was space an issue, but the actual identification of "Indians" was also very difficult, due to the prevalence of Mestizos throughout the country.

It is this fact that lay at the heart of the distinction between Indian identity in Mexico and Canada. In Mexico, the biological distinction between Indian and White was not clear. As Adams states, "The emergence of Mestizos and the importation of black slaves injected confusing elements that were neither indigenous nor European" (Adams, 2005, p. 135). Being Indian could not simply be about biology, it also had to have a social meaning. That social element was class. Indian came to be symbolic of a rural worker who was integrated into the social order at its lowest level with little, if any, political and economic power. Thus, more than skin colour, it was clothing, occupation, consumption and lifestyle that came to symbolize Indian-ness in Mexico. This was particularly the case during the Cárdenas era (1934–1940) when "campesino" (peasant) and "Indian" became synonymous. These ideals came to be reflected in the education system, from the textbooks used to the promotion of indigenismo. The mantra seemed to hold that with education indigenous people could become modern, productive members of Mexican society.

In contrast, "Indian" in Canada remained a biologically-based label. The continued isolation of indigenous groups was achieved through social policy aimed at maintaining two separate gene pools. State policy reflected the idea that there was little to be done to help the indigenous people of Canada, since they were biologically inferior. Researcher Malik stated that, "the discourse of race helped recast social differences as natural ones, externalizing what were historically contingent features" (cited in Adams, 2005, p. 134). These ideas were very clear in government reports of the late nineteenth century, including the Davin Report which became the basis upon which the education system for indigenous people was built, and continued on through the twentieth century with the various Indian Acts. The education system in Canada was not meant to help indigenous people become active members of Canadian society. It was meant to teach them basic skills to adjust to life on the reserves and create as few disturbances as possible within the expanding nation. Adams sums it up with the following quote, "Inferior peoples had to be dealt with as such, and education was of limited use because inferior people could not be changed" (Adams, 2005, p. 137). This was very much the principle behind the establishment of the Canadian education system in relation to indigenous people. "Indian" was used as a racist term to justify isolating some of the poorest people in the nation.

Perhaps more than any other institution, the education system reflects the underlying ideals of a government. The historic development of education in Mexico and Canada demonstrates the varying regimes' approaches to the indigenous peoples of the nations. It is through an examination of the history of education policy that one can truly appreciate how governments sought to isolate (Canada) or integrate (Mexico) conquered groups within their midst.

REFERENCES

Adams, R. N. (2005). The evolution of racism in Guatemala: Hegemony, science and anti-hegemony. In R. Darnell & F. W. Gleach (Eds.), *Histories of anthropology annual* (Vol. 1, pp. 132–180). Lincoln: University of Nebraska Press.

Archibald, J. A. (1993). Resistance to an unremitting process: Racism, curriculum and education in Western Canada. In J. A. Mangan (Ed.), *The imperial curriculum: Racial images and education in the British colonial experience* (pp. 93–107). London: Routledge.

Barman, J., Hébert, Y., & McCaskill, D. (1986). The legacy of the past: An overview. In J. Barman, Y. Hébert, & D. McCaskill (Eds.), *Indian education in Canada Vol. 1: The legacy* (pp. 1–22). Vancouver: University of British Columbia Press.

Coates, K. (1992). *Aboriginal land claims in Canada: A regional perspective*. Toronto: Copp Clark Pittman.

Corrigan, P., & Sayer, D. (1985). *The great arch: English state formation as cultural revolution*. Oxford: Blackwell.

Davin, N. (1879). *Report on industrial schools for Indians and half-breeds*. Ottawa.

Dawson, A. (2001). "Wild Indians," "Mexican Gentlemen," and the lessons learned in the Casa del Estudiante Indígena 1926–1932. *The Americas, 57*(3), 329–361.

de la Peña, G. (2002). Anthropological debates and the crisis of Mexican nationalism. In W. Lem & B. Leach (Eds.), *Culture, economy, power: Anthropology as critique, anthropology as praxis* (pp. 47–58). Albany, NY: State University of New York Press.

Fournier, S., & Crey, E. (1997). *Stolen from our embrace: The abduction of First Nations children and the restoration of aboriginal communities*. Vancouver: Douglas and McIntyre.

Gramsci, A. (1971). *Selections from the prison notebooks of Antonio Gramsci* (Q. Hoare & G. N. Smith, Eds. & Trans.). New York: International Publishers.

Kirkness, V. (1992). *First nations and schools: Triumphs and struggles.* Toronto: Canadian Education Association.

Mallon, F. (1995). *Peasant and nation.* Berkeley, CA: University of California Press.

Morales-Gómez, D. A., & Torres, C. A. (1990). *The state, corporatist politics, and educational policy making in Mexico.* New York: Praeger Publishers.

Rockwell, E. (1994). Schools of the revolution: Enacting and contesting state forms in Tlaxcala, 1910–1930. In G. M. Joseph & D. Nugent (Eds.), *Everyday forms of state formation: Revolution and the negotiation of rule in modern Mexico* (pp. 170–208). Durham, NC: Duke University Press.

Royal Commission on Aboriginal Peoples. (1996). *The report on the royal commission on aboriginal peoples.* Ottawa: Minister of Supply and Services Canada.

Sayer, D. (1994). Everyday forms of state formation: some dissident remarks on "Hegemony." In G. M. Joseph & D. Nugent (Eds.), *Everyday forms of state formation: Revolution and the negotiation of rule in modern Mexico* (pp. 367–377). Durham, NC: Duke University Press.

Schoenhals, L. (1964). Mexico experiments in rural and primary education: 1921–1930. *The Hispanic American Historical Review, 44*(1), 22–43.

Suchlicki, J. (2001). *Mexico: From Montezuma to the fall of the PRI.* Washington, DC: Brassey's.

Vaughan, M. K. (1982). *The state, education and social class in Mexico, 1880–1928.* DeKalb, IL: Northern Illinois University Press.

Vaughan, M. K. (1997). *Cultural politics in revolution.* Tucson, AZ: University of Arizona Press.

Wilson, D. N. (1972). *University of Canada North: Promise for an alternative university structure.* Unpublished paper prepared for The Comparative and International Education Society of Canada.

Wilson, D. N. (1991). *Creating educational environments supportive of health.* Ottawa: Health and Welfare Canada.

Wilson, J. D. (1986). "No blanket to be worn to school": The education of Indians in nineteenth-century Ontario. In J. Barman, Y. Hébert, & D. McCaskill (Eds.), *Indian education in Canada* (Vol. 1, pp. 64–87). Vancouver: University of British Columbia Press.

Kelly Crowley-Thorogood
Faculty of Education
The University of Western Ontario

YAACOV IRAM, NAVA MASLOVATY* AND ELI SHITREET

9. MANAGING DIVERSITY THROUGH INTERCULTURAL TEACHING AND LEARNING

Acculturation of Youth in Israel

Preface by Yaacov Iram

The project discussed in this chapter is very much in line with David's longtime worldwide interest in multiculturalism and acculturation of immigrants through education. David expressed particular interest in developments in Israel and especially in vocational education and the integration of immigrants and students of under privileged background into mainstream society. These were our shared research interests. While on a visit in Israel, David was invited to lecture and advise the Ministry of Education on issues of vocational education.

Recalling our meetings in different countries in different parts of the world, during conferences and invited events, I came to know of his outstanding personality both as a scholar and a friend. He encouraged me to establish the Israeli Comparative Education Society and its joining the CESE and the WCCES. The term that most fit David's personality is expressed in the Yiddish term: A MENTCH—someone to be proud of, a decent human being, an honourable person with integrity and concern for the individual and humanity, a real humanist.

*Since the submission of this chapter, Dr. Nava Maslovaty has passed away. This chapter is to honour her scholarship and memory.

INTRODUCTION

Multicultural societies face a major and complex problem: how to integrate groups from highly varied cultures into a civil society with well-defined behavioural norms, a common language, and a clear conception of political rights and obligations, without coercing these groups to give up their own sense of cultural identity (Iram, 2003; Bommes & Schiffauer, 2006).

This first section of the paper gives a brief overview of the worldwide phenomenon of multiculturalism and acculturation, particularly in the context of education. The case of Israel as a pluralistic society is then discussed. The next section presents the findings of some previous studies of the acculturation and adaptation processes of former Soviet Union (FSU) and Ethiopian immigrants in Israel. The authors then propose a study in which these processes could be examined in schools comprising immigrants and native-born (i.e. non-immigrant) students.

V. Masemann et al., (Eds.), A Tribute to David N. Wilson: Clamouring for a Better World, 129–142.

The scope of this study would explore simultaneously values, attitudes and social awareness of veteran and newcomer students as well as the school context with the aim of improving the acculturation processes among both groups.

OVERVIEW: MULTICULTURALISM AND ACCULTURATION

The faster pace and huge volume of immigration and global interaction is a well documented worldwide phenomenon (Adler & Gielen 2003). Migration and emigration have prompted a greater awareness of cultural diversity (Joppke & Morawska, 2003; Swain, 2007). While this awareness has given wider scope to the expression of such diversity, it has also permitted the representation of differences such as hierarchy, domination and conflict. Difference is often used as an excuse for intolerance, hatred and the exclusion of others. Yet the very same differences, in the framework of political equality, human rights and responsibility for others, can— and often do—offer the opportunity to explore new horizons and to enrich our lives (UNESCO, May 2001).

The former United Nation's Secretary-General, Kofi Annan stated that "One of the great challenges faced by multi-ethnic and multicultural societies is to reconcile democracy and human rights with respect to diversity" (Kofi Annan, UN September, 2006).

Likewise, the well-known Canadian philosopher and political scientist, Will Kymlicka claims that "We are currently witnessing the global diffusion of multiculturalism, both as a political discourse and as a set of international legal norms. States today are under increasing international scrutiny regarding their treatment of ethno-cultural groups, and are expected to meet evolving international standards regarding the rights of indigenous peoples, national minorities, and immigrants" (Kymlicka, 2007).

According to Berry (1997), the acculturation process involves a dynamic contact activity which occurs during and after continuous and first-hand interaction between cultures. Berry (1997) developed a fourfold model of acculturation strategies which immigrants can adopt in the process of their interaction with the host society: *assimilation, integration, separation,* and *marginalization* (see Figure 1). He argues that in plural societies, individuals and groups often confront two important issues during acculturation. The first issue pertains to the maintenance of one's ethnic or cultural distinctiveness (identity) in society. This involves deciding whether or not one's own cultural identity is of value, and whether it should be retained. The other involves the desirability of inter-ethnic contact. This means deciding whether positive relations with the larger society are of value, and therefore should be sought. For conceptual purposes, these decisions have been treated as dichotomous ("yes" and "no") decisions, thus generating a fourfold model: integration, assimilation, separation, and marginalization (Figure 1).

Acculturation is a bidirectional process with changes occurring within both host and immigrant groups. Bourhis, et al. (1997) claim that acculturation strategies of ethnic minority members are interrelated with the acculturation orientations of host-majority members, with the latter group having a stronger impact on the acculturation

Is it considered to be of value to maintain relationships with larger society?

		Yes	No
Is it considered to be of value to maintain one's identity and characteristics?	Yes	Integration	Separation
	No	Assimilation	Marginalization

Figure 1. Acculturation strategies.

Source: Berry, 1997

preferences of the newcomers. Concordance and discordance profiles yield different relational outcomes. Berry (1997; 1999; 2001) refers to acculturation as changes that take place in individuals or groups in response to social and cultural demands. He also distinguishes between psychological adaptation and social-cultural adaptation in the new society.

Indeed social-cultural acculturation occurs when two distinct groups interact continuously over an extended period of time. This results in changes in either or both groups. Berry (2001) uses the term "psychological acculturation" when referring to the adaptation of individuals.

ISRAEL: A PLURALISTIC SOCIETY

One of the most striking characteristics of the State of Israel is its being an immigrant society comprising immigrants from more than one hundred countries, cultures and languages. Israel has experienced rapid growth of its population since its establishment. Immigration accounted for more than 50 per cent of the increase in the Jewish population of Israel between 1948 and 1977, and more than 25 per cent from 1972 to 1982. Israel's ethnic composition, religious and cultural character, and its socioeconomic structure were affected profoundly by the various waves of immigration, both before and after the establishment of the state in 1948. Immigration and its integration (*klitat aliyah*) continue to play an important role in Israel's national agenda.

Thus in 2008 Israel's population was more than 7 million (Israel Central Bureau of Statistics, 2009) compared to 806,000 in May 1948, when the state of Israel was formally established. The growth rate of its population was 8 per cent annually in the first decade of independence, about 2 per cent in the 1980s, rising to more than 3 per cent in the 1990s with the waves of immigration from the former USSR. In the early 2000s Israel's population growth rate was 2.4 per cent which is high when compared to the growth rate of 0 (ZPG) in many European countries and 1 per cent in North America. About forty per cent of Israel's population growth since statehood stems from immigration.

Another related feature of Israel is the pluralistic composition of its society, evident in almost every aspect. In terms of nationality in 2000, there was a Jewish majority (about 81 per cent) and a non-Jewish, predominantly Arab, minority (about 19 per cent). The non-Jewish minority is religiously diverse: Moslem, Druze, and Christian. Hebrew and Arabic are both official state languages. As a result of national, religious, and linguistic pluralism, separate education systems emerged: Jewish, Arab, and Druze.

The Jewish majority is also diverse ethnically, religiously, culturally, and educationally. Ethnically—in the sense of country of origin—there is a division between "Orientals" "Easterners" or "Sephardim" (born in Asian, African, and Middle Eastern countries) and "Westerners" or "Ashkenazim" (born in America, Europe, and South Africa). Religiously, Israeli Jews are divided into those considered "religious", strict observers of Jewish practices and obligations, and those considered "non-religious", non-observers of religious commandments (Mitzvot) in daily life, although they may honour some Jewish customs.

Culturally, the different ethnic groups bring with them different customs, ceremonies, attitudes, values, and ways of life from their countries of origin. Educationally, the differences in religious observance have caused the development of three subsystems of Jewish education: State Education, State Religious Education, and Independent Education of Agudat Israel. The latter is an ultra-orthodox party that maintains its education system under the category of "non-official recognized schools" of the State Education Law of 1953 (Iram & Schmida, 1998).

There have been alternating periods of harmonious cooperation and tension, coexistence and conflict between "Orientals" and "Ashkenazim", as well as between religious and non-religious Jews, on issues of socio-economic equality and cultural identity.

The heterogeneity of the Jewish majority within Israeli society has raised a dilemma regarding the socio-cultural function of education. The question is, should education serve as a "melting pot", to assimilate immigrants into the dominant ruling groups, or rather as an instrument to encourage immigrants to integrate socially within the pluralistic society and to encourage cultural identity of the different groups? These two conflicting attitudes of mono-culturalism vs. multiculturalism have found expression in different strategies of immigrant absorption (Eisenstadt, 1985), as well as in educational policy (Iram 1992; Iram & Schmida, 1998).

The changing nature of immigration to Israel since 1948 has made it imperative to change cultural conceptions, strategies of absorption and to modify educational policies. The educational absorption of immigrants, by providing both quality and equality of educational opportunities for all, has been a major concern for politicians, educators, sociologists, political scientists and researchers. During different periods since 1948 there has been a special focus on specific "under-privileged" groups of immigrant children, such as Orientals in the 1950s and 1960s, immigrants from Asian republics of the U.S.S.R. (i.e., Georgians) in the 1970s, and Ethiopians in the 1980s and 1990s. The continuous flow of students from extremely diverse back-grounds posed a challenge to the integrity of the education system, stimulating ideological, conceptual, administrative, pedagogical and curricular changes, and sometimes even radical transformation. The "Ethiopian phase" of educational absorption has raised again the issue of the proper balance between the need to preserve unique lifestyles and religious practices, which are different from those of Oriental and Western Jews, in order not to hinder Ethiopian immigrants' adjustment to

Israeli society. This brought to light the need to find appropriate ways and means to strengthen the principle of cultural pluralism, to enable fruitful coexistence between the various unique groups as well to find common elements and characteristics of the emerging Israeli society. This challenge was in addition to that of seeking fruitful co-existence between the Jewish majority and Arab-Palestinian minority (Horowitz & Kraus, 1987; Iram, 1992; 2003).

STUDIES ON ACCULTURATION IN ISRAEL

Research in the early 1990s, after the arrival of large groups of immigrants into Israel from the Former Soviet Union and from Ethiopia, suggests that while these newcomers knew that they need to learn Hebrew and become familiar with basic elements of Israeli culture, many of them placed great value on their earlier cultural traditions (Shuval & Leshem, 1998). Both groups found certain elements of the local culture unattractive in comparison with parallel aspects in their respective traditional cultures. Thus, several processes take place simultaneously when immigrants relocate within their new country: socialization, de-socialization and re-socialization (Tatar, et al., 1994; Horowitz & Naftalie, 1997).

Young migrants find themselves abandoning their friends, language, culture, and aspirations for the future. They become "illiterates" overnight. The main task facing adolescents in modern society is the formation of their values and identity through a process of individuation and increasing autonomy. These difficulties have been documented in research (Maslovaty & Shitreet, 2003; Merkens & Wessel 2003). Findings from these studies confirmed five issues adolescent immigrants have had to cope with upon entering Israeli society: gender roles, education, acquiring a profession and financial independence, social and emotional maturity, and value system formulation. Literacy barriers are another problem newcomers have had to face. In the vast majority of mixed classes as well as in special classes of newcomers, a gap was found between the verbal ability of native-born and newcomer students (Shuval & Leshem, 1998). This finding is of great concern, since language is the gateway to communicating with one's surrounding. Hence, literacy barriers play a role in immigrants' acculturation process and how they integrate into a new environment and its culture.

Acculturation and Adaptation Processes among Youth in Israel

Shitreet (2006) examined the relationship between acculturation strategies and adaptation in Israel. His study looked at Ethiopian-born adolescents studying in different youth villages and in a day school as well as teachers teaching in these schools. Shitreet's study supports Berry's theory which claims that, when transitioning to different cultures, immigrants embrace four strategies within the acculturation process. The "integration" strategy in this study was also found to be connected to an increase in social, behavioural and general adaptation among the adolescent populations. The "marginalization" strategy was found to be connected to a decline in most of the adaptation measurements, mainly among adolescents in the day school. The "assimilation" strategy was found to be connected to a decline in social, behavioural and general adaptation only among the population of adolescents in the day school. For the "separation" strategy, no clear trend was found in relation to the different adaptation measurements. In a recent research study in Germany, inter-ethnic friendships were found as an indicator for social integration of immigrant youth (Reinders & Mangold, 2005; Reinders, et al., 2006).

The Attitudes of the Absorbing Society (Adolescents)

The native-born Israeli perceives the adaptation and change processes as short and rapid, while in reality this is a continuous process of crises and learning. It is important that the host community takes an active and positive role in the acculturation and adaptation of the newcomers. Tzabar Ben-Yehoshua et al., (1997) found in their study that one-third of the host population perceive the immigrants positively, but immigrants' language and culture were perceived as foreign to the Jewish values and culture. An assimilation pattern best describes the Israeli views towards Russian immigrant students (Shamai & Ilatov, 1998). They found that inclination of native-born students to socialize with the immigrants was low. Horowitz (1992) found that native-born students from lower socio-economic backgrounds demonstrated more hostile attitudes towards the immigrants compared to students from middle and higher socio-economic groups.

Alt's (2006) findings reinforce and add to the finding that ethnic origin plays a role in attitudes toward student immigrants as well as gender differences. Regarding the relationship between gender and civic attitudes and moral reasoning, Schulz, Bar and Selman (2001) found that girls scored significantly higher on relationship maturity and civic attitudes and participation, and boys had significantly more self-reported fighting behaviour and racist attitudes than girls. These findings coincide with Selman (2003), whose theory of social awareness defines social interactions—from the intimate and personal to the public and political—as central to the experience of being human. His study focused on the coordination of social perspectives—how immigrants and the host society come to identify their own needs, wants and feelings; understand those of others; and act to manage differences and conflicts, as well as closeness, within relationships.

Furthermore, Selman (2003) theorizes that an individual's core operational capacity to coordinate attitudes toward common social experiences develops in reciprocal interaction with each of the three distinct, but closely related psychological competencies, as follows:

- The general level of understanding that individuals have of the facts about the nature of the risk in the context of social relationships.
- The repertoire of interpersonal strategies that individuals have available to manage risks.
- The self-awareness that individuals have of the personal meaning of the risks that they take in connection to the quality of the personal relationship they maintain (Selman, 2003).

The adaptation of newcomer students is an interactive process and takes place simultaneously in four areas (see Figure 2).

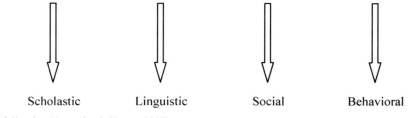

| Scholastic | Linguistic | Social | Behavioral |

(following Horowitz & Kraus, 1987)

Figure 2. Adaptation areas.

Shitreet (2006) developed a multi-dimensional model to show the pattern by which immigrants in Israel are absorbed in schools (see Figure 3). According to the model, schools operating according to an innovative-active model (i.e. schools dealing with the absorption of immigrants from an integration approach) should have the following characteristics:
– the task of absorption is centrally located in the school's long-term school plans;
– the enrolment of immigrants is perceived as a change in direction;
– and the school implements a strategy of initiative.

In schools that follow this model, the social adaptation was found to be very high, the behavioural adaptation was medium to very high and there was a mixed trend in the level of learning adaptation. In contrast, schools working according to partial models showed a very low to medium level of adaptation. Schools embracing the "integration" approach were found to be more efficient in the process of absorbing immigrants from Ethiopia than schools embracing the "assimilation" approach. There is a need to study this model further regarding other immigrant groups.

Recent studies have shown that contextual factors such as the composition of school classes, as well as teachers' expectations and their ability to assess achievement, have considerable effects on student achievement, but it is impossible to distinguish the social and ethnic effects (Konsortium Bildungsberichterstattung, 2006, 161ff). Thus, the adaptation of Shitreet's (2006) multi-dimensional model might provide innovative insights regarding the capacity of schools to absorb immigrant students.

The unique contribution of this study is specified both in its aims and in the research model as follows (Figure 3).

Coping strategies	Perception of the goal	Significance of enrolment	The basic approach to absorption
1. Initiative	1. Central	1. Directional change	1. Integration
2. Routine	2. Marginal	2. Additive change	2. Assimilation

X1111>X2222
(Tater, et al; developed by Shitreet, 2006)

Figure 3. A multi-dimensional model to absorb immigrants in schools.

A PROPOSED RESEARCH STUDY

The following section describes a proposed research study on the acculturation processes of immigrant and native-born youth in Israel.

Aims of the Research

The aims of the proposed research are as follows:
− to analyze relationships between the values, attitudes and social awareness systems of native-born and immigrant students towards the acculturation process.
− to analyze relationships between acculturation strategies and scholastic, linguistic, social and behavioural adaptations.
− to identify factors that contribute to successful acculturation in schools.
− to analyze attitudes of teachers and principals towards absorption and adaptation.
− to identify school acculturation processes and successful models for absorption and adaptation of immigrant students.
− to explore relationships between linguistic competence and social interaction between native-borns and immigrants.

Research Methods

This research would employ quantitative and qualitative methods (see Figure 4).

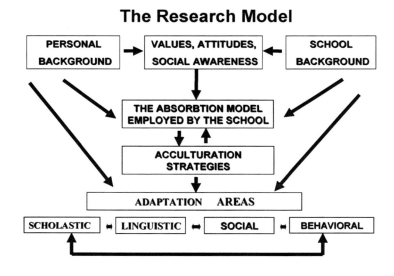

Figure 4. The research model.

Participants

The research group would include participants from different family ethnic origins, length of residence and countries of origin. Ethnic origin would be determined up to the second generation. Several sub-groups would be studied, for example, Native Israeli (Eastern, Western and mixed), Ethiopian immigrants and Former Soviet Union immigrants.

Instruments

The research instruments that such a study would employ may comprise a series of closed questionnaires, such as the ones described below, followed by in-depth participant interviews.

Schools Acculturation Processes - Models of Absorption of Immigrant Students

This questionnaire (Shitreet, 2006 based on Eisikowitz & Beck, 2001; Tatar, et al., 1994) is based on a multi-dimensional model to absorb immigrants in schools (Shitreet, 2006): assimilation vs. integration, centralization vs. marginalization, additive change vs. directional and routine entrepreneurships. It consists of 38 items, divided into 8 sub-scales. The reliability (Cronbach Alpha) of the questionnaire is 0.72.

The Acculturation Strategies of Students' Questionnaire

The model for this questionnaire claims that when transitioning to different cultures, immigrants embrace four strategies in the acculturation process. The questionnaire examines students' assimilation and integration, according to parameters of integration, marginalization, assimilation, and separation strategies. The questionnaire consists of 38 items, divided into 4 sub-scales, according to Berry's (1999) conception: The reliability (Cronbach Alpha) of the scale is 0.85.

The Adaptation Questionnaire

This questionnaire (Shitreet, 2006) consists of 37 items and examines adaptation to the school context across three domains: learning, social and behavioural. The reliability (Cronbach Alpha) of the questionnaire is 0.89.

The Values System Questionnaire

This 40 item questionnaire (one question per value) is based on Schwartz's intercultural theory on the structure of the value system (Schwartz & Bilsky, 1990; Schwartz, Lehmann & Melech, 1999) and has been validated in 90 samples. The reliability (Cronbach Alpha) of the questionnaire, as found by Shitreet (2006), is 0.85.

Values that lay at the core of attitudes and behaviours have been explored by Maslovaty and Shitreet (2003) confirming the Schwartz, Lehmann and Melech (1999) theory (see Figure 5). Schwartz (1992) suggests a universal typology in the

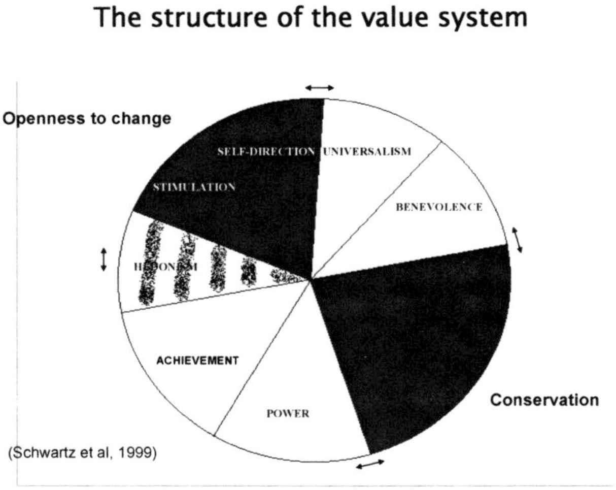

The structure of the value system

Figure 5. The structure of the value system.

form of conscious goals. The questionnaire employs the ten distinct motivational types of values that were derived; power, achievement, hedonism, stimulation, self-direction, universalism, benevolence, tradition, conformity and security. The questionnaire also employs the basic structure of four higher order value types, organized on two bipolar continua; the first, "conservation" versus "openness to change", and the second, "self-enhancement" versus "self-transcendence" (Schwartz, Lehmann & Melech, 1999).

They found that although the structure of values of native-born and immigrant adolescents was similar, they differed in the ranking of motivational type values and their intensity. In their study, Ethiopians emphasized significantly more universalism and power while native-born Israelis emphasized benevolence and motivation (Maslovaty & Shitreet, 2003).

The Relationship Questionnaire

This questionnaire (Selman, 2003; Schultz, et al., 2001) can be employed to measure social awareness. It is a 24-item multiple-choice instrument that measures the developmental level (0–3) of interpersonal development on 5 scales: perspective taking, interpersonal understanding, hypothetical negotiation, real-life negotiation and personal meaning. The Cronbach Alpha reliability coefficient is 0.75.

Attitudes towards Immigrants and Minorities Questionnaire

This questionnaire (Torney-Purta, 2002 a/b; Torney-Purta & Barber, 2004; Ichilov, 2000) examines perceptions and attitudes towards multiculturalism and social equality. It consists of eight questions that deal with attitudes regarding democracy, minorities and immigrants.

Following the questionnaire stage, in-depth interviews with teachers and students would be employed to gain insight into acculturation processes, adaptation of students, perceptions towards and acceptance of the others (by both native-born and immigrant students). The purpose of the in-depth interviews of key individuals and policymakers in the education system would be to better understand educational policy regarding absorption and acculturation of immigrant students

Procedure

To further test this model, 35 classes (ages 10, 11, 14 and 17) would be sampled according to the age groups, from a national list of schools. About 4 schools would be sampled for each age group. The composition of these classes and schools would reflect the socioeconomic background and ethnic immigration origin of its students.

In addition, in-depth interviews of 10 students would be conducted. Each student would be interviewed three times, to enable researchers to examine changing processes that the students have undergone while attending these schools. Ten teachers would also be interviewed.

Expected Results

The goal of such a project would be to improve the social and educational interventions that promote the integration of migrants into their host society. To this end, the project would comprehensively explore student and school variables that relate to absorption of newcomers into Israeli society.

The project would explore values, attitudes and behaviours of native-born and newcomer students as well as exploring acculturation models of Israeli schools. It is believed that the project would lead to valuable complementary information to the research results also expected in the evaluation of the Model Project. The findings of the project would serve to develop tolerance and social awareness within native-born and newcomer students.

Based on the projects' findings, we plan to construct practical models which could be tailored to different kinds of educational contexts. We will also suggest intervention programmes to the education system, for native-born as well as newcomer students. To widen the project's impact and to contribute to already existing work, we intend to conduct scholarly and public discussions on the educational policies regarding integration. School principals, teachers and students would also be involved in these dialogues.

It is expected that the models developed in this study could also be adapted to specific contexts of other education systems. We believe that this research project, which examines acculturation and adaptation processes of students who hailed from the former Soviet Union and from Ethiopia, might contribute to a better under-standing of their absorption process in Israel.

However, the contribution of this project spans beyond Israeli society. It is hoped that the multidimensional model to absorb immigrant students in schools and acculturation strategies of adaptation (scholastic, linguistic, social and behavioural)

139

will provide both a theoretical and practical base for coping successfully with the global issue of integrating new-comer students into the mainstream society.

CONCLUSION

Societies differ in their attitudes towards ethnically diverse migrants and particularly minority groups. These attitudes span a spectrum, varying from rejection through passive tolerance, to support and positive encouragement of variety, diversity and pluralism (Iram, 2003; Bommes & Schiffauer, 2006).

Many studies have dealt with the perspectives of newcomers towards the host society in the acculturation processes. However, the few studies that explored the attitudes of native-born students in Israel revealed their hostile attitudes towards newcomer students (Horowitz, 1992; Tzabar, et al., 1997). Fewer studies have explored acculturation processes within different models of school contexts. Shitreet (2006) identified several dimensions of successful acculturation of newcomer students at schools. These schools were characterized by the centrality of absorption of new-comer students in their curricula and educational road maps. Only a few schools are implementing successful acculturation models.

A study, such as the one proposed in this chapter, would explore values, attitudes and behaviours of native-born and newcomer students as well as acculturation models within Israeli schools. The central research question of such a study could follow Berry's (1997) acculturation strategies, discussed earlier. The findings of this study would assist in constructing varied acculturation models in educational contexts in order to develop tolerance and social awareness among both native-born and newcomer students.

REFERENCES

Adler, L. L., & Gielen, U. P. (Eds.). (2003). *Migration: Immigration and emigration in international perspective.* Westport, CT: Praeger Publishers.

Alt, D. (2006). *The contribution of personal background and media literacy to the civic-democratic system of concepts, attitudes and behaviors among Israeli high school students.* Submitted in partial fulfillment of the requirements at the pre-requisite course for the PhD degree. School of Education, Bar-Ilan University, Ramat-Gan.

Annan, K. (2006, September). *Migration and development: United Nations high-level dialogue.* Report of the Secretary-General on International Migration and Development (A/60/871).

Berry, J. W. (1997). Immigration, acculturation, and adaptation. *Applied Psychology: An International Review, 46,* 5–34.

Berry, J. W. (1999). Intercultural relations in plural societies. *Canadian Psychology, 40,* 12–21.

Berry, J. W. (2001). A psychology of immigration. *Journal of Social Issues, 57,* 615–631.

Bommes, M., & Schiffauer, W. (2006). *Migrationsreport 2006: Fakten-analysen-perspektiven.* Frankfurt, Germany: Campus Verlag GmbH.

Bourhis, R. Y., Moise, L. C., Perreault, S., & Senecal, S. (1997). Towards an interactive acculturation model: A social-psychological approach. *International Journal of Psychology, 32*(6), 369–386.

Central Bureau of Statistics. (2009). *Statistical abstract of Israel 2008.* Jerusalem, Israel: Central Bureau of Statistics.

Eisenstadt, S. N. (1985). *The transformation of Israeli society.* Bolder, CO: Westview Press.

Eisikovitz, R. A., & Beck, R. H. (2001). Models governing the education of new immigrant children in Israel. *Studies in Education, 55*, 30–50.

Horowitz, T. R., & Kraus, V. (1987). Violence at school: Situational factors or social input. *School Psychology International, 8*, 141–147.

Horowitz, T. R. (1992). The two worlds of childhood: Israel and the Soviet Union (the Soviet child in a state of dissonance). In R. Weller (Ed.), *Between two worlds: Anthology for enriching parent counselors on the issue of absorbing parents from the Soviet Union* (pp. 25–33). Jerusalem, Israel: Ministry of Education & Culture, Division of Adolescents, Unit for Parents, Family and Community.

Horowitz, T. R., & Naftalie, M. (1997). Achievement motivation and level of aspiration: Adolescent Ethiopian immigrants in the Israeli education system. *Adolescence, 32*, 169–179.

Ichilov, O. (2000). *Citizenship orientations of 11th grade students and teachers in the Israeli Hebrew and Arab high schools*. Research report, submitted to the steering committee of the IEA Civic Education Study and to the Israeli Ministry of Education.

Iram, Y. (1992). Russian and Ethiopian immigrants in Israel: A comparative perspective on educational absorption. *Education and Society, 10*(1), 85–93.

Iram, Y., & Schmida, M. (1998). *The educational system of Israel*. Westport, CT: Greenwood Press.

Iram, Y. (2003). Education of minorities: Problems, promises, and prospects: An international perspective. In Y. Iram (Ed.), H. Wahrman, (asst. Ed.), *Education of minorities and peace education in pluralistic societies* (pp. 3–13). Westport, CT: Praeger Publishers.

Joppke, C., & Morawska, E. (Eds.). (2003). *Toward assimilation and citizenship: Migration, minorities and citizenship*. New York: Palgrave Macmillan.

Konsortium Bildungsberichterstattung. (2006). *Bildung in Deutschland. Ein indikatorengestützer Bericht mit einer Analyse zu Bildung und Migration*. Bielefeld (W. Bertelsmann).

Kymlicka, W. (2007). *Multicultural odysseys: Navigating the new international politics of diversity*. New York: Oxford University Press Inc.

Maslovaty, N., & Shitreet, E. (2003). A comparison of the value systems of Ethiopian-born emigrants and Israeli-born adolescents: Origin and gender. *Education and Society, 21*(2), 55–74.

Merkens, H., & Wessel, A. (Eds.). (2003). *Zwischen Anpassung und Widerstand. Zur Herausbildung der Sozialen Identität Türkischer und Deutscher Jugendlicher Baltmannsweiler*. Schneider-Verlag.

Reinders, H., Mangold, T., Greb, K., & Grimm, C. (2006). Entstehung, Gestalt und Auswirkungen Interethnischer Freundschaften im Jugendalter. In *Diskurs Kindheits - und Jugendforschung, 01*(01), 39–58.

Reinders, H., & Mangold, T. (2005). Die Qualität Intra- und Interethnischer Freundschaften bei Mädchen und Jungen Deutscher, Türkischer und Italienischer Herkunft [Intra- and interethnic friendship quality of boys and girls of German, Turkish and Italian origin]. *Zeitschrift für Entwicklungspsychologie und Pädagogische Psychologie, 37*(03), 144–155.

Schwartz, S. H., & Bilsky, W. (1990). Toward a theory of the universal content and structural values: Extensions and cross-cultural replication. *Journal Personality and Social Psychology, 58*, 887–891.

Schwartz, S. H. (1992). Universals in the content and structure of values: Theoretical advances and empirical tests in 20 countries. In M. P. Zanna (Ed.), *Advances in experimental social psychology* (Vol. 25, pp. 1–65). New York: Academic Press.

Schwartz, H., Lehmann, A., & Melech, G. (1999). *Validation of a theory of basic human values with a new instrument in new populations*. Jerusalem, Israel: The Hebrew University of Jerusalem.

Schultz, L. H., Barr, D. J., & Selman, R. L. (2001). The value of developmental programmes: An outcome study of facing history and ourselves. *Journal of Moral Education, 30*, 3–27.

Selman, R. L. (2003). *The promotion of social awareness*. New York: Russell Sage Foundation.

Shamai, S., & Ilatov, Z. (1998). Attitudes of Israeli and Canadian students towards new immigrants from Russia. *Education and Society, 16*(1), 27–36.

Shitreet, E. (2006). *Acculturation processes and adaptation to studies and society of Ethiopian-Born adolescents in state religious youth villages. Submitted in partial fulfilment of the requirements for the PhD degree*. Ramat-Gan: Bar-Ilan University.

Shuval, J. T., & Leshem, E. (1998). The sociology of migration in Israel: A critical view. In E. Leshem & J. Shuval (Eds.), *Immigration to Israel: Sociological perspectives* (pp. 3–50). New Brunswick, NJ and London: Transaction Publishers.

Swain, C. M. (Ed.). (2007). *Debating immigration*. New York: Cambridge University Press.

Tatar, M., Kfir, D., Sever, R., Adler, C., & Regev, H. (1994). *Integration of immigrant students into Israeli elementary and secondary schools: A pilot study*. Jerusalem: The NCJW Institute for Innovation in Education, School of Education, The Hebrew University. (Hebrew).

Torney-Purta, J. (2002a). Patterns in the civic knowledge, engagement and attitudes of European adolescents: The IEA Civic Education Study. *European Journal of Education, 37*, 129–141.

Torney-Purta, J. (2002b). The school's role in developing civic engagement: A study of adolescents in twenty-eight countries. *Applied Developmental Science, 6*, 202–212.

Torney-Purta, J., & Barber, C. H. (2004). *Education for democracy citizenship 2001–2004, democratic school participation and civic attitudes among European adolescents: Analysis of data from the IEA Civic Education Study*. College Park, MD: University of Maryland College of Education.

Tzabar Ben-Yehoshua, N., Resnik, G., Shoham, E., & Shapira, R. (1997). Encounters of Native-borns and new comers: Is that the case? Lessons learnt from school reality. *Social Security, 50*, 85–103.

UNESCO. (2001, May). *Dakar framework for action*. Paris: UNESCO.

Yaacov Iram
UNESCO/Burg Chair in Education for Human Values, Tolerance and Peace
Faculty of Education, Bar-Ilan University

Nava Maslovaty
Faculty of Education, Bar-Ilan University

Eli Shitreet
Faculty of Education, Bar-Ilan University

SECTION IV: POLICY

NORMA TARROW

10. EDUCATION OF THE BEDOUIN OF THE NEGEV FROM 1977 to 2007

INTRODUCTION

My dear friend and colleague, David Wilson, and I shared an attachment to the Land of Israel as well as a profound interest in the treatment of indigenous groups who, as a result of political actions beyond their control, have become minorities in their own land. The Bedouin of the Negev are a prime example of this phenomenon and for many hours, at many conferences, their situation was discussed with David. He was most interested in my early work and I'm sure would have been most interested in this follow-up study, which examines the impact of differing policies and practices on opportunities and educational outcomes of the Negev Bedouin over the last 30 years of Israeli rule. A review of socio-political factors and the realities and challenges identified by the author in 1977 provides the background and basis of comparison for the current study. The fieldwork undertaken includes school observations, interviews with teachers, parents and administrators and data from the Ministry of Education in 2007. The study examines such issues as access, attendance and dropout rates, educational objectives, budget and staffing as well as the relationship of the "land issue" to the provision of education to children in "government-planned", "recognized" and "unrecognized" sectors of Bedouin society.

BACKGROUND

Who are the Bedouin of the Negev? For most westerners, the image commonly conjured is that of a simple nomad, astride his colourfully saddled camel, wandering with his small flock, his family and possessions from watering place to watering place through the arid and hostile desert. Traditionally, the Bedouin have been nomads with a superbly developed facility for adapting to changing conditions (Bernstein-Tarrow, 1978).

Bedouin history is a long one—too long for more than a brief overview in this paper. Most scholars agree that they have inhabited the Negev since at least the fifth century. The first school for Bedouin children, in which Turkish was the language of instruction, was established under Ottoman rule and lasted until the end of the Ottoman empire in 1917 (Abu-Rabi'a, 2001). A critical legacy of the Ottoman era that has socio-economic, political *and* educational ramifications until today has its origin in the 1858 Turkish law, which defined uncultivated land that did not belong to anyone and that was more than 1.5 miles from the nearest government-planned

V. Masemann et al., (Eds.), A Tribute to David N. Wilson: Clamouring for a Better World, 145–162.
© *2010 Sense Publishers. All rights reserved.*

townships as *mawat* (dead land) (Falah, 1989). This constraint, combined with Bedouin tradition, kept most Bedouin from registering their land during the Ottoman era. During the Mandate era (1917–1948),

> The Bedouin did not register their land in Tabu (the Land Registry Office) for the following reasons: (1) fear of the burden of government taxes; (2) aversion to publicizing details about private property and (3) failure to see the need to record land on a piece of paper as proof of ownership. In that period, proof was, literally, through the sword. (Abu Rabi'a, 2002, p. 205)

Meanwhile, throughout this period, the Jewish National Fund (established in 1901) pursued a policy of purchasing land in Palestine, largely from absentee Arab landowners for settlement of the Jewish population. This policy continued both during the remaining years of Ottoman rule and the British mandate era.

As for education under the British Mandate, in addition to private schools, a dual system of national education developed along linguistic (Arabic and Hebrew) and ethnic lines (Arabs and Jews). Special provision for the Bedouin provided teachers who lived with the tribes and taught the three "Rs" and the Koran to boys in groups gathered in a tent or under a tree. From 1920 to 1940, the Mandatory administration maintained schools for Bedouin boys in five tribal areas. In the final decade, there were over 20 schools, with half the costs borne by the tribes and half by the British administration. From the 1930s until the end of the Mandate period, those who completed lower forms at tribal schools could attend upper elementary schools as boarders in Beersheba. Most of these were sons of sheikhs or wealthy Bedouin. Informal education of sons by their fathers included all the skills necessary for their lives in the desert. Girls were only informally educated by their mothers in such skills as weaving, food preparation, child-care, raising crops and tending livestock (Abu Rabi'a, 2001).

In 1947, the United Nations recommended partitioning Palestine into Jewish and Arab states, a plan which Arab leaders rejected. The creation of the State of Israel in 1948 and its victory over five Arab armies signified the beginning of the events referred to by the Arabs as *Al Nakba* (the catastrophe). For the Arab population as a whole, this abrupt change in status from a majority with awakening national aspirations in mandatory Palestine to one of a dominated minority was, and remains, traumatic. According to Abu-Rabi'a (2002), by the end of the war, the Bedouin population of the Negev was reduced from approximately 100,000 to about 11,000 people in nineteen tribes, whose heads were recognized as sheikhs by the government. Twelve of these tribes were removed to a "reservation" where, under military governance, there was large scale confinement to a designated area.

In this area, Abu-Saad (2006a) describes the imposition of curfews, special permits required to leave villages, physical and administrative separation of Jews and Arabs, and a separate military court system with no right of appeal. He enumerates control techniques such as no representative share in policy-making and planning, dependency on the Jewish sector for employment, and co-option of Bedouin elite who determined appointment of teachers, access to secondary education, colleges and universities. Abu-Saad (2006a) claims that, with the dismantling of the military government in 1966, the government developed other means of maintaining a strategy of segmentation, dependence and cooption (i.e. creation of urban settlements) perpetuating the legacy of the military government.

Confined to a prescribed area under military rule from 1948 to 1966, followed by removal starting in 1968, to government-planned urban settlements, the Bedouin of the Negev experienced the impact of migration in the most powerful way—without actually leaving the land they considered to be theirs, living in a "new" country surrounded by an alien culture, with borders and boundaries defined by the new inhabitants. Thus, "they arrived in a new and strange land without the physical journey" (Givati-Teerling, 2007, Introduction). Since those who refused to move off what they consider to be their land are living in what the government refers to as "unrecognized settlements", they were not, and are still not, entitled to basic services. Therefore, provision of services generally considered essential for health and education have been made contingent upon their relinquishing claims to land and acceding to a policy of moving into government-planned settlements. As will be seen below, this situation affects between 40 to 50 per cent of the current Bedouin population.

It was not until 1981 that the Bedouin Education Authority (BEA) was established to enforce the 1949 national compulsory education law in the Bedouin sector. It was charged with setting up, building and maintaining schools; assuring appropriate and adequate teaching personnel; provision of furniture, equipment, water supply; teaching materials; and student registration (Swirski & Hasson, 2006). The BEA was later superseded by the Abu Basma Regional Council. Established by government decision in January 2004, it operates under the direction of a Jewish former Director of the Interior Ministry with three Bedouin in administrative positions. The Council has responsibility for both recognized and unrecognized villages. Currently, there are nine newly recognized settlements (30,000 people), with two more about to be recognized. Including those in the 30 to 45 still unrecognized settlements, there are about 80,000 people under their jurisdiction. As of 2006, the Abu Basma Regional Council assumed responsibility for education in all locations

Table 1. Settlement chart as per government categorization

Permanent (original) settlements	Recognized settlements	About to be recognized settlements	Unrecognized settlements (estimated)
Tel Sheva	El Sayed	Al Arash	30 – 45 additional
Arara in the Negev	Tarabin	Mariet	
Laquia	Abu Krinat		
Rahat	Kaser a Ser		
Hura	Drigat		
Segev Shalom	Abu Kaf		
Kaseifa	Beer Adag		

Source: Abu Basma Regional Council, May 2007

for which it bears responsibility. The original seven government planned townships operate independently outside of their jurisdiction and are responsible for all social services, including education, within their townships. (See Table 1 for listing of government planned townships and recognized settlements.)

THE STATE OF ISRAEL AND THE EDUCATION OF THE NEGEV BEDOUIN

1948–1977

From 1948 until the late 1960s, the State of Israel was more occupied with issues of national defence, absorption of immigrants and building its own education system than attending to the educational needs of Arab citizens. The latter were also not accustomed to the Jewish tradition of local communities accepting major fiscal and organizational responsibility for education (Bernstein-Tarrow, 1980). Almost no educational facilities were available to the Bedouin who, as mentioned above, were confined to a reservation-like area under military administration until 1966. It also must be noted that while in the early days of statehood, "The Israeli government was slow in establishing public schools for the Bedouin ... the Bedouin themselves initially showed very little interest in this new form of education, since its relevance was not immediately apparent to them" (Abu-Saad, 2001, pp. 247–248). Still, expansion of educational facilities continued:

> In 1960, there were seven schools serving a total of 556 Bedouin pupils. In 1965, there were 14 schools serving approximately 1100 pupils, of whom about 100 were girls. There were five Bedouin teachers. There were still no facilities for secondary schooling other than distant boarding schools. (Marx, 1967, cited by Bernstein-Tarrow, 1978, pp. 144–145)

Not until 1968 were there schools for every tribe—none with more than four grades (Abu-Saad, 1991). By 1973, for the first time, Bedouin children attended kindergartens in three schools. An academic high school was available to day students. Girls were represented only in the primary grades (Bernstein-Tarrow, 1978).

1977–2007

By 1977, this author noted that the Israeli government had provided the Negev Bedouin community with access to 22 schools serving 6,552 children. There were 14 kindergartens, 249 teachers, and 14 Bedouin principals as well as one vocational high school program, and two classes for training Bedouin teachers offered at a Teachers' Seminar in Beersheba. There were few girls attending schools, and difficulty in convincing fathers to allow their daughters to serve as aides in newly formed kindergartens. Teachers were overwhelmingly Arabs from the north of Israel who had limited knowledge of Bedouin culture and knew little about the families of their pupils. There were no supervisors to provide support for inexperienced young teachers, and no guidance for those dealing with children with special needs. During all lessons observed by the author, teachers used teacher-centered instructional methods, especially memorization and repetition. Educational materials produced for urban Jewish schools bore little relation to the life experiences of desert-reared Bedouin children. Physical facilities of schools visited were primitive, with out-houses and no running water or electricity. Although there was almost unlimited space around each school, there were no playgrounds and no playground equipment. (The arrival of the researcher with playground balls was a major event for the children.) Neither food nor transportation was provided, and many children walked long distances across the desert to arrive in class. Consequently, bad weather, illness or family responsibilities contributed to irregular attendance of pupils. Health facilities were very limited, and illness of pupils or younger siblings was widespread. Parents were not convinced of the value of formal education for their children and efforts at parent education and involvement had not yet been instituted. Certainly, education at the secondary level was neither a priority of the State nor of the Bedouin community, and the only viable option was one school offering vocational education. As a result of fieldwork in 1973–74 and 1976–77, the author identified areas urgently needing attention and suggested the following for prioritization by government educational authorities:

- Provision of subject matter and special services supervisors;
- Physical facilities—more classrooms better suited to desert climate, with sanitary facilities and water on premises;
- Transportation for children living long distances from schools;
- Food programme to provide school lunches;
- Long range planning jointly by government and local education authorities;
- Updating and revision of curriculum, educational materials and text books to make them more relevant to Bedouin students;
- Provision for some emphasis on Bedouin culture;
- Facilities for special education, and guidance for teachers with special needs children in class;
- Use of teaching methods involving active learning;
- Physical-motor equipment—playground and sports areas;
- Parent education and community involvement;
- More opportunities for vocational education;
- Attention to health issues with provision of school nurses, health education and health facilities;
- Upgrading of teachers' qualifications with pre- and in-service training;
- Access to higher education (requiring attention to student retention and alleviating the barrier of matriculation examinations). (Bernstein-Tarrow, 1978, pp. 146–147)

In the 30 years since Bernstein-Tarrow's investigation, much has been published regarding education of the Bedouin of the Negev. A decade later, Abu-Rabi'a (1987) reported that the number of Bedouin children enrolled in school had grown from 150 in 1950 to about 16,000 in 1986. Girls made up 40 per cent of elementary and 25 per cent of secondary enrolment in the 29 elementary and 3 secondary schools staffed by 626 teachers, approximately half of whom were Bedouin (Abu-Rabi'a, 1987).

In 1993, researchers found that 23,276 Negev Bedouin were enrolled in 37 schools—29 primary, 3 junior high schools, 2 comprehensive schools (grades 7–12), 2 high schools and 1 vocational school (Abu-Rabiy-ya, al-Athauna & al-Bador, 1996).

In 1994, Abu-Rabi'a (1994) claimed,

> There has been progress in the number of schools and teachers provided, the number of children in the schools, the attendance of girls, the awareness of parents of the importance of education, and the willingness of parents to send their children to schools. (p. 16)

By 1995, according to Abu-Saad (1995), there were 24,790 students in 38 Bedouin schools (30 elementary, three intermediate, two secondary and one vocational school).

As a result of a survey in 1996, Abu-Rabyya and colleagues (1996) identified a number of areas needing attention. It is interesting to note the similarity to those identified in 1977 by Bernstein-Tarrow, as described above. These included:

- Level of teacher training and familiarity with curricula, noting that there were significant differences between permanent and temporary settlements in the preparation of teaching staff and that half of the teachers surveyed received "certification" from a supervisor, usually after one or two classroom visits, rather than from an institution of higher learning.
- Scholastic achievement—noting a decrease in number of students taking the matriculation exams, which the researchers related to the principals' wish to maximize the rate of success of their schools. Most of those who did take the exams obtained a low level certificate not recognized by the higher education system.
- Kindergarten and school attendance rates—in a society where kindergarten attendance among other population groups is nearly universal, more than one quarter of five year old Bedouin children did not attend kindergarten.
- Gender differences—boys outnumbered girls; drop-out rates were higher among girls, and only 20 per cent of teachers in post-primary schools were women.
- Provision for weak pupils—although there was a high rate of children with special needs, principals reported no assistance in dealing with these pupils. No systematic records were kept on these students, and only five of 413 teachers in the survey were trained in special education.
- School and community relations—many of the non-Bedouin Arab teachers had a condescending attitude towards the local parents, little contact with the parents, and a low level of expectation of the students. More than one third of teachers surveyed believed parents were in need of assistance to make them better parents.
- Some teachers alleged that teachers and principals are appointed primarily on the basis of political and tribal considerations. (Abu-Rabyya et al., 1996)

The physical conditions of the schools have been described as follows:

> The physical conditions in Negev Bedouin schools are not up to Israeli
> standards. This is true not only for schools in "temporary" localities but also
> for those in government-planned townships...The construction of appropriate
> school buildings, as well as health service facilities, should be the first and
> perhaps the major step towards keeping the promise to provide Bedouin who
> move to government-planned townships with the full range of state services
> that, officials claim, are hard to deliver to a nomadic population group.
> However, even if appropriate school premises are built in the government-
> planned townships, the Ministry of Education is still duty-bound to provide
> such buildings in the temporary settlements as well....In Israel, it is the local
> government's task to provide buildings for schools. Because of the residents'
> low socioeconomic level, however, the Bedouin local governments generally
> lack the resources to do this, and the temporary localities have no such govern-
> ments at all. Thus it is the duty of the Ministry of Education to honour Israel's
> promise to eliminate educational disparities by allocating larger sums to
> improve the physical conditions of the Negev Bedouin schools (Abu-Rabyya et
> al., 1996, p. 33).

Abu-Saad (1996) notes that another investigator identified the following needs:

- Improvement at elementary and secondary levels through equalization of
  material & human resources to provide students with needed skills;
- More relevant curricula and textbooks (dealing with Arab culture and
  identity and issues related to the radical social upheaval of Bedouin
  community;
- Education to fit social and economic needs of community, provide security,
  pride in heritage and confidence in skills;
- Dropout issue to be addressed with special educational programs, especially
  directed at girls;
- Programs to better prepare high school students to succeed in matriculation
  exams;
- Review of university admission policies for unfair cultural bias, recruitment
  programs, a national scholarship program for Bedouin students, assistant-
  ship and grant programs, loan incentive programs, programs for re-entry
  and career changes and special support for students accepting jobs in their
  Bedouin communities;
- Public and private sector prepared to absorb Bedouin graduates into fields
  appropriate to their training; directed efforts at filling leadership positions
  in development of community. (pp. 532–533)

Twenty years after Bernstein-Tarrow's recommendations, Abu-Saad (1997) noted
that, "While accessibility to education has improved greatly over the last 30 years
for Negev Bedouin-Arab children, the quality and success rate of the Bedouin
schools remains very low" (p. 35). Also, while there was more stability in the teaching
staff, with 60 per cent of the teachers from the Bedouin community, some only had

a high school education and more than 23 per cent of the teachers were unqualified. Abu-Saad (1997) made five recommendations for improving the educational situation:

- Equalization of material & human resources;
- Training a qualified staff able to understand the community's needs and problems;
- Revision of curricula and textbooks to be more relevant to Arab culture and identity and to the radical social upheaval of Bedouin community;
- Special educational programs involving parents to counter drop-out and improve student retention;
- Special training of teachers and administrators to deal with integration of school and community (p. 36).

It is notable that many of the areas highlighted in the 20 years between 1977 and 1997 are still identified as needing attention by those involved with the education of Bedouin children and youth in 2007. From 1967 to the present, the government has been attempting to move the Bedouin into planned settlements with the stated objective of providing municipal services, including education. Excluded from consultation, between 40 and 60 per cent of Bedouin families affected have resisted this policy, claiming its objective is to secure land rather than supply services. Factors that have had a major impact on the Bedouin community include

- Educational policies towards Arab citizens in general;
- A slow-to-develop interest in education on the part of the Bedouin;
- Land acquisition policies allocating social and educational services only to Bedouin willing to relinquish land claims (with what they view as minimal compensation) and relocate into concentrated urban settlements;
- Demographic issues—keeping up with a population that doubles every 13–15 years;
- Geographic issues—providing services over a vast geographic area containing widely scattered small settlements.

THE CURRENT SITUATION

Analysis of the educational situation in 2007 (30 years after the previous investigation of the author) is based on review of an extensive literature that has accumulated, statistics available from various sources, field work including school visitations, meetings, and interviews with teachers, administrators, municipal and regional authorities, teacher educators, university faculty and civil rights activists. A general overview of the current situation is followed by a particular focus on accessibility, educational objectives, budget, staffing, and the issue of attendance/dropout.

Accessibility

It is clear that while the number of schools and classrooms, of children in schools, and of teachers and others serving these children has grown exponentially, so has the (Bedouin) population of the region (from an estimated 11,000 in 1948 to between 150,000 and 200,000 today. Thus, the growth in provision of facilities and services merely reflects the growth in school population. And the authorities are having difficulty in keeping up with the population growth. According to one educator,

> In recent years, there has been a huge expansion of the educational system in response to an approximately six per cent birthrate. In each village there needs to be a new school every year. About 60 per cent to 70 per cent of the population are under age 16. The system simply cannot cope with such growth (College President, personal communication, June 3, 2007).

Yet, "while accessibility to education has improved greatly over the last 30 years for Negev Bedouin children (and especially for girls), the quality and success rate of the Bedouin schools remains very low" (Abu-Saad, 1997, p. 35). Abu-Saad, (1997) identifies the main problems as unqualified teachers, weak links between school and community, a curriculum that is irrelevant to students, and the invalidity of the Bagrut (Matriculation examination) for this particular population, noting that the low rate of success eliminates the incentive for completing high school.

In 2004, the Center for Bedouin Studies at Ben Gurion University estimated that one third of the classrooms in the seven government-planned townships for Bedouin in the Negev were unsound. Also in both recognized and unrecognized villages there were few or no libraries, laboratories, or facilities for sports or recreational activities. Many unrecognized villages lack a school of any kind, and, according to some reports (Coursen-Neff, 2004), more than 6,000 Bedouin children must travel dozens of kilometres to school every day. Long travel distances tend to have a disproportional effect on girls' ability to go to schools.

As of 2007, the Director of the Abu Basma Regional Council claimed that educational facilities have been provided in all newly-recognized settlements (then numbering nine) with two additional settlements about to be recognized and provided with educational facilities, and more to follow. Since education was added to the charge of the Abu Basma Regional Council, the Council is responsible for 24 primary schools with a population of 12,117 students, 122 preschools and kindergartens serving 3,650 children, and two high schools serving 305 pupils in grades 9–12. According to the Director, transportation is provided for 20,550 pupils within the area (personal communication, May 20, 2007).

Progress in current and future building of school facilities was evident through interviews with administrators of the Council and visits to schools. Three schools have been completed, including a state-of-the art, two-storey high school which opened in 2007 in Abu Krinat with electricity supplied by generator, water and an access road in the process of being completed. (A visit to this school provided evidence of computer and science laboratories, but these did not contain any equipment.) Another high school about to open will further supplement the high schools in the original settlements of Rahat, Laqia and Tel Sheva. A holistic regional centre is being planned to include youth services, sports facilities, a new K-12 school, leadership training, and a college.

Visits to the school in Abu Kaf and interviews with the Director and staff members provided the following information: The school houses approximately 1,200 students from Kindergarten to grade 9. In order to complete high school, students need to travel to Laqia. There are 56 teachers, 34 of whom are Bedouin. The rest are Arabs from the north plus one Jewish teacher for sports. There is a generator for electricity and water from main pipes supplied by the State (the quality of which seems to be open to question).

Visits to the technological high school in Hura provided an example of secondary education offering an option of single-sex facilities (to overcome the problem of fathers refusing to allow their daughters to attend co-educational secondary schools). The school includes grades 9–12, has 25 teachers, all of whom are certified, and all teaching the subjects they were trained to teach, according to the Director. Thirteen are Bedouin, the rest Arabs from the north. There are no Jewish teachers. Curriculum includes options for nursing and electrical professions. The Director pointed out that while the top students want to go on to universities to prepare for careers in high-tech industries, the psychometric examination appears to be even more of a barrier than the Bagrut (matriculation exam). The school has computers, a laboratory for mechanics and automobile repair and a library. There is also a programme for children with special needs (primarily in reading and writing) in a separate building.

Educational Objectives in Israel

Established in 1949 and amended in 2000, the educational objectives continue to emphasize Jewish values, history and culture with no parallel aims for the education of Arabs in Israel (Abu-Saad, 2006b). Abu-Saad (2005) also points out that alienation of students is the norm since, within the schools, there is little attention to their own (Bedouin/Arab) culture. Brous (2005), confirming that the disregard of the Palestinian-Arab narrative lessens the relevance of educational experience for all Arab students, notes that most of what Bedouin youngsters learn in school will never be of real use to them. Brous (2005) states that,

> Despite extensive High Court rulings, reports from the State comptroller, media exposés and the continuous work of NGO pressure groups, Israel has failed to change its ethnocratic educational system (p. 260).

One example to the contrary was observed in the recently recognized village of Abu-Kaf where an environmental educator works with children in grades 4–6, on such subjects as waste management and planning of open space. In an interview with this educator, she indicated that she tries to look for subjects relevant to the children. "For example, we work with small gardens—choose plants that are suited to terrain and climate, planning our village and this is very relevant to them" (an environmental educator, personal communication, June 6, 2007). She noted that there is a lot of discussion in lessons where children plan their settlement (and bring to the surface much of the dissatisfaction they hear at home).

It must be noted that while formally-stated educational objectives remain directed at the Jewish sector, field work in 2007, involving visits to elementary, secondary and teacher training institutions provided some examples of activities and units of study based on Bedouin culture and traditions. One school had a week of activities based on Bedouin life, culminating in a school-wide rotation of students to learning centres with parents involved in numerous activities. However, the majority of educational administrators noted that the focus on Jewish values, history and culture and lack of attention to Arab history, tradition and culture are major factors in the alienation of Arab and Arab/Bedouin students.

Budget

Abu-Saad (2004) highlights discrimination in budget allocation from the Ministry of Education, which spends more per child in the Jewish sector and further notes that these schools receive additional state and state-sponsored private funding for special programmes. He claims that five-year plans of the Ministry of Education designed to correct imbalances were only partially implemented and even if they were fully implemented would not be enough to equalize the gap between the two systems without some form of affirmative action (Abu-Saad, 2004). Abu-Saad, (1995) pointed out that there were no Bedouin educators in the higher echelons of the Ministry where policy, curriculum, resource management and budgetary decisions are made, although recently a special department for Bedouin Education was formed, under the direction of Dr. Muhmad Al-Haip, a Bedouin from the north.

As a signatory to the Convention on the Rights of the Child, Israel is required to submit status reports to the Committee on the Rights of the Child. In its 2004 report, the government acknowledged that for Arab education it spends about 60 per cent of what it spends on Jewish education. Fewer teaching hours are also allocated for Arab children at every grade level. More teachers per capita are allocated to Jewish schools, and the number of kindergarten children per full-time teacher was twice as high in Arab kindergartens (39.3 as compared to 19.8 in Jewish kindergartens). Coursen-Neff (2004) notes the following:

> Data show that each year officials at the Ministry of Education consciously decided to allocate core education funds unequally, and each year the Knesset approves a budget that makes this unequal allocation explicit (p. 760).

Educational Staff

Accordingly, with the aforementioned population growth, increased interest in education and consequent increase in numbers of schools and classroom, there has been a proportionate rise in the number of teachers. With an education system at the bottom of every scale, the Negev Bedouin community has not been able to produce a sufficient quantity of certified teachers to staff these schools. Arab communities in the north and the "Triangle" area of Israel, however, with a longer tradition of and interest in higher education, are producing large numbers of graduates of higher education facilities—primarily in the humanities and social sciences. Since the limited career options for these graduates direct many into the field of education, the population growth in their local areas cannot absorb the number of available teachers. Consequently, many are sent to staff schools in the Negev Bedouin communities—usually for a period of three years. Interviews and visits to the apartments of several of these teachers indicate that most are in their first or second year of teaching. They live in shared apartments in Beersheba, subsidized by the government, which also covers the cost of their daily transportation to and from their schools and for travel back to their family homes on weekends. In terms of equality with the Jewish sector, they receive the same salary as their Jewish colleagues with extra pay to those who hold the Bachelor of Education degree and additional stipends to those who teach more than one grade level (for example English teachers of grades 4, 5 and 6). When asked "What would you like to change about your school?" one very responsible teacher replied,

> I would like to change some teachers. Some teachers are not qualified enough to teach or don't have conscience (are not conscientious). They don't internalize that these pupils are their responsibility. They don't teach as they should teach. Some are not interested. The environment is different from their own environment in the north and they don't do their best. They stay three years, get tenure and then leave for jobs in the north. They don't 'invest' in the schools to which they are assigned here (English teacher, personal communication, June 3, 2007).

Conscious of the value of producing and employing teachers from the local Bedouin community, and hampered by the limited number of Bedouin going on to higher education, or even completing high school, administrators in the early years placed willing but uncertified Bedouin teachers in their schools. In recent years, there has been a concerted effort to provide both pre- and in-service programmes, to prepare beginning teachers as well as to provide certification for those who entered the system without adequate academic or pedagogic background. A senior education official in Rahat (personal communication, May 10, 2007) indicates that most of the teachers in Rahat are Bedouin when he states,

> At the Kindergarten level, all are Bedouin. We have a branch of Achva College here for teachers. Five hundred thirty eight people have completed the three year Kindergarten teachers' course since 1994. This year we have the report. Most of them are women (80). Two hundred are teaching in Rahat.

Attendance and Dropout Issues

Teachers report irregular attendance for a variety of reasons. One teacher noted,

> Many are absent as much as 30 days a year. For any occasion, they don't come to school. If they want to go buy clothes, they miss school that day, then they go on a trip and miss school and the day after they come back they also don't come to school (personal communication, May 3, 2007).

As for the problem of student retention, an Arab teacher from the north stated,

> The level of students here is so much lower than in the north...Here the parents don't encourage teaching. They care about their source of living because they have many children. They don't think education will help improve their living. There are so many who drop out from school (personal communication, May 3, 2007).

Keeping children in school is one of the biggest problems facing educators in the Bedouin sector. Yet counselors trained to deal with students and parents who have dropped, or are about to drop, out of school are rare in the Bedouin community. According to Coursen-Neff (2004), "In January 2005, the Supreme Court found that counselor positions were assigned unequally to Bedouin towns in the Negev and that the difference in dropout rate between Jewish and Bedouin pupils made that inequity even more severe" (p. 785).

Statistics abound on the issue of school dropout and can be used to "prove" whatever point its distributors wish to make. In one school, the director claims a zero per cent dropout rate. This apparently means for example, that, of the students who have managed to make it to ninth grade, all who began the semester completed it. This does not take into account the number of youngsters of ninth grade age who never even began the semester. In another school with a "zero per cent dropout rate" the school is located in a very homogeneous community, where the school director is a respected tribal leader who knows, and has a strong influence on, the parents of his students. In the largest urban Bedouin community, Rahat, official statistics acknowledge a dropout rate of 33.4 per cent. "Official" statistics from the Ministry of Education compare the dropout rates of the Bedouin community with those of the larger Arab sector, with the Druze minority, and with the Jewish sector. These statistics indicate that the percentage of dropouts in the Bedouin sector has been reduced to 28 per cent, while still the highest dropout rate of the four sectors of Israeli society and reduced from an extraordinarily high rate of 71 per cent in 1990. (See Table 2 below.)

Table 2. Dropout rates among Jews, Arabs, Bedouin and Druze (in percentages)

Year	Jews	Arabs	Bedouin	Druze
1990	19	48	71	49
1991	22	43	74	51
1992	22	44	72	44
1993	21	45	71	39
1994	17	44	68	39
1995	16	43	67	35
1996	11	43	59	29
1997	12	42	57	31
1998	16	33	50	24
1999	14	27	43	16
2000	10	29	37	20
2001	12	34	37	20
2002	15	26	40	19
2003	7	25	36	15
2004	4	17	31	19
2005	1	21	28	17

Source: Israeli Ministry of Education, Culture and Sport. May 2006

CONCLUSIONS AND RECOMMENDATIONS

Thirty years ago, this investigator noted that,

> education plays a key role in...mediating between the basic character of the society and the current processes of adaptation. Although the provision of schools and services has grown rapidly to meet this challenge, there is an urgent need for short- and long-range educational planning. This planning should be in consultation with Bedouin leaders and educators in order to bring about many needed changes and refinements to provide education that is effective and relevant for Bedouin children (Bernstein-Tarrow, 1978, p. 147).

In considering what has improved since 1977, Ben-David (2009), a well-known and early Israeli investigator of Bedouin society, points out that the last two governments have begun taking steps to solve the problems with unprecedented determination and allocation of the necessary funds. A Ministerial Committee for the Advancement of Bedouin Affairs has been set up with a budget of billions of NIS (New Israeli Shekel) for implementation of new programmes. Ben-David (2009) claims that within a single generation, the Bedouin of Israel have reduced illiteracy from 95 per cent to 25 per cent; those still illiterate are aged 55 and above.

In response to the question, "What do you see as 'improvements' since my research here in 1977?", one Bedouin educational leader replied,

> A lot has improved. Now at Soroka hospital we have some of the best doctors (Bedouin) who studied in Romania, Jordan, and Germany...At Ben Gurion University, we have four Bedouin Department heads—Social Work, Education, Middle East, Studies and Computer Science. Two girls from Rahat are studying medicine (in Beersheva). Three girls are studying abroad...We have twenty one schools—thirteen elementary, three intermediate, four high schools, one special education school, and one technological school (Director of Education, Municipality of Rahat, personal communication, May 16, 2007).

Another educational administrator said,

> Improvements? Students have more school hours. More students are getting to Bagrut. More students are in colleges of technology, of education, and at university. Many more girls are studying. (Originally they didn't arrive in these centres.) Teachers used to be mostly from the north. Now about 50–60 per cent are from here. They are well-prepared (school principal, personal communication, May 16, 2007).

Yet, when questioned about where their children were enrolled in school, it became clear that quite a few of these educational leaders of the Bedouin community have themselves studied outside the Bedouin community and/or have placed their children in Jewish schools.

> It pains me very much and is a big problem for me but I have to choose between a really backward education if I send them to traditional Bedouin schools or if I prepare them for life in the present century, hoping they will

keep their traditions. The Bedouin schools are not bad because the children are poor pupils or the teachers are not good but due to the interest or lack of interest of the parents (as compared to the Jewish sector). The home, which should be the FIRST school, does not exist as a school and doesn't put an emphasis on education. This is also related to the socio-economic situation. I have one son who is a master in judo. He would not have been able to develop this talent in a Bedouin school. Another son has advanced work in mathematics. So I have to send them to the better schools and extra programs and, as a father try to keep them in the framework of their tradition (High School Principal, personal communication, May 20, 2007).

Responses to the question, "What are your priorities for improvements you would like to see in the immediate future?" The most frequent responses of interviewees were the following, with items also identified in the 1977 study marked with *:

- *More involvement of Bedouin in developing policy and programs;
- *Better classrooms;
- Smaller classes;
- Smaller schools;
- * Curriculum more relevant to Arab and Bedouin culture;
- Curriculum expanded to learn more about the world;
- * Less frontal and more activity-based teaching/learning;
- More resources for special projects;
- Computers;
- School libraries;
- * Provision for special education;
- Language development – reading & writing in Arabic to succeed in all subjects;
- * Sports facilities;
- * Better teacher preparation;
- Training for teachers who teach in areas other than their specialization;
- Training for teachers for activity-based group learning;
- * Supervisors to work with the teachers;
- * Improved access to higher education (modification of entrance exams);
- Separate sex high schools as an option;
- * Parent education and involvement;
- * Courses in cooking to involve parents and to provide school lunches;
- Business/job training;
- Better economic situation for families; and
- Improved infrastructure of the towns.

It must be noted that there certainly has been an increase in the number of classrooms, schools, and students. There has also been an increase in the number of Bedouin teachers, who are familiar with their culture and an increase in attention to that culture in the schools—although educational objectives and curriculum are still heavily weighted with irrelevant Israeli-Judaic material, and are sorely in need of revision to reflect the culture and narrative of Bedouin society.

As the Department of Bedouin Affairs within the Ministry of Education grapples with the problems of educating the burgeoning number of Bedouin children, this investigator recommends prioritizing parent education and involvement of Bedouin educators and parents in developing policy and practice for their schools. School attendance (and the corollary absenteeism), the dropout phenomenon, and the continuation of girls from primary to secondary and higher education are all related to parent recognition of the importance of education for the future betterment of the lives of their children and for the society as a whole. Also critical on the part of the Ministry is better teacher preparation and continued in-service education, including mentoring and constructive supervision as well as greater equity in allocation of resources. And certainly attention must be paid to equalizing resources allocated to the Arab and Arab/Bedouin sectors of Israeli society.[1]

Finally, one must recognize that Israel, surrounded by hostile neighbors has, in its 60 years of existence, expended enormous resources on its defense and survival as well as absorption of immigrants requiring a multiplicity of social services. Currently it faces internal conflicts over the occupation, the creation of a Palestinian State and between its religious and secular sectors—all of which also have fiscal ramifications. Its self-definition as a democratic Jewish state, however, requires recognizing its multicultural composition and providing equitable treatment of all its minorities.

In terms of the Bedouin, Israel continues to struggle with demographic, geographic and political factors in providing education for a sector of its society that is spread over a wide geographic area, and that doubles its population every 13–15 years. Yet, education is a basic human right, and as such, it should be entirely separate from politics. Access to adequate schools, teachers and resources is the right of all citizens and should not be employed as a weapon to carry out a political agenda and enforce acquiescence to land acquisition policies.[2]

Thirty years ago, there was concern that forced urbanization constituted a danger to Bedouin tradition. From the hindsight of 30 years, one would have to conclude that there is less danger of the Bedouin succumbing to government efforts to assimilate them into a totally western, urban lifestyle and more danger of an eruption of a formerly loyal minority into active revolt against systemic discrimination in school and society.

NOTES

[1]. It is important to note that on November 23, 2008, the Israel Supreme Court unanimously criticized the Education Ministry for delaying implementation of High Court of Justice ruling to cease current practices in budget allocation that discriminate against Arab locales. The Ministry was ordered to fully implement budget allocation practices, within nine months, that conform to the principle of equality for communities defined as being in need of bolstered educational infrastructure.

[2] On December 11, 2008, a significant recommendation was submitted to the Housing Minister by a special committee overseen by a former Chief Justice of the Supreme Court. It calls for formal recognition of illegally constructed Bedouin villages in the Negev; allowing villages that do not gain

formal recognition to move to alternate sites; compensating some Bedouin monetarily or with land; and establishing a committee to formally recognize illegally constructed buildings in Bedouin villages (which have been subject to destruction by government authorities). This would hasten connection to water and sewage systems and provision of social services.

REFERENCES

Abu-Rabi'a, A. (1987). *Education development among Bedouin tribes of the Negev Desert*, ERIC # ED339560.

Abu-Rabi'a, A. (1994). The Bedouin refugees in the Negev. *Refuge, 14*(6), 15–17.

Abu-Rabi'a, A. (2001). *Bedouin century: Education and development among the Negev tribes in the twentieth century.* Oxford: Berghahn Books.

Abu-Rabi'a, A. (2002). Displacement, forced settlement and conservation. In D. Chatty & M. Colchester (Eds.), *Conservation and mobile Indigenous peoples: Displacement, forced settlement, and sustainable development* (pp. 202–211). New York: Berghahn Books.

Abu-Rabiyya, al-Athauna, S. F., & al-Bador, S. (1996). *Survey of Bedouin schools in the Negev.* Tel Aviv: ADVA Center.

Abu-Saad, I. (1991). Towards an understanding of minority education in Israel: The case of the Bedouin Arabs of the Negev. *Comparative Education, 27*(2), 235–242.

Abu-Saad, I. (1995). Bedouin Arab education in the context of radical social change: What is the future? *Compare, 25*(2), 149–160.

Abu-Saad, I. (1996). Provision of public educational services and access to higher education among the Negev Bedouin Arabs in Israel. *Journal of Education Policy, 11*(5), 527–541.

Abu-Saad, I. (1997). The education of Israel's Negev Bedouin: Background and prospects. *Israel Studies, 2*(2), 21–39.

Abu-Saad, I. (2001). Education as a tool for control vs. development among indigenous peoples: The case of Bedouin Arabs in Israel. *Hagar; International Social Science Review, 2*(2), 241–259.

Abu-Saad, I. (2004). Separate and unequal: The role of the state education system in maintaining the subordination of Israel's Palestinian Arab citizens. *Social Identities, 10*(1), 101–127.

Abu-Saad, I. (2005). Education and identity formation among indigenous Palestinian Arab youth in Israel. In S. Champagne & I. Abu-Saad (Eds.), *Indigenous and minority education: International perspectives on empowerment* (pp. 235–256). Beer-Sheva, Israel: Negev Center for Regional Development, Ben-Gurion University of the Negev.

Abu-Saad, I. (2006a). Palestinian education in Israel: the legacy of the military government. *Holy Land Studies, 5*(1), 21–56.

Abu-Saad, I. (2006b). Bedouin Arabs in Israel: Education, political control and social change. In C. Dyer (Ed.), *Education of nomadic peoples: Current issues, future prospects* (pp. 141–158). New York: Berghahn Books.

Ben-David, Y. (2009). *The Bedouin in Israel.* Retrieved May 23, 2007, from http://www.jewishvirtual library.org/jsource/Society_&_Culture/Bedouin.html

Bernstein-Tarrow, N. (1978). Education of the Bedouin of the Negev in the context of radical socio-economic change. *Compare, 8*(2), 141–147.

Bernstein-Tarrow, N. (1980). The education of Arab children under Israeli administration. *Canadian and International Education, 9*(1), 81–94.

Brous, D. (2005). The uprooting: Education void of indigenous "location-specific" knowledge among Negev Bedouin Arabs in southern Israel. In S. Champagne & I. Abu-Saad (Eds.), *Indigenous and minority education: International perspectives on empowerment* (pp. 257–265). Beer-Sheva, Israel: Negev Center for Regional Development, Ben-Gurion University of the Negev.

Coursen-Neff, Z. (2004). Discrimination against Palestinian Arab children in the Israeli educational system. *New York University Journal of International Law and Politics, 36*(4), 749–815.

Falah, G. (1989). Israeli state policy toward Bedouin sedentarization in the Negev. *Journal of Palestine Studies, 18*(2), 71–91.

Givati-Teerling, J. (2007, February). *Negev Bedouin and higher education: At the crossroads of a community in transition.* Sussex Migration Working Paper No. 41. Sussex, UK: University of Sussex Centre for Migration Research.

Israeli Ministry of Education, Culture and Sport. (2006, May).

Swirski, S., & Hasson, Y. (2006). *Invisible citizens: Israel Government policy toward the Negev Bedouin.* Beer Sheva, Israel: Adva Center, Center for Bedouin Studies & Development Research Unit, Negev Center for Regional Development, Ben Gurion Universiy of the Negev.

Norma Tarrow
California State University, Long Beach

RUPERT MACLEAN AND JOHN FIEN

11. EDUCATION FOR SUSTAINABLE DEVELOPMENT

Lessons from the Private Sector[1]

INTRODUCTION

Professor David Wilson worked closely with the United Nations Educational, Scientific and Cultural Organization (UNESCO), and in particular the UNESCO-UNEVOC International Centre for Technical and Vocational Education and Training (UNESCO-UNEVOC) in Bonn, Germany, on numerous occasions as a valued consultant who provided assistance concerning the promotion of best and innovative practices regarding skills development for employability. David had a special interest in the area of Technical and Vocational Education and Training (TVET) and its contribution to sustainable social and economic development, and in the role of private-public partnerships and the business sector in strengthening and upgrading skills development for employability.

UNESCO is not a development agency that funds anti-poverty projects. That is the role of bodies such as the United Nations Development Programme (UNDP). Rather, like the World Health Organization (WHO) and the International Labour Organization (ILO), UNESCO is a standards-setting organization and a catalyst to innovation for sustainable human development. UNESCO works primarily through establishing collaborative relationships between countries and by catalysing partnerships with governments, civil society groups and the private sector. David Wilson was a strong believer in the UNESCO approach to partnership building as evidenced by his many contributions not just to UNESCO but also through his significant international leadership in comparative education and TVET. He was also very conscious of the many intellectual, commercial, ethical and practical challenges faced in building partnerships, especially with the private sector. He recognised that there can be fundamental tensions between the unfettered drive for profit maximization of many businesses and the public good goals of education and sustainable development. He also recognised that without the reorientation of business and industry towards sustainable pathways to the future, there would be little likelihood of the Millennium Development Goals (MDGs) being achieved. Indeed, when it comes to reorienting the forms of economic development and finding appropriate education and training approaches to support them, he recognised that business and industry can contribute many of the concepts and tools we need to meet these challenges.

As a tribute to David Wilson and in recognition of his commitment to partnership building, this chapter stresses the importance of the private sector in supporting education, training and capacity building for sustainable development.

V. Masemann et al., (Eds.), A Tribute to David N. Wilson: Clamouring for a Better World, 163–175.

WORK AND THE MILLENNIUM DEVELOPMENT GOALS

The world of work—those who create employment opportunities, the employees and workers themselves, and the educators and trainers who provide the skills needed for employability—is central to achieving sustainable development. At its base level, achieving sustainable development means achieving the Millennium Development Goals adopted by 189 countries at the special September 2000 session of the General Assembly of the United Nations (UN). Skilled workers are central to achieving all the eight goals and associated targets in the MDGs (Box 1).

Box 1: The Millennium Development Goals

Goal 1: Eradicate extreme poverty and hunger

Target 1A: Halve, between 1990 and 2015, the proportion of people whose income is less than one dollar a day

Target 1B: Achieve full and productive employment and decent work for all, including women and young people

Target 1C: Halve, between 1990 and 2015, the proportion of people who suffer from hunger

Goal 2: Achieve universal primary education

Target 2A: Ensure that, by 2015, children everywhere, boys and girls alike, will be able to complete a full course of primary schooling

Goal 3: Promote gender equality and empower women

Target 3A: Eliminate gender disparity in primary and secondary education, preferably by 2005, and to all levels of education no later than 2015

Goal 4: Reduce child mortality

Target 4A: Reduce by two-thirds, between 1990 and 2015, the under-five mortality rate

Goal 5: Improve maternal health

Target 5A: Reduce by three-quarters, between 1990 and 2015, the maternal mortality ratio

Goal 6: Combat HIV/AIDS, malaria and other diseases

Target 6A: Have halted by 2015 and begun to reverse the spread of HIV/AIDS

Target 6B: Achieve, by 2010, universal access to treatment for HIV/AIDS for all those who need it

Target 6C: Have halted by 2015 and begun to reverse the incidence of malaria and other major diseases

Goal 7: Ensure environmental sustainability

Target 7A: Integrate the principles of sustainable development into country policies and programmes and reverse the loss of environmental resources

Target 7B: Reduce biodiversity loss, achieving, by 2010, a significant reduction in the rate of loss

Target 7C: Halve, by 2015, the proportion of people without sustainable access to safe drinking water

Target 7D: By 2020, to have achieved a significant improvement in the lives of at least 100 million slum dwellers

---

Box 1 (Continued)

Goal 8: Develop a Global Partnership for Development

Target 8A:	Develop further an open, rule-based, predictable, non-discriminatory trading and financial system
Target 8B:	Address the special needs of the least developed countries
Target 8C:	Address the special needs of landlocked countries and small island developing States
Target 8D:	Deal comprehensively with the debt problems of developing countries through national and international measures in order to make debt sustainable in the long term
Target 8E:	In co-operation with developing countries, develop and implement strategies for decent and productive work for youth
Target 8F:	In co-operation with pharmaceutical companies, provide access to affordable, essential drugs in developing countries
Target 8G:	In co-operation with the private sector, make available the benefits of new technologies, especially information and communications

Source: United Nations Development Programme, 2000, accessed 2007

The MDGs include halving extreme poverty and hunger; achieving universal primary education and gender equity; reducing under-five mortality and maternal mortality by two-thirds and three-quarters respectively; reversing the spread of HIV/AIDS; halving the proportion of people without access to safe drinking water; and ensuring environmental sustainability. They also include the goal of developing a global partnership for development, with targets for aid, trade, and debt relief.

As a strategic vision, the MDGs are steps towards a longer-term vision of building human, social, economic and environmental capital, especially in developing countries. Maintaining and building social, economic and environmental capital depends upon human capital—and upon the institutions for TVET that develop work-ready human capital that is the engine for sustainable development over the long run.

Achieving the MDGs necessitates action on issues such as poverty, hunger, education, gender equality, child and maternal mortality, HIV/AIDS, safe water, upgrading slums, and global partnerships for development that include technology transfer. Effective TVET is integral to finding and implementing solutions to all of these issues. In this way, TVET underpins every one of the MDGs and the achievement of sustainable development. It is impossible to think of making gains in poverty reduction, job creation, health or environmental concerns without a focused TVET policy. It is equally true that a well-articulated and focused TVET policy can lead to huge improvements in education, gender equality and living conditions. Much of the improvement in human welfare over the last century is due to technological innovation in the fields of public health, nutrition, and agriculture. These improvements have reduced mortality rates and improved life expectancy. Similarly, improvements in areas such as environmental management will also increasingly rely on the generation and application of new knowledge. In essence, implementing the MDGs will require the development of appropriate forms of Technical and Vocational Education.

A key outcome of the 2002 World Summit on Sustainable Development was the establishment of a special United Nations Decade of Education for Sustainable

Development, from 2005 to 2014, with the primary goal of making sustainable development central to education and training, across all sectors, by refining and promoting the transition to a sustainable future through all forms of education, public awareness and training. UNESCO was designated as the lead UN agency for the Decade and has catalysed key initiatives in all parts of the world.

THE UNESCO-UNEVOC INTERNATIONAL CENTRE

The UNESCO-UNEVOC International Centre for Technical and Vocational Educa-tion and Training is the body responsible for supporting education, training and capacity building for sustainable development in relation to the world of work. The Centre works with UNESCO's 193 member states to strengthen and upgrade their TVET systems. UNEVOC is driven by the following three concerns:
- The acquisition of skills for work, and for citizenship and sustainability, is crucial for economic and social development because 80 per cent of the world's workforce use technical and vocational skills in their work.
- Ideally, TVET should be relevant to the needs of the labour market, be of high quality, and be broadly accessible to all. However, this ideal is not being met in many countries and so UNESCO-UNEVOC gives priority to working with those with the greatest need: developing nations, economies in transition, and those in a post-conflict situations.
- UNESCO-UNEVOC particularly focuses on contributing to overarching UNESCO goals in TVET. These are to assist Member States to improve and integrate TVET as part of the global Education for All (EFA) Campaign, and to assist in the alignment of TVET with the tenets of sustainable development. (www.unevoc. unesco.org)

UNESCO-UNEVOC is also the hub of a world-wide network of over 250 key organizations and institutions specialising in TVET in 166 countries worldwide. UNEVOC Centres act as focal points for the dissemination of ideas and as the key institutions for local, national and regional training on the skills needed for implemen-ting these ideas. Further, through regional and international meetings of UNEVOC Centres, UNESCO learns about the needs and concerns of different countries and convenes meetings to begin the process of developing ideas for responding to them, sharing good practice between and among countries, and working with partners to build capacity where needed.

As an example, the area of health involves the need to train people to work in the environmental health sector which has been identified as a key priority, especially by developing countries. "Health" is chosen here since, when it comes to thinking about sustainable development and the workplace, we can draw lessons from the UNEVOC experience of stimulating education, training and capacity building in the area of health and work. In May 2008, UNESCO-UNEVOC and the World Health Organization (WHO), along with other partners, co-hosted a conference on "Health in the Workplace". A number of very important areas of concern about health in the workplace were identified that are relevant to the focus on sustainable development:
- Clean air (dust, toxic chemicals, cigarette smoking, etc.);

- Clean water;
- Sanitation and personal hygiene practices: adequate toilet facilities; hand-washing etc.;
- HIV/AIDS;
- Disposal of chemicals, garbage etc.;
- Physical dangers: safety clothing;
- Food in workplace canteens;
- Psychological problems (values in the workplace).

The discussions on the potential contributions of the corporate sector focused on
- promoting a healthy workplace;
- supporting staff through health insurance;
- teaching health education in the workplace; and
- teaching health education in the community.

TVET and Sustainable Development

These examples of modalities through which business and industry are promoting worker and community health are examples of sound Corporate Social Responsibility (CSR) policy and practice. There are many other ways in which companies are using education, training and capacity building as modalities for CSR as part of their sustainable development strategy. UNESCO-UNEVOC came to recognize the importance of these activities from one of its early initiatives in promoting the reorientation of TVET towards sustainable development. This was to convene an International Experts' Meeting in 2004 on "Learning for Work, Citizenship and Sustainability" to prepare for the United Nations Decade of Education for Sustainable Development. David Wilson was co-rapporteur of this meeting and a co-author of the Discussion Paper prepared by UNESCO-UNEVOC for the meeting (UNESCO-UNEVOC 2004a). Participants at this meeting recognised the need for new paradigms of both development and learning for the world of work, and declared education and training for and through the workplace to be the "master key that can alleviate poverty, promote peace, conserve the environment, improve the quality of life for all and help achieve sustainable development" (UNESCO-UNEVOC 2004b, p. 1).

The responsibilities of national systems for Technical and Vocational Education and Training in advancing sustainable development through workforce development were discussed at follow-up meetings in Thailand (2005), Bahrain (2005), and Viet Nam (2006). With our partner, InWEnt (Capacity Building International, Germany), UNESCO-UNEVOC is now beginning to engage very closely with the private sector to explore ways education and training for sustainable development can be integrated into training and capacity building endeavours in corporate environmental management and corporate social responsibility. As Michael Hopkins (2007) argues, "improving people's skills in a myriad of ways is undoubtedly the best way to create sustainable development. Education, training, skill development, capacity development are all aspects of the same issue .... There is no substitute" (p. 14).

Similarly, the UNESCO Asia Pacific Programme of Educational Innovation for Development (APEID) (2006) identified that,

> many initiatives undertaken by businesses and their partners in the area of sustainable development can contribute considerably to the area of Education for Sustainable Development. In particular, sustainable business models resulting in the improvement of the quality of local life, sustainable supply chain management, corporate social responsibility (CSR) initiatives and development of local sustainable development initiatives could inform educational practices of business schools, training provided by companies, labour unions, NGOs and other business-related organizations. (p. 1)

In order to draw lessons from the private sector's work in this area, this paper analyses several case studies of the activities of companies with a strong record of engagement in education and training for sustainable development. The case studies were presented by companies and organizations that participated in a UNESCO-UNEVOC meeting in Bonn in May 2007. Participating companies included the following:

- Untouched World Foundation
- DaimlerChrysler
- National Health Service (UK)
- D. Swarovski & Co.
- Wuppertal Institute Collaborating Centre on Sustainable Consumption and Production
- Cap Gemini
- Garment 10 Joint Stock Company
- Newmont Mining Corporation
- Fraunhofer Institute
- Shell
- CISCO Systems
- Vocational Training Institute of the Construction Industry, North Rhine Westphalia
- World Business Council for Sustainable Development

The case studies presented by these companies included activities such as
- providing corporate training programmes for employees;
- establishing training programmes for clients and employees of firms along their supply chains;
- partnering local organizations with NGOs to provide community development and education programmes; and
- assisting schools, TVET institutions, and universities with sustainability related teaching.

The next sections provide examples of these activities as well as examples from other companies that UNESCO is linking with. A range of issues that have emerged from a meta-analysis of these case studies are also discussed, including the motivations, opportunities and drivers underlying private sector involvement in education and training for sustainable development; the corporate and broader sustainability benefits this involvement brings; the barriers faced and ways in which they are addressed; and lessons for other firms to guide their future involvement in education and training for sustainable development. Full details of the case studies and discussions from this meeting may be found on the UNESCO-UNEVOC website (http://www.unevoc.unesco.org).

1. CORPORATE TRAINING PROGRAMMES FOR EMPLOYEES

The training of staff in environmental, social and related responsibilities associated with their tasks and the company's wider operations is the most fundamental of all CSR activities. Sustainability training is also vital to broader industry sustainability.

For example, the construction industry in the North Rhine Westphalia region of Germany comprises over 500 companies. The industry association recognizes the challenges posed by looming energy shortages, climate change and the need for energy efficiency in buildings. It also recognises the business opportunities in responding to the fact that 75 per cent of Germany's building stock was built before 1949, and is therefore highly energy inefficient.

There is a popular German slogan that the country aspires to the "3-litre house", i.e. a house that consumes three litres of oil per cubic metre per year. At the present time, the average German residence is consuming 18 litres of oil per cubic metre per year. As a result, the construction industry has intervened in the curriculum of the Vocational Training Institute of the Construction Industry, North Rhine Westphalia, with a goal of "sustainable development education for every apprentice, trainer, expert and member company". Thus, it is now compulsory for all in the industry to understand
- how to use the right materials to avoid unnecessary energy consumption;
- how to behave and work to minimise energy consumption; and
- how to identify, source and use new, more efficient materials to save energy.

It is a similar case in the Viet Nam textile industry. For example, the Garment 10 Joint Stock Company, Garco10, is a leader in environmental training for its employees. The company employs 7,500 workers across 13 factories in six provinces and has a turnover of US$ 85 million, manufacturing clothing for companies such as Perry Ellis, Columbia, JCPenney, Gap, Van Heusen, Walmart and K-Mart. Recognising the need to integrate into global standards, especially since Vietnam joined the World Trade Organization (WTO), Garco10 has obtained certification for quality and management as well as for environment protection through the International Organization for Standardization (ISO). Garco 10 also received certification from Social Accountability International (SAI), a global standard-setting non-profit human rights organization dedicated to improving workplaces and communities. Training is central to all these; thus Garco10 runs its own training academy for 500 new employees each year, with social and environmental responsibility as part of the core curriculum.

2. CORPORATE TRAINING PROGRAMMES FOR EMPLOYEES OF FIRMS ALONG THEIR SUPPLY CHAINS TO ENSURE THEY HAVE THE CAPACITY TO ACHIEVE CORPORATE SUSTAINABILITY GOALS

A key feature of a globalized economy is outsourced production with many companies now having very complex supply chains. These chains often involve the employment of workers in developing countries where industrial and environmental standards are lower than in a company's home base, but also where opportunities for investment and employment to enhance human development are immense.

Traditional ways of handling issues relating to industrial and environmental standards, e.g. by codes of conduct and factory inspections, are not working well.

Thus, much effort is now being spent into management and employee training with an emphasis on assisting workers to know their own rights, to protect themselves, as well as training in dispute resolution and communications. As the 2006 UNESCO-Asia Pacific Programme of Educational Innovation for Development (APEID) report on the corporate sector and education for sustainable development states, "These types of skills are entirely consistent with the skills required for engaging in the challenges of sustainable development" (p. 24). The transnational textile, clothing and footwear companies operating in China are world leaders in this field. Take the case of Reebok, for example.

Reebok organizes training workshops in its worldwide network of factories on issues such as strengthening compliance with standards for non-discrimination, acceptable working hours, no forced or compulsory labour, fair wages, no child labour, freedom of association, non-harassment, and safe and healthy working environments. Outside experts and Non-Governmental Organizations (NGOs) are commissioned to help worker representatives to understand their rights and to improve their communication and problem solving skills.

Toyota provides an example of training along the supply chain in the more economically developed world in that Toyota collaborates with the Coordinating Committee for Automotive Repair (CCAR) to host a website called CCAR-GreenLink. This website provides their dealers with environmental information and compliance assistance related to requirements for the storage and disposal of their waste steam materials, the way to implement their own waste management programmes and other ways of operating their businesses in an environmentally responsible manner. Additional support is provided through a telephone hotline and newsletters.

3. PARTNERING LOCAL ORGANIZATIONS AND NGOS TO PROVIDE COMMUNITY DEVELOPMENT AND EDUCATION PROGRAMMES

For companies to operate sustainably there is a need for the communities in which their operations are located to appreciate the companies' goals and for the communities to have the skills for sustainable community development. This is not only part of the "licence to operate" but also a way to ensure that employees and their families and communities can obtain maximum benefit from local economic development. The following are three examples of corporate sector involvement in promoting sustainable community development.

Shell is a major stakeholder in the Sakhalin Energy Investment Company (SEIC). Despite its vast oil and gas reserves and the significant economic, social and environmental transformations that the oil and gas industry has brought, Sakhalin is characterised by
- limited understanding and acceptance of the aims and activities of the oil and gas industry, among wide sectors of the public;
- widespread mistrust and suspicion towards "foreign companies";
- limited experience and capacity of key social actors in Sakhalin to effectively address challenges posed by the activities and impacts of the oil and gas industry;
- very limited knowledge about (or experience of) sustainable development;

- very limited tradition of civil society participation in decision-making on development issues; and
- very limited experience of government consultation on development issues.

Shell engaged the United Kingdom (UK) NGO, Living Earth Foundation (LEF) to assist with such issues. LEF carried out public initial introductory presentations to mixed audiences of local and regional government officials, academics, local entrepreneurs, students, and representatives of the oil and gas industry. These activities centred on basic concepts and principles of sustainable development. In parallel, LEF started engaging staff at Sakhalin State University (SSU) to work together to promote sustainable development on Sakhalin Island, in the Russian Far East. In 2005–2006, LEF and SSU implemented an initial education for sustainable development (ESD) project with 24 local and regional government officials of Sakhalin. The course included the following activities:

- Teaching practical skills for multi-stakeholder dialogue, negotiation and consensus-building;
- Practical exercises and field trips to explore stakeholders' concerns and to promote consultation and shared reflection in decision-making processes;
- A learning visit to the UK by key Sakhalin stakeholders to share experiences with different stakeholder groups associated with the impacts of the oil and gas industry in the North Sea during the past 35 years or so;
- Small pilot-projects to enable different stakeholder groups (among which there is little experience of cooperation) to learn to work together to design, implement and monitor modest local projects based on multi-stakeholder consensus and joint responsibility.

The following three case studies provide examples of corporate engagement in sustainable community development projects in Indonesia, Cambodia, South Africa and Turkey.

Adaro Indonesia's mining and port activities in South Kalimantan are supported by a community education and development programme that includes equipping schools and hospitals, staff training, and scholarships for high school, agricultural college and university study. Adaro also provides training and loans to support the establishment of farming and plantation activities, aquaculture, automotive and light engineering and local cooperatives. These are supported by a procurement policy optimizing the use of local goods and services, thus ensuring market viability in the initial phases of development.

In Cambodia, the Swedish clothing company H & M organizes a HIV/AIDS Awareness and Prevention Program. Activities include health promotion sessions, and training of 300 peer educators providing education to 3000 factory employees on the issues of HIV/AIDS and reproductive health.

BSH Bosch und Siemens Hausgeräte GmbH (BSH) is a German corporate group operating worldwide which manufactures home appliances. In South Africa, BSH supports the Buskaid Soweto String Project that provides musical training for students in classical music forms as well as their own composition and interpretations of traditional and modern African forms. In Turkey, the firm has developed a highly trained rescue team to assist community organizations develop skills in managing disasters and providing assistance to victims. Fire fighters at the BSH Fire Department also hold training sessions for schools to raise public awareness of fire prevention techniques to improve safety at school and at home.

4. ASSISTING SCHOOLS, TVET INSTITUTIONS AND UNIVERSITIES WITH SUSTAINABILITY RELATED TEACHING

Many companies have been assisting schools, TVET institutions and universities with sustainability related teaching for a long time. The following are three examples directly related to education, training and capacity building for sustainable development in and through corporate assistance to the formal education sector.

Newmont Mining Corporation has Indigenous programmes in remote areas of Australia that are based upon a sustainable and effective Indigenous training and employment strategy. Newmont has developed a comprehensive programme of pre-vocational and mine access training, guaranteeing successful graduates a job with Newmont upon completion. These are based upon key principles which include development of a culturally appropriate literacy and numeracy assessment tool; engagement of land councils and Traditional Owners in participant selection and programme evaluation; and, participant, supervisor, and post-graduate mentoring to ensure strong retention rates. The programme also involved Cross Cultural Awareness training to assist in providing a culturally safe work environment for Indigenous employees with the objective of creating a culturally competent and culturally safe work place. As well as providing direct employment in the company (or through its contractors), Newmont supports local Indigenous business enterprises through partnerships that deliver sustainable benefits to local communities.

BP's initiatives in the formal education sector range from projects to help schoolchildren learn about the environment in the UK, the United States and China to high-level academic work in Russia and China. BP's signature programme in California and Texas, A+ for Energy, provides $2.5 million in grants and training for teachers for the enhancement of energy education and has reached more than 3,000 teachers. In China, the Environmental Educators' Initiative (EEI)—a partnership between the Chinese Ministry of Education, the World Wide Fund for Nature (WWF) and BP—is embedding environmental education in China's national school curriculum through teacher training, pilot schools that test new materials and approaches, and 21 environmental education centres at teacher training universities. In June 2005, a 10-year, $16-million commitment was made to the BP Energy and Environmental Programme to provide education and training to emerging leaders in the fields of conservation and development.

In Hong Kong, HK Electric Holdings Ltd. runs "Education Tours on Renewable Energy" for students in Hong Kong in partnership with the Education and Manpower Bureau of the Hong Kong SAR Government under the "School-Business Partnership Programme". HK Electric is one of more than 130 companies delivering education on environment and sustainable development in this programme. Through visits to the company's wind station and exhibition centre on the Lamma Island of Hong Kong, engineers of the company educate secondary school students on the operation of windmills as well as the wider use of renewable energy.

LESSONS FROM THE CASE STUDIES

At the UNESCO-UNEVOC conference in May 2007, after the corporate represent-atives presented their case studies, they were asked to participate in a meta-analysis of their experiences in order to identify any patterns and recurring issues. This section presents a summary of their discussions.

Interpretations of Sustainability

It was noted across the case studies that a variety of interpretations of the term "sustainability" was being used. There were limited examples of integrating social, economic, environmental and cultural perspectives within each case study, with most commonly focusing upon the environment. The participants believed that the lack of a common understanding of terms, principles, underlying concepts and visions for the future within a company can be a major impediment to both its corporate social responsibility and its education and training activities.

Corporate Sector Motivations

Across the cases there was a range of reasons why the corporate sector was engaged in various education activities associated with sustainability. The case studies identified five major categories.

The first reason identifies business opportunities that create a market by capturing future consumers through innovative marketing using an indirect link to sustainability. Several case studies showed that business also became involved because of direct cost savings.

The second reason concerned promoting a brand and identifying the brand as a good corporate citizen through a link to sustainability, thus impacting on positive customer relationships.

A third reason placed a high value on staff professional development and protection of talent to promote employee retention and attraction and ensure a future talent pipeline.

The fourth reason identified specific political motivations, costs and damage control associated with the concept of business standing on a burning platform.

The fifth reason was the impact of the enlightened or aware business leaders who are passionately committed to bringing about change for sustainability because they understand the importance of a healthy planet to achieve broad business outcomes. They promote the concept of education for the planet, for people and for the economy. Furthermore, they recognise that knowledge, skills and key competencies associated with sustainability are an essential element of education for the future.

Barriers

Several potential barriers were identified that limited corporate sector engagement in Education for Sustainable Development (ESD). The availability of resources such as funding, time and expertise were viewed as critical factors. While funding and time were business issues, the lack of expertise was viewed as a potential business and education sector problem. Commitment from senior management was considered in many cases as essential for in-depth engagement.

A lack of understanding about the full benefits and drivers for corporate sector engagement in ESD was viewed as the main issue. Learning to work in collaborative partnerships and working with people with different perspectives, needs and end goals or outcomes was viewed as a limiting factor, especially in developing a common language across cultural difference, use of terminology and differing contextual backgrounds. Thus knowledge and understanding about ESD and the differing perspectives and values placed on the economic, social and environmental aspects of ESD caused confusion.

There was also the perception that many business managers may lack the knowledge and understanding of how to start to engage in ESD, how to start partnerships and how to access the knowledge to navigate the management change process. Thus, a key competency/skill for future managers is the ability to change as things around them change. In other words they remain capable as things around them become more complex.

Conflicting interests between the economic, social and environmental agendas were considered a major limitation. Conservative views towards sustainability and education for sustainable development were viewed as contributing towards a lack of understanding around the broader objectives of ESD. They often led to cynical perspectives and "green-washing" to appease or show that "something" was being done to contribute towards sustainability.

Addressing the Barriers

The first solution suggested by participants was to develop a strong business case for increasing corporate sector engagement in education for sustainable development. This involves identifying the drivers, benefits and potential outcomes to increase motivation and capacity for business. Second, it was suggested that consideration needs to be given to packaging key benefits and outcomes (production of the bottom line) to boards and management. Greater access to knowledge and understanding was required to provide a frame of reference for engagement in sustainability and ESD.

As a consequence the participants believed that increased access to mentors, organizational expertise, potential partners, NGOs and the World Sustainable Business Council for sustainable Development were critical to identifying and sharing positive models of engagement and examples of good practice to help overcome cynical perspectives and avoid potential conflicts within business and between business and wider community interests.

CONCLUSION

The case studies discussed here show that we are living in exciting times. The "challenge of sustainability" brings an urgency that cannot be ignored.

We would like to conclude with a short quotation from the American educator, David Orr, who said,

The crisis of sustainability, the fit between humanity and its habitat, is manifest in varying ways and degrees everywhere on earth. It is not only a permanent feature on the public agenda; for all practical purposes it is the agenda. No other issue of politics, economics and public policy will remain unaffected by the crisis of resources, population, climate change, species extinction, acid rain, deforestation, ozone depletion, and soil loss. Sustainability is about the terms and conditions of human survival, and yet we still educate at all levels as if no such crisis existed. The content of our curriculum and the process of education, with a few notable exceptions, has not changed....Those presuming to lead—whether it be in government, business or education—simply cannot stand aloof from the decisions about how and whether life will be lived in the twenty-first century. To do so would be to miss the Mount Everest of issues on the historical topography of our age. (Orr, 1992, p. 83, p. 145)

Let us go forward and climb Mount Everest together!

NOTES

[1] Speech presented at the 12th International Business Forum 2007 held at the InWEnt and the World Bank Institute, World Bank, Washington, DC, 8–10 October, 2007.

REFERENCES

Hopkins, M. (2007). *Corporate social responsibility and international development: Is business the solution?* London: Earthscan Publications Ltd.

Orr, D. (1992). *Ecological literacy: Education and the transition to a postmodern world.* Albany, NY: State University of New York Press.

United Nations Educational, Scientific and Cultural Organization-UNEVOC. (2004a). *Orienting technical and vocational education and training (TVET) for sustainable development.* Discussion paper presented at the International Experts Meeting on Learning for Work, Citizenship and Sustainability, Bonn, Germany.

United Nations Educational, Scientific and Cultural Organization-UNEVOC. (2004b). *The Bonn declaration.* Bonn, Germany: UNESCO-UNEVOC.

United Nations Educational, Scientific and Cultural Organization (UNESCO)-Asia-Pacific Programme of Educational Innovation for Development (APEID). (2006). *Education for sustainable development: Private sector engagement.* Bangkok: UNESCO-APEID.

United Nations. (2000). *Millennium declaration.* Retrieved September 5, 2007, from http://unstats.un.org/unsd/mi/pdf/MDG%20Book.pdf

Rupert Maclean
Director of the Centre for Lifelong Learning Research and Development
Chair Professor of International Education
Hong Kong Institute of Education

John Fien
Professor of Sustainability
Royal Melbourne Institute of Technology (RMIT) University

MELISSA WHITE

12. POLICY AND PRACTICE

Retraining Initiatives for Displaced Workers
in Economically Depressed Areas

PREFACE

This chapter draws primarily from my doctoral dissertation, which I completed at the Ontario Institute for Studies in Education (OISE) of the University of Toronto (White, 2004). The focus of my research was training in the context of changing economies. During my time at OISE, Professor David Wilson wrote on a variety of areas relating to training with his later works focusing on training and the new or knowledge economy. He was interested in the preparation of workers for participation in the new economy and the international standardization of the skills and knowledge required for this new economy. David's work contributed to my understanding of both the theoretical analyses and the practical implications of the changing nature of work, which was an integral part of the dissertation.

INTRODUCTION

Education and training are often viewed as the solutions for many social and economic problems. In recent years, with an increasingly globalized economy, education and training are seen, perhaps second only to liberalized markets, as the key to winning entry into and succeeding within the globalized economy. Education and training are put forth not only as the cure for social ills and the ticket to participation in the international market place, but as the panacea for chronic unemployment. The underlying assumption is that an educated and trained population, in and of itself, will lead to economic development and participation in the global marketplace.

This chapter presents one of two case studies undertaken to investigate government programs intended to address needs arising in communities affected by industrial decline. This chapter draws on a case study of The Atlantic Groundfish Strategy (TAGS) introduced in 1995 by the Canadian government following a moratorium on the Northern Cod fishery, which effectively closed the industry. The Program was intended to restructure the industry, support economic development in the region and provide re-training for those displaced by the closure. Interviews for this research were conducted with participants involved in the development and implementation of the Program at both national and local levels. Government documents relevant to the TAGS program were also analyzed. Participants cited in this chapter have been assigned pseudonyms.

V. Masemann et al., (Eds.), A Tribute to David N. Wilson: Clamouring for a Better World, 177–189.

This chapter begins with an overview of the literature on education and training, changing economies and regionalism in Canada. This will provide for an understanding of the context within which this Program was developed and implemented. In drawing together the economic and political contexts of the problem in addition to the role of education and training, this chapter illustrates the need for a multi-faceted approach to the complex problem of economic (re)development.

EDUCATION AND TRAINING

The extent to which education and training are seen as the key to successful economic development and participation in the global economy is amply evident in the documentation of many national and sub-national levels of government and international organizations and the scholarly literature. Discussions of the "knowledge" and "new" economy are replete with references to training and education as the key to participation in the global economy. A Human Resources Development Canada (HRDC)[1] report from 2002 states, "Countries that succeed in the 21st century will be those with citizens who are creative, adaptable and skilled" (p. 5). The belief in the relationship between education, training and economic development is pervasive. "In some cases, this link is conceived in quite simple terms: conventional wisdom has emerged, wherein 'better' education or training is assumed to lead automatically to improved economic performance" (Ashton & Green, 1996, p. 11). Albo (1998) notes the belief that "the creation of a supply of skilled labour will lead to the effective demand for the commodities produced, and ultimately, to good jobs and full employment for all" (p. 113). He continues,

> The acquisition of appropriate skills by workers is conventionally put forth by government departments and business associations as a simple proposition; that individuals improving their skill attributes will better their prospect of being hired in the labour market. (Albo, 1998, p. 200)

The assumption underlying training policy and provision is that an educated and trained population, in and of itself, will lead to economic development. This assumption is widely held and evidenced by the profusion of research and studies undertaken on human capital investment over the past 40 years. Though there have been many significant critiques of human capital theory—that it ignores the role of social structures in economic growth and is difficult to quantitatively measure[2]— the emphasis placed on education and training as the key to economic development illustrates the continuing popularity of this theory, especially among policy makers.

RE-TRAINING

The re-training of displaced workers is a common governmental response to industrial decline, increased unemployment and community depopulation. The goal of government retraining programs is to enable displaced workers to obtain skills and knowledge that will facilitate their transition into new employment. These initiatives have met with varying levels of success. While traditional re-training programs may meet the needs of the unemployed in general, anecdotal evidence shows they can often be insufficient in meeting the training needs of workers displaced by industry-wide closures. Unemployed individuals with existing and transferable skills may benefit from the kinds of skill-upgrading and job search assistance schemes traditionally offered through government programs. The needs of workers permanently displaced by industry closure, however, differ significantly. It is not uncommon for workers displaced by industrial closure to have low levels of education. This is particularly so in the case of resource extraction industries, like fishing, where high levels of education are often not necessary for the vast majority of jobs these industries provide. These workers often have a skill set that is not easily transferable to other employment and industries. Workers of certain trades in these industries may have skills that would be applicable to other industries if they have the opportunity to up-grade these skills to recognized industry standards. Obtaining industry-recognized qualifications can be a time-consuming and expensive venture. Without industry recognized qualifications, these workers are unlikely to find employment. Many more displaced workers, however, require comprehensive re-training from basic numeracy and literacy to the acquisition of skills.

The more significant problem is the lack of alternative employment opportunities in many regions affected by industrial decline. In such areas, there is little chance for re-employment, not because of a lack of training opportunities but because of a lack of employment opportunities. "Training for what?" is an often-asked question in these regions. If displaced workers are to find alternative employment, economic development and job creation must occur in concert with re-training initiatives. Therefore, training policies must aim "to create mechanisms which encourage the establishment of a long-term approach to planning and development, underpinned by institutional stability (Rainbird, 1992, p. 7).

A reliance on re-training and a skilled populace may not be enough to generate economic development. Atlantic Canada is a good example. For decades, various Atlantic Canadian industries have been in decline. Steel manufacture, mining and fishing have all been affected. The Canadian government has instituted re-training programs in the hope of ameliorating the problem. However, unemployment rates remain high in areas of Atlantic Canada, and many regions remain economically underdeveloped. The International Labour Organization (ILO) World Labour Report (1995), "Learning to start afresh: The challenge of re-training", states, "Retraining is not a panacea for the problems of structural adjustment" (p. 1). Just as education is seen as a panacea for social problems, so re-training is seen as a panacea for structural adjustment problems. In both instances, it is not enough.

Very little research on re-training in relation to policy has been undertaken, with the exceptions of Lauzon (1995), Addison (1991), Leigh (1989), for example. The research that exists is, to a large extent, focused on the analysis of statistics associated with worker displacement such as wage levels, re-employment percentages, earning loss, etc., and on labour market issues. In the realm of policy, this work provides prescriptive policy solutions or options with little attention to analysis of what influences actual policy decisions.

A good deal of the literature on training and re-training is concerned with re-training programs in and of themselves and the implications of both displacement and re-training for the worker, their families and, to some extent, their communities. For example, Zippay (1991) reports on the re-training experiences of displaced workers in Pennsylvania. Her research discusses barriers that displaced workers face in pursuing re-training such as low levels of education and lack of personal assets to support re-training as well as variables that encouraged displaced workers to pursue re-training such as spousal income. She found that workers who made successful transitions from displacement through re-training and re-employment generally had higher levels of education initially than did workers who were less successful. She discusses worker relocation experiences with regard to both their success in finding employment following relocation and the reasons some chose not to relocate.

Research on training also focuses on outcomes and rates of return for training (see Baran, Bérubé, Roy, & Salmon, 2000). This approach is relevant for issues discussed in this chapter only insofar as it influences decisions to invest in training, particularly at the national level. Research on training does not, however, provide for an understanding of or a rationale for the continued emphasis on training—human capital investment—even with evidence, in some instances, of low rates of return for the individual and the state.

CHANGING ECONOMIES

Widespread worker displacement is an increasing phenomenon in many Western, industrialized countries. While industrial sectors often experience periods of growth and decline, the difference today is that many sectors are not recovering as they did in the past. Where workers once experienced temporary unemployment in times of decline and could expect to be re-hired for the same job or within the same industry, this is no longer the case in many regions. Whether as a result of globalization, increased competition, improved technology or resource depletion, large numbers of workers are being permanently displaced from work.

Lauzon (1995) writes that one of the central issues in discussing the situation of displaced workers is defining what is meant by displacement. Writing about displacement in the context of the United States, he notes that researchers studying the issue since the 1982 recession have developed a more definitive definition limiting displacement to workers who have suffered job loss through "structural decline and whose re-employment opportunities were minimal without some form of public intervention" (p. 8). Further, this definition refers to workers displaced from "locally declining industries" (Lauzon 1995, p. 8). For the purposes of this chapter, *permanently displaced workers* refers to workers "who have lost their jobs through no fault of their own *and who are likely to encounter considerable difficulty finding comparable employment*" (Browne cited in Lauzon, 1995, p. 8; emphasis in Lauzon).

The problem of widespread worker displacement is compounded in regions and communities where the employment and economic base is centred on a single industry. In many mono-industrial communities, there is little chance of re-employment. Single-industry closures are often followed by the closure of local businesses indirectly dependent on the industry for survival. Employment opportunities outside of the industry decline as a result, leaving little alternative employment for displaced workers. Economic diversity is not generally a feature of these communities. The existence of the industry often meant there was little need for economic diversity as the industry provided sufficient employment for the population. The lack of economic diversity and poorly developed economic structures leaves little on which to build.

In addition to problems associated with an undiversified economy, many single industry communities, particularly those dependent on natural resources, are geographically isolated. Geographic isolation presents several problems. Distance from larger employment centres means displaced workers may have to choose between commuting and relocating. Both financial and family commitments can make relocating a difficult choice for many. Geographic isolation can also be a significant barrier for economic development in these communities. The distance from major economic centres and the costs associated with that distance, particularly transportation, may prohibit new investment and the development of new businesses and industry. Thus, for many communities, dependence on a single industry, an undiversified economic base and geographic isolation further complicate the problem and add to the complexity necessary in addressing the need facing these communities.

As greater numbers of workers face displacement, the nature of work itself is changing. Many writers and theorists claim that the age of industry is in decline. (See, for example, Krahn & Lowe, 1998; Russell, 1999.) They suggest that industrialized countries have entered a period of post-industrialization and that this has a dramatic impact on the ways in which we work. Traditional "Fordist" ways of working, understood to be primarily assembly line production, are passing; and new, more flexible methods of working are on the rise. This new way of organizing society and work, according to Russell (1999), requires "nothing less than a total revision of our notions of welfare, citizenship, rights and social wages" (p. 18).

Industrial countries worldwide have seen their manufacturing, resource extraction and heavy industries decline. In particular, the traditional economic bases of steel and auto manufacturing, fishing, mining and farming have been affected by changing consumer demand and technological change as well as organizational and economic restructuring. With regards to the changing nature of work in Canada, Krahn and Lowe (1998) note that, "Industrial restructuring involves interrelated social, economic and technological trends. The shift from manufacturing to services is crucial. Canada's service industries have rapidly grown in recent decades compared with declining employment in agriculture, resource and manufacturing industries" (p. 26). Krahn and Lowe (1998) call this phenomenon de-industrialization, which they define as "declining employment due to factory closures or relocation, typically in once-prominent manufacturing industries" (p. 26).

The decline of manufacturing, resource extraction and heavy industries, the rise of service and technology-based industries and the advent of the new and knowledge economy have changed the nature of work. Vickerstaff (1992) suggests we will no longer have the same job for the duration of our working life. "The emphasis then will be on re-training, flexibility, multi-skilling, the ability to adapt to new technologies, new work processes and new products" (Vickerstaff, 1992, p. 257).

REGIONALISM AND GOVERNMENT STRUCTURE

In a country as regionally divisive as Canada, economic development programs that target specific regions are always a contentious issue. The research from which this chapter draws (White, 2004) shows that government structure and regional division are key elements that influence policy decisions and program development in Canada.

> Regionalism is a pervasive feature of Canadian society and politics—it is everywhere to be found: in our politics, in the structure of the economy, in our associative life, in Canadian culture and identity. It is entrenched in our political institutions, in party and electoral politics, in federal-provincial relations, in government policy and in the composition of the federal government itself. Finally, but certainly not least important, regions are present in Canada's constitution, wherein special regional rights are recognized (Bickerton, 1999, p. 209).

In a federal state, the national government must contend with provinces of varying economic strength and political power. Provincial parties in power may or may not be the same as the party in power at the federal level, a situation which may or may not ease negotiations between the two levels. Public perception holds that having a provincial government of the same political party as the federal government generally bodes well for that province. This belief is particularly widely held in Atlantic Canada, an economically depressed region with little economic or political clout. Similarly, having a federal member of parliament (MP) elected to the ruling federal party is also seen as beneficial, particularly if that MP is given a senior cabinet portfolio or a portfolio of importance for that province. For example, Brian Tobin and John Crosbie served as federal MPs representing ridings in the province of Newfoundland and Labrador. Both served as federal Minister of Fisheries, a critical portfolio for Newfoundland and Labrador.

Political negotiations in Canada are a complicated and delicate process at and between the two levels of government. The relationships between federal and provincial governments, different jurisdictions of responsibility—not always clear-cut—and the division of power add complex layers of negotiations to the development of social and economic development programs and policies. The federal system in Canada creates an environment of struggle for power and authority.

Harris (1998) provides an excellent discussion of the effects of the division of power in Canada on the fishing industry. Both federal and provincial governments control the fishing industry. The federal government has jurisdiction over the fish while provincial governments have jurisdiction over fish processing. In an effort to increase employment opportunities, provincial governments in Atlantic Canada expanded fish processing plants and pressured the federal government to increase fish quotas to ensure employment. Both levels of government used the fishing industry for their own political advantage, and many would claim they did so to the detriment of the industry.

The unconscionable expansion of the fishery at the expense of disappearing fish stocks was made possible by the way the industry is regulated in Canada... where the federal and provincial governments lock horns for political rather than fisheries reasons, which in turn pits inshore against offshore [fisheries], province against province and community against community. (Harris, 1998, p. 70)

Regionalism has a significant impact on policy choice in Canada, partly as a by-product of the federal/provincial divide but also due to the large geographic size of the country. The size and number of regions in Canada as economically weak as Atlantic Canada—the North, the Prairies (Alberta excepted) and large sections of other provinces—mean greater competition for scarce government resources. The varying economic and political strength of Canada's regions heavily influences public perceptions of the "validity" of who gets what. This has contributed to a certain degree of resentment and a "what about us?" attitude. Reactions to government aid in response to the outbreak of SARS (Severe Acute Respiratory Syndrome) in Toronto, in the spring of 2003, and the case of Mad Cow Disease (Bovine Spongiform Encephalopathy or BSE) in Alberta later that spring, illustrate the depth of regional resentment in Canada. The federal government provided financial assistance to the city of Toronto to deal with the SARS crisis. The western Canadian provinces affected by the case of Mad Cow Disease called on the federal government for financial assistance to the beef industry and cited the funding given to Toronto as part of the rationale:

Western leaders are seeking $400 million from Ottawa to help the cattle industry recover from the fallout over the Mad Cow scare...The western leaders said that unlike the SARS outbreak in Toronto...the western beef industry has been left to fend for itself. ("Western leaders call for $400M mad cow bailout", 2003)

The use of this example is not meant to negate the seriousness of either SARS or BSE. It does, however, illustrate the extent of regionalism in Canada when politicians are willing to use so serious an issue as leverage for federal funding. Regionalism plays a role not only in terms of federal attempts at regional balance but also in the level of public and, in turn, political support a regional program would receive.

Atlantic Canada has had its fair share of various forms of government subsidies over the past 50 years. Regional subsidies are a particularly contentious point in Canada, and the TAGS program was no exception. Having lived in the region for most of my life, I can say that regional tensions between wealthier provinces, the "haves", and poorer provinces, the "have-nots", can run high. There is a perception in some areas that Atlantic Canada has long been overly dependent on federal subsidies (McMahon, 2000). Given the political structures in Canada, it is unlikely that such sentiments would not influence political decisions regarding programs such as TAGS. The next section of the chapter looks at the TAGS program specifically, in the context of the above discussions.

THE TAGS PROGRAM

Following years of over-fishing, both foreign and domestic, incorrect quota calculations, bad policy choice, and political brinkmanship between the federal and provincial governments, the Canadian federal government declared a moratorium on the Northern Cod fishery in the mid-1990s, which effectively closed the industry in much of Atlantic Canada. The resulting loss of employment was immediate and widespread. Whole communities were threatened as thousands of workers were left without employment, and businesses supported by the income generated through the fishery suffered.

To address the problem, the Canadian government implemented The Atlantic Groundfish Strategy (TAGS) in 1995. TAGS was a five-year program with a funding total of $1.9 billion. The intent of the Program was to restructure the fishing industry, provide funding for economic development, and provide displaced workers with income, training and employment assistance. Displaced workers did receive training and some found employment, though this employment was generally less well-paying than the fishery and often less secure with minimum benefits, if any. It is somewhat difficult to measure the success of economic development initiatives that were to be implemented through the TAGS program in part because responsibilities, reporting mechanisms and strategic plans were not well-developed and partly because overall program coordination was lacking (Auditor General of Canada, 1997).

TAGS was primarily the responsibility of two government departments: Human Resources Development Canada (HRDC)—the federal employment ministry—and the Department of Fisheries and Oceans (DFO). Economic development initiatives under the Program were the responsibility of one quasi-governmental agency, The Atlantic Canada Opportunities Agency (ACOA). Little has been recorded on the success of economic development initiatives in the region that were to be implemented under the auspices of the TAGS program. As previously stated, this is largely because of poor reporting structures between the federal government and the agency responsible for economic development. There has been development in the region in the years since the moratorium but, to a large extent, this development has occurred in larger, more urban centres and largely comprises small business development and a good many call centres. Larger businesses have come to the region; however, this cannot be attributed solely or directly to efforts undertaken within the TAGS Program.

Efforts to restructure the industry relied heavily on workers' early retirement and on the re-training of workers in the industry. The idea behind restructuring was to reduce the size of the overall fishery to something that matched the amount of fish available for harvesting. Strictly speaking, industry restructuring was a success in that the numbers of fishers and plant workers in the industry were significantly reduced. However, the industry has not recovered to the extent anticipated. Thus, the interpretation of success is ambiguous. Government miscalculations as to the numbers of eligible participants meant the Program had to be reorganized to one of simply income supplements at the three-year mark. Nonetheless, the rate of displaced workers eligible to participate in re-training was 38 per cent at that three-year mark.

One research participant noted the numbers would have increased had the Program continued to its full five-year term. If the goal of the Program was to re-train workers out of the industry, the goal was achieved. On the other hand, if success is measured in terms of industry recovery, then the Program could be said to have been a failure.

TRAINING AND EMPLOYMENT UNDER THE TAGS PROGRAM

HRDC's (1999) final evaluation report shows training was by far the largest adjustment measure of the TAGS program. A wide variety of training opportunities was available to TAGS participants. In consultation with local HRDC offices, TAGS clients could pursue training ranging from literacy and numeracy, general education upgrading such as high school equivalency, skills training at community colleges and university degrees.

Under the TAGS Program, clients could undertake training for longer periods than had been allowed in previous HRDC programs. Training was restricted to institutions recognized and accredited by the various provincial governments. Education in Canada falls under provincial jurisdiction. One of the participants in the original research commented on the level of support and cooperation received from one provincial education department (White, 2004). This department facilitated training, most particularly through its adult education division, and actively encouraged training providers to accept TAGS participants. The department also paid TAGS clients' tuition fees, later recovering the costs from HRDC. This active encouragement and a guarantee of tuition payment facilitated access to training and education for many TAGS participants in this province. While the reorganization of the Program eliminated training opportunities, research participants mentioned individual client successes with regard to training as in the following two examples:

> Looking back at some of these individuals and some of the training they participated in, there are numerous success stories that have taken place throughout this region. Only yesterday I was talking to an individual who spent 14 years in the fishing industry and when the moratorium came in 1992, this individual realized that there may not be any immediate future in the groundfish fishery and he went to university and obtained his Bachelor's and Master's degrees in biology and is now gainfully employed in his respective profession. So you can see, this Program has many success stories. (Simon)

> ...most of our students were successful and one year, one of our TAGS students was valedictorian. Many others graduated with honours and the award for high proficiency in various trades. (Jennifer)

Despite some individual success stories, the Atlantic Groundfish Strategy was problematic from the outset. Implemented within a short time frame, much of the Program was undeveloped at the time of implementation. As noted by the Auditor General of Canada (1997), "The partnerships needed to implement the Strategy's proposed components still had to be negotiated and TAGS components related to industry restructuring had not been finalized" (16.20). Economic development initiatives remained unclear for a full two years into the Program. "Community economic development was a missing link in the adjustment process" (HRDC, 1998, 1.13). Further, the responsibilities of organizations and agencies involved with implementing the Program were not clearly defined or formally agreed upon. Integrated strategic plans identifying and scheduling the activities of the various bodies involved were not developed, nor were measures put in place to coordinate the Program (Auditor General of Canada, 1997, 16.88). Participants interviewed gave contradictory information as to whether the federal government consulted departments, organizations and agencies with interests in the issue during the development and implementation of the Program. Nonetheless, as the report of the Auditor General of Canada (1997) makes clear, there was no formal or clearly defined understanding of who would be responsible for what, and no coordination plans put in place for the Program. Both of these elements (responsibility and coordination) would be equally as important to the success of a program as broad-based consultation, particularly in a country as geographically large and with such divided, and divisive, areas of provincial and federal jurisdiction as Canada.

A number of factors influenced the success, and the perceived success, of the Program. Although evaluation documents make reference to the Program's objective as adjusting 50 per cent of workers to employment outside of the industry, this fact was not widely publicized nor understood. Andrew noted, that by the time the Program was reorganized, more than half of the 50 per cent target participants were in the process of adjusting out of the industry. Approximately 38 per cent of TAGS participants were involved in training and, thus in the process of adjustment, before the Program was reorganized. With an additional three years, Andrew suspected that they would have, in all likelihood, achieved the 50 per cent adjustment objective.

Study participants indicate that the catchment area for TAGS was unnecessarily large. Areas less dependent on groundfish and with other species-rich fisheries were included in the TAGS program largely as a result of political pressure. Participation eligibility criteria were developed not only for individuals but also for regions. Not all of Atlantic Canada depended on the groundfish industry, so measures were put in place to restrict the Program to areas affected by the moratorium. Some Human Resources Centre (HRC) personnel believed that TAGS should have been restricted to industry communities with high unemployment. In the end, the decision about which areas would be included was based on the industry—whether areas had an active groundfish fishery—and not level of unemployment (Andrew). Unemployment in the region is always a contentious political issue, and it would not sit well with constituents if a politician did not secure TAGS benefits for his or her riding.

Participant eligibility criteria were broad-based and inconsistently implemented in the region; thus TAGS clients across the region were treated differently. Broad-based eligibility criteria and inconsistent implementation also led to situations where some individuals with easily transferable skills and questionable need under the Program took advantage of training and adjustment measures.

...they allowed everyone associated with the fishery. We enlarged that to include accountants, refrigeration mechanics, in some cases automotive repair people, people who had transferable skills. And for me, that's a critical area because if you had transferable skills, why retrain them in something? The fish filleters didn't have transferable skills, the guys who drove the boats didn't have transferable skills, so why would you do that? (Andrew).

The Atlantic Groundfish Strategy was a politically "hot" topic in the region. Years of failed government intervention in the region left people with little hope that TAGS would be any different. The perception that the Program was doomed to fail from the start left little room for success in the minds of many. Research participants commented on the level of negative media publicity the Program received not only at the regional level but at the national level as well. The failings of the Program were widely reported, while success stories went unnoticed.

It appears that factors such as political party affiliation—whether the various provincial governments in power were the same as or in opposition to the federal government—and the sometimes acrimonious relationship between the provinces and the federal government—had greater influence on how the Program was perceived politically and publicly rather than whether displaced fisheries workers benefited, or the actual failures or successes of the Program.

Determining whether TAGS was successful is, to a large degree, a matter of perspective. If the Program's objectives were to restructure the industry, and to facilitate economic development, income support and adjustment to employment outside the fishery, then success was mixed. Industry restructuring was not achieved to the level anticipated. The ability of the government to buy back fish licenses was negatively affected by budgetary demands from income support and adjustment measures. Fisheries workers did not opt for early retirement in the numbers originally predicted (Auditor General of Canada, 1997). The fact that the federal government subsequently announced the closure of what remained of the Northern Cod fishery is clear evidence that industry restructuring, as envisioned in the TAGS program, did not occur.

In the end, perhaps the greatest barrier the Program faced was a lack of employment opportunities in the region. Even if the Program had not been beset with development and implementation problems, it would still have been a difficult challenge given the economic situation in the region. This is illustrated by the comments of a research participant when he noted that,

it was almost impossible to create whole bunches of new jobs in Trepacy or in Canso. Much easier in North Sydney, much easier to do down in South West Nova. Difficult to do in northern New Brunswick...I guess what I'm saying is there's very little they could have done. (Andrew).

CONCLUSION

There were many elements that contributed to the demise of the Northern Cod fishing industry in Atlantic Canada, the development and implementation of the TAGS program and its ultimate failure. White's research (2004) shows that while training and education were said to be key elements of this Program, in the end the need for training was overshadowed by government mismanagement resulting in the early closure of the Program. The lack of public support for the Program and the complicated nature of political negotiation in Canada meant there was a lack of political will to keep the Program going or to keep in on the political agenda. The ad hoc nature of the Program and lack of long-term planning contributed to the overall failure of not only the Program but of economic development and labour market alternatives in the region. While there were some successes in that some displaced workers received training and the industry was, in effect, restructured, overall the TAGS Program ultimately became merely an income subsidy program, which did nothing to ameliorate the structural and economic problems that resulted from the collapse of the industry in Atlantic Canada. The Atlantic Groundfish Strategy is a compelling example of the need for integrated, long-term and multi-faceted approaches to the economic recovery of communities affected by industrial decline.

NOTES

[1] The name of this government department has been changed twice since 2002, with both changes clearly illustrating the Department's emphasis on skills development. In 2004 the Department was renamed Human Resources and Skills Development Canada. Two years later, in 2006, under a change of government (and political party), the Department became known as Human Resources and Social Development.

[2] See Fägerlind & Saha, 1989, and Langelett, 2002.

REFERENCES

Addison, J. (Ed.). (1991). *Job displacement: Consequences and implications for policy.* Detroit, MI: Wayne State University Press.

Albo, G. (1998). "The cult of training": Unemployment and capitalist employment policy. In J. Wheelock & J. Vail (Eds.), *Work and idleness: The political economy of full employment* (pp. 183–203). Boston: Kluwer Academic Publishers.

Ashton, D., & Green, F. (1996). *Education, training and the global economy.* Cheltenham, England: Edward Elgar Publishing Limited.

Auditor General of Canada. (1997). *Report of the Auditor General of Canada: Atlantic groundfish fisheries.* Ottawa, ON: Minister of Public Works and Government Services Canada.

Baran, J., Bérubé, G., Roy, R., & Salmon, W. (2000). *Adult education in Canada: Key knowledge gaps.* Ottawa, ON: Human Resources Development Canada.

Bickerton, J. (1999). Regionalism in Canada. In J. Bickerton & A. G. Gagnon (Eds.), *Canadian politics* (pp. 209–235). Peterborough, ON: Broadview Press.

Fägerlind, I., & Saha, L. J. (1989). *Education and national development: A comparative perspective* (2nd ed.). Toronto: Pergamon Press.

Harris, M. (1998). *Lament for an ocean: The collapse of the Atlantic cod fishery: A true crime story.* Toronto: McClelland & Stewart Inc.

Human Resources Development Canada [HRDC]. (1998). *Evaluation of the Atlantic Groundfish Strategy (TAGS): TAGS/HRDC final evaluation report.* Ottawa, ON: HRDC. Retrieved June 2, 2001, from http://www.11.hrdc.drhc.gc.ca/edd/TAGS.1html

Human Resources Development Canada. (1999). *Final report: Audit of TAGS grants and contributions.* Ottawa, ON: HRDC.

Human Resources Development Canada. (2002). *Knowledge matters: Skills and learning for Canadians: Canada's innovation strategy.* Ottawa, ON: HRDC. Retrieved February 17, 2002, from http://www.hrdc.drhc.ca

International Labour Organization. (1995). *Learning to start afresh: The challenge of re-training. World Labour Report* (Press Kit). Retrieved November 21, 2000, from www.ilo.org

Krahn, H., & Lowe, G. S. (1998). *Work, industry, and Canadian society* (3rd ed.). Scarborough, ON: Nelson Canada.

Langalett, G. (2002). Human capital: A summary of the 20th century research. *Journal of Education Finance, 28,* 1–24.

Lauzon, D. (1995). *Worker displacement: Trends, characteristics and policy responses.* Ottawa, ON: HRDC.

Leigh, D. (1989). *Assisting displaced workers: Do the states have a better idea?* Detroit, MI: W.E. Upjohn Institute for Employment Research.

McMahon, F. (2000). *Retreat from growth: Atlantic Canada and the negative sum economy.* Halifax, NS: Atlantic Institute for Market Studies.

Russell, B. (1999). *More with less: Work reorganization in the Canadian mining industry.* Toronto: University of Toronto Press.

Rainbird, H. (1992). *The effectiveness of training boards: A case study of the United Kingdom.* (Discussion Paper No. 99) Geneva: International Labour Organization.

Vickerstaff, S. (1992). Training for economic survival. In P. Brown & H. Lauder (Eds.), *Education for economic survival: From Fordism to Post-Fordism?* (pp. 244–267). London: Routledge.

Western leaders call for $400M mad cow bailout. (2003, June 9). *CTV.ca News.* Retrieved July 26, 2003, from http://www.ctv.ca/servlet/ArticleNews/story/CTVNews/1055166501314_75/

White, M. (2004). *Re-training in the post-industrial era: A comparison of government responses to widespread worker displacement in Canada and Britain.* Unpublished doctoral dissertation, University of Toronto.

Zippay, A. (1991). Job-training and relocation experiences among displaced industrial workers. *Evaluation Review, 15*(5), 555–569.

Melissa White
Centre for Labour Market Studies
University of Leicester

ANTHONY R. WELCH

13. AUSTRALIAN EDUCATION IN AN ERA OF MARKETS AND MANAGERIALISM

A Critical Perspective

David N. Wilson used to fondly reminisce about his time in Australia, even at times speculating about the idea of retiring there. Awarded a Social Science and Humanities Research Council of Canada (SSHRC) Leave Fellowship for research on occupational training in Singapore and Malaysia for 1980–81, he spent several months as a Visiting Fellow in the Centre for Comparative and International Studies in Education, La Trobe University, in Melbourne, Australia, with his wife and four children.

Over the almost 30 years since, much has changed both at La Trobe and more generally. The Comparative Education department at La Trobe—at that time one of the world's largest and better known—is no more. The large and vigorous faculty of which it was a part has shrunk significantly. This is only one index of change in Australian higher education, which is now a vastly larger system, and far more internationalized, than during David's visit. The schooling system has also changed significantly, and in much the same direction—towards marketisation and managerialism. To many who have lived through the reforms, it seems that educational priorities, policies, and institutions have been re-fashioned substantially, all-too-often by forces outside of the education field, and according to principles that have little to do with it.

To be fair, the sets of reforms and reform principles discussed below are not uniquely Australian. Several of the traditional centres of Comparative Education research have retreated or disappeared (Welch, 1997b); while others have flourished, most particularly in East Asia. Within the North, the ebullience of the post-war decades has largely gone, with the post-war Keynesian settlement replaced by a much more austere and technicist world of markets and managerialism (Clarke, Gewirtz & McLaughlin, 2000; Considine & Painter, 1997; Gee, Hull & Lankshear 1996; Yeatman 1997). Within the South, too, including in some socialist states transitioning to a market economy, markets and managerialism have been seen as key strategies with which to promote development, to reform the rigidities of the state socialist model, and to leapfrog directly into a modern knowledge economy. However, as some scholars have pointed out, this sequence has not been the case in all states (Carnoy, 2006; Welch & Mok, 2003; Welch, 2000, 2007c, 2008).

Nonetheless, within education, the determination that post-war capitalist or post-revolutionary socialist generations would not be disfigured by structures and

V. Masemann et al., (Eds.), A Tribute to David N. Wilson: Clamouring for a Better World, 191–205.

ideologies that created and sustained class, ethnic, and gender inequalities has now been largely overtaken by a fissiparous reform programme that often sets groups, such as institutions, teachers, parents, and students, against one another. This is not to say that the former more egalitarian ideologies were always successful in achieving their goals; rather that the goals were different, and equality was accorded a higher priority.

The current chapter sketches some of the main tenets of this renascent ideology, making the point that it is not the first time that such ideologies have *re*formed (and arguably *de*formed) education. Some of the mainsprings of markets and managerialism are first outlined. A sketch of earlier episodes of the introduction of business efficiency schemes into education, both in Britain and the colonies, and the effects on pedagogy, curriculum and financing of education, as well upon teachers and pupils, is followed by some select examples of contemporary reform programmes within schooling and higher education systems in Australia. The sketch of major reform moments in Australian education serves to illustrate the capacity of contemporary ideologies of markets and managerialism to transcend political and cultural differences, and levels of development.

MAINSPRINGS

After briefly tracing core assumptions underlying markets and managerialism, I outline some of the likely ways in which each finds expression in education. Educational markets are understood in more theoretical terms and seen to rest on theories of choice, while managerialism is seen to offer a technology of implementation, including benchmarks to measure progress towards the attainment of market goals. While in each case, contra to the claims of hyper-globalists such as Ohmae (1991, 1995), state strategies do make a difference (Carnoy, 2006; Weiss, 1998; Welch & Mok, 2003), it is equally true that the agendas of major global agencies such as the World Bank, Asian Development Bank, and the Organisation for Economic Co-operation and Development (OECD) have been significant in pressing, for example, "a less interventionist ...state, ... and a preference for market-like mechanisms over bureaucratic methods of service delivery" (World Bank, 1995).

Markets

Markets in education are justified by an appeal to the notion of choice, and the argument that state-dominated systems deny much, even all, choice to families, parents and students. By contrast, it is argued that individuals should be free to select an education that they believe best caters to their interests and aspirations, and they should also be responsible for the outcomes of that choice. According to this argument, individuals and families compete for advantage in education. Within market discourses, education is seen as a positional good, in which those who have the knowledge and opportunity use education for purposes of achieving greater status and a better position in the socio-economic hierarchy (Gewirtz, Ball & Bowe, 1995). Choices are often made more on the status of an educational institution, whether school, college or university, rather than the quality of education it offers. Individuals gain advantage through accessing prestige education, but (it is sometimes admitted) this is at a cost to others: "Positional competition…is a zero-sum game. What winners win, losers lose" (Hirsch, 1976, p. 52). Despite substantial evidence that class effects mean that the more sophisticated chooser can compound their social and educational advantages, while those whose cultural capital equips them less well in the competition stakes fare much less well, market ideologies continue to thrive. As a result, a more fissiparous society eventuates, where the gap between the "haves" and "have nots" widens, as a direct result of the extension of educational markets.

This is not the whole story, of course: it is not just individuals who comprise the market. Institutions, too, increasingly compete. It is now often said that, rather than students choosing schools, schools are often choosing students, through carefully orchestrated marketing campaigns. As a result, more advantaged schools (in terms of location, social class composition, or with low proportions of children whose first language is not that of the majority) are able to trade on these attributes to forge further ahead. In contrast, schools in poorer areas (rural environments, or with high proportions of migrant children who must learn the majority language as their second language) often fall further behind, becoming less and less attractive to both parents and funding agencies. Parents and children frequenting such schools are then effectively blamed for their own failure to choose a better school.

In Australia, the fostering of a market ideology in education, as in other social policy arenas, has been a concomitant of a changed view of the shape and role of the state. There had long been a significant private sector in Australia, most particularly at the secondary level (Campbell, 2007). The rise of a more economistic ideology in the latter part of the nineteen eighties saw the increasing subordination of education to the language and logic of a scientistic economics, and the subsequent progressive extension of marketisation to the public sector.

Managerialism

Managerialism in education is arguably an outgrowth of wider neo-liberal reform programmes of the past decade or two (Pusey, 1991). Such programmes have not merely led to greater privatization and decentralization (although as some have pointed out, the directed character of the latter means the process might be better characterized as centralized decentralization), but have also—in an apparent paradox—led to increased regulation of educational institutions. It is the latter process that interests us here. In an era in which funding per student for public sector educational institutions has remained static or declined in many systems, education has come under increasing pressure, but also paradoxically, under increasing scrutiny or surveillance. As much as a decade or more ago, the effects of this ideology were being pointed out in countries such as Australia:

> while hard-pressed staff in schools and universities must do more and more with less and less, they are less free to engage in democratic action and resistance. They are increasingly beset by detailed external and internal demands

which affect both how they spend their time, and which increasingly impose directly upon curricula, evaluation and pedagogy—all in the name of account-ability or devolution. (Welch, 1997a, p. 17)

The basis for managerialism rests on an appeal to technicist principles of efficiency and economism (Habermas, 1971, 1974, 1976, 1978; Pusey, 1991; Welch, 1997a, 1998) that represent the historical triumph of a means-ends, instrumentalist ratio-nality over older forms of reason that enshrined ethical concerns about the social good. That of the ancient Greeks, for example, whose maxim "Man is the measure of all things" was expressly countered by the new logic of efficiency and economism. An alternative account was offered by Lyotard (1984), whose notion of perfor-mativity critiqued the historical process whereby knowledge has become commodified and transformed into one of the principal productive forces in society. Under such conditions he argued, notions of productivity like "optimising the system's performance" (Lyotard, 1984, p. xxiv) become the ultimate goal, and the relevant system technology is drawn from the discourse of business and management. Enhancing worker productivity, such as in the compulsory use of new technologies such as ICTs, forms the new techno-logic of performativity. Performance targets are set, and individual workers compete against each other for rewards and punishments. This new regimen means that questions drawn from the discourse of business efficiency come to dominate: "Is it efficient?" or "Is it saleable?" become more important and more common questions than "Is it true?" (Lyotard, 1984, p. 51).

HISTORICAL ANTECEDENTS

As I have argued above, a key technology of managerialism is the idea of rewarding workers according to quantitative performance targets. While this process provides a starting point for understanding why they were introduced and what influence they have on educational policy, what remains is to chart their effects in practice. In the Anglo-American democracies described above (such as in New Zealand, Canada, the UK and Australia), performance indicators have flourished in recent decades, to the point where they have become an integral weapon in the mana-gerialist armory—within education, just as in health, welfare and other public policy arenas. But not for the first time: before managerialism, there was efficiency. A brief review of one or two examples of efficiency movements in education from the nineteenth and early twentieth century serve not merely to show the principal effects of this ideology, but are also excellent reminders of the lessons of history, at least for those who still wish to learn.

Payment by Results

Importing policies from the UK or elsewhere is by no means new. The first example is drawn from the mid-nineteenth century. Like much educational baggage of the time, it was imported by numerous colonies from England. Among other things, it also serves as a timely warning to current hyper-globalists who insist that the impact of globalization effects on current policy agendas is an entirely novel phenomenon.

The Revised Code, or "Payment by Results" as it came to be widely known, was introduced into British education around the 1860s. Its rationale was encapsulated in the proud boast of its proponent to the British parliament: "If it is not cheap it shall be efficient; if it is not efficient it shall be cheap" (Maclure, 1974, p. 79–80). Its legitimacy stemmed from the strong prevailing current of business accountability and efficiency that informed education inquiries of the time: "The Commissioners held the common view of the period, that the notion of accountability, so vital to a well-run business, should be applied vigorously to all forms of government expenditure" (Musgrave, 1968, p. 35). Within years, it had been introduced into several of the Australian colonies (Miller, 1986; Rodwell, 1992; Turney, 1969) as well as to India (Allender, 2006; D'Souza, 1976).

The original British scheme was largely inspired by middle-class fears of rising calls upon state funds for elementary schools (provided for the working class), at a time of swelling demand for education by and for that group. In an effort to rein in justified rises in expenditure, the needs of a "business age" specified that a "standard" be established which each child had to attain to pass at that level (Musgrave, 1968). This standard was based upon the assumed needs of industry for a literate workforce and bourgeois assumptions about a curriculum appropriate to the working class: the three R's, suffused by Christianity.

The effects of the scheme were swift and dramatic. In the face of rising demand, the state grant for primary education promptly fell by more than a quarter, and a sharp decline ensued in numbers of pupil teachers, and teachers' college trainees. The teacher-pupil ratio worsened profoundly from 1:36 in 1861 to 1:54 five years later (Maclure, 1974).

Other perverse effects included inducing teachers, whose annual salaries were now tied to the numbers of pupils in their classes and to their performance at particular exams, to cheat. When an inspector's visit was imminent, teachers drilled their pupils mercilessly on test items (Hyndman, 1978). Some secretly trained their pupils in classroom tricks that would create a more favourable impression. Others falsified enrolment registers to keep numbers of pupils artificially high. Sick children were dragged along to school to satisfy attendance requirements, upon which teachers' salaries were dependent (Hyndman, 1978), while teachers now had to negotiate their salaries directly with school managers (Welch, 2007a).

Cramming rather than teaching, became the means to ensure a teacher's livelihood, weakening pupils, teachers, and pedagogy. Hence, a further product of the Revised Code was a narrowing of the curriculum and a narrow instrumentalism with respect to educational aims. Overall, while the scheme was justified by appeals to the principle of "efficiency", it was introduced largely as a means of curbing justifiable growth in state expenditure on education.

As with the Indian experience (Allender, 2006, D'Souza, 1976), and at much the same time, the Australian schemes inherited all the weaknesses of the British. In the introduction of the so-called "Standards of Proficiency" into New South Wales for example, officials insisted that teachers follow set requirements scrupulously, and submit to a similarly detailed examination of requirements by inspectors. The effect on both teachers and inspectors was to mechanise the labour process. Teachers, whose promotional prospects were directly tied to their pupils' results in the test, were led to implement "rote learning and...mechanical modes of instruction" (Turney, 1969, p. 230) while "the work of the inspector largely became one of mechanical examining and his reports became mainly based on statistical analysis of results" (Turney, 1969, p. 231). In the colony of Victoria for example, payment by results was acknowledged to have achieved "the encouragement (of)...memorization rather than reasoning, (of) formal, mechanical teaching methods, and...keeping the curriculum narrow" (Barcan, 1980, p. 107; see also Rodwell, 1992; Welch 2007a).

Taylorism or Scientific Management

The "payment by results" schemes in England, India, and various Australian colonies in the 1860s were not the only ones to use business efficiency to promote ideological reforms in education. *Taylorism* or *scientific management* cut a swathe through American schools and universities in the period around World War I. Originally introduced into the manufacturing industry as an attempt to boost productivity (the amount produced per worker), the success of scientific management in extracting more output per input attracted those concerned to hold back or reduce spending on education. Business interests were particularly concerned, under the banner of efficiency, to reduce state educational costs (termed "wastage"), while also shifting the financial burden of apprenticeships away from industry, which had been their traditional training ground.

The imposition of this "cult of efficiency" as it was dubbed (Callahan, 1962; Welch, 1998) impoverished education. But not just costs were reduced: the curriculum was narrowed to become more like vocational training, while the education system's capacity to respond to diversity—African Americans (then called negros or blacks), rural dwellers, poor whites, and the growing ranks of American immigrants—was equally attenuated.

The rationale for implementing scientific management in schools and universities was based squarely on an argument which consisted of making unfavourable comparisons between the schools and business enterprise, of applying business-industrial criteria (e.g. economy and efficiency) to education, and of suggesting that business and industrial practices be adopted by educators (Callahan, 1962).

Within years, not only had the *Atlantic Monthly* championed the introduction of scientific management into education, but *The National Education Association* had also done so. By 1907, popular books on education argued that classroom management could be seen as a "business problem". By 1910, it could be claimed that

Our universities are beginning to be run as business colleges. They advertise, they compete with one another, they pretend to give good value to their customers. They desire to increase their trade, they offer social advantages and business openings to their patrons. (Callahan, 1962, p. 7)

School Boards were made smaller, sometimes considerably, and became dominated by businessmen interested in reforming school administration along financial lines.

This process represented a profound retreat from earlier reforms of some of the best-known school administrators such as William T. Harris, Horace Mann, and Henry Barnard.

A final change provoked by the rising tide of business ideology in American education at this time was curriculum reform to make the curriculum "more practical". Major business moguls, such as Andrew Carnegie, Cornelius Vanderbilt, and John D. Rockefeller argued that their success had nothing to do with "book learning" but was based on good old-fashioned common sense, married to the kind of business acumen that could not be taught in schools. Carnegie was particularly scornful of college study as he stated, "in my own experience I can say that I have known few young men intended for business who were not injured by a collegiate education" (Callahan, 1962, p. 9). According to this ideology, Business English should be substituted for composition, and business principles, contracts, and bookkeeping should be introduced into schools. At least for those not proceeding to high school, and arguably for all pupils, the "love of learning" should be subordinated to the "love of earning" (Callahan, 1962, p. 10), a view that also licensed a proliferation of vocational courses in schools.

The preceding historical examples of the implementation of "efficiency" policies in education serve as useful pointers to more modern ideologies of markets and managerialism in education. Among principal effects of earlier episodes were
– a narrowing of the curriculum, and heightened emphasis upon vocationalism;
– lower quality teaching, caused by cramming and "teaching to the test";
– significant cost reductions in real terms leading to much higher class sizes and fewer teaching recruits; and
– less effective capacity to respond to cultural diversity and working class pupils.

Markets and Managerialism in Australian Education

Notwithstanding the above, we should not be too surprised that the bleak results of earlier episodes, when education came to be dominated by ideologies of business efficiency, have little influenced populist politicians, selected educational critics, and media hacks who peddle similar principles in modern guise. The following examples from Australian education, both secondary schooling and higher education, underline not only the easy popularity of such schemes but also the failure of the policy process to attend to the lessons of history.

Notwithstanding the corrosive critiques of the incorporation of business efficiency models into the world of social policy by figures such as Habermas and Lyotard, managerialism has been widely implemented in the Australian state (Painter, 1997) and its reform agenda widely touted, including within education (Miller, 1995a, 1995b). Entire management technologies such as Total Quality Management, borrowed from the commercial world, have been used to regulate educational institutions. A recent variant to be incorporated into some schools and universities is the "Balanced Scorecard" management technology, replete with Key Performance Indicators and coloured flags that indicate progress towards goals. Red indicates danger, of course.

The rise of markets in education has had a profound effect on Australian universities, technical and further education (TAFE), and schools in recent years as institutions (both private *and* public) increasingly compete for students, or at least for a greater share of certain kinds of students. Hence the birth or expansion of performing arts high schools, academically selective high schools, sports high schools, technology high schools, schools that offer an international curriculum such as the International Baccalaureate, and institutions that market a curriculum based on a particular religion (Christian or Muslim schools, for example). Universities are also enmeshed in this market, competing vigorously for both local and international enrolments (Welch, 2002c).

Justified by an appeal to choice, the Australian strategy was two-fold. Since choice entailed more than choice within the public sector, the first strategy was to expand the private sector in education. While most of the energy here has been expended on shifting resources from public schools to the private sector (Sydney Morning Herald [SMH], 2000a, 2000b, 2000c; Welch 2003, 2007a,), the beginnings of such moves in higher education (which in Australia has traditionally been entirely public) may now be discerned.

In the process, whereas marketing was formerly restricted to the private sector, both the principle and practice of marketing have now become firmly ensconced within the public sector, with vigorous competition for the best students. This process is made more intense because school populations are predicted to decline significantly over the next decade or more (Bonnor & Caro, 2007). In some states (it should be reiterated that, like Canada, the USA and Germany, Australia is a federal system), the process of competition within the public sector has been deliberately intensified by the creation of selective high schools, at least in some states, which now often attract many more applicants than they could conceivably accommodate. The effects on the mainstream neighbourhood high school of this retreat from the former idea of a common school have been predictable, with research revealing their progressive residualisation (Campbell, 2007; Campbell & Sherington, 2006; SMH, 2008b). Within the Australian university system, the former fiction that all universities were much the same has now been exploded by the formation of various splinter groups within the sector: the Group of Eight (Go8), a group of eight Australian tertiary institutions considerd the most prestigious, which (like the Russell Group in the UK) collectively dominate the race for research income; the New Technology Universities, and other such groupings.

The second strategy was to induce a climate of market competition within the public sector, whose schools were to be encouraged to compete vigorously not only with other state schools but also with private sector institutions. Hence, the successful academically selective state high schools in New South Wales, most of which were created in the past twenty years, now tout academic results often outshining those of wealthy private sector academies, which charge fees as high as A$ 20,000 per annum. Mainstream state high schools are now encouraged to compete against low-fee denominational high schools, which have proliferated over the last decade, as seen below. In such circumstances, the effects are well known (Campbell & Sherington, 2006, Freund, 2005; Gewirtz, Ball & Bowe, 1995).

Seeing education as a positional good, middle-class parents engage in sophisticated strategies to maximize their opportunities (Bonnor & Caro, 2007), while poor parents continue to send their children to the local school, as they always have.

In the name of choice and marketisation, further reforms in Australian education were evident in specific attempts by state and federal governments to foster the private schooling sector. However, "choice" was used as a tool by state and federal governments to make more public funds available for the purpose of extending the private sector, a process that has resulted in a plethora of new, largely low-fee Christian schools being founded from 1996 to 2006, the decade of the conservative Howard federal government. Private sector schools receive between 42 and 82 per cent of their funds from the public purse (Bonnor & Caro, 2007; Vickers, 2005).

Preston's data show a similar trend in relation to enrolments in government and non-government schools over the last two decades: in most states, the proportion of enrolments in government schools fell from around three-quarters to about two-thirds from 1986 to 2006, with the largest growth evident in the non-Catholic private school sector (Preston, 2007). A recent survey by the Principals' Association of New South Wales showed that in that state widespread flight by Anglo middle classes from local public schools was evident (Sydney Morning Herald [SMH], 2008a). The changes indicated in table 1, in Preston's analysis, and in the Principals' Association survey were underpinned by specific funding mechanisms introduced over the last decade or so, such as the now notorious Enrolment Benchmark Adjustment (EBA) formula, introduced by the former Howard federal government, soon after coming to power in 1996. The formula transferred significant federal government funds from a public school to any private school to which a pupil transferred. The parallel de-regulation of the criteria for the establishment of new private schools (that previously had to establish a case based on need and insufficient educational resources existing in the area) allowed seventy-six new schools to be established within four years, in the most populous

Table 1. Number of schools by sector and percentage of change, Australia 1984–2004

Year	Government		Catholic		"Independent"	
	N	% change	N	% change	N	% change
1984	7544		1705		776	
1994	7159	-5.3	1699	-0.4	821	+5.5
2004	6938	-3.2	1695	-0.2	982	+16.4

From Campbell, 2007, p. 223

Note: In Australia, the "Independent" sector embraces a small number of Catholic, non-systemic schools, as well as those run by other religious sects (mostly Christian, but also Jewish, Muslim, etc.) and some progressive schools (such as Steiner, or Montessori). As such, the term "Independent" is something of a misnomer, and might be better termed "state subsidised". Fees range from moderate to highly exclusive.

state alone (Welch, 2007a). In the face of widespread criticism, the EBA was abandoned, in favour of the so-called Socio-Economic Status (SES) formula, introduced in 2000. The SES formula was also widely criticized for failing to take into account the actual wealth of parents who subscribe to such schools, depending only on the blind law of SES averages for that community (Welch, 2003). In this way, for example, wealthy rural parents could well have their children's enrolment at high-fee, socially exclusive private secondary schools effectively subsidized. Current figures show that 69 per cent of Commonwealth (i.e. federal) government funding to schools is directed to private schools, which is a major reversal of the situation some 30 years ago or so, when in 1974, 70 per cent of its funding went to public schools, paralleling enrolment proportions (Connors, 2007). By 2004, the situation had been reversed: Commonwealth funding of the independent non-government sector (accounting for 13 per cent of enrolments) totalled A\$ 7.6 billion, while public schools, with around two thirds of total enrolments, were scheduled to receive A\$ 7.2 billion (Connors, 2007). Such profligate use of public taxpayers' resources meant that, while total expenditure per student was roughly similar between public and private sectors, there was great variation among the latter:

> 27 per cent of independent non-government school students in the survey attended schools where the income from tuition fees also exceeded the average resources per student in government schools. These schools received \$368 million per year in government grants that assisted in raising their average resources per student to more than 62 per cent above average government school resources. Overall, 55 per cent of independent school students attend schools where the total average resource level per student is higher than that of the average government school. (Connors, 2007, p. 17)

The actual rationale that lay behind the creation of an educational market by the federal government was illustrated in the comment of a recent federal minister of education:

> We have to realize...that parents who send their children to non-government schools are saving taxpayers a vast amount of money—about two billion dollars a year, more than that...and that money is then available for the funding of government schools. (Welch, 2003, p. 276)

The parallel introduction of the federal schemes sketched above to divert funds from public schools to private ones, without increasing the size of the budget in real terms, ensured that the monies "saved" by the taxpayers did not extend support of public schools.

An example of the insistence upon managerialist performance indicators was seen in the actions of an Australian Federal Minister of Education, who, in 2005, used the threat of withholding funding to state governments as a means to introduce compulsory reports on performance by schools across the country. At the same time, the same federal minister pushed strongly for teacher attendance and productivity records, and the return to an "A, B, C, D, E" grading system. Three billion dollars were at risk in the most populous state (New South Wales) alone, until the state government finally relented, demanding that their schools "tell it like it is" (SMH, 2005a, 2005b). While parents may well appreciate more information from schools about their children's performance, the introduction of the machinery of testing and grading can end up distorting rather than strengthening the core education and mission of better quality teaching and learning, as illustrated by the historical examples previously mentioned. The arbitrary use of such indicators, such as the number of pupils at a school that achieve in the top ten per cent of literacy or numeracy tests, represents another example (Welch, 2007a). Assumed in this ideology of managerialism is that success in meeting such performance targets equates to improved quality of education, something that the historical examples treated above show to be at best dubious. Nonetheless, it is by such measures that the performance of educational managers (school principals, heads of department, Faculty Deans) is often now evaluated.

Reforms to Australian universities over the past decade or so have tended in much the same direction, motivated by the same basic principles. Universities have become used to the practice of competing against each other, on a range of performance criteria that are increasingly mandated by the federal government. In the process, the old fiction that all Australian universities are the same has been laid bare. Competition between universities intensified so greatly that it is increasingly difficult for the organization that represents Australian university leaders (the Australian Vice Chancellors Committee [AVCC]) to speak with a single voice. Now, different subgroups such as the New Technology Universities or the Group of Eight each sing a somewhat different song.

The Vice-Chancellor of one of the country's largest and more successful universities recently underlined the effects of a decade of neglect of university funding by the Commonwealth government:

> The last dozen or so years have been a tumultuous time for Australian universities. The investment by the federal government in support of the university education of its citizens fell by about 30 per cent (a) student in real terms between 1996 and 2004. As public funding fell, student-staff ratios have increased from 14 to one to 20 to one. [In order for] Australian universities to be 'real players' in the knowledge economy of the 21st century, Professor Larkins also calls for an extra $2 billion from annual federal budget surpluses to be invested until the higher education endowment fund reaches $20 billion. (The Australian, 2008)

OECD data show that, when comparing higher education expenditure as a proportion of GDP over the decade 1995–2003, Australia was the only country to experience a decline, whereas the OECD average increased by 48 per cent (OECD, 2007; National Tertiary Education Union [NTEU], 2007). While overall revenue to universities rose from A$ 7.9 billion to A$ 13.9 billion over the decade 1996–2005, federal funding in the form of Commonwealth grants increased by less than A$ 1 billion, while the Higher Education Contribution Scheme (HECS) increased from A$ 933 million to A$ 2,333 million, and income from other sources increased from

A\$ 2.4 billion to A\$ 6.05 billion, largely in the form of income from international student fees (NTEU, 2007). Expressed as a proportion of overall university revenue, Commonwealth funding fell from 57 per cent in 1996 to 41 per cent in 2003 (AVCC, 2005).

CONCLUSION: A NEW CULT OF EFFICIENCY IN EDUCATION?

What is evident from the previous analysis? Perhaps the first point is that, in many ways, little has changed. A depressing failure to attend to the lessons of history, which show that attempts to force educational markets and business concepts of administrative efficiency upon educational institutions in the mid-nineteenth and early twentieth centuries, led to a decline in both quality and morale within the institutions as well as a reduced capacity to deal with difference effectively. This has meant that many of the same mistakes were being repeated at the end of the twentieth century and the beginning of the twenty-first. While the transition to a new federal government in late 2007 was accompanied by promises to redress the years of intentioned neglect of higher education, it is, at the time of writing this paper, premature to be confident about results. There is no evidence that the existing and highly divisive funding schemes that have overseen the growth of the private schooling sector at the cost of the public over the past decade will be abolished by the new government, which has promised only to hold an inquiry. The need for reform is urgent in the face of what even senior educational administrators admit is "residualisation"—the process whereby better-off students leave certain schools and create a dumping ground of harder-to-educate children (SMH, 2008b; also see SMH 2008c; Connors, 2007). Effectively, middle class choice is being purchased at the cost of removing choice from poorer families, who, as always, are more likely to send their children to the local public school.

Second, it is important to reiterate that such reforms and trends are not unique to Australia, and are being introduced to different degrees in a number of settings, including both post-communist states transitioning to a form of social democracy and socialist market states such as China and Viet Nam. This is by no means to deny important differences in history and ideology (Weiss, 1998) that help shape different social and educational trajectories at the national level (Carnoy, 2006). However, it is highly significant that, despite profound differences between China and Australia, for example, markets and managerialism triumphed in each at the end of the twentieth century, underlining the capacity of this ideology to transcend political and cultural differences (Welch, 2008). Indeed, the rise of these ideologies parallels wider trends in the Asia Pacific region (Welch, 2005, 2007b), notwithstanding significant differences in the responses to this agenda by individual states (Weiss, 1998; Welch & Mok, 2003). While the diversity of response forms a useful cautionary tale for the hyper-globalists, the widespread rise of current ideologies of markets and managerialism is both impressive and worrying. The coalescence of markets and managerialism in contemporary Australian education has been shown, above, to have reduced the quality and effectiveness of education, at least for many students, as well as the morale of educationists, in institutions that are increasingly subjected to associated technologies of regulation. The underlying goal of increasing productivity, as measured in economic terms, leaves education poorer in every sense, something that David N. Wilson would certainly have lamented.

REFERENCES

Allender, T. (2006). *Ruling through education: The politics of schooling in the colonial Punjab.* Delhi: Sterling Publishers Pvt. Ltd.

Australian, The (2008, February 27). Larkins calls for right to set fees.

Australian Vice Chancellors Committee (AVCC). (2005). *University funding and expenditure.* Retrieved January 15, 2009, from www.universitiesaustralia.edu.au/documents/publications/stats/Funding &Expenditure.pdf

Barcan, A. (1980). *A history of Australian education.* Melbourne: Oxford University Press.

Bonnor, C., & Caro, J. (2007). *The stupid country: How Australia is dismantling public education.* Sydney: University of New South Wales Press.

Callahan, R. (1962). *Education and the cult of efficiency.* Chicago: University of Chicago Press.

Campbell, C. (2007). Schools and school choice. In R. Connell, C. Campbell, M. Vickers, A. Welch, D. Foley, & N. Bagnall (Eds.), *Education, change and society* (pp. 211–238). Oxford University Press.

Campbell, C., & Sherington, G. (2006). *The comprehensive public high school: Historical perspectives.* New York: Palgrave Macmillan.

Carnoy, M. (2006). Rethinking the comparative and the international. *Comparative Education Review, 50*(4), 551–570.

Clarke, J., Gewirtz, S., & McLaughlin, E. (Eds.). (2000). *New managerialism, new welfare.* London: Sage.

Connors, L. (2007). *Making federalism work for schools: Due process, transparency, informed consent.* Sydney: NSW Public Education Alliance.

Considine, M., & Painter, M. (Eds.). (1997). *Managerialism: The great debate.* Victoria, Australia: Melbourne University Press.

D'Souza, A. (1976). *Anglo Indian education: A study of its origins and growth in Bengal up to 1960.* Delhi: Oxford University Press.

Freund, M. (2005). *Making morals: Creating order in the first year of school.* Unpublished Ph.D., University of Sydney.

Gee, J., Hull, G., & Lankshear, C. (1996). *The new work order: Behind the language of the new capitalism.* Sydney: Allen and Unwin.

Gewirtz, S., Ball, S., & Bowe, R. (1995). *Markets, choice and equity in education.* Milton Keynes: Open University Press.

Habermas, J. (1971). *Technology and science as ideology: Toward a rational society.* London: Heinemann.

Habermas, J. (1974). *Theory and practice.* London: Heinemann.

Habermas, J. (1976). *Legitimation crisis.* Boston: Beacon Press.

Habermas, J. (1978). *Knowledge and human interests.* London: Heinemann.

Hirsch, F. (1976). *Social limits to growth.* Cambridge: Harvard University Press.

Hyndman, M. (1978). *Schools and schooling in England and Wales: A documentary history.* London: Harper and Row.

Lyotard, J.-F. (1984). *The postmodern condition: A report on knowledge.* Minneapolis, MN: University of Minnesota Press.

Maclure, J. (1974). *Educational documents: England and Wales, 1816–1967.* London: Chapman & Hall.

Miller, H. (1995a). States, economies and the changing labour process of academics: Australia, Canada and the UK. In J. Smyth (Ed.), *Academic work: The changing labour process in higher education.* Buckingham: Society for Research in Higher Education/Open University Press.

Miller, H. (1995b). *The management of change in universities: Universities, state and economy in Australia, Canada and the UK.* Buckingham: Society for Research in Higher Education/Open University Press.

Miller, P. (1986). *Long division: State schooling in South Australian society.* Adelaide: Wakefield Press.

Musgrave, P. (1968). *Society and the curriculum in Australia.* Sydney: Allen and Unwin.

National Tertiary Education Union [NTEU]. (2007). *The funding of Australian universities, 1996–2005: An examination of the fact and figures.* Melbourne: NTEU.

Ohmae, K. (1991). *The borderless world: Power and strategy in the interlinked economy.* London: Fontana.

Ohmae, K. (1995). *The end of the nation state: The rise of regional economies.* London: Harper Collins.

Organisation for Economic Co-operation and Development [OECD]. (2007). *Education at a glance.* Paris: OECD.

Painter, M. (1997). Public management: Fad or fallacy? In M. Considine & M. Painter (Eds.), *Managerialism: The great debate* (pp. 39–43). Melbourne: Melbourne University Press.

Preston, B. (2007). *The social makeup of schools: Family income, religion, indigenous status and family type in government, Catholic, and other nongovernment schools.* Victoria, Australia: Australian Education Union.

Pusey, M. (1991). *Economic rationalism in Canberra: A nation-building state changes its mind.* Cambridge: Cambridge University Press.

Rodwell, G. (1992). *With zealous efficiency: Progressivism and Tasmanian state primary education, 1900–1922.* Darwin: William Michael Press.

Sydney Morning Herald (SMH). (2000a, August 23). Richest schools to 'Reap Rewards' of federal law.

Sydney Morning Herald (SMH). (2000b, September 29). *'Kemp finds new formula to give more to richest schools.*

Sydney Morning Herald (SMH). (2000c, October 19). 37,000 to choose private schools.

Sydney Morning Herald (SMH). (2005a, June 29). Order to all state schools: Tell it like it is.

Sydney Morning Herald (SMH). (2005b, July 1). Reports required from all schools.

Sydney Morning Herald (SMH). (2008a, March 10). White flight from schools.

Sydney Morning Herald (SMH). (2008b, March 10). Overcoming disadvantage. The No. 1 priority being tacked from the top.

Sydney Morning Herald (SMH). (2008c, January 9) 'School Funding Flaws Hidden'.

Turney, C. (Ed.). (1969). *Pioneers of Australian education.* Sydney: Sydney University Press.

Vickers, M. (2005). In the common good: The need for a new approach to funding Australia's schools. *Australian Journal of Education, 49*(3), 264–277.

Weiss, L. (1998). *The myth of the powerless state: Governing the economy in a global era.* Cambridge: Polity Press.

Welch, A. (1997a). Reform or crisis in Australian education? In Welch, A. (Ed.), *Class, culture and the state in Australian education: Reform or crisis?* (pp. 1–31). New York/Berlin: Peter Lang.

Welch, A. (1997b). Things fall apart: Disintegration, universities and the decline of disciplines. Problematising Comparative Education in an Uncertain Age. In C. E. A. Kodron (Ed.), *Vergleichende Erziehungswissenschaft. Herausforderung - Vermittlung - Praxis* (pp. 182–191). Cologne/Vienna: Böhlau Verlag.

Welch, A. (1998). Education and the cult of efficiency: Comparative reflections on the reality and the rhetoric. *Comparative Education Review, 34*(3), 157–176.

Welch, A. (2002). Going global? Internationalising Australian universities in a time of global crisis. *Comparative Education Review, 46*(4), 433–471.

Welch, A. (2003). Globalization, structural adjustment and contemporary educational reforms in Australia: The politics of reform or the reform of politics. In K.-H. Mok & A. Welch (Eds.), *Globalisation and the re-structuring of education in the Asia Pacific* (pp. 262–301). London: Palgrave Macmillan.

Welch, A. (2005). Korean higher education in international perspective: Internationalised or globalised? In K.-H. Mok & R. James (Eds.), *Globalization and highereducation in East Asia* (pp. 99–136). London: Marshall Cavendish.

Welch, A. (2007a). Making educational policy. In R. Connell, C. Campbell, M. Vickers, A. Welch, & N. Bagnall (Eds.), *Education, change and society* (pp. 1–31). Oxford: Oxford University Press.

Welch, A. (2007b). Governance issues in South East Asian higher education: Finance, devolution and transparency in the global era. *Asia Pacific Journal of Education, 27*(3), 237–253.

Welch, A. (2007c). *Ho Chi Minh meets the market: Public and private higher education in Viet Nam.*

Welch, A. (2008). Mammon, markets and managerialism: Asia Pacific perspectives. In R. Cowen & A. Kazamias (Eds.), *International handbook of comparative education.* Amsterdam: Springer.

Welch, A., & Mok, K.-H. (2003). Conclusion: Deep development or deepening division? In K.-H. Mok & A. Welch (Eds.), *Globalisation and the re-structuring of education in the Asia Pacific* (pp. 333–356). London: Palgrave Macmillan.

Welch, A. R. (Ed.). (2000). *Quality and equality in third world education.* Garland, New York.

World Bank. (1995). *Higher education: The lessons of experience.* Washington, DC: World Bank.

Yeatman, A. (1997). The concept of public management and the Australian state in the 1980s. In M. Considine & M. Painter (Eds.), *Managerialism: The great debate.* Melbourne: Melbourne University Press.

Anthony R. Welch
Director of International Institute for Educational Development
Faculty of Education and Social Work
University of Sydney

MINA O'DOWD

14. THE BOLOGNA PROCESS AND THE RE-STRUCTURING OF HIGHER EDUCATION

Who will bear the Brunt of Unexpected Outcomes?

This chapter deals with an issue that I would have enjoyed discussing with David Wilson. Over the years, David and I have had many discussions on a variety of issues. David's voice, as he critically addressed important issues in education, will be missed. This chapter is written in appreciation of David Wilson's commitment to change and his readiness to voice his well-informed critique.

There can be no doubt that the ongoing restructuring of Higher Education (HE) in Europe, known as the Bologna Process, has already had an influence on the lives of innumerable teachers, students, and administrators in many European Union (EU) member states. Recognizing the immense work that has thus far taken place due to the Bologna Process, Keeling (2006) states,

> the Bologna reforms, with their main focus on students, have entailed hard work for the academic community. The rapid transformations in European higher education over the last five years have necessitated an often painful restructuring of working practices and in many cases a loss of professional autonomy in both teaching and research. (p. 214)

The far-reaching work entailed with the standardisation of Higher Education in the context of European Union (EU) member states has thus far constituted a burden for many, requiring re-thinking, re-structuring, re-writing and re-constructing national education systems throughout this part of the world. This is the greatest systemic education re-structuring ever to occur and many questions arise regarding its success thus far. Future research will no doubt provide answers to many questions and reveal a number of factors that at present remain unclear. Some questions, such as those that follow, have already been answered. How did the Bologna Process come about? What arguments were advanced that convinced so many Ministries of Education to embark on the Bologna express?

Given the massive re-structuring entailed in the Bologna Process, other questions persist: Is the Bologna process an education reform? Is it a large-scale economic restructuring strategy? Is its purpose to further mobility and Europe's competitive edge? The aim of this chapter is to reflect upon the latter questions, with the hope of providing some insight into this ongoing process. The central question of this chapter is as follows: if the Bologna process is an education reform, does it meet

V. Masemann et al., (Eds.), A Tribute to David N. Wilson: Clamouring for a Better World, 207–220.

the criteria for a successful and effective education reform? In other words, what constitutes a successful and effective education reform, and how does the Bologna process fulfil these criteria? Using Torsten Husén's extensive work on education reform in Sweden and internationally, an attempt will be made herein to answer these questions. First, however, a brief introduction of the Bologna Process is undertaken.

PROJECT EUROPE

For over almost three decades supporters of European integration have been seeing the promotion of a European consciousness and the creation of a European identity as a crucial policy goal. In the early seventies several leading politicians have placed the development of a supra-national identity on top of the EC [European Commission] political agenda during debates on the future of European integration. (Weiner, 1996, p. 19 as cited in Jacobs & Maier, 1998, p. 5)

This ambitious project lost momentum in the early 1980s, only to gain momentum again in the late 1980s when it was "translated in[to] a large scale European public relations campaign and the introduction of a wide variety of Eurosymbolism" (Jacobs & Maier, 1998, p. 6). It gained full momentum in the early 1990s, "actualized in the signing of the Treaty of Maastricht and the introduction of the so-called European citizenship" (Jacobs & Maier, 1998, p. 6). The introduction of European citizenship was followed by the introduction of the common currency, which Irish politician Mary O'Rourke commented upon in the following manner: "While the single currency will have the most significant impact on people's identification with the Union, there remains a pressing need to bring together European citizens on non-economic grounds" (O'Rourke, 1996 as cited in Jacobs & Maier, 1998, p. 7).

What, then, is Project Europe? The concept of Project Europe is a construction which is comprised of three different projects. According to Jacobs and Maier (1998),

[a]t present, there are mainly three conflicting projects for a future Europe within the institutional framework of the European Union: The first one wants Europe to be (again) an important power factor in the world. The second one, in partial opposition to the first one, conceives a social Europe underlining human rights and democracy. A third one, in opposition to both former projects, attempts to defend the existing national states or would even prefer to strengthen them. (p. 7)

Since Jacobs and Maier wrote this statement, it has become apparent through the measures taken by the European Union (EU) that Project Europe has increasingly been defined in terms of the first project, while the second and the third projects have become less pronounced. It is argued here that this re-alignment of the definition of Project Europe, i.e., "Europe as a political and military entity...an efficient economic world power" (Jacobs & Maier, 1998, p. 2), can be attributed to what is commonly referred to as the Bologna Process. What, then, is the Bologna Process?

THE BOLOGNA PROCESS

In June 1999, the Bologna Declaration was signed by the Ministers of Education of 29 European countries. This declaration constitutes a commitment taken by the Ministers of Education in these countries to reform their systems of higher education. To date, as many as 46 European countries have made this commitment, which entails
- the development of a European knowledge area;
- the education of individuals who are included in Europe, defined as a common social and cultural area;
- increased student, teacher and researcher mobility; and
- the professionalization of higher education (Siedersleben & Dahl, 2003).

Following the Bologna Declaration, the Lisbon Summit in 2000 laid the ground for what Dale (2006) calls the "Lisbon agenda". The Lisbon agenda constitutes "the iconic representation" of the "development of neo-liberal globalisation, and especially what has come to be known as the Knowledge Economy" (Dale, 2006, p. 29). In short, it was at the Lisbon summit that "the EU set itself the task of becoming the most dynamic, competitive knowledge-based economy in the world, capable of sustained growth, with more and better jobs and greater social cohesion" (Dale, 2006, p. 29). The conclusion of the Lisbon presidency is important in this context, as it is here that "[e]ducation and [t]raining were accorded a strong and central role in attaining these goals, and... the Lisbon presidency emphasised that this contribution could only be met at the level of Community as whole and not at the level of the individual MS [Member State]" (Dale, 2006, pp. 29–30).

The insistence on a Community-level operationalisation of the Lisbon agenda was based on "a lack of confidence in the existing MS education systems to meet the challenges laid down by the Lisbon agenda" (Dale, 2006, p. 30). This lack of confidence was clearly documented in the Commission's 2004 report (European E-skills Forum, 2004 as cited in Dale, 2006, p. 31). Dale (2006) reminds us that the Lisbon agenda is "made up of at least five distinct discourses, each with their own histories and trajectories, and separate implications for education, its purposes and how they are to be attained" (p. 30).

According to Dale (2006), the five discourses are as follows:
- competitiveness;
- knowledge-based economy;
- sustainable growth;
- more and better jobs; and
- greater social cohesion (p. 30).

Of all these, competitiveness is "the master discourse" (Dale 2003a, 2003b, 2006; Radaelli, 2003; Rosamond, 2002).

THE CONSTRUCTION OF "PARALLEL UNIVERSES"

The Bologna Declaration specified the creation of a mobile European Higher Education Area (EHAE), to be accomplished by 2010. It aims to achieve this goal through the use of three instruments: the introduction of the three-cycle system, Quality Assurance and the recognition of qualifications and periods of study (European Union, 2008a).

It is maintained that through these three instruments, the re-construction of higher education is to be accomplished, transforming HE in Europe into a transparent, standardized system that will further the aims of the Community, as specified in the Lisbon agenda, thereby, "becoming the most dynamic, competitive knowledge-based economy in the world, capable of sustained growth, with more and better jobs and greater social cohesion" (Dale, 2006, p. 29). Through these three instruments, competitiveness is further strengthened as "the master discourse". The Framework for Qualifications in the European Higher Education Area (EQF-HE) was approved by Ministers of Education at a summit in Bergen, Norway in 2005 (BWG-QF, 2005), whereby it became the central coordinative structure in the Bologna Process. In 2006, the EU Commission proposed a comprehensive European Qualifications Framework for Lifelong Learning (EQF), in which Europass Mobility (EUROPASS), the European Credit Transfer System (ECTS), European Credit System for Vocational Education and Training (ECVET) and quality assurance through the European Network for Quality Assurance and the European Network for Quality Assurance in Vocational Education and Training (ENQA-ENQAVET) initiatives are introduced. This framework has been approved by both the European Parliament and the Council and was published in April 2008 (European Communities, 2008, European Union, 2008b).

Against this background, it appears naïve to maintain, as do Dahl, Lien and Lindberg-Sand (2008), that "the Bologna Process is not an EU initiative" (p. 2). The authors qualify this statement by maintaining that "the commitments, goals and instruments fit a lot of the EU initiatives" (p. 2). However, as Kallo & Rinne (2006) assert, it is only in a highly technical sense that the Bologna Process can be viewed in this manner, disregarding the interplay between and the influence of supranational regimes such as the Organisation of Economic Co-operation and development (OECD), the EU, United Nations Educational, Scientific and Cultural Organization (UNESCO), the World Bank and the World Trade Organization (WTO). Dale (2006) maintains, and I concur, that "[t]heoretically,…the Lisbon declaration made attaining the educational goals of Lisbon a Community matter", although "it did not and could not (because it is enshrined in the Treaty) alter the formal application of subsidiarity in the case of education: this means that education is a national and not a Community responsibility" (p. 34). Despite this fact, "the Bologna and Lisbon Processes have significantly broadened the European Comm-ission's base for involvement…these developments have confirmed the increasingly central role of the Commission's policy texts in shaping higher education discourse in Europe" (Keeling, 2006, p. 203). The EU strategy employed to insert itself into the HE sector resembles the creation of a "parallel universes" (Dale, 2006, p. 35). Dale has adapted the phrase used by Adelman (2000), albeit using it to describe EU strategies for higher education. Dale (2006) also argues that

the existence of parallel rather than overlapping education sectors was a means by which there was only minimal terrain on which turf wars could take place. This is especially important in an area like education, which has not only been considered formally a national responsibility, but is widely perceived as the key means of ensuring the reproduction of national culture and national identity. (p. 35)

One may ask how this process has been undertaken. According to Dale (2006), the process has been furthered by what Lukes calls the 2nd and 3rd dimensions of power (Lukes, 1974, as cited in Dale, 2006, p. 31). Dale (2006) notes that

> the power to set the agenda on which decisions will be taken (2nd dimension), and the exercise of power through influencing preference, or through controlling the rules of the game (3rd dimension). The second dimension of power is ubiquitous in the EU; indeed, it might be said that that is both the raison d'être and its most prominent mechanism. (p. 31)

However, as Dale has shown with his discussion of the EU's Open Method of Coordination which was designed by the Lisbon summit, the EU has also made use of the 3rd dimension of power.

Two other features of the Bologna Process are important to note as regards its implementation in EU member states: the speed with which the Process has been undertaken (Keeling, 2006; National Unions of Students in Europe [ESIB], 2005; Neave & Amaral, 2008; Reichert & Tauch, 2005) and the monitoring of the progress of the Process, its aim and form, especially as these relate to "methodological niceties" (Neave & Amaral, 2008, p. 48). Neave and Amaral (2008) maintain that the speed with which the Bologna Process has been implemented can be attributed to the use of "the strategy of competitive emulation":

> Competitive emulation is a gambit well tried in "leverage reform", employed as much by national authorities responsible for higher education as by the intergovernmental agencies with a similar remit. "Competitive emulation" displays a certain generic similarity to what was once known in the terrible and heroic days of constructing the Soviet Union as "Stakhanovism" or, in its American variation, Taylorism....Stakhanovism and Taylorism both involve the rationalism of work to better increase productivity. The ways "rationalisation" is induced are interesting. Competitive emulation involves suasion, conditionality and incentives, physical in the case of Stakhanovism, moral in the case of Taylorism...Moral suasion, shaming, and the implicit threat that backsliding or non-compliance bring such pressure to bear that exceptional performance by the few becomes the expected norm for the many. Competitive emulation is an exceedingly versatile strategy. It may be applied at all levels of the administrative process, across different sectors in the nation's provision of higher education, to the individual establishment, depending on the sophistication and adaptability of the national statistical office or the national organs of evaluation. (p. 43)

Concern has also been expressed as regards "the quality of the translation of the Bologna goals at the university grass-roots" (Keeling, 2006, p. 208), notably by the student unions and other groups (National Unions of Students in Europe [ESIB], 2005; Reichert & Tauch, 2005).

THE INTERACTION BETWEEN THE EU'S RESEARCH AGENDA
AND THE BOLOGNA PROCESS

Keeling (2006) shows "the Lisbon-based research agenda and the Bologna Process have assisted the Commission to disseminate an influential European discourse of higher education. A richly-elaborated language for discussing higher education is circulated through the Commission's Calls for Proposals, its policy documents, and also by its consistent participation in policy discussion at a European level" Keeling, 2006, pp. 208–209). Keeling cites Commission President Barroso who maintains "we're the only constant in this project...we're always sitting there" (Barroso, 2005 cited in Keeling, 2006, p. 209). Furthermore, Keeling stresses that the Commission's multileveled involvement in "the 'language games' (Mottier, 2005) of research policy and the Bologna Process have contributed significantly to the development of a widening pool of 'common sense' understandings, roughly coherent lines of argument and 'self-evident' statements of meaning about higher education in Europe" (Keeling, 2006, pp. 208–209).

Moreover, Keeling (2006) argues that

> The European higher education discourse promoted by the European Commission is thus a complex hybrid of research and Bologna elements. Although deriving from different policy origins, the Bologna reforms and the EU's research agenda thus mutually reinforce each other—discursively and politically. The framing of EU research policy as consistent with the Bologna Process enhances the political legitimacy of the Lisbon objectives in education and research, as Bologna has become the guiding framework for universities in many countries...The effective blending of these two policy fields has allowed the hybridised Bologna-research policy discourse employed by the Commission rapidly to become a widely—accepted— even hegemonic—perspective for higher education at the European level. (pp. 211–212)

Keeling (2006) emphasises that the coordination between the Bologna Process and the European research agenda has contributed to the construction of a discourse on higher education with the following characteristics: higher education is *purposeful*, it *leads somewhere*, it is *an inherently productive activity*, the outcomes of which are *measureable*, while higher education itself is *economically beneficial* (p. 209). Wain (2006) maintains that

> the discourse of performativity has infiltrated the world of education at all levels, that it has become the dominant discourse in Europe and that, notwithstanding protestations to the contrary, it largely informs the EU's lifelong learning agenda which has, over recent years, very significantly, abandoned the socially oriented notion of the learning society and replaced it with the technocratic notion of a knowledge-based society. (p. 108)

THE THREE PHASES OF THE BOLOGNA PROCESS

The Bologna Process can be more clearly understood if one views it in terms of three phases: phase one (1999–2003), phase two (2003–2007) and phase three (2007 onwards). It was in phase one that the "broad-front approach" and a rapid tempo for implementation were utilized. Phase two was characterized by an attempt to engage academia in the re-structuring process, which had not been undertaken in phase one. This attempt "eventually took place in 2005 at the Bergen Ministerial Meeting, six years after the launching of the Declaration" (Neave & Amaral, 2008, p. 52). Throughout phases one and two, the impression of expediency and success was dependent upon the use of competitive emulation: "In effect, the Bologna strategy of competitive emulation relies as much upon the *image* conveyed of advancing achievement and achievement advanced as it does on the often-meagre reality of what indeed has been achieved" (Neave & Amaral, 2008, p. 48). If we accept this argument, it is interesting to note, as do Neave and Amaral, that competitive emulation has outlived its usefulness in phase three of the Bologna Process. Unlike the first two phases of the Bologna Process, phase three has necessitated paying attention to "methodological niceties" (Neave & Amaral, 2008, p. 50), previously subordinated to the production of an *image* of success in the two previous phases.

This change, however, has consequences for the Bologna Process: it calls into question the legitimacy of the Bologna Process itself and the information gathered to legitimize it in the first two phases:

> In the quest for consensus and through consensus, demonstrable progress, little attention was paid to views that questioned the ways to achieve the Bologna objectives…The striking feature of the Bologna strategy in its third stage is the recognition that while instant success may encourage effort, it is a gambit limited in usefulness and applicability. (Neave & Amaral, 2008, p. 55)

An arguably more important aspect of the third phase is the issue of "whether or not the Bologna strategy is easily reconcilable with academia's daily life. Or, indeed whether or not the interpretation that national governments placed on Bologna and the opportunities it presented for the furtherance of national policy were reconcilable" (Neave & Amaral, 2008, p. 56).

TORSTEN HUSÉN AND EDUCATION REFORM

Of central importance in educational reform during the 20th century was Torsten Husén, not only in Sweden, but in a wide range of international contexts. Husén's career, which ended with his demise on July 2, 2009, was an extraordinary one, dedicated to improving understanding of what education can and should be and how to achieve this end. It goes without saying that this Swede was an internationally acclaimed educator we would do well to take into consideration to study the Bologna Process.

In Sweden, a country with a long history of education reform, the Bologna process has entailed a massive restructuring of the Swedish higher education system and a re-alignment to the intentions of the EU Commission. Swedish government policy documents support the Bologna Process in its construction of a European Higher Education Area and the construction of the European citizen through education (Fejes, 2008). The only point of disagreement that the Swedish government has expressed with the overall aims of the Bologna Process regards the introduction and use of the 7 grade scale European Credit Transfer System (Fejes, 2008).

The extensive education reforms implemented in Sweden during the 20th century through the centralized education authorities have been either praised or critiqued, depending on varying political orientations. For those who perceived Sweden as "a Socialist paradise", the extensive reform efforts were often viewed as "social engineering". For the more erudite, Sweden's relative success was based on what was called a "mixed economy"—a capitalist economy the profits of which were used to finance social reforms (Fägerlind & Saha, 1989; Lindbeck, 1974).

Education and social reform were devised and implemented in a closely linked process, in close cooperation with research and researchers. This model was developed in keeping with and was dependent upon consensus, the conviction being that broad consensus was vital for the success of reform.

In 1994, Torsten Husén wrote extensively on education reform, saying that to be effective reforms should meet a number of criteria. Husén (1994) also poses the question, "what is it that constitutes a successful or an unsuccessful reform?" (p. 227). His thoughts on this topic are the results of many years of work both nationally and internationally throughout his long career as an educator. As Husén writes, "naturally, it is not possible to identify a universal 'paradigm' for the implementation of education reform" (Husén, 1994, p. 227) because historical, cultural and economic conditions vary so greatly between and within different countries. This fact necessitates that the "specific policy and technique that is used for the planning and implementation of reforms are re-thought anew for every national education system" (Husén, 1994, p. 227). However, after years of being actively engaged in the evaluation of education reform around the world, Husén (1994) maintains that a number of "general rules" can be identified, which taken together appear to constitute a "strategy that can succeed, if the rules are taken into consideration when planning, implementing and evaluating reforms....the rules are especially important in cases in which radical reforms of structure, enrolment and curriculum are concerned" (Husén, 1994, p. 227–228).

First Husén (1994) stresses that education reform should be considered in relation to its socio-economic context, a process which necessitates awareness that education reform is not and cannot be a substitute for social and economic reform: "An education reform cannot in itself lead to greater social justice or an increase of quality of life" (Husén, 1994, p. 228).

The second principle of education reform, according to Husén (1994), has to do with "the *tempo* with which the reform is introduced and implemented" (p. 228). Citing examples of attempts made in Sweden and France to implement education reform quickly, Husén (1994) concludes that there are lessons to be learned from past mistakes. For instance, time is needed to test an education reform before it is implemented. Further, education reforms require the cooperation of those involved, i.e., students, teachers and pupils, "not least in order to inform them of what the new measures entail" (Husén, 1994, p. 229). In other words, education reform is best implemented after it has been thoroughly discussed by all the actors involved thus achieving a working consensus prior to its implementation. It should be noted that the examples that Husén cited in Sweden and France were education reforms that, despite a relatively long period of time involved, nevertheless did not effect the changes expected.

Husén's third rule for education reform is that financial and human resources are needed. As Husén (1994) points out, investments in education entail a very long-term perspective. Whether or not a reform has been successful can first be clearly seen only after many years, even as far in the future as when students have reached the "productive age". Education reform entails that investments are needed for infrastructure, for example, the education of teachers, the development of new methods, the procurement of new buildings, and the development of new forms of leadership. Last, but not least, education reform requires a comprehensive research base upon which to determine beforehand the appropriate methods, their short-comings and how to adjust for them, possible consequences of the reform, as well as funds with which to monitor the implementation of the reform process itself.

In a lecture given at the Institute of International Education, Stockholm University, in the spring of 1994, Husén elaborated on the above "general rules". It is important to note Husén's clarification that education reform yields "unexpected outcomes". Despite the use of a comprehensive research base for development of reform policy, invariably "unexpected outcomes" have been the result. Therefore, in the context of Sweden, pre-testing has been conducted to determine probable outcomes, prior to wide-spread implementation, termed broad-front implementation. Based on the pre-test results, it has been possible to adjust for negative results, correcting malfunctions immediately, before large-scale implementation was undertaken. Research was conducted collaboratively with the research community and interested parties throughout the implementation process to determine and document the effects of the reform.

THE GENERAL RULES OF EDUCATION REFORM AND THE BOLOGNA PROCESS

With only two years left before the mobile European Higher Education Area (EHAE) is to be accomplished, it is interesting to reflect upon the Process(es) thus far as they relate to the work cited in this chapter and Husén's "general rules" for education reform.

Husén (1994) cites as the first rule that education reform is to be considered in relation to its socio-economic context and necessitates awareness that education reform is not and cannot be a substitute for social and economic reform. Given that the Bologna Process attempts to combine social, economic and education reform within the context of one, albeit massive, restructuring reform, it may arguably fail, because it is too broad, too complex, and too massive. As the Bologna Process progresses, it increasingly resembles an economic reform, despite rhetoric to the contrary. The purpose of the reform is to re-model the EHEA on market principles by re-defining higher education, replete with a "master discourse" of competitiveness, at the same time as a New Europe is constructed—a Europe envisioned "as a political and military entity…an efficient economic world power" (Jacobs & Maier, 1998, p. 2).

As the second rule, Husén (1994) proposes that education reform is to be introduced and implemented slowly, giving time to test the reform and engaging all the actors involved prior to broad front implementation. As several sources have pointed out, the Bologna Process has been characterised by rapidity and no pre-testing has taken place prior to broad-front implementation. Furthermore, it was only in phase 2, six years after the broad-front implementation had begun that an attempt was made to inform and engage the academic community in the Bologna Process (Neave & Amaral, 2008).

Husén's third rule stipulates the necessity of investments, and the awareness that assessing returns to investments in education require a very long-term perspective. Although the EU has neither the authority nor the mandate as regards the regulation or legislation of education, it has effectively inserted itself in the education sector in the role guaranteed in the Treaty to be the sole concern of the nation state. Furthermore, implementation of the Bologna Process has required substantial investments at the university level, investments of financial and human resources that have not been supported by national governments or the EU.

If one is to take Husén's "general rules" seriously, the consequences of the reform—which have not been taken into account during the implementation process and have not been adjusted for throughout the process—may result in far-reaching problems for individual students, universities and higher education systems. As Ash (2006) points out, "the creation of a European higher education sphere is a fascinating project, likely to result in something far different from and in many respects more interesting than the 'Anglo-Saxon' system with which it has supposed, erroneously, to be compatible" (p. 262). The three-cycle university system with Bachelor, Master's and Ph.D. share only names in common with degrees in the American and British systems. Substantial differences as regards length and content distinguish the degrees from one another.

The manner in which this comprehensive re-structuring process has been undertaken appears to further complicate the issue of "unexpected outcomes", especially as these relate to individual students, individual universities and individual higher education systems. Students are already discovering, much to their understandable dismay, that—despite the similarity of degree names—there are serious unresolved questions regarding content and length, which stand in the way when students aspire to transfer from the EHEA to American universities (Ash, 2006, p. 261). Another serious problem yet to be resolved seems to be labour market acceptance of Bologna "Bachelor" degrees. As Ash (2006) notes,

> policy-makers appear to be agreed that this is one of the major problems of the Bologna Process thus far. One of the goals stated in the Glasgow Declaration [2003], for example, is to work on making government employment systems accommodate the new first- and second-cycle degrees. (p. 262)

The optimism with which the Bologna Process was intentionally enveloped may prove to be a further problem in the future. Resistance to the restructuring of European higher education systems was not encountered in what Neave and Amaral (2008) term as phases one and two. This lack of resistance may be attributed to the fact that the process effectively by-passed interested parties, such as students, teachers, and universities as well as Ministers of Education who appear to have been quick to commit their countries without reservation to the cause. The reasons for ministry commitment were many: for example, the promise of the chance to rectify problems with their higher education systems that had thus far proved difficult to solve, the conviction that commitment entailed advantages and financial benefits, and the euphoria of being part of Project Europe. Last, but not least, there was the chance to re-write their responsibilities for higher education:

> By discursively referencing the Commission's broad objectives for higher education, national governments can articulate additional justifications for their withdrawal from their traditionally active responsibilities for higher education, moving to arms-length steering and the provision of incentives, rather than centralized control. (Keeling, 2006, p. 213)

By creating "parallel universes", the EU has effectively made use of the 2nd dimension of power—the power to set the agenda on which decisions will be taken—and the 3rd dimension of power—the use of competitive emulation—to pressure Member States to "willingly" re-structure their higher education system. This strategy has effectively put the EU and the Member States in the position of controlling the processes without being responsible for the outcomes.

Who, then, will bear the brunt of the unexpected outcomes? It is worrisome to reflect upon the way the European Commission (EC) has inserted itself in the education sector: Given that it has no legal grounds to stand on, engaging Ministers of Education in this process has effectively functioned to re-define both the roles of ministries vis-à-vis education as well as providing space for the EU to construct "parallel universes" in which it could assume an ever-growing role in the construction of Europe. This strategy has provided the EU with a position of power, without having to assume responsibility for failure, since legally, responsibility rests with the nation state, as stipulated in the Treaty. Ministries, eager to get on the Bologna Process bandwagon, have made use of competitive emulation to bring pressure to bear on their own universities. At the university level, the Bologna Process has been implemented most often at the expense of faculty and staff. At the national level, there is little or no funding for universities to implement the Bologna Process. Nor is there funding for research to be conducted throughout its implementation. Monitoring of the Process has been criticed for disregarding "methodological niceties" (Neave & Amaral, 2008, p. 48). Funding provided by the Commission has been targeted to support and to legitimise the implementation of the Bologna Process itself: from "financial incentives for higher education cooperation and reform projects in line with the Bologna objectives...as well as funding national Bologna Promoters and Bologna information activities" (Keeling, 2006, p. 208).

There do not appear to be any measures put in place, either by the European Commission or at the national level, to determine what unexpected outcomes may result from the implementation of the Bologna Process. As implementation of the Process progresses, one can not help but be concerned that the transformation of European higher education systems is, in effect, a reform project with serious implications that have thus far received little or no attention.

The Bologna Process—through the speed with which it has been introduced and implemented, the fact that the academia was first brought into the Process six years after it has begun, the inadequacies of the data used for the monitoring process, the lack of research-based results to guide this reform project and the focus on performativity and competitiveness—has thus far identified the united efforts of ministries and the European Commission as an economic re-structuring process. Its purpose is to quickly put into place a New Europe, the defining characteristics of which are Europe (again) as an important power factor in the world. Left behind are the Project(s) Europe as a social Europe underlining human rights and democracy and a Europe that defends the existing national states or would even prefer to strengthen them.

The implications for university education are very serious. There is reason for concern, given what Wain terms "the unquestioned and unquestioning all-around allegiance" (Wain, 2006, p. 107) in Europe as regards this massive reform project and the European Commission's overall perspective on the role of higher education, its goals and its purposes. As Keeling (2006) writes,

> its identification of "indicators" and its use of "benchmarking", in relation to both research and higher education reform, break open the formerly unique status of universities. Higher education institutions are constructed by the Commission as organizations like any other, participating in and competing on an open market, and measurable in terms which transcend the education sector. (p. 209)

CONCLUSION

The Bologna Process does not follow the three general rules that Husén has recommended as necessary to ensure effective education reform. This conclusion raises serious questions as to the future of higher education in Europe, a fact that is even more disturbing given Husén's warning: "the rules are especially important in cases in which radical reforms of structure, enrolment and curriculum are concerned" (Husén, 1994, p. 228). The Bologna Process involves many radical reforms undertaken within many different higher education systems. It is a Process that appears, for all intents and purposes, to disregard the socio-economic and cultural diversity of Europe and its member states as well as the unique role of higher education in "the reproduction of national culture and identity" (Dale, 2006, p. 35). The Process is a massive reform conceived, introduced, and implemented without forethought to the distinctive role of higher education and the diversity of Europe and its different higher education systems.

Implementation of the Process will undoubtedly result in unexpected outcomes. Ash (2006) and Purser and Crosier (2007) argue that students face problems when transferring to other higher education systems and entering the labour market. Moreover, the Bologna Process has entailed "restructuring of working practices and in many cases a loss of professional autonomy" (Keeling, 2006, p. 214) for teachers and researchers.

There are also grounds for concern as to "the quality of the translation of the Bologna goals at the university grass-roots" (Keeling, 2006, p. 208). One can also question whether or not the Bologna Process is "easily reconcilable with academia's daily life", and if "the interpretation that national governments placed on Bologna and the opportunities it presented for the furtherance of national policy were reconcilable" (Neave & Amaral, 2008, p. 56).

With national governments withdrawing "from their traditional active responsibilities for higher education" (Keeling, 2006, p. 213) and the EU with no legal responsibility for education, it seems appropriate in the context of the European Higher Education Area, as it has increasingly been defined through the Bologna Process, to issue the warning: *Caveat emptor* or "Let the buyer beware".

REFERENCES

Adelman, C. (2000). *A parallel postsecondary universe: The certification system in information technology.* Jessup, MD: Office of Educational research and Improvement, U.S. Department of Education.

Ash, M. G. (2006). Bachelor of what, Master of whom? The Humboldt myth and historical transformations of higher education in German-speaking Europe and the US. *European Journal of Education, 41*(2), 245–267.

Barroso, J. M. (2005, September). *Speech presented at the Open Forum for Commission Staff.* Belgium: Brussels.

Dahl, B., Lien, E., & Lindberg-Sand, A. (2008, March). *Changing grading-scales in higher education as a part of the Bologna Process- the case of Denmark, Norway and Sweden.* Paper presented at the Nordic Educational Research Association Conference, Copenhagen, Denmark.

Dale, R. (2006). Policy relationships between supranational and national scales: Imposition/resistance or parallel universes? In J. Kallo & R. Rinne (Eds.), *Supranational regimes and national educational policies: Encountering challenges.* Finland: Finnish Educational Research Association.

Dale, R. (2003a, March). *The Lisbon declaration, the reconceptualisation of governance and the reconfiguration of European educational space.* Paper presented at the RAPPE Seminar on Governance, Regulation and Equity in European Education Systems, Institute of Education, London University.

Dale, R. (2003b, July). *Globlisation, Europeanisation and the 'competitiveness' agenda: Implications for education policy in Europe.* Paper present at the GENIE conference, Cyprus.

European Communities. (2008). *The European qualifications framework for lifelong learning (EQF). Luxembourg: Office for official publications of the European Communities.* Retrieved March 12, 2008, from http://ec.europa.eu/education/policies/educ/eqf/eqf08_en.pdf

European Union. (2008a). *The Bologna process: Towards the European higher education area.* Retrieved March 12, 2008, from http://ec.euopa.eu/education/policies/educ/bologna/bologna_en.html

European Union. (2008b). *ECTS-European Credit Transfer and Accumulation System.* Retrieved March 12, 2008, from http://ec.europe.ey/education/prorammes/socrates/ects/index_en.html

Fägerlind, I., & Saha, L. J. (1989). *Education and national development: A comparative perspective.* London: Pergamon Press.

Fejes, A. (2008). European Citizens under Construction. The Bologna process analysed from a governmentality perspective. *Educational Philosophy and Theory, 40*(4), 515–529.

Husén, T. (1994). *Skola och universitet inför 2000-talet. En utbildningsforskares perspektiv.* [School and The University in the 21st Century. An educational researcher's perspective]. Stockholm: Atlantis.

Jacobs, D., & Maier, R. (1998). *European identity: Construct, fact and fiction.* In M. Gastelaars & A. de Ruijter (Eds.), *A united Europe. The quest for a multifaceted identity* (pp. 13–34). Maastricht: Shaker. Retrieved May 20, 2008, from http://home.planetinternet.be/~ecitoyen/europa.pdf

Kallo, J., & Rinne, R. (Eds.). (2006). *Supranational regimes and national educational policies: Encountering challenges.* Finland: Finnish Educational Research Association.

Keeling, R. (2006). The Bologna process and the Lisbon research agenda: The European Commission's expanding role in higher education discourse. *European Journal of Education, 41*(2), 203–223.

Lindbeck, A. (1974). *Swedish economic policy.* Berkeley, CA: University of California Press.

Mottier, V. (2005). From welfare to social exclusion. In D. Howarth & J. Torfing (Eds), *Discourse theory in European politics: Identity, policy and governance* (pp. 255–274). Houndsmills: Palgrave MacMillian.

National Unions of Students in Europe [ESIB]. (2005). *The black book of the Bologna process.* Bergen: ESIB.

Neave, G., & Amaral, A. (2008, January/April). On process, progress, success and methodology or the unfolding of the Bologna process as it appears to two reasonably benign observers. *Higher Education Quarterly, 62*(1/2), 40–62.

Purser, L., & Crosier, D. (2007, March). *Trends V: Key messages.* 4th Convention of European Higher Education Institutions, Lisbon (power point presentation).

Radaelli, C. (2003). *The open method of coordination: A new governance architecture for Europe?* Stockholm: Swedish Institute for European Policy Studies.

Reichert, S., & Tauch, C. (2005). *European universities implement Bologna.* EUA Trends IV Report. Brussels: European University Association.

Rosamond, B. (2002). Imagining the European economy: Competitiveness and the social construction of "Europe" as an economic space. *New Political Economy, 7*(2), 157–177.

Siedersleben, W., & Dahl, B. (2003). Chronology of education and training policy within the European Union. In D. Phillips & H. Ertl (Eds.), *Implementing European Union education and training policy- A comparative study of issues in four member states* (pp. 319–329). Dordrecht: Kluwer Academic.

Wain, K. (2006). Some reflections on the learning society in a postmodern world. In J. Kallo & R. Rinne (Eds.), *Supranational regimes and national educational policies: Encountering challenges* (pp. 101–114). Finland: Finnish Educational Research Association.

Weiner, A. (1996). *Practicing citizenship beyond modern frontiers. The resources of Union citizenship.* Paper presented at the European University Institute (EUI) European Forum on Citizenship, European Citizenship: An Institutional Challenge, Florence, Italy.

Mina O'Dowd
Division of Education
Department of Sociology
Lund University

RATNA GHOSH AND PAROMITA CHAKRAVARTI

15. WOMEN'S EDUCATION IN INDIA AT THE START OF THE TWENTY-FIRST CENTURY

Implications of the National Knowledge Commission Reports

Preface by Ratna Ghosh

It is a great privilege to be part of a Festschrift that honours David Wilson, who helped shape the field of Comparative and International Education through his publications as well as his leadership as President of the Canadian Comparative and International Education Society (twice), as President of Comparative International Education Society and also President of the World Council of Comparative Education Societies.

Although David's specialization was in Technical and Vocational Education, he had vast international experience and an immense interest in equity issues. While he did not focus on women's inequalities in particular, the increasing importance given to technical and vocational education in the National Knowledge Commission Report (NKC 2006–2008) in India reminded me of David, and I contribute a gender analysis of this important blueprint for India's future as it would have undoubtedly interested David. The goal of this analysis was to develop a grassroots critique of the recommendations of the NKC Report that would have *a* major impact on women's educational opportunities, disciplinary choices, career options and life choices. I conducted the study with my colleague, Paromita Chakravarti, in India.

INTRODUCTION

India is said to be at the forefront of the knowledge revolution and one of the fastest growing economies in the world. Yet, it has a quarter of the world's poorest people and the largest number of illiterate women (over 40 per cent). In 2005, India was ranked 62 among 108 developing countries listed in the Gender Development Index (GDI) (UNDP, 2007). Despite many advances for women since India's independence (1947), in 2001 245 million Indian women were illiterate and 40 per cent of Indian girls younger than 14 years of age did not go to school (Census, 2001). These figures indicate that nearly half the brain power represented by women in India is not being utilized for the country's development.

The authors of the recently presented National Knowledge Commission (NKC) Reports, 2006–08, envisage a comprehensive and radical programme of educational

V. Masemann et al., (Eds.), A Tribute to David N. Wilson: Clamouring for a Better World, 221–236.

reform at all levels of education in India needed to bring the country into the new knowledge economy. The proposed changes have significant implications for women engaged in education whether as students, teachers, educational administrators or parents of students. However, the Reports do not explore the embedded gendered impact of their recommendations, especially on the vast majority of women. In spite of various Constitutional guarantees and international treaty obligations promising gender equity, women's issues continue to take a backseat in governmental policies in India.

Given that India has the largest number of illiterate women of any other country worldwide, the motivation for this analysis was to study national education policy regarding women's and girls' education and the implications of the NKC Reports to emphasize the need to tap women's talents adequately for national development.

Our aim was to study the gender implications of the National Knowledge Commission Reports in the State of West Bengal with the stakeholders who are most directly affected by these changes—women students, teachers, administrators and policy makers. Since education in India is a responsibility of both central and state government, our research focuses on one state (West Bengal) that has been led by a left-wing government for the last thirty years.

CONTEXT

The NKC Reports, 2006–08, should be seen in the context of the changes that have been taking place in the Indian education system since the late 1980s. These changes can be linked to the processes of economic liberalization which entailed the gradual privatization of public sector enterprises such as education and brought in the economic regime of the General Agreement on Trade in Services (GATS). The latter classified education as a part of the "service" sector: in essence, education for those who can pay.

In post-independence India, education was considered a key factor for the overall development of individuals, communities, and the nation. The State's democratic responsibility to educate all citizens and provide a funded and subsidized higher education system was recognized. During the pre-reform period, higher education was defined as a public good in India and financed almost totally with public funds, either from the central government or from state governments. However, since the late 1980s the impact of the Structural Adjustment Programme (SAP) led to the erosion of the Nehruvian ideal of a socialist, welfare state aiming for a just society. Sweeping changes in the economy led to cuts in government expenditure in many areas, notably education, and particularly higher education. There was a sharp increase in the demand for both professional and general university education which facilitated the entry of private players in higher education mostly as "for profit" businesses. In the post-reform period, education increasingly came to be recognized as an investment and demand for education began to be determined solely on the basis of its expected return. The income-generating role of education might have led to the decline in the demand for women's enrolment since women who were not going to work for pay did not enrol (Upadhyay, 2008).

In 1997, the government-sponsored Ambani-Birla Report asserted that higher education was a marketable commodity and proposed "full cost recovery from students and immediate privatization of the entire higher education [system]" (2000, p. 120). The educational landscape, particularly within professional and technical education, was transformed in the 1990s by a huge growth of private colleges. In 2001, 42 per cent of the higher education institutions in India were privately owned, catering to approximately 37 per cent of the students enrolled in this sector (Kaul, 2006). Private colleges outnumber the government-affiliated colleges in many states although the degree of privatization varies greatly among states.

These changes in higher education brought about by globalization have serious repercussions for women students. The majority of private institutions are for-profit with very limited resources and dubious standards. Other factors which affect women are the creation of a two-tier system, one catering to the rich and the other to the poor, a large number of whom are girls and women. Emphases on marketable skills serve the global economy and devaluation of non-professional disciplines, particularly the liberal arts which have a majority of women students. The emphasis on English as an important criterion for higher educational access means that those who lack English skills (largely female students who are sent off to the cheaper government-run vernacular medium schools) are structurally discriminated against.

The educational goals of the 1980s that envisaged education as a radical tool for empowering women seem to have shifted toward a more instrumentalist understanding of education only serving to produce skilled personnel for a new economy. Not much attention is being paid to issues of equal access and opportunities, equitable growth, and particularly to the crucial role that education plays in transforming women's lives. Women and girls are the most neglected segment of the population in the Indian democracy (Ghosh, 2008). Much of this neglect is also due to culturally entrenched gender-discriminatory practices which constrain women's own perception of their fundamental right to education and equality of opportunities. The highest illiteracy and dropout rates in India are still among women and girls. While some urban English-educated women from the affluent classes are benefiting from the opening of the economy and the privatization of higher education, vast numbers of Indian women are affected negatively.

While the Commission has emphasized the urgent need to expand higher education in science and technology, there has been a steady decline in the allocation of government expenditures for higher education over the past few decades: 0.75 per cent of the GDP in 1990–91, 0.6 per cent in 1997–98, and 0.35 per cent in 2003–04. Much of the proposed expansion of education in science and technology will therefore be done through private players who are unlikely to provide affordable education to the masses. The exorbitant fees of private institutions push higher education beyond the reach of many in India, where the per capita income is Rs. 29,642 (US$ 605) per annum (Press Information Bureau, 2008). This trend would particularly affect women students adversely. Viewed in the context of India, this model of educational development does not appear to be sustainable.

IMPLICATIONS OF THE NKC, 2006, FOR WOMEN'S EDUCATION

The National Knowledge Commission is a high-level group convened by the Indian Prime Minister and entrusted with the task of preparing "a blueprint to tap into the enormous reservoir of our Knowledge base so that our people can confidently face the challenges of the 21st century" (NKC, 2009, p. 1). Chaired by a technology expert and consisting of high-powered academics and members of industry, the Knowledge Commission submitted its reports between December 2006 and 2008. Its recommendations included a comprehensive plan for revamping higher education with implications for school education, the creation of libraries and knowledge networks and national portals, and the transformation of vocational education and e-governance to respond to the changing needs of a globalizing economy. Instead of playing a critical and leading role in providing a balanced vision of future national development, the report simply emphasizes the need for trained, English-speaking technical personnel for global corporations, validates privatization, and justifies the focus on the techno-sciences and the expanding information technology (IT) sector at the expense of the social sciences and humanities (SSH). The report uses the discourse of efficient management, maximizing productivity, downsizing institutions and rationalizing operations rather than of educational goals, social responsibility, accommodating diversity and providing equity, access and justice. As such, it does not treat gender issues with any degree of seriousness. The definition of knowledge within the report is limited, uncritical, and abstract, and is not located in the grounded realities of oppression and marginalization in Indian society. The fallouts for women's education, empowerment and their life chances are many.

First, the report commodifies knowledge as capital to maintain a "competitive edge" in the new global world. Science and technology, "relevant" education which will produce trained workers for the industry, Intellectual Property Rights and innovation form the core of this document to the near exclusion of the social sciences and the humanities, which have the greatest number of women students and academics in their programmes.

Second, the authors elaborate on the benefits of globalization, arguing how information technology can be used for democratic ends by making knowledge more accessible through computer-aided distance learning, e-governance, data sharing between universities and digital library networks. However, the report places those who are least likely to have access to technology—the poor, women and the margin-alized—at the other side of what is already being perceived as the "digital divide".

Third, a major concern in the NKC report is with language. English is described as a "determinant to access" thus disadvantaging those who do not attend schools that use English as the language of instruction (private schools), many of whom are girls. Education in the vernacular language is a constitutional right, and most government schools use the vernacular as the language of instruction. The emphasis on English in higher education disadvantages female students as many attend the free, government schools. Thus, an educational "apartheid" is created between the urban rich whose children attend schools with English as the language of instruction and the rural and urban poor whose children attend free schools with the vernacular as the language of instruction.

Fourth, the report clearly states that universities should follow a "needs blind policy" in admitting students and charging fees. By charging fees, access to higher education will be beyond the reach of poor students, particularly women. While provisions of fee waivers have been suggested for "needy" students, there is no reference to the social and cultural context and factors that discriminate against women. For example, many parents, even when they can afford to cover the costs of schooling, are not inclined to invest in their daughters' education due to socio-cultural reasons.

Finally, gender issues do not figure in the entire body of the Report. In fact, women are never mentioned as a social category. Gender is left to a section titled "Potential Future Areas" which is to be discussed in the future along with public health, environment, and teacher training.

CONCEPTUAL FRAMEWORK

The broad conceptual framework guiding this analysis was derived from gender and feminist critiques of globalization and development. The researchers used qualitative means of data collection such as discourse analysis of the NKC Report (2006), a survey questionnaire, interviews and workshop discussions.

Over the last two decades, a body of feminist research has contested the gender neutral discourses of globalization and development, which failed to address the uneven impact of pervasive economic changes on men and women (Tinker, 1990; Sen, 1992, 1995; and Nussbaum, 2002). This work has documented and theorized the underside of globalization through women's experience of the Structural Adjustment Programme in Asia, Africa and Latin America. These studies have focused not on large macro-economic policies but on globalization as a lived, everyday experience that transforms women's lives, livelihoods, and relationships (See Afshar & Denis, 1992; Banerjee, 1991, 1996; Stromquist, 1995; Moser, 1993; Sparr, 1994). Feminist critiques of development have also been particularly attentive to differences among women, between the middle-class, urban woman who in many respects is the beneficiary of the opening up of the economy, and the rural, poor woman who is excluded from the fruits of economic growth (Afshar & Barrientos, 1999; Elson, 1988; Rege, 2003; Chakravart & Sangari, 1999; Davids & Van Driel, 2001). Feminist philosophers like Martha Nussbaum (2002) have challenged the model of growth by suggesting the basic needs approach. Marxist feminists and eco-feminists like Maria Mies and Vandana Shiva (1993) have also critiqued globalization and development as projects that promote inequity between men and women.

THE STUDY

The objective of our study was to look primarily at two areas of the recommend-dations to see how they might have an impact on women. One area was the proposed privatization of higher education. The second was the focus in the NKC on science and technology often at the expense of the women-dominated disciplines of the social sciences and humanities which are neglected because they are not regarded as useful for the new "knowledge economy". Both of these issues involved gender discrimination in higher education institutions through unequal access as well as other more obvious discriminatory practices within institutions and disciplines and also within communities and families.

Research Context

We conducted workshops in five private colleges and seven government-funded institutions in the State of West Bengal. We interviewed 138 students from private colleges. 269 female students from government institutions participated in the workshops and responded to the questionnaires.

There are no private institutes in West Bengal (and generally in the country) offering Bachelor degrees in Arts, Science, and Commerce. They offer a wide range of programmes including Bachelor degrees in Technology, Business Administration, Computer Applications, Hospitality Management, and Optometry.

Government-funded institutes offer a range of programmes including Bachelor degrees in Technology, Engineering, Arts, Science and Commerce. Most of these institutes also offer Master's-level degrees in all these streams.

The fee structure in private engineering and management institutes ranges from Rs.18,000 to Rs. 33,000 per semester. In the government-funded institutes, the fees range from Rs.360 to Rs. 14,800 per annum.

Our data include participants' views on the proposed privatization model, social sciences and humanities as disciplines, and gender discrimination. We also sought information about the socio-economic background of the students who were coming into private as well as government colleges. The purpose was to prepare a profile of the typical student who can afford access to a private institution and one who goes to the considerably more affordable government institutions. We demonstrate our findings with illustrative vignettes.

Socio-economic profile of female students in private and government-funded institution. The socio-economic background of the students in private colleges and in government-funded institutions revealed a stark difference of socio-economic conditions.

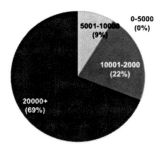

Figure 1. Socio-economic background of students in private colleges (by family income in rupees/month).

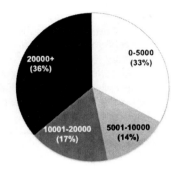

Figure 2. Socio-economic background of students in government-funded colleges (by family income in rupees/month).

Source: Figures compiled from questionnaire data on income of students' parents.

The average family income of students attending private colleges was higher than those attending government-aided colleges. In our sample, 69 per cent of students in private institutions and 36 per cent of students in government-aided institutions came from families with average family incomes of Rs. 20,000 and above per month. Only 9 per cent of students in private institutions had an annual family income of Rs. 5,000 to Rs. 10,000 in comparison to 14 per cent of students in government institutions. 36 per cent of students in private institutions had family incomes of Rs. 5,000 and below while 54 per cent of students in government-aided colleges come from low-income families.

The following vignettes illustrate the difficulties many women students from private engineering colleges faced when paying high fees, an inevitable aspect of private education. All names are fictional.

> *Anita Banik* attends a private engineering college. She has to pay a hefty sum of Rs.25,000 per semester for her education. Since Anita's family income is Rs.8,000 per month, her family has had to go through many difficulties to sustain her education. Anita wrote in the questionnaire, *"It is very tough to pay the fees."* She also told us about the various problems that she has been facing ever since joining college because of her financial situation.

> *Binodini Pattanaik* studies in a private engineering college. Like Anita, her monthly family income is Rs.7,000 while she has to pay semester fees of Rs. 39,000. She has had to overcome problems at home. She said that her *"close relatives made obstructions...because my family is facing a financial crisis for six years."*

Anita and Binodini exemplify the problems faced by many students, especially female students, who are studying engineering in private institutes. With low incomes, students' families find it hard to finance the costs associated with their childrens' education. In many cases, female students also face barriers from within their family (like Binodini) when they want to pursue the educational programme of their choice. Often, the families take bank loans to pay the fees of these institutions, which add to their already existing financial pressures. Little or no guarantee of employment, even after completing the course, also adds to the anxieties of the students studying in private institutions.

> ***Pooja Kundu*** studies engineering in a government college where the fees are Rs. 7,400 per semester. Her father is a farmer and her family's income is Rs. 1,200 per month. She said that the only reason she has been able to continue her studies is because it is a government institution where the fees are significantly lower than that of private institutions and financial support is available for needy students.

> ***Manju Saha*** attends a private college where she has to pay approximately Rs. 200,000 per annum. She has a family income of Rs. 30,000 per month. Despite being able to afford studying in a private college, Manju said, *"Privatization of higher education has put a barrier in the path of education. India is not rich and there are many people below poverty level. I do not support privatization. Privatization will make conditions worse for women's education."*

The quality of education differs greatly between government institutions and most privately run institutions which lack credible systems of accreditation and monitoring of academic standards. It is popularly believed, even by prospective employers, that there are no norms for admissions in place and anybody can attend these institutions by paying "capitation fees" which refers to money charged over and above what the institution needs by way of revenue and capital expenditure plus a reasonable surplus. Also, in West Bengal the standard of higher education is almost uniformly lower in private institutions (which have repeatedly come under government scrutiny) compared to that of government institutions.

Privatization. The NKC proposed both privatization and the Public-Private Partnership (PPP) model for educational development. While the NKC stated that it does not encourage setting up for-profit educational institutions by private players (NKC, 2006), it also would like the higher educational infrastructure to be like that of private business.[1] In the PPP model, the government will provide the land on which to build the educational institutions and the private sector will provide the other required finances (NKC, 2006).

While privatization and PPP represent a major shift in the funding pattern of higher education and its goals for India, the NKC recommendations were hardly debated either in Parliament or among stakeholders—academics and students. PPP has already entered planning documents and is well on the way to being implemented.

While private investment may be necessary (either as PPP or in its entirety) for expansion of the higher education system, it will lead to further problems of access to the tertiary level for students from disadvantaged sectors, especially females, because privatization increases fees. Currently, the recovery rate of university expenditure from student fees is below 10 per cent in publicly funded institutions. The NKC recommends that fees should cover at least 20 per cent of the total expenditure in universities (NKC/FAQs, 2006).

The National Knowledge Commission (2006) suggests that the government provide 100,000 scholarships for students who are unable to pay the admission fees to government institutions (presumably, in addition to those available for disadvantaged groups such as Scheduled Castes and Scheduled Tribes). These scholarships are not designated for female students but are available to all students and are far too few for the large numbers of students who should be in higher education. The expenditure of the Central Government for scholarships has steadily declined in the past few decades from 0.5 per cent in 1990–91 to 0.27 per cent in 2000–01 (Tilak, 2003).

In a society where gender inequities are ingrained and there is a reluctance to invest in girls' education, the government needs to take affirmative action to make higher education cheaper and more accessible for women rather than following the privatization model which would deny access to the majority of female students, especially within the science and technology fields. A further issue is related to the uneven quality of private education that makes a government college degree more valuable to the students than one from a private institution. Our findings indicate that privatization is likely to have a differential impact on men and women's higher education because of socially and culturally ingrained gender disparities.

Figures 3 and 4 show the opinions of female students in government and private colleges regarding privatization. As many as 92 per cent of female students in government colleges and 55 per cent in private colleges are opposed to privatization; and 67 per cent of women teachers in private colleges and 100 per cent in government colleges had the same opinion. Many respondents, even though they had opted for a private college themselves, felt that wide-scale privatization would adversely affect poorer women students who comprise the majority of the student population at these colleges.

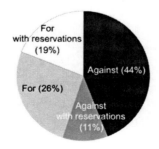

Figure 3. Female private college students' opinions of privatization.

229

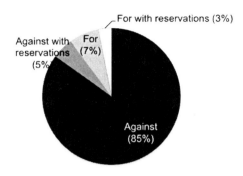

Figure 4. Female government-funded college students' opinions of privatization.

Gender issues arising from cultural factors. Not only has the NKC failed to consult the stakeholders on the proposed privatization model of higher education, it has not considered the differential impact that the privatization model might have on men and women's education. Given entrenched social and cultural disparities of gender, the national education policy should plan for affirmative action for women rather than glossing over gender differences. One of the major educational goals articulated in the Approach Paper to the last Five Year Plan (2002–07) was to reduce the gender disparity in education. But rather than address gender issues, gender seems to have gradually been dropped out of the national educational agenda. Gender disparities seem to remain a concern only at the elementary education and school level (the NKC refers to problems of access for girls at this level only), as if to suggest that girls and women need only literacy and primary education. Tables 1 and 2 which follow show the literacy rates and gross enrolment ratios. It also seems that government policy makers are reluctant to address the issue of women's employment in the formal sectors and their contribution to the highest reaches of the economy. This is, however, not to suggest that women's literacy is no longer an issue or that it deserves any less attention. Women's illiteracy remains one of the major issues in Indian society.

Table 1. Literacy rate

Year	Country	Male (%)	Female (%)
1971	India	46	22
2001	India	76	54
	West Bengal	78	60

Source: Census, 2002

Table 2. Gross enrolment ratio, primary level, 2004–05

Country		Male (%)	Female (%)	Total (%)
India	Rural	10	6	8
	Urban	28	26	27
West Bengal		15	10	13

Source: Srivastava, 2007

Table 1 shows that there has been a significant increase in the number of literate women in India in the three decades since 1971, yet the difference between the literacy rates of men and women has remained more or less constant. There is a gap of 18 per cent between men and women in West Bengal, and this is a major area of concern, especially because the National Knowledge Commission does not address this disparity at all.

Table 2 shows the disparity between the gross enrolment ratio (GER) of male and female students in rural as well as urban areas. This is evident at both the level of the state (West Bengal) and the country.

Responding to a question on gender disparity,[2] the NKC Chairman said, "there is no gender divide." This comment illustrates the stark reality of how gender discrimination within families, communities, and higher education institutions seems to have escaped policy makers and planners.

Our data, with regard to particular difficulties faced by women students, indicated that many faced financial hardships. In addition, the lack of affordable hostel facilities particularly in the private institutions made it difficult for poor, rural girls to go and live in the city in order to study. Sometimes the female students mentioned how their families were reluctant to invest in their futures and sent their brothers to expensive private colleges while they were sent to government institutions. Most female students encountered the problem of overwork because they were expected to help with household chores in stark contrast to their brothers who not only were not expected to do so, but rather were catered to. The vignettes below exemplify the problems faced by female students.

Roshni Mondal studies in an Industrial Training Institute where the monthly fee is Rs.30. Her family income is Rs. 1,250 per month. Roshni said, *"My mother is ill...being the only daughter; I have to complete household chores before I can come to study."* Roshni's case makes it apparent how difficult it already is for a girl from a poor family to come into the purview of higher education and to complete a course. Roshni has opted for a vocational training course because, with the burden of housework, she has no hope of being able to pursue a higher degree.

Another problem that rural girls face is the reluctance of their families to allow them to go to the city to pursue higher education. This factor, coupled with the special restrictions on girls' mobility, makes it imperative that they should be provided with cheap and safe accommodation in hostels. Sometimes they have to abandon hopes of pursuing higher education because living and boarding expenses become unaffordable.

> ***Jhilli Das*** studies in a government engineering college. Her father is a labourer and the monthly income of her family is Rs. 1000. She said, *"Coming to a city and studying is very expensive. Since I come from a rural area, the only problem I faced in the course of pursuing higher education was a financial one."*

> ***Soma Ghatak*** is enroled in a vocational programme at an Industrial Training Institute where the fees are Rs. 30 per month. Soma comes from a family whose monthly income is Rs. 1,500 per month. Despite having the marks and desire to pursue a Master's degree, she could not do so because *"There are many problems for girls coming from rural areas like boarding, transport expenses etc. I would have had to stay in a hostel that required a lot of money. So I had to opt for...this course."*

> ***Bela Bose*** studies in an Industrial Training Institute where the fees are Rs.30 per month. In stark contrast, her brother is studying for a BBA in a private engineering college where the fees are Rs. 23,000 per semester. Her family income is Rs. 20,000 per month.

> ***Malini Ghosh*** studies in a government college where the annual fees are Rs.1,500. Her family income is Rs.17,000 per month. Although Malini wanted to study engineering, she mentioned that she did not want to be a burden on her father because her brother is already studying in a private engineering college.

The cases of Bela and Malini highlight the discrimination that many girls face from their families when it comes to higher education, particularly technical education. If privatization causes fees to increase even more, young women like Bela or Malini will be even less likely to afford to study beyond secondary school when free schooling ends. However, so deeply internalised is the son preference that girls themselves do not see this as gender discrimination in their family. In many cases, even mature women who had been teaching for many years were unaware of the gender discrimination they faced both within their family and workplace.

A majority of the students and teachers said that they had faced no gender discrimination. However, we came across a few cases, including those of Bela and Malini, where it is clear that they are facing gender discrimination but the situation is normalized and internalized to such a great extent that they themselves are unable to recognize it and do not regard equality of status within and outside the family as a fundamental right.

In a context where women themselves are unsure and unaware of their right to equal opportunities to education and employment, educational policies should be aimed at correcting these entrenched gender disparities in families, communities and educational institutions by taking affirmative action rather than ignoring them. The lack of gender sensitivity in the National Knowledge Commission Reports, 2006–08, has the potential to aggravate the gap that already exists.

Social sciences and humanities. The second area of our research is the virtual neglect of the social sciences and humanities in the NKC recommendations that focus on innovation, entrepreneurship, intellectual property, science and technology, copyrights and trademarks. The focus is on training students to fit within a consumer economy rather than acquiring a well-rounded education. Women are the largest stakeholders in the discipline of social sciences and humanities both in terms of the number of students and the number of teachers and administrators. Most all-female colleges focus on social sciences and humanities.

The Approach Paper to the Eleventh Five Year Plan, taking its cue from the National Knowledge Commission, focuses only on science and technical education. They go so far as to propose to relegate "non-laboratory subjects" to the realm of open and distance education, suggesting that students use internet kiosks at will to study those subjects—despite the basic prerequisite needed for open and distance education being the availability of computers and access to digital technology. The lack of electricity and access to computers in rural areas and the digital gender divide have not been taken into account by the educational planners who are using the NKC reports as a blueprint.

Furthermore, a salary differential between social science/humanities (SSH) and science/technology teachers is being proposed. Given that the highest concentration of female academics is in the SSH, it is clear that they will become the first casualties of this move. Moreover, all incentives in terms of fellowships and awards for both teachers and students have been concentrated in the disciplines of science and technology.

Are social sciences relevant in higher education and do they serve any purpose in social development? Our survey results indicated that 95 per cent of female students in government colleges and 85 per cent in private colleges think that there is a need to have social science and humanities (SSH) programmes in their institutions. Overall, 88 per cent of students who were in science and technology programmes thought that SSH were important. Among female teachers, 100 per cent in both private and government institutions felt it was important to have those programmes. Students' comments reveal that the Bachelor of Arts (BA) course in a government college was the most affordable option for poor students who wanted a higher education degree.

> *Tumpa Kundu* has a family income of Rs. 1,600, and is currently pursuing her BA degree in a government institution. Tumpa said, *"A BA course is less expensive. In a country like ours, such courses are needed."*

233

> **Smita Das** studies Sanskrit in a government-funded college. Her family income is Rs. 1,000 per month. She says, *"After leaving school, I wanted to study Geography but because of financial crisis I was forced to study Sanskrit."*

For many students like Tumpa and Smita, a humanities course is their only means to access higher education in the country. Although Smita cannot afford to study a laboratory-based subject like Geography, which has higher course fees, she still had the option of pursuing a BA degree. If these disciplines are marginalized, the large number of female students and teachers in the SSH would suffer the most. But more generally speaking, all students from economically-depressed sections will be denied the opportunity of higher education.

CONCLUSION

The issue of gender disparities in education has to be addressed at all levels, not only at the primary and secondary school levels. Gender gaps in higher education mean that women have less entry ways to participate in the formal workforce. In a country where women's work remains confined to the informal and unorganized sectors, higher education is one path enabling women to enter the organized labour market and to provide women with the skills to deal with challenges within the workplace, such as exploitation.

Gender issues in education cannot be considered in isolation. They need to be understood in terms of class as well as geographical location. It is important to look at women's issues as crosscutting with other disparities and disadvantages. When policy makers assert that the gender divide does not exist, they think primarily of urban, upper middle class women and rarely of the majority of poor, rural women.

Gender discrimination can have specific cultural characteristics as well. Even if a family is not necessarily poor, it might be reluctant to invest in a daughter's higher education. It is important to be attentive to these entrenched cultural factors. A concerted and widespread effort is needed to address the deep-rooted traditions of boy-preference. The Government will need to strengthen efforts against giving dowry, female feticide, and child marriage—all of which are still practiced despite being illegal.

The deeply internalized patriarchal notions even among educated women also need to be addressed through gender sensitization. Women need to be made aware of their right to equal educational opportunities and to employment so that they may recognize cases of discrimination.

The larger question of educational goals needs to be addressed and discussed. Is the goal of effecting social transformation through education to be totally abandoned to privilege the need to supply recruits for the newly emerging global markets? Surely, innovative education reforms can incorporate market needs as well as social needs.

NOTES

[1] As declared by Sam Pitroda at a Dissemination workshop on December 16, 2008, in Swabhumi, Kolkata. This workshop was, organized by All India Management Association (AIMA).

[2] The workshop was organized by All India Management Association (AIMA) on the National Knowledge Commission Report on the 16th of December 2008 in Kolkata.

REFERENCES

Afshar, H., & Barrientos, S. (Eds.). (1999). *Women, globalization and fragmentation in the developing world*. New York: Palgrave Macmillan.

Afshar, H., & Denis, C. (1992). *Women and adjustment policies in the Third World*. New York: St. Martin's Press.

Ambani, M., & Birla, K. (2000). *Report on a Policy Framework for Reforms in Education: Special subject group on policy framework for private investment in education, health and rural development*. New Delhi: Prime Minister's Council on Trade and Industry.

Banerjee, N. (1991). *Indian women in a changing industrial scenario*. New Delhi: Sage.

Banerjee, N. (1996). The structural adjustment programme and women's economic empowerment. In N. Rao et al. (Eds.), *Sites of change*. New Delhi: Tulika.

Chakravart, C., & Sangari, K. (1999). *From myths to markets: Essays on gender*. New Delhi: Manohar.

Davids, T., & Van Driel, F. (2001). Globalisation and gender: Beyond dichotomies. In F. Schuurman (Ed.), *Globalisation and development studies: Challenges for the 21st century* (pp. 153–177). Vistaar: New Delhi.

Elson, D. (1988). *The impact of structural adjustment on women: Concepts and issues*. Manchester Discussion Papers in Development Studies, International Development Centre, University of Manchester, UK.

Ghosh, R. (2008). Education, women and development: The anomaly of women's education in India. *Journal of Education and Development in the Caribbean, 10*(1), 58–80.

India, Government of. *Census of India (1951–2001)*. New Delhi: Government of India

Kaul, S. (2006). *Higher education in India: Seizing the opportunity*. Working Paper, 180. New Delhi: Indian Council for Research on International Economic Relations.

Mies, M., & Shiva, V. (1993). *Ecofeminism*. London: Zed Books.

Moser, C. (1993). Adjustment from below: Low-income women, time and the triple role in Guayaquil, Ecuador. In S. Radcliffe & S. Westwood (Eds.), *'Viva': Women and popular protest in Latin America* (pp. 173–196). New York: Routledge.

National Knowledge Commission (NKC). (2006). *FAQs on NKC recommendations on higher education*. Retrieved April 23, 2009, from http://www.knowledgecommission.gov.in/downloads/documents/faq_he.pdf

National Knowledge Commission (NKC). (2006). *Report to the nation*. New Delhi: Government of India.

National Knowledge Commission (NKC). (2008). *Second report to the nation*. New Delhi: Government of India.

National Knowledge Commission (NKC). (2009). *Foreword to the report to the nation 2006–2009* (p. 1). New Delhi: Government of India.

Nussbaum, M. (2002). *Women and human development: A capabilities approach*. Cambridge, UK: Cambridge University Press.

Press Information Bureau. (2008). *Advance estimates of national income. 2007–08*. Retrieved January 23, 2009, from the government of India: http://mospi.nic.in/press_release_7feb08.pdf

Rege, S. (2003). *Sociology of gender: The challenge of feminist sociological thought*. New Delhi: Sage.

Sen, A. (1995). Agency and well-being: The development agenda. In N. Heyzer, S. Kapoor, & J. Sandler (Eds.), *A commitment to the world's women* (pp. 103–112). Washington, DC: UNIFEM.

Sen, A. (1992). *Inequality re-examined*. Oxford, UK: Clarendon Press.

Sparr, P. (Ed.). (1994). *Mortgaging women's lives: Feminist critiques of structural adjustment*. London: Zed Books.

Srivastava, R. (2007). *Disparities in access to higher education in India*. Retrieved April 24, 2009, from http://www.ukieri.org/docs/kolkata-presentations/Disparities%20in%20Access%20-Ravi%20Srivastava.pps

Stromquist, N. (1995). The theoretical and practical bases for empowerment. In C. Medel-Añonuevo (Ed.), *Women, education and empowerment: Pathways towards autonomy* (pp. 13–22). Hamburg: UNESCO Institute for Education.

Tilak, J. B. G. (2003). Privatization of higher education. In J. B. G. Tilak (Ed.), *Education, society, and development: National and International Perspectives* (pp. 557–574). New Delhi: National Institute of Educational Planning and Administration.

Tinker, I. (1990). (Ed.). *Persistent inequalities: Women and world development*. New York: Oxford University Press.

Upadhyay, S. (2008). *On the economics of higher education in India, with special reference to women*. Retrieved April 23, 2009, from http://www.eSocialSciences.com/data/articles/Document12992008220.3985559.pdf

UNDP. (2007). *Human development report 2007–2008. Fighting climate change: Human solidarity in a divided world*. New York: United Nations Development Programme.

Ratna Ghosh
McGill University

Paromita Chakravarti
Jadavpur University

SECTION V: COMPARATIVE EDUCATION

CARLOS ALBERTO TORRES

16. NEOLIBERAL GLOBALIZATION AND HUMAN RIGHTS

Crises and Opportunities

INTRODUCTION

This chapter aims to address a number of crises that, combined together, reveal some of the outcomes of more than 25 years of neoliberal globalization. The latter has deepened the onset of these crises which, connected with the development of capitalism, affects profoundly the lives of people, communities, and nations. These are, by implication, the pressing issues of our times.

There is no question that if we want to expand the horizons of tolerance and human rights, we need to address these crises and, hopefully, solve them as part of a civilization revival. Education and the politics of culture have a major role to play in this endeavour.

A SCENARIO OF CRISES: CRISIS IS OPPORTUNITY

The comprehension of the limits of educational practice requires political clarity on the part of educators in relation to their project. It demands that the educator assume the political nature of her practice (Freire, 1998, p. 46).

There is a fundamental tension in modern civil and political societies between regulation and emancipation. In addition to these secular tensions, modern societies are confronting multiple crises. These include but are not restricted to a moral crisis, a crisis of regulation (sometimes referred to as the ungovernability of democracies), a fiscal crisis of the state, a financial mega crisis bringing about the demise of models of deregulation as the guiding light of globalization, a crisis of emancipation and solidarity, a planetary crisis of the environment, a crisis of productivity in solidarity, a crisis in the politics of culture related to immigration and multiculturalism, and an epistemological crisis.

In the limited space of this paper, five key crises are identified and discussed:

1. a moral crisis;
2. the crisis of deregulation;
3. the crisis of human rights, immigration and multiculturalism as the bedrock of citizenship;
4. the planetary crisis; and
5. the epistemological crisis.

V. Masemann et al., (Eds.), A Tribute to David N. Wilson: Clamouring for a Better World, 239–246.

All of these crises are connected to the deepening of neoliberal globalization over more than a quarter of a century, and its impact on the politics of culture and education. Yet, these crises are intimately related to the convoluted and contradictory development of capitalism. It could be said that neoliberalism is simply one of the most advanced phases of capitalism.

A Moral Crisis

There is a serious moral crisis in modern societies. We are reminded of this moral crisis by the constant reference to the "moral hazard" or the risk to help, with the plan to rescue banks in the recent financial mega-crisis, without major punishment of those bankers, speculators, managers and financiers who brought about the mega-crisis in the first place through unethical speculation and shady financial instruments. They made fortunes in the process, leaving it to the taxpayers to foot the bill of rescuing the financial institutions, particularly the banking system, and further leaving behind an increasingly impoverished population.

A large number of youth, children, and adults have been experiencing these crises on several levels affecting different aspects of their lives. There is also a most serious conflict of ethnicities, religious beliefs, class, gender, and of course racial and ethnic exchanges in our educational institutions and practices. That conflict is also aggravating the way children, youth, and adults cope with the moral and cognitive crises that they experience in their societies.

Lost in the struggle for meaning and identity is the same notion of tolerance that we have indulged as one of the premises of the Enlightenment—despite its failures and weaknesses. Some political scientists will also argue that one of the effects of this moral crisis is a growing crisis in the ability to govern democracies.

There are many other symptoms of this crisis, such as the pervasive corruption in so many public sectors and the lack of transparency and checks and balances in the business world. The latter has been revealed by the extraordinary gaps in remuneration between the employees and the CEOs both in industrially advanced and emerging societies, and also indicated by the greedy and predatory business practices that led to the macro-financial crisis that began in 2008. Further, there is the presence and action of narco-traffic as a parallel power in many societies; the merchants of death selling arms and feeding militias of many different political and ideological signs; and the systematic annihilation of populations and genocides such as the most recent experience of Darfur, Sudan. Unfortunately examples abound.

Cornel West (1996) talks about this crisis speaking of an undeniable cultural decay in the United States that frightens him more than anything else: "By unprecedented cultural decay I mean the social breakdown in nurturing children, and/or the inability to transmit meaning, value, purpose, dignity, and decency to children" (p. 196).

It is tantamount to address these crises in order to solve the dilemmas of our time; and no government, organization or individual should remain neutral. Dante Alighieri in the *Divine Comedy, The Book of the Inferno*, claimed that God has reserved the darkest places in hell for those who maintain their neutrality in times of moral crisis.

The Crisis of De-regulation

Neoliberal models of deregulation promote notions of open markets, unchecked free trade, a reduction of the public sector, and the decrease of state intervention through regulations on the economy and the de-regulation of markets. This agenda includes a drive towards privatization and decentralisation of public education, a movement toward educational standards based on decontextualized definitions of quality of education, and the testing of academic achievement usually through multiple choice exams to determine the quality of education at the level of students, schools, and teachers. Accountability, defined more as a means of social control than as a pedagogical device, is another key tenet of the model. The financial and policy prescriptions of de-regulation models are now being challenged with a reorganization of the world system, and predictably, will have an impact on the politics of culture and education.

Critics of current regulatory models and their global trends support educational alternatives that will preserve local languages and cultures, ensure progressive educational practices that will protect the poor against the rich, and continue to strive for gender parity in education. These alternatives consider models of equality, equity, and fairness that are appropriate in the social context of people's lives, and seek to protect the environment and human rights as the bedrock to citizenship.

However, achieving educational expansion does not guarantee an agenda of inclusion, equality, and fairness:

> The last half century has seen a dramatic expansion in access to primary, secondary, and higher education in many nations around the world. Educational expansion is not only viewed as desirable for a country's economy and as beneficial for educated individuals themselves, but it is also valued as a strategy for social inclusion, a step towards greater social harmony. The hope is that expanding educational access can mitigate economic inequality, increase upward social mobility, and lessen class and other social antagonisms. (Attewell, 2008, p. 1)

One of the clear indications of this moral crisis is that the last century has seen a dramatic expansion of educational access, but this has been coupled with also a dramatic expansion in social inequality. Thus the moral question is how to link the inclusion agenda that has been the focus of this dramatic expansion with a fairness agenda, focusing on class, income, gender, and race/ethnicity disparities in educational opportunity and performance in all educational and learning systems in the world. The red light is on when education expansion has become an important mechanism generating social exclusion.

The Crisis of Human Rights, Immigration, and Multiculturalism as the Bedrock of Citizenship

The perennial question of how to relate education and inter-group relations has been key in defining the premises of citizenship in modern society. Interculturalism and multiculturalism are two of the principal frameworks that address the question of inter-group relations. The situation of indigenous people who are now demanding that inequalities of the past be redressed have situated the debate of inter-group relations, in terms of ethnicity and race, at the center of the political and peda- gogical debate, particularly in the American continent. However, the question of immigration related to multiculturalism and citizenship has taken central stage everywhere:

> Immigration represents the emerging aspects, probably the most evident, of the wide process which characterizes more and more the whole planet— globalisation. Migrations represent more than a phenomenon, a historical certainty that can be found today, though with different features, in all countries and, in particular, in the most developed. Migration phenomena are becoming more and more important within the Mediterranean basin. (Foundazione Laboratori Mediterraneo, 1997, p. 551)

The question of human rights in education, both in the frameworks of intercul- turalism and multiculturalism, has become a central question for citizenship and democracy, and indeed for adult learning education. Yasemin Nuhoglu Soysal's (1994) analysis of the limits of citizenship in the era of globalization highlights some of these issues. She argues that "the logic of personhood supersedes the logic of national citizenship [and] individual rights and obligations, which were historically located in the nation state, have increasingly moved to a universalistic plane, trans- cending the boundaries of particular nation-states" (Soysal, 1994, pp. 164–165).

Yasemin Nuhoglu Soysal's (1994) analysis of the limits of citizenship has implications at three levels. The first is the level of citizenship, where notions of identity and rights are decoupled. Second is the level of the politics of identity and multiculturalism, where the emergence of membership in the policy "is multiple in the sense of spanning local, regional, and global identities, and which accommodates intersecting complexes of rights, duties and loyalties" (Soysal, 1994, p. 166). Finally, given the importance of the international system for the attainment of democracy worldwide, Soysal highlights the emergence of the third level, what could be termed cosmopolitan democracies, that is, international political systems relatively divorced in their origin and constitutive dynamics from the nation-states' codes.

For instance, within the discourse of cosmopolitan democracies, critical stances from feminist perspectives criticize the concept of human rights *per se*, because "It's Western, it's male, it's individualistic, its emphasis has been on political and not economic rights". Yet, despite these criticisms, human rights are seen as "a powerful term that transforms the discussion from being about something that is a good idea to that which ought to be the birthright of every person" (Bunch, 2001, pp. 138–139).

If the agenda for human rights is reconfiguring the boundaries of nations and individual rights of national citizens, and they are seen as a precondition to attain basic equality worldwide, there are implications for education. Education systems, lifelong learning and Adult Learning Education (ALE) will reflect more and more, the tension between human rights as a globalized ideology of cosmopolitan democracies, and the growing nationalistic feeling in many education systems— systems that were originally built as powerful tools of the Enlightenment.

This tension is also projected in questions of identity and the rights of cultural and religious values to be upheld independently of the ideology of human rights and its demands upon education systems. Once again, lifelong learning and ALE have a major role to play *vis à vis* identity, multiculturalism, human rights, and citizenship.

The Planetary Crisis

Any discussion about a planetary crisis seems to be a *non sequitur* considering the policy debates and empirical evidence on global warming, pesticides as water pollutants, the exhaustion of natural non-renewable resources, the ever-thinning of the ozone layer, and the greenhouse effect. Also on this list are the food crisis and desertification of several areas of the globe particularly in Sub-Saharan Africa, the disappearance of plants and animals, and the growing endangerment of species or the devastation of the Amazon and tropical rainforests. In one sentence, the planetary crisis relates to the difficulties of establishing lasting foundations for the sustainable development of the planet.

The United Nations Educational, Scientific and Cultural Organization (UNESCO) declared 2005–2014 the *Decade of Education for Sustainable Development*. Sustainable development means "caring for the needs of the present without compromising the possibility for future generations to satisfy their own needs" (Lopez-Ospina, 2003, p. 42).

The following needs demand immediate attention for sustainable development in the South: "sustainable livelihoods; secure housing rights; and freedom from violence and intimidation on the basis of social identity" (Mahadevia, 2001, p. 78). Macro-level sustainable development must ensure:

(i) effective government policies to reduce inequality within cities themselves and between the rural and urban areas; (ii) democratic urban development processes that meet the needs of the disadvantaged, and in which the most disadvantaged can participate; (iii) economic growth through activities that are non-polluting and labor-intensive; (iv) a sound, participatory regulatory mechanism to check unsustainable activities; and (v) government responsibility for promoting human development. (Mahadevia, 2001, p. 78)

The simplest definition of sustainable development can be found in the report *Our Common Future* (1987):

sustainable development is a transformation process in which the use of natural resources, the direction given to investments, the orientation given to technological development and institutional change get in harmony with each other and reinforce the present and future potential, in order to fulfil human needs and aspirations. (United Nations World Commission on Environment and Development, 1987)

It is a very wide concept. The report *Our Common Future* does not give details, and that caused ambiguity, leaving the concept open to creativity and ideological disputes (Gadotti, 2008).

The Epistemological Crisis

The crisis of epistemology is brought about by the crisis of positivism as normal and hegemonic science, with its premise that science is independent from culture. This dovetails quite nicely with the premise in most educational establishments that education is independent from politics. Many scholars have argued that the cultural assumptions of normal science are not neutral, and that one may question the degree, process, and methods to achieve objectivity in science; yet science is never neutral. Thomas Popkewitz (1988) says this very well:

> The view of society as composed by "possessive" individuals provides a basis for organizing schooling. Attitudes, knowledge, and skills are conceived of as the personal property of the individual. The psychology of a possessive individual is incorporated into contemporary curriculum through the use of behavioral objectives, notions of affective and cognitive learning, taxonomies of knowledge and processes, and psychological testing and measurement. Methods of teaching are to enable individuals to develop particular attributes and abilities and to internalize some logical state which they "own" as one would objects or commodities. (p. 86)

The premise that there is no basis for a methodological differentiation between the natural and the social sciences or that the natural scientific model of causality and invariant laws is the logical basis of all inquiry are increasingly questioned. Also challenged is the view that knowledge is built on a growing accumulation of facts rather than a perception of the world characterized by discontinuities and small results with gradual consequences. The ownership of knowledge opposes the growing calls for an open and public science. The idea of value-free research, sponsoring neutrality, and the apolitical nature of the researcher are being contested by new paradigms that argue that science is never neutral. Boaventura de Souza Santos, following 17th century philosopher Gottfried Leibniz, called these premises an "indolent reason" that produces monocultures: the monoculture of knowledge and rigor (that only rigorous knowledge is scientific knowledge), the monoculture of lineal time (the idea that history has a direction, a sense, and that the developed societies lead the pack and the rest of the countries should follow), the monoculture of naturalization of differences (hiding classifications through naturalization hierarchies, that is racial and ethnic classification, sexual classification, gender classification, caste classification, etc.), the monoculture of the dominant scale (where the universal and global emerges as dominant and hegemonic, and the local and particular remains invisible or disposable), and the monoculture of capitalist production (seen as the only way to produce).

Against these monocultures, Boaventura de Sousa Santos (2007; 2009) proposes an ecology of wisdom. This means science in dialogue with the popular cultures, the lay cultures, with indigenous knowledge, with the knowledge of elders, with the campesino and urban marginal knowledge. This also implies an ecology of multiple times, including the voice of our ancestors, and an understanding of people's histories. Then Boaventura de Sousa proposes the ecology of recognition, employing post-colonial approaches to de-colonize the minds. There is also the ecology of multiple scales, assuming the differences in the local, regional, national, continental, and global. Finally, there is the ecology of productivity, recuperating traditional and alternatives models and methods of production (de Sousa Santos, 2007; 2009).

Many of these premises are currently being advocated by a large number of social movements, NGOs, grass-roots organizations and community organizations as well as critical intellectuals and contesting forces in institutions of higher education. This narrative is beginning to make inroads in political parties as well.

CONCLUSION

While educational institutions and paradigms could provide leadership and moral, ethical, and practical examples, they cannot by themselves be the lever of development or the exclusive source of morality and ethics. There is obviously a need for a world system and compatible national strategies to confront these planetarian crises, discussed in this chapter, one by one and in their entirety.

This *Festschrift* for David Wilson's life work reminds us of the struggles that he fought in trying to prevent the onset and deepening of these crises. There is always a sense of joy and agony in academic work when we try to do our best to follow insights, theoretical inspirations, and ethical values that have marked our lives.

David's life and work, that we are honouring here, advanced educational research in so many areas and in original ways that would be difficult to summarize. Yet, he was particularly concerned about issues of importance in educational research, and how education could make a difference in preventing what seems, at least to this writer, as an inevitable development debacle if these civilisational crises are not addressed head on and with the radicalism that is needed.

The theses advanced in this chapter would please David's lifelong search for the truth. Yet he probably would also have disagreed with several emphases or analytical and political directions of what I have written. Alas, if he were still here, he would have continued the dialogue, with a sense of purpose, of friendship and love that we dearly miss because of his untimely departure.

REFERENCES

Attewell, P. (2008). Inequality in an era of educational expansion. In P. Attewell & K. S. Newman (Eds.), *Growing gaps: Educational inequality around the world.* Unpublished manuscript submitted to Oxford University Press.

Bunch, C. (2001). Women's human rights: The challenges of global feminism and diversity. In M. Dekoven (Ed.), *Feminist locations: Global and local, theory and practice.* Piscataway, NJ: Rutgers University Press.

Freire, P. (1998). *Politics and education* (P. L. Wong, Trans.). Los Angeles: UCLA-Latin American Center Publications.

Foundazione Laboratori Mediterraneo. (1997). *obiettivi e mezzi per il parternariato europeo.* Il Forum Civile EuroMed, Naples, Magma. Foundazionee Laboratorio Mediterraneo.

Gadotti, M. (2008). *Education for sustainability: A critical contribution to the decade of education for sustainable development.* São Paulo, Brazil: University of São Paulo-Paulo Freire Institute.

Lopez-Ospina, G. (2003). *Planetary sustainability in the age of the information and knowledge society: Working toward 2015 for a sustainable world and future.* Paris: UNESCO.

Mahadevia, D. (2001). Sustainable urban development in India: An inclusive perspective. *Development in Practice, 11*(2/3), 242–259.

Popkewitz, T. S. (1988). Educational reform: Rhetoric, ritual and social interest. *Educational Theory, 38*(1), 78–83.

Santos, Boaventura de Sousa. (2009). The World Social Forum: Towards a counter-hegemonic globalization. In J. Sen, A. Anand, A. Escobar, & P. Waterman (Eds.), *The World Social Forum: Challenging empires* (pp. 235–245). Retrieved May 5, 2009, from http://74.125.113.104/search?q=cache: mGxNSWAhhmcJ:www.choike.org/documentos/wsf_s318_sousa.pdf+Sociology+of+absences&hl=es &ct=clnk&cd=1&gl=ar&client=firefox-a

Santos, Boaventura de Sousa. (2007). *Another knowledge is possible: Beyond Northern epistemologies.* Londres: Verso.

Soysal, Y. N. (1994). *Limits of citizenship: Migrants and postnational membership in Europe.* Chicago: University of Chicago Press.

United Nations World Commission on Environment and Development. (1987). *Our common future.* Oxford: Oxford University Press.

West, C. (1996). *Prophetic thought in postmodern times.* Monroe, ME: Common Courage Press.

Carlos Alberto Torres
Director, Paulo Freire Institute
University of California-Los Angeles

LOUISE GORMLEY

17. THE ROLE OF FOREIGN LANGUAGE FLUENCY IN COMPARATIVE EDUCATION RESEARCH

The Sapir-Whorf hypothesis states that some elements of language, for example, vocabulary or grammatical systems, influence speakers' and listeners' perceptions of the world, rendering language as a strong determinant of their attitudes and behaviours (Bonvillain, 1997; Whorf, 1973). While some scholars argue that thought and language are universal and independent of each other (Chomsky, 2006; Pinker, 1994), the so-called "weak version" of the Sapir-Whorf hypothesis subscribes to the view that language plays a substantial role in influencing our perceptions and thoughts. Applying this hypothesis to academia, the dominance of the English language in the field of comparative international education suggests that its research has been determined and limited by English-language conceptual frameworks (Gormley, 2005; Pinar, 1995; Schugurensky, 1999). David Wilson, however, was among those who championed the inclusion of other languages into our research and practice. In 2003, in a series of email correspondence with me on this issue, he wrote,

> I might also add that in Comparative Education, I have written about the linguistic competence of some of the greats, e.g. Isaac Kandel, William Brickman, Harold Noah, George Bereday, Jürgen Schriewer, who are my "role models" for learning other languages and working in other cultures. (July 30, 2003, personal communication)

In this chapter, I will touch upon the stances taken by Kandel, Brickman, Noah, Bereday, Schriewer and Wilson with respect to the role that linguistic fluency plays in being a "great" comparative education scholar, while interweaving my reflections on how aspects of the Spanish and English languages influenced my doctoral research in Mexico.

While pursuing my Ph.D. in Comparative, International and Development Education at the Ontario Institute for Studies in Education at the University of Toronto from 2001 to 2006, I had the privilege of learning from several renowned academics, including Philip Nagy, Joseph Farrell, Daniel Schugurensky, Vandra Masemann, and David Wilson. For the purposes of this chapter, I will focus on my intellectual journey with David Wilson in particular, with whom I shared an affinity on several subjects, including his love of travel and foreign languages. As described in *The Toronto Star*,

V. Masemann et al., (Eds.), A Tribute to David N. Wilson: Clamouring for a Better World, 247–259.

> [David Wilson] worked, lived or travelled in more than 110 countries. He spoke French, Spanish, Swahili, German, and Portuguese well, plus bits and pieces of four other languages. He was learning Mandarin because he said it was the language of the future. (Dunphy, 2007)

Within our student-professor relationship, I felt that David Wilson was also a true friend, someone whose opinion I sought out on a wide variety of topics, and with whom I felt completely at ease. With his wry sense of humour, he would poke fun at the vagaries of life in academia and at an increasingly complex world often rendered awry by topsy-turvy global politics. But it was with foreign languages that David Wilson was truly like a child at play—in the best sense of the metaphor. He took secret joy, I believe, in deftly rolling the Spanish alveolar trill "*rr*" off his tongue and was amused at the idiosyncrasies of certain phrases. Whenever an opportunity arose to talk with a speaker of a language that he had studied, he would eagerly jump into a non-English conversation simply because he found it fun to do so. For him, communicating in another language was a recreational activity. Upon first meeting me and learning of my years spent in Taiwan and Mexico, David's initial words to me were greetings in Mandarin Chinese, followed by Spanish.

Many of us who were personally acquainted with David Wilson were aware of how he embraced the study of foreign languages as a vital aspect of comparative and international education. Some of his writings also reflect this belief. For example, in an article discussing the evolution of the field of comparative and international education, he begins by detailing the contributions of Sir Michael Sadler and Isaac Kandel, and then points out the unfortunate fact that, historically, Western readers have been unaware of the heritages of other languages in comparative and international education:

> It has generally been recognized that the "modern" and "scientific" period of comparative education in Western nations dates from Sir Michael Sadler (1900)....Another milestone was the publication of Isaac Kandel's *Studies in Comparative Education* in 1933. Hayhoe (2001:10) indicates that four different books entitled *Comparative Education* were published by Chinese scholars in Chinese between 1929 and 1934 (See also Bray and Gui 2001: 454). Western readers are only now learning that communications in other languages also comprises our heritage in comparative and international education. (Wilson, 2003, p. 20)

In the same article, David Wilson (2003) commends efforts that support the dissemination of educational research in languages other than English.

> My OISE colleague, Joseph Farrell, was also instrumental in assisting colleagues in Latin America in the 1980s with the establishment of REDUC (Red Latinamericana de Documentación y Información en Educación), the Latin American version of ERIC that facilitates electronic searches of educational articles and books in Spanish and Portuguese. Canadian participation in the REDUC project received assistance from the Canadian International Development Agency (CIDA). Projects of this nature have helped Latin America to reduce the hegemony of English on the Internet. (p. 26)

Given David Wilson's stance that it was important "to reduce the hegemony of English on the Internet" as well as his penchant for foreign languages, it is only fitting that I mention an important decision that David Wilson helped me make *vis-à-vis* language in my doctoral research.

My research was a case study of issues of success in four public primary schools in a low-income region of northern Mexico. Based on insights from interviews, classroom observations, questionnaires, school visits, students' final grades, and an informal survey of maternal schooling, my study had three main goals. Its first aim was to describe the research setting and selected aspects of the Mexican public education system. Its second aim was to analyze concepts of educational success held by three of the main stakeholders: principals, teachers, and parents. Its third aim was to present Mexican perspectives from primary Spanish-language sources as often as possible. It is this third aim that is most relevant to this chapter.

When I began my fieldwork in Mexico in 2003 and 2004, the words of curriculum theorist William Pinar reverberated through my mind. Pinar and others argue that too many international education studies neglect those primary sources in native languages that originate from the country or geographical locale under examination, and instead consider only secondary English language sources (Gormley, 2005; Pinar, 1995; Schugurensky, 1999). When this neglect occurs, the resulting monograph is likely to possess a world view—a conceptual scheme of reality—that leans more towards the beliefs of the English-speaking authors cited than of the research participants (Dei, 1999; Pinar, 1995; Scheurich & Young, 1997; Stanfield II, 1993, 1994; Tuhiwai Smith, 1999). Pinar strongly recommends inclusion of insider "native language" publications that are more likely to possess epistemological resonance.

> The problem becomes acute when English-speaking scholars limit their international research to secondary English sources...This matter illustrates a tendency towards ethnocentrism in the First World, especially English-speaking nations. The significance of employing primary sources in the study of education internationally must be emphasized. (Pinar, 1995, p. 795)

In 2003, I shared Pinar's quote with David Wilson, and he and I discussed the dominance of the English language in educational research. Was I on the right path, I asked him in an email, in trying to gather mostly primary, Spanish-language sources for my research? He answered with a resounding yes, that I was most definitely travelling down the better path, even if it was one that lately was in want of wear. He expounded on the virtues of comparativists being multilinguists, citing Kandel, Brickman, Noah, Bereday, and Schriewer as his role models in this regard. While acknowledging that others may have also made significant contributions in promoting the role of language in comparative education research, I will confine my discussion mainly to the above scholars' stance on languages in order to pay homage to David Wilson's role models. Then I will reflect upon the role that the Spanish language played in my research.

249

"ROLE MODEL" COMPARATIVE SCHOLARS ON MULTILINGUALISM

This journey begins with Isaac Kandel (1881–1965), who was "the biggest of the men who made the flowering of interest in the study of foreign educational systems possible in our time" (Bereday, 1966, p. 147). In addition to being the first Jew to be appointed to the professoriate at Teachers College, Kandel "became known as America's leading authority on comparative education and international education. Many people credit him with the founding of comparative education in the U.S." (Null, 2004, p. 10).

> It is Kandel who first brought to bear upon education the disciplines of philosophy, history, political science, and to some extent sociology. It is he who perfected the art of comparison, not describing, nor even classifying, but freely shuttling from country to country, unhampered by the binding shackles of inadequate language, infrequent travel and scant training in academic disciplines. (Bereday, 1957, p. 14)

To conduct the type of educational research that he produced, Kandel needed to be able to read and write fluently in numerous languages (Null, 2004, 2007). "He was fluent in at least nine languages: English, German, French, Spanish, Latin, Greek, Portuguese, Dutch, and Norwegian" (Null, 2004, p. 14). During the war, he put his translation skills to national use by translating laws and administrative regulations from foreign schools to help Americans understand education systems in other countries. Kandel placed great importance on the ability to read primary documents in their original languages. "Kandel's contribution to comparative education is well-known…He advocated meticulous attention to primary documents, a sort of comparative *explication de texte*, which is regrettably becoming rare at present" (Bereday, 1966, p. 149).

Next under consideration is William Brickman (1913–1986), another of David Wilson's linguistic role models. He was founder, first president (1956–1959) and president again in 1967–68 of the Comparative International Education Society, which then was called the Comparative Education Society. Fluent in multiple languages, he deemed such abilities to be a crucial skill of a comparative scholar:

> Brickman drew on the fields he knew—literature, history, and foreign languages. A linguist fluent in classical Greek and Latin, German, Hebrew, Yiddish, Danish, Swedish, Russian, Polish, Hungarian, Portuguese, Rumanian, and Bulgarian, as well as several Asiatic and African tongues, he frequently assumed linguistic skills lacking in his American students, an assumption that presented practical problems. But he did not waver in the belief that documentary research in original languages was the most important feature of comparative education. (Sherman Swing, 1987, p. 3)

Brickman, like Kandel, placed importance on "meticulous attention to primary documents" (Bereday, 1966). Brickman's belief "that documentary research in original languages was the most important vehicle for teaching comparative education" (Sherman Swing, 1987, p. 3) and Kandel's emphasis on this type of research are reminiscent (and are arguably precursors) of Pinar's stance on "the significance of employing primary sources in the study of education internationally" (1995, p. 75).

It is also interesting that just as Brickman would assume linguistic skills of his students, he also assumed the same ability of his readers. Brickman evidently did not anticipate his readers needing any English translations, at times writing in German and Spanish only such as in his article *John Dewey in Russia* (1960) when he analyzes societal perceptions of John Dewey's work across six continents:

> A German Professor Erich Hylla, declared that Dewey belonged "zweifellos zu den bedeutendsten pädagogischen Führern aller Zeiten" (1928). An Argentine, Professor Lorenzo Luzuriaga, described Dewey more recently as "el pensador más ilustre y al mismo tiempo el defensor más eminente de la democratización educativa de nuestra época" (1946). Other examples of more recent date may be cited to show the esteem with which Dewey has been held and is still held throughout the world. (Brickman, 1960, p. 83)

George Bereday (1920–1983), another of David Wilson's linguistic role models, was founder-editor of the *Comparative Education Review* and "as much as anyone, responsible for the emergence of comparative education as an academic field in the United States" (Noah, 1984, p. 1). Bereday's stewardship of this journal determined and firmly established its orientation and character (Noah, 1984). "Bringing his phenomenal mastery of foreign languages to bear [on educational research], George managed to do in one life what it might well take half-a-dozen ordinarily strong men good and true to accomplish" (Noah, p. 1). In his landmark book *Comparative method in education* (1964), Bereday championed the importance of multilingualism in young scholars, illustrating the value of being able to read about an event or phenomenon in various languages and therefore, from multiple national points of view. Bereday (1964) believed that "a knowledge of language lets one in on the intimate secrets of the nation under study" (p. 139).

As an aside, one may criticize Bereday's statement which hints at self-interested motivations of espionage, instead of more peace-oriented research goals of global understanding. However, even if Bereday did look at the value of uncovering a nation's "secrets" from a surveillance viewpoint, perhaps this view is more a reflection of the Cold War era in which his works were published. Certainly he promoted language study as a privilege and as "a lesson in humility":

> To be privileged to read each and the same day about current events, not in one but in two or more languages, not from one but from several national points of view, is a lesson in humility and understanding not easily matched anywhere. (Bereday, 1964, p. 139)

In her analysis of the role of language in comparative education, Ruth Hayhoe delves into Bereday's stance on foreign language mastery. "Bereday devoted a whole chapter to arguing for the importance of mastering several languages for comparative education research, and the need to use that linguistic understanding in the interpretation of educational data before comparative analysis could proceed"

(Hayhoe, 1998, p. 9). Hayhoe also identifies Bereday's plea that all aspiring comparative educators see language education as essential, and particularly that Americans, given their history, should be multilingual:

> A seal of approval for those aspiring to be specialists should include language skills. The Russians have recognized this by instituting experimental schools at which language experts are trained almost entirely in a language of specialization beginning from the second grade. The loss of potential that occurs when Americans, a great many of whom have had at least one foreign grandparent, fail to utilize their national heritage should not be permitted to continue. Given their history, Americans should be a nation of polyglots. (Bereday, 1964, p. 142)

Harold Noah, another polyglot whom David Wilson greatly admired, is widely recognized as a distinguished authority in the field of comparative education. Working with his long-standing co-author Max Eckstein, Noah is known for promoting the use of empirical methods in comparative education (Noah & Eckstein, 1998). In *The use and abuse of comparative education* (1984), Noah begins his article with an anecdote that plays upon the difficulties of translating Spanish into Russian, as a way to ridicule the notion that the objective of comparative study of education is to find an easy solution abroad to complex problems at home. This amusing story, however, can only be fully appreciated by readers who are familiar with both of these languages; and therefore, one can see that Noah, like Brickman, also assumed certain linguistic skills of his readers:

> My favourite anecdote in comparative study is from the field of comparative philology. One day, the story goes, a Spanish-speaking student of Russian language went to her professor and asked him: "Professor, do you have in Russian any equivalent of our Spanish word 'mañana'?" After brief reflection, the professor said to her: "Why, yes. In Russian we have twenty-seven equivalents for 'mañana', but none of them I think conveys the same sense of urgency!" (Noah, 1998, p. 57)

Jürgen Schriewer, the fifth of David Wilson's linguistic role models, and a professor at Humboldt University in Berlin, is another comparativist polyglot. In his article *Globalisation in education: Process and discourse* (2003), Schriewer discusses an investigation in "degree and dimensions of the 'internationalisation' of educational knowledge in societies that differ considerably in terms of civilisational background and modernisation path" (p. 271). He compared Spanish, Russian (Soviet) and Chinese education journals over a period ranging from the early 1920s to the mid-1990s. Such an inquiry presupposes researcher fluency in Spanish, Russian, and Chinese—not to mention the fact that Schriewer's findings were published in English. Interestingly, his data manifested significant variations. "These variations are not only discerned *between* [italics in original] Spanish, Russian (Soviet), and Chinese educational discourse, but they are also identified, in terms of considerable fluctuations over the whole period under scrutiny, *within* [italics in original] each of these discourse constellations" (Schriewer, 2003, p. 279). Such powerful insights could have not been revealed in a unilingual research endeavour. Among his conclusions, Schriewer (2003) advocates for the importance of "assuring each individual's capacity for society wide communication" (p. 281):

> [An educational system's outward performance] consists of *assuring each individual's capacity for society-wide communication* [italics in original]... [because] present-day communication requirements extend well beyond national frontiers. The complexity of present-day social realities...requires an individual's capacity for society-wide, i.e. area-encompassing communication to be operative at all levels, the local, the national, the regional, and the world level. This certainly presupposes strengthening linguistic skills; this also presupposes, however, developing appropriate mental attitudes; finally this presupposes assuring the proper understanding of basic "languages"—scientific, technological, social, political as well as artistic—which prevail in today's world. (Schriewer, 2003, p. 281)

For Schriewer, the "strengthening of linguistic skills" is a foundational skill upon which an individual can then move on to a proper understanding of other "basic languages." In fact, he considers it an *a priori* condition upon which other understandings can build.

In addition to David Wilson's linguistic role models, other comparativists have addressed issues of language; however, as Ruth Hayhoe demonstrates, such concerns have been considered to a varying lesser or greater degree in the field of comparative education. In the previously alluded to article *Language in comparative education: Three strands* (1998), Hayhoe explores approaches to language within three different strands of comparative education: positivist, cultural, and dependency. Within these respective strands, language is viewed as a translating challenge, a necessity for cultural understanding, and as a transforming agent:

> Within the positivist strand, language is seen to be neutral, a challenge for translators when educational achievement is being measured objectively across numerous societies, also a potential barrier to modernization in specific historical situations. Within the cultural strand language issues are given greater importance, both in the literal sense of the need to learn languages for in-depth comparative studies and in the metaphorical sense of a concept sensitive approach to understanding education in different societies. Within the dependency strand of comparative education, language is seen as a potential instrument of power and exclusion, on the one hand, and of awakening and national self-assertion, on the other. (Hayhoe, 1998, p. 1)

Space considerations preclude a lengthy discussion in this chapter but it is debatable whether Kandel, Brickman, Bereday, Noah, and Schriewer's approaches to language would fall into the cultural or the dependency strands of comparative education. Certainly, however, all stressed the need for comparative scholars to study foreign languages.

Other comparative education scholars have similarly drawn on their knowledge of foreign languages to substantiate a point. In a comparative word analysis, Joseph Farrell (1999) demonstrates the importance of family to the concept of education in the Spanish language. He references Villenas and Dehyle (1999) who, in their review essay of ethnographic studies of Latino family education, note that the term "education" has a much different connotation in the Spanish language than in the English one:

> In common English usage "education" refers to schooling and book learning (when we say to a young person "get an education" we mean go to school, stay there as long as possible, and become good at what they do there). In Spanish usage the word "educación" has a much broader sense, including manners, moral values, sense of responsibility to the family and the community, generally how to comport oneself with dignity and respect in the broader community. Much of this is done informally in the home, principally through consejos (narrative advice or homilies). (Farrell, 1999, p. 407)

The difference in nuance between the English "education" and the Spanish "educación" highlights the importance of considering Pinar's advice regarding "the significance of employing primary sources in the study of educational internationally" (1995, p. 795). When a researcher fails to do so, the potential for misunderstandings is greatly increased.

I see a complementary relationship between Pinar's stance and the Sapir-Whorf hypothesis regarding the influence of language on world views and eventual attitudes and behaviours:

> Human beings do not live in the objective world alone, nor alone in the world of social activity as ordinarily understood, but are very much at the mercy of the particular language that has become the medium of expression for their society. The fact of the matter is that the real world is to a large extent unconsciously built up on the language habits of the group. (Sapir, 1949, cited in Bonvillain, 1997, p. 52)

While agreeing with Sapir and Bonvillain that some elements of language (for example, vocabulary or grammatical systems) influence perceptions of the world (Sapir, 1949, cited in Bonvillain, 1997), my stance is that the native language is a most clear window for any outsider to catch a glimpse, however fleeting, of another culture's reality. From an ontological point of view, a comparative researcher (from a dominant or marginalized position) must listen/speak/read/write (as applicable) with participants in their mother tongue to get closer to the goal of more fully understanding their real world (Gormley, 2005).

Language fluency should be viewed as an important entry point into a deeper understanding of philosophies, history, and culture, rather than a final destination (Chang, 1974; Dlaska, 2000). Although language and culture are inseparable, knowing or learning a language does not automatically lead to a heightened cultural awareness (Dlaska, 2000).

It is important to note that in comparison to the amount of research conducted in other foreign languages (such as Chinese, Spanish, and French), indigenous languages are even more marginalised. "There is an emerging academic awareness these days that 'local' knowledge is being marginalised to the detriment of all players"

(Findlow, 2004, p. 403). Addressing this dilemma begins with advocating for more support (financial and otherwise) for local researchers doing their own research in their own languages (Findlow, 2004; Latapí Sarre, 2000, 2003; Schmelkes, Lavín, Martínez & Noriega, 1999; V. Masemann & N. Truong, personal communication, February 3, 2008)

Sometimes participants may speak a language that does not employ a script, so that no written texts in the primary language are available. In such an oral culture, it would be tempting to rely almost exclusively on interpreters and translators. However, nuances and subtleties of meaning are best teased out from participants' words in their local languages so comparative researchers need to be native speakers or need to strive towards native-like fluency (Gormley, 2005).

THE ROLE OF LANGUAGE IN MY DOCTORAL RESEARCH IN MEXICO

As I embarked upon my doctoral research, bolstered by David Wilson's belief in the importance of primary language sources (as well as joining him in his admiration for multilingual comparativists), I resolved to write about such issues in my thesis (Gormley, 2006). As a response to the criticisms of Pinar (1995), I decided to construct two chapters for my literature review—one for English-language literature and another for Spanish-language literature. In my third chapter, I reviewed literature not more than five years old that was published in Mexico in the Spanish language and was generally intended for a Mexican readership. The topics analyzed were a reflection of debates in Mexican circles from 2003 to 2005. My wish was to honour Mexican perspectives by presenting selected Mexican literature in its own chapter.

I purposefully pluralized "Mexican perspectives" in the previous sentence as a way of recognizing that there is not a single Mexican outlook, but rather multiple, often contradictory ones: "Aztec, Spanish, Catholic. Pre-Hispanic, civil, religious. A triple cosmology, founded upon the sun god and human sacrifice, rape and conquest, Christianity and the Napoleonic Code. No wonder being Mexican is complicated" (Cohan, 2000, p. 83). In spite of the beautifully rich complexity of Mexican viewpoints and identities, I was nevertheless able to discern some common themes in the literature I reviewed. Two language reviews were conducted to ensure that readers were not restricted to a purely English-language interpretation of Mexico. Readers thus had an inkling of the Mexican mindset on some of the educational issues whose themes were related to my case study. I aspired to approach my case study with the wider ontological lens that came from interweaving two languages and two conceptual frameworks of the world. To that end, a perusal of the works cited within my thesis shows numerous Spanish language sources.

Compared to the copious quantities of English-language literature written by mostly USA- and Canada-based authors on the intersection of poverty and education, the amount of Spanish-language literature written by Mexican researchers on this topic was relatively small. One probable interpretation for this difference in quantity is that educational research in Mexico is a developing field that requires more funding, support, and attention (Latapí Sarre, 2000, 2003). The challenges facing educational researchers in Mexico include low salaries at universities, the dismantling of official research organizations, the dropping of journal subscriptions to cut costs, "and the flight of qualified Mexican educational researchers to other countries where they will receive far more lucrative opportunities" (Latapí Sarre, 2000, p. 53). Discovering this discrepancy in itself made it worth conducting my literature reviews in two languages.

Many of my English-language sources originated from research conducted within Mexico and offered important insights, but since Spanish-language sources are written usually for a primarily Mexican readership (as opposed to English language sources which are written usually for an English-speaking or international audience), I considered my Spanish-language sources to be particularly valuable when representing Mexican perspectives on educational and societal themes. I did not naively proclaim my investigation to be free of issues related to conducting research across lines of gender, social class, and race especially since my status as an academic from the First World doing research with low-income participants from the Third World was rife with potential power differentials (Dei, 1999; Patai, 1992, Scheurich & Young, 1997; Stanfield II, 1993, 1994); however, I do believe my study can be introduced as a sincere attempt to avoid the historical tendency of many international researchers who rely only on English-language secondary sources—a practice that runs a higher risk of producing monographs plagued with First World ethnocentrism (Pinar, 1995).

Although my thesis was written in English, all of my data collection (interviews, classroom observations, questionnaires, etc.) was conducted in Spanish. Thus, many of my sources were indeed primary. My high degree of fluency in Spanish, the result of having a Mexican mother, enabled me to gather insights that would not have been possible had I needed to use a translator. For example, in one section of my thesis, I illustrated the high degree of respect accorded to principals (who were mostly in their forties and fifties) by the teachers (who were mostly in their twenties) in the four schools of my case study. I explained that in order to get along well in their schools, teachers must informally acknowledge a principal's authority in countless interpersonal ways, including the use of respectful language. Next I discussed an *El Norte* newspaper article on the symptoms of job stress experienced by young persons in Mexico, in which the journalist discussed the socially-unacceptable action of using *tu por tu,* that is, communicating with one's superiors using the informal form for "you" (*tu*) instead of the formal *Usted,* among other behaviours of resistance (Molina, 2004). People, especially young persons, who engage in *tu por tu* use language as an act of defiance, rashly position themselves on an equal (rather than inferior) footing as their bosses. In my illustration of principals' authority in the four schools of my case study, I deconstructed the linguistic behaviour of participants:

> To a reader who is unfamiliar with the Spanish language, this explanation of terms of address may seem a digression, but I include it because an under-standing of this custom is imperative in the real-life context of a Mexican public school. A foreigner who is a beginner learner of the Spanish language would be quickly forgiven for any linguistic faux-pas towards the principal, but a native speaker would not so easily escape criticism.

At these four schools, I never once heard any teacher engage in *tu por tu* towards the principals—even though these beginning teachers at least in theory might have had difficulty outwardly accepting the traditional *status quo* of their new workplace. Rather, teachers (and parents and students) always addressed principals employing the respectful pronoun for "you" of *Usted* (or they conjugated the verb in a manner appropriate for *Usted*). In contrast, principals always addressed their teachers using the *tu* pronoun (or they conjugated the verb in a manner appropriate for *tu*, which can be interpreted as a mutual recognition of teachers' subordinate position relative to principals. Such minute details on culturally acceptable forms of address speak volumes on the type of sociolinguistic deference that teachers are expected to accord their principals. Ordinary verbal exchanges are embedded in concepts of social stratification, with principals at the top of the school pyramid and teachers positioned below principals. (Gormley, 2006, pp. 220–221)

Such insights into ordinary verbal exchanges would have remained unearthed without Spanish fluency. Thus, I mostly concur with Bereday (1964) that being privileged to understand "current events [and phenomena], not in one but in two or more languages, not from one but from several national [or community] points of view is a lesson in humility and understanding not easily matched anywhere" (p. 139). Truly being "let in on the intimate secrets of a nation [or community]" (Bereday, 1964, p. 139) is perhaps an impossible goal, given the complexities of conducting research across potentially conflictive lines of social class, gender, race, and life experiences (Dei, 1999; Patai, 1991; Scheurich & Young, 1997; Stanfield II, 1993, 1994). Nonetheless, in spite of the difficulties of most outside comparative researchers to grasp the ontologies of a given group as well as perhaps an insider can, language fluency is one way such a researcher can at least climb a little higher in order to see more of the landscape.

This chapter has travelled over much territory, beginning with David Wilson's discussion on the contributions of foreign languages to the heritage of comparative and international education and Pinar's views on the importance of using primary language sources in educational research. Next were forays into the stances held by Kandel, Brickman, Bereday, Noah, and Schriewer—listed by David Wilson as his role models for bringing their foreign language skills to bear on comparative international education research. After briefly touching upon the work of other comparativists such as Farrell and Hayhoe, I then interwove my views on language with my doctoral research experience in Mexico. Finally, I conclude that fluency in a community's language will help a comparative researcher better to understand that group's conceptions of reality.

On December 10th, 2006, I was privileged to be at David Wilson's burial at Pardes Shalom Cemetery, north of Toronto, alongside an intimate group of his family, friends, and colleagues. Somehow, it seemed fitting that this globe-trotting and multilingual man should be laid to rest surrounded by the quiet and rugged beauty of our northern land of Canada, the country of so many newcomers and their languages. His many contributions to the field of comparative international education have been detailed elsewhere, so the purpose of this chapter is to be a testament to David Wilson's belief in the importance of foreign language study in comparative international education research. May we, his students who represent the next generation(s) of comparative scholars, attempt to follow in his footsteps in this regard and, like him, encourage others in our field to do likewise.

REFERENCES

Bereday, G. Z. F. (1957). Some discussion of method in comparative education. *Comparative Education review, 1*(1), 13–15.

Bereday, G. Z. F. (1964). *Comparative method in education*. London: Holt, Rinehard and Winston Inc.

Bereday, G. Z. F. (1966). Memorial to Isaac Kandel (1881–1965). *Comparative Education, 2*(3), 147–150.

Bonvillain, N. (1997). *Language, culture, and communication: The meaning of messages*. Upper Saddle River, NJ: Prentice Hall.

Brickman, W. (1960). John Dewey in Russia. *Educational Theory, 1*(1), 83–86.

Chang, T. (1974). Thought, language and culture. In J. Somer & J. F. Hoy (Eds.), *The language experience* (pp. 45–57). New York: Dell Publishing.

Chomsky, N. (2006). *Language and mind* (3rd ed.). Cambridge, MA: Massachusetts Institute of Technology Press.

Cohan, T. (2000). *On Mexican time*. New York: Broadway Books.

Dei, G.J.S. (1999). Knowledge and Politics of Social Change: The Implications of Anti-Racism. *British Journal of Sociology of Education 20*(3), 395-409.Dlaska, A. (2000). Integrating culture and language learning in institution-wide language programmes. *Language, Culture and Curriculum, 13*(3), 247–263.

Dunphy, C. (2007, January 18). David Wilson, 68: Educator travelled the world. *The Toronto Star*. Retrieved November 14, 2007, from http://www.thestar.com/News/article/172046

Farrell, J. P. (1999). Twin/multiple mythologies posing as curricular truth. *Curriculum Inquiry, 29*(4), 405–411.

Findlow, S. (2004). Comparative and international perspectives on educational 'spaces.' *European Educational Research Journal, 3*(1), 400–414.

Gormley, L. (2006). *A case study of issues of success in four public primary schools in a low-income region of northern Mexico*. Unpublished doctoral dissertation, Ontario Institute for Studies in Education of the University of Toronto, Toronto, Canada.

Gormley, L. (2005). Insights for comparative education researchers from the anti-racism education discourse on epistemology, ontology, and axiology. In G. J. Sefa Dei & G. S. Johal (Eds.), *Critical issues in anti-racist research methodologies* (pp. 95–123). New York: Peter Lang.

Hayhoe, R. (1998). Language in comparative education: Three strands. Hong Kong institute of education. *Hong Kong Journal of Applied Linguistics*. Retrieved October 29, 2007, from sunzi1.lib.hku. hk/hkjo/view/5/500045.pdf

Latapí Sarre, P. (2000). *La investigación educativa en México* [Educational research in Mexico]. Mexico City, Mexico: Fondo de Cultura Económica.

Latapí Sarre, P. (2003). Un siglo de educación nacional: Una sistematización. In P. Latapí Sarre (Ed.), *Un siglo de educación en México, volume I* [A century of education in Mexico, volume I] (pp. 21–42). Mexico City, Mexico: Fondo de estudios e investigaciones Ricardo J. Zevada, Consejo Nacional para la cultura y las artes, Fondo de cultura económica.

Molina, A. (2004). *Enfrentan jóvenes esters ante incertidumbre laboral* [Youth stressed over uncertain workforce]. *El Norte*, p. 1D.

Noah, H. J. (1984). In Memoriam: George Z. F. Bereday. *Comparative Education Review, 28*(1), 1–3.

Noah, H. J. (1998). The use and abuse of comparative education. In H. J. Noah & M. A. Eckstein (Eds.), *Doing comparative education: Three decades of collaboration* (pp. 57–67). Hong Kong, China: Comparative Education Research Centre, The University of Hong Kong.

THE ROLE OF FOREIGN LANGUAGE FLUENCY

Noah, H., & Eckstein, M. (1998). *Doing comparative education: Three decades of collaboration.* Hong Kong, China: Comparative Education Research Centre, University of Hong Kong.

Null, J. W. (2007). *Peerless educator: The life and work of Isaac Leon Kandel.* New York: Peter Lang.

Null, J. W. (2004). *An introduction to Isaac Leon Kandel: Who he was and why he matters.* Paper presented at the 2004 Annual Conference Midwest History of Education Society, Chicago.

Patai, D. (1991). US academics and third world women: Is ethical research possible? In S. B. Gluck & D. Patai (Eds.), *Women's words: The feminist practice of oral history* (pp. 137–153). New York: Routledge.

Pinar, W. (1995). *Understanding curriculum: An introduction to the study of historical and contemporary curriculum discourse.* New York: Peter Lang.

Pinker, D. (1994). *The language instinct: How the mind creates language.* New York: Harper Collins.

Scheurich, P., & Young, M. (1997). Coloring epistemologies: Are our research epistemologies racially biased? *Educational Researcher, 26*(4), 4–16.

Schmelkes, S., Lavín, S., Martínez, F., & Noriega, C. (1999). *La calidad en la educación primaria: Un estudio de caso* [Quality in primary education: A case study]. Mexico City, Mexico: Fondo de Cultura Económica

Schriewer, J. (2003). Globalisation in education: Process and discourse. *Policy Futures in Education, 1*(2), 271–283.

Schriewer, J., & Holms, B. (1988). *Theories and methods in comparative education.* New York: Peter Lang.

.Schugurensky, D. (1999). Higher education restructuring in the era of globalisation: Toward a heteronomous model? In R. F. Arnove & C. A. Torres (Eds.), *Comparative education: The dialectic of the global and local* (pp. 283–304). Lanham, MD: Rowman & Littlefield.

Sherman Swing, E. (1987). In Memoriam: William W. Brickman, 1913–1986. *Comparative Education Review, 31*(1), 1–6.

Stanfield II, J. H. (1993). Epistemological considerations. In J. H. Stanfield II (Ed.), *Race and ethnicity in research methods* (pp. 16–36). Newbury Park, CA: Sage.

Stanfield II, J. H. (1994). Ethnic modelling. In N. K. Denzin & Y. S. Lincoln (Eds.), *Handbook of qualitative inquiry* (pp. 175–188). Newbury Park, CA: Sage.

Tuhiwai Smith, L. (1999). *Decolonizing methodologies: Research and indigenous peoples.* London: Zed Books.

Villenas, S., & Deyhle, D. (1999). Critical race theory and ethnographies challenging the stereotypes: Latino families, schooling, resilience and resistance: An essay review of 7 books. *Curriculum Inquiry, 29*(4), 413–446.

Wilson, D. (2003). The future of comparative and international education in a globalised world. In M. Bray (Ed.), *Comparative education: Continuing traditions, new challenges, and new paradigms* (pp. 15–33). New York: Springer.

Whorf, B. L. (1973). *Language, thought and reality: Selected writings of Benjamin Lee Whorf.* Cambridge, MA: Massachusetts Institute of Technology Press.

Louise Gormley
Educational Researcher, Toronto, Ontario, Canada

DAVID A. TURNER

18. THE TWIN FIELDS OF COMPARATIVE AND INTERNATIONAL EDUCATION

INTRODUCTION

In his 1994 Presidential Address to the Comparative International Education Society (CIES), David Wilson addressed the topic, "Comparative and International Education: Fraternal or Siamese Twins? A Preliminary Genealogy of Our Twin Fields". He examined what each field contributes to the other, and what both contribute to the development of "academic-practitioners". To paraphrase Einstein, "Comparative without International is lame: International without Comparative is blind".

Even in the thirteen years since that address, internationalisation and globalization have developed apace. To review just a few of those changes that have occurred since 1994, Wilson was speaking at a time when the Cold War had only recently ended (1989) and the World Wide Web had just been established (1990). The North American Free Trade Agreement (NAFTA) was established in 1994. Since 1995, the number of member countries within the Association of Southeast Asian Nations (ASEAN) and the European Union almost doubled, from 6 to 10 and from 12 to 27 respectively. International travel is cheaper in real terms, regional and international organizations have grown in strength, and all fields of higher education have a palpably international context.

In the light of these changes, it is appropriate to revisit the theme, and ask again: Can or should the Comparative and International Education twins be separated? In this chapter, I argue that a *comparative sensibility* is a necessary complement to an *international environment*. At the same time, the impulse toward amelioration, often associated with international engagement, is an essential discipline to the comparative imagination.

BACKGROUND

Change has been so rapid over the past twenty years that it is perhaps worth recounting those changes that have taken place in our field in recent decades. These changes began much earlier than 1994, when David Wilson chose to review the relationship between comparative and international education, and his comments need to be seen against an evolving background. Although both comparative and international education have a much longer heritage, it seems sensible to start with a review of that changing background with the founding of the United Nations in 1945.

V. Masemann et al., (Eds.), A Tribute to David N. Wilson: Clamouring for a Better World, 261–270.
© 2010 Sense Publishers. All rights reserved.

As Noah and Eckstein (1998) note in their overview of comparative education, "Since World War II these trends have accelerated and the empirical orientation of the social sciences has begun to reshape comparative education" (p. 17).

The late 1940s saw the creation of the United Nations Educational, Scientific and Cultural Organization (UNESCO) and the World Bank, two major institutions concerned with international education. The same period saw Joseph Lauwerys appointed to the first chair of comparative education at the Institute of Education, University of London, while comparative education in the United States received an additional impetus to expand, in part as a result of the GI Bill of 1944. As Epstein (2008) notes, "Beginning with the 1950s, however, courses [in comparative education] began to shift gears" (p. 10). These developments eventually led to the creation of the professional and academic bodies that represent the bulwarks of academic comparative education: the various societies of international and comparative education that make up the membership of the World Council of Comparative Education Societies (WCCES), together with the journals these bodies publish. This was not so much the beginning of either field, but it was a time of expansion and institution building. Before 1950, an individual, such as Joseph Lauwerys, could engage fully with the academic field of comparative education and be involved in the development of UNESCO. After 1950, the twin fields of comparative and international education, as Wilson described them, were becoming too large to be influenced by a single individual.

From the 1960s through the 1980s, the two fields followed divergent paths from their common origins. Comparative and international education were increasingly characterised by different concerns, pursued by different groups of people who expressed their views through different institutional frameworks. By way of illustration, Coombs (1985) notes that, "this expanding worldwide common market of high-level intellectual exchanges is probably doing a more thriving business today than ever before" (p. 331). He follows this remark by devoting the next section of his chapter to "The worrisome decline of international studies" and omits any mention of comparative education.

To caricature the situation, from the 1960s into the 1980s comparative education and international education were very different kinds of activities. Comparative education was largely an academic study based in postgraduate schools of education in universities, and primarily concerned with theory. In principle, it was recognised that comparative study offered a viable alternative to controlled, laboratory-type experiments. However, there was no agreement about the practicable arrangements and intellectual frameworks that would make it possible to take advantage of those comparative insights. The 1960s saw the publication of a range of position statements on this question, and the disputes over theory and methods dominated discussions in comparative education. The focus of attention was inwards, towards the identification of what made comparative education a discipline, a field of study, or an activity that was in any way justifiable.

In contrast, international education was primarily focused on direct intervention that would promote development. Attitudes and activities that had first led to the implementation of the Marshall Plan for the reconstruction of Western Europe were extended to other regions of the world. This work was carried out most obviously through the World Bank, but subsequently by the European Bank for Reconstruction and Development as well. With less patience for introspective, theoretical discussions, international educationalists wanted to obtain results "in the field", meaning in real schools in developing regions, not simply in the discipline. International educationalists tended to be dismissive of scholastic, methodological discussions and had a track record of working for international or bilateral agencies. Their idea of a good piece of research was more likely to be a project evaluation than a monograph on method.

Even when international education was based in a university, the concerns and backgrounds of those involved showed a large and possibly growing division between the twins. If they started out as Siamese twins in 1945, by the 1970s comparative education and international education were well on the way towards separation.

As noted above, however, this is a caricature of the situation. There were individuals in both fields of study who straddled the divide. David Wilson was one himself, who had extensive engagement with aid agencies and was engaged in the academic study and teaching of comparative education. He was initially an educational planner and international educationalist who then made the transfer into comparative education. Others might also be identified as ones who straddled the line, but whose movement was more in the other direction, from a background in academic comparative education into work with international aid agencies. Philip Jones' (1992) work with the World Bank might be one example. But in neither case does the notion of movement from one field into the other really capture the way these individuals managed to integrate the concerns of both fields in their work.

It was this complex area of interest which David Wilson sought to map in his 1994 Presidential Address, and in subsequent work. He thought that this task could best be approached by tracing personal influences and connections: where individuals had studied and with whom, and with which institutions they were affiliated. At that time, comparative education could be characterised as a number of prominent schools based in institutions such as Teachers College Columbia University, the Ontario Institute for Studies in Education of the University of Toronto, or the Institute of Education University of London. Powerful personalities led those schools and gave their adherents a firm grounding in methodological approaches. For doctrinal reasons, or the lack thereof, international education was less easy to characterise as a number of schools, but the two fields were not practised in isolation. Many international educationalists have studied in one of the schools of comparative education, at least to the Master's level.

A RAPPROCHEMENT

Sometime around the end of the 1980s, this general tide started to turn. The twins, which had been growing apart so rapidly, started to look to what they had in common, and what they could gain by closer relationships.

This process might be exemplified by changes in the United Kingdom (UK). In 1983, the British Comparative Education Society (BCES) changed its name to the British Comparative and International Education Society (BCIES). This trend, started by CIES which added "international" to its name in 1968, and the Comparative and International Education Society of Canada (CIESC), which had "international" in its name from its foundation in 1967, was pursued subsequently by a number of other professional societies in the field. In 1998, BCIES joined with the British Association of Teachers and Researchers in Overseas Education to form the British Association of International and Comparative Education (BAICE) (Sutherland, Watson & Crossley, 2007). It could be argued that the name changes of these British education societies were no more than symbolic. However, other parallel changes also indicated that the gulf between the different schools of thought was narrowing. The British Comparative Education Society had been caught up in those "paradigm wars", and was very definitely not seen as a welcoming home for those who belonged to the Institute of Education University of London camp. Those from the latter were more likely to be encouraged to see their academic affiliation within the Comparative Education Society in Europe than in the British Society. Later, the foundation of the London Association of Comparative Educationalists reified that split between London and the rest of Britain in a more concrete form, but the two societies were more the result than cause of different interests. The inclusion of the word "international" in the title of the society could even be seen as part of the fragmentation of the field, an assertion against the methodological purism which was seen to hold sway in London.

By 1988 however, the London Association had disappeared. Many of the key positions on the executive of the British Association were held by individuals who had studied at the London Institute and had been members of the London Association. They were involved in the discussions that eventually led to the creation of the British Association for International and Comparative Education. Thus, in microcosm, changes in the organization of comparative and international education in the UK reflected and illustrated changes that were happening worldwide.

This reconciliation within the field of comparative education and its move towards the attitudes of international education should not be linked, entirely or in part, to the retirement or the decline of influence of certain individuals. By the 1980s, one can see an attempt at synthesising different approaches, and of producing a "multicultural" comparative education (see in particular, Holmes, 1981). To be sure, this exercise could be partly seen as a hegemonic attempt to reduce other people's methods to one's own. However, it could also be seen in part as a genuine recognition that too much energy had been spent on emphasising differences in approach.

Incidentally, it should be noted that these events point to one of the weaknesses of David Wilson's approach of tracing influence. Knowing who a scholar has studied with is not an infallible indicator of the views of that scholar. A good number of students have subsequently found it desirable or necessary to repudiate the work of their former teacher; others have simply ignored their teachers' views in their own work. Studying with one or more of the participants in the methodological debates of the 1960s produced rather uncertain outcomes in terms of influence, as the various schools of thought were themselves fluid and changing.

When the twins started to come together, the movement was from both sides. The British Association of Teachers and Researchers in Overseas Education had acquired a journal, the *International Journal of Educational Development*. "Acquired" rather than "founded" is used here because the journal had an independent existence for some time before becoming the organ of the society, but the final impact was the same. The journal reflected the interests and concerns of the Association: above all that international education was no longer just about doing, but about developing an academic understanding of doing.

A further development of the rapprochement between comparative and international education in the UK was the establishment of the Oxford Conference, a biennial event designed to bring together practitioners of the two fields. This may have been expressed in different terms—the integration of theory and practice, discussions between academics and policy makers in the field of education for development, or the exchange of ideas among practitioners in the two fields—but the net effect was the same, a strengthening of the links between the fraternal twins.

As any comparativist would expect, similar developments occurred in other countries, although they have been institutionalised in different ways. The annual conference of the CIES in North America has attracted growing numbers of participants, including researchers whose primary area of interest would once have been described as international education. In some countries the word "international" has been added to the name of the academic association; in others this has not been thought necessary, perhaps because the term is already implicit. In the francophone world, as in the UK, there are two bodies representing the different constituencies. Both are affiliated to the WCCES, suggesting that, at some level, they have interests in common. So nearly separated in the 1970s, the two twins are now part of a more comprehensive field of comparative and international education, or at the very least are more willing to recognise their interdependence.

In that process of re-integration, much has been gained. Comparative education is no longer so inward-looking, and international education recognises the importance of critical scrutiny and theoretical analysis. However, unfortunately, much has also been lost. At a personal level, I regret the end of the paradigm wars. This is not because I particularly relish personal antagonism, or the view that one perspective is right and all others wrong. But it did concentrate the mind on the theoretical foundations of any study. Too often nowadays, it seems that there is an attitude of "get on and do the study" rather than worry about the methodological frameworks. This mindset leads to work which is poorly developed in a theoretical sense and which omits discussion of the lines of thought which make up the development of our field. However, the complaint that younger scholars are ignorant of what has gone before, which may reflect a genuine change in the field or may simply be the perennial complaint of older scholars, is not my primary concern in this paper.

265

If the twins, whether fraternal or Siamese, had once moved so far apart as to be ideal typical poles on a spectrum—with theory-driven, ivory tower comparative education at one pole, and action-driven, "can do" international education at the other—what happens as they move towards the centre ground of theoretically-based, policy-related studies? What has been happening outside our field (and perhaps within it) as a result of that rapprochement?

WATCHING OUR FLANKS

The argument being posed here is that comparative and international education have so integrated over the last fifteen years that what is of interest now is much less the relationship between those two fields, and much more what is happening at their margins. Or perhaps the question is more specifically what is happening at the edge of the field of comparative and international education field which threatens to push this whole field to the margin.

The growth of international activity in education has far exceeded the rate at which the influence of the field of comparative and international education can spread. International student numbers have grown dramatically since 1990. For example, the number of international students in Australian institutions rose from 35,000 in 1994 to 172,000 in 2006 (Commonwealth of Australia, 2006). More and more academics are taking part in international projects funded by multilateral funding bodies, such as the European Union (EU). For example, the EU consolidated its support for international collaboration on research into the Research, Technology development and Demonstration (RTD) Framework Programmes. The fourth Framework Programme (FP4) operated from 1994 to 1998 and had a total budget of 13,215 million Euros. The sixth Framework Programme (FP6), which functioned from 2002 to 2006, had a total budget of 17,500 million Euros (European Union, 2007)

Engagement with overseas systems of education on the basis of practical action but with hardly any theoretical intellectual understanding of the methodological issues involved in working across cultural boundaries is becoming the norm rather than the exception. If comparative educationalists once thought that international educationalists paid insufficient attention to theoretical issues, then we currently face a whole new host of activists who make the international educationalists of yesteryear look positively bookish and disinterested.

Universities have international offices bent on recruiting students overseas or expanding the university's offshore activities into other regions of the globe. They have research offices devoted to securing funding for international projects. Subject specialists of every stripe rush to work in international environments, armed only with the assumption that their subject discipline must be the same everywhere—after all, do they not attend international conferences with delegates from all around the world? There are also quality agencies and offices to evaluate the equivalence of qualifications (or lack thereof), attempting to redress some of the anomalies which this headlong rush into international activity on the part of academics has sparked.

Nor has the comparative branch of the family been immune from this growth in international activism. The international studies most widely known to the general public are the simple-minded, league-table comparisons derived in the mass media from the Programme for International Student Assessment (PISA) and the Trends in International Mathematics and Science Study (TIMSS), developed by the Organisation for Economic Co-operation and Development (OECD) and the International Association for the Evaluation of Educational Achievement (IEA) respectively (OECD, 2008; IEA, 2008). Policy recommendations based on these studies rarely get far beyond the level of sophistication of, "Finland (or Singapore or Japan) is at the top of the league tables, so we should copy some aspect of their educational system" (BBC, 2004).

This increase in international activity and interest in simplistic grading of outcomes is not unique to comparative/international education. It is part of a general confusion over the ends and the means of education. Or rather, it is part of a process whereby what once were means have been elevated to the status of ends. So, where academics once sought research grants so that they could do interesting research, today securing the research grant is the end in itself. Similarly, where universities once sought to recruit overseas students to provide a service for countries other than their own, and to enrich the diversity of their own learning culture, today it is enough simply to recruit overseas students. When Michael Sadler (1900) and Pedro Roselló (1943) wrote about comparative education, their concern was to come to a wiser and more subtle understanding of educational issues. Artificially manipulating the education of young people to learn more about the processes involved was deemed to be immoral. On the other hand, comparison offered the use of "natural experiments", cultural studies that would use naturally occurring cultural differences to illuminate an understanding of how processes operated in education. In short, comparative education was studied for a purpose, and that purpose was to gain a better understanding of one's own system. Now, comparisons seem to be made for no purpose at all, beyond knowing who is top of the various league tables.

There may have been no way to avoid this situation. The sphere of international education and international links in general is expanding so rapidly, it may have been inevitable that it would outstrip the rate at which the intellectual influence of comparative/international education could ripple out into a broader academic universe. Or it may have been that, by losing its specific, theoretical focus on how one can make sense of cross-national and cross-cultural activity, comparative/international education lost its grasp on the one instrument that it could legitimately have offered to the broader community of academics involved in international developments. Then again, an academic field focused inwards on methodological influence might have had still less influence beyond its own borders.

However one may evaluate the possible influence of comparative education within a wider area of educational activity, it clearly would be unwise to ignore the current situation. Perhaps one answer is to become more focused on international educational activity in general, and to ask what comparative educationalists can contribute to this growing area of activity within academe.

While the international nature of education has changed, and international education has ceded ground to the barbarian hordes who believe that all education can be assimilated to the standards of their own national conception, the situation has been no better on the flank of comparative education. The theoretical constructs which dominate the comparative education field now predominantly come from the sociology of education. "Globalization", "international capitalism" and "trans-national corporations" are mentioned with growing frequency in the literature. At the macro-level, comparative education now tells a story, which is universally applicable to the whole world, of international trends and forces which transcend the frontiers of individual states. To that extent, comparative education has ceased to be comparative at all.

There is a reason why the paradigm of comparative education is comparison at the national level (even though there are doubtless valuable comparisons to be made at both the level of larger and smaller units). The reason is that national (or in a federal system, provincial or state) legislatures set the legal framework within which international or global trends in education are worked out. One does not need to believe that a sovereign government is free from all external influences in order to see that the laws that they pass are crucial to what happens in the schools within their territory, and will set the framework within which debates will happen, local decisions will be made, regulations prescribed, and policies implemented or ignored. Globalization and other similar trends can only have an effect through the specificity of national and local institutions.

In moving towards a stronger policy orientation, with less insistence upon theoretical and methodological purism, comparative/international education has ceded ground to an understanding of education which is not only outside of the framework of comparative education, but is also fundamentally damaging to the project of comparative education.

While psychologists have sought to explore the nature of humanity through the study of the universal mechanisms of the individual intellect, sociologists have sought to explore the nature of the individual through the relationship of each to the global necessities of association. In contrast with both of these approaches, comparative educationalists have sought to understand how individuals relate to the specificities of the society in which they happen to find themselves, and how those cultures relate to the global system. Comparative education has eschewed the resort to facile answers, whether in the form of universal psychology or global trends. In the search for answers both more complex and more interesting, comparative education has faced violent debate and discussion. Perhaps it is time to recognise once again that one of the most important gifts that comparative/international education can bring to the study of global phenomena in education is unsettling and disquieting debate.

CONCLUDING REMARKS

In his CIES Presidential Address of 1994, David Wilson directed attention to the relationship between international and comparative education, and used the metaphor of fraternal or Siamese twins to depict the relationship between the two aspects of our joint field. Perhaps it looked as though the field were in the midst of sibling rivalry at that time, exacerbated by the fact that both twins were passing through an awkward adolescence. Probably what was needed then was the application of some soothing balm, and time for old wounds to heal. It could be that was the treatment that David Wilson was trying to apply.

In hindsight, however, I would suggest that even in 1994, turbulent adolescence was coming to an end and the family was coming together into a more functional unit. But, to extend David Wilson's metaphor to breaking point, like many families, there were tender subjects which would not be wise to raise, or which should only be raised with the anticipation of provoking a bitter fight. And so, as in many families, things remained unsaid to be forgotten or left to fester.

It must be remembered though that, by suppressing lively debate, we may leave ourselves open to being pushed to the margins by others who have less insight into the issues in the field than we have.

I think of myself as a comparative educationalist, even though I rarely, if ever, actually engage in explicit, national comparisons. However, I think that the spirit of comparative education rests in the desire to understand how the things that we would not choose to do ourselves make sense to somebody else. As Broadfoot (1999) describes it, comparative education is not so much a context, more a way of life. And more than the desire, comparative education provides some of the intellectual tools for accomplishing that most difficult of tasks, while international education provides some of the experience that keeps theory grounded and makes sure that we do not become lost in flights of theoretical fancy. Together the twin fields are stronger.

But perhaps more importantly, together, comparative and international education can provide a valuable corrective to much of the work that goes on in fields close to its centres of interest. This work includes not least the Gadarene rush to internationalise education for commercial reasons and for reasons of reputation, and the theoretical flights of fancy which constitute the sociology of education. Nor should one forget the current rise in genetic explanations of every conceivable aspect of society, including education, to which comparative study and international education might offer a valuable counterpoise.

David Wilson was undoubtedly right when he suggested that we need, periodically, to examine our field and be clear that we can see how the parts interact. In 1994 he focused on the internal relationships of the field, and that was probably completely appropriate to the time. However, at the present time, when we review the relationships of our field, the external relationships may be more important. It may be time to risk opening some old debates and to arm ourselves against encroachment from outside. By thoughtfully revisiting some of the methodological debates that shaped the field of comparative and international education, though hopefully without replaying some of the more acrimonious and heated scenes, it may be possible to find the tools to resist the encroachment of universalising analysis from sociologists, economists, and psychologists. It may also be possible to resist the encroachment of international educational activism which is little more than a renewed form of "travellers' tales". Our flanks may still be protected, but only if we use the full resource available in comparative and international education to resist simplistic and globalizing analysis, and certainly not if those who care about comparative and international education connive in its colonisation by other intellectual fields.

REFERENCES

BBC. (2004, December 7). *Finland tops global school table*. British Broadcasting Corporation. Retrieved October 30, 2007, from http://news.bbc.co.uk/1/hi/education/4073753.stm

Broadfoot, P. (1999). Not so much a context, more a way of life? Comparative education in the 1990s. In R. Alexander, P. Broadfoot, & D. Phillips (Eds.), *Learning from comparing: New directions in comparative educational research* (pp. 21–31). Oxford: Symposium Books.

Commonwealth of Australia. (2006). *2006 Annual international student statistics*. Canberra: Department of Education, Science and Training. Retrieved October 30, 2007, from http://aei.dest.gov.au/AEI/MIP/Statistics/StudentEnrolmentAndVisaStatistics/2006/2006_TimeSeriesGraph_pdf.pdf

Coombs, P. H. (1985). *The world crisis in education: The view from the eighties*. Oxford: Oxford University Press.

Epstein, E. H. (2008). Crucial benchmarks in the professionalization of comparative education. In C. Wolhuter, N. Popov, M. Manzon, & B. Leutwyler (Eds.), *Comparative education at universities worldwide* (pp. 9–24). Sofia: Bureau for Educational Services.

European Union. (2007). *CORDIS guidance and support*. Luxembourg: Community Research and Development Information Service. Retrieved October 30, 2007, from http://cordis.europa.eu/guidance/services_en.html

Holmes, B. (1981). *Comparative education: Some considerations of method*. London: George Allen and Unwin.

International Association for the Evaluation of Educational Achievement. (2008). *International association for the evaluation of educational achievement reports and publications*. Retrieved September 24, 2008, from http://www.iea.nl

Jones, P. W. (1992). *World Bank financing of education: Lending, learning, and development*. London: Routledge.

Noah, H. J., & Eckstein, M. A. (1998). *Doing comparative education: Three decades of collaboration*. Hong Kong: Comparative Education Research Centre, University of Hong Kong.

Organisation for Economic Co-operation and Development. (2008). *OECD Programme for International Student Assessment (PISA)*. Retrieved September 24, 2008, from http://pisa.oecd.org

Rosselló, P. (1943). *Les Précurseurs du Bureau International d'Education*. Geneva: International Bureau of Education.

Sadler, M. (1900). *How far can we learn anything of practical value from the study of foreign systems of education?* Guildford: Surrey Advertiser.

Sutherland, M. B., Watson, K., & Crossley, M. (2007). The British Association for International and Comparative Education (BAICE). In V. Masemann, M. Bray, & M. Manzon (Eds.), *Common interests, uncommon goals: Histories of the World Council of Comparative Education Societies and its members* (pp. 155–169). Hong Kong: Springer and the Comparative Education Research Centre, University of Hong Kong.

Wilson, D. N. (1994). Comparative and international education: Fraternal or Siamese twins? A preliminary genealogy of our twin fields. *Comparative Education Review, 38*(4), 449–486.

David A. Turner
University of Glamorgan

NOTES ON THE CONTRIBUTORS

EDITORS

Kara JANIGAN is a Ph.D. candidate in the Comparative, International and Development Education Programme at OISE-UT. Her doctoral research focuses on gender issues and schooling in rural Tajikistan. As a teacher and teacher educator, Kara has worked in Canada, Eritrea, Ethiopia, and Malawi.
Correspondence: Comparative, International and Development Education Programme, Room 7-104, OISE, University of Toronto, 252 Bloor St. West, Toronto, ON, M5S 1V6, Canada.
Email: kjanigan@oise.utoronto.ca

Suzanne MAJHANOVICH is Professor Emerita/Adjunct Research Professor at the University of Western Ontario. She is a former President of the Comparative and International Education Society of Canada (CIESC), is Editor of the Society's journal, *Canadian and International Education*, and is also Chair of the WCCES Publication Standing Committee.
Correspondence: Faculty of Education, Room 1122A, University of Western Ontario, 1137 Western Rd., London, ON, N6G 1G7, Canada.
Email: smajhano@uwo.ca

Vandra MASEMANN was a colleague of David Wilson's from 1972. Like him, she was President of the World Council of Comparative Education Societies, and President of the US-based Comparative and International Education Society (CIES), and President of the Comparative and International Education Society of Canada (CIESC).
Correspondence: Comparative, International and Development Education Programme, Room 7-107, OISE, University of Toronto, 252 Bloor St. West, Toronto, ON, M5S 1V6, Canada.
Email: vmasemann@oise.utoronto.ca

Nhung TRUONG has is currently an Assistant Programme Specialist in education at the UNESCO Institute for Statistics and a graduate student in the Comparative, International and Development Education Programme at OISE/UT. She has also been a researcher at the UNESCO International Bureau of Education.
Correspondence: Comparative, International and Development Education Programme, Room 7-104, OISE, University of Toronto, 252 Bloor St. West, Toronto, ON, M5S 1V6, Canada.
Email: truonghuenhung@gmail.com

AUTHORS

Kingsley BANYA is former Interim Dean and Professor of Curriculum Theory and Comparative & International Education at Florida International University in Miami, Florida, USA. He has published extensively about his research on NGOs, development projects, higher education, and educational reform in Africa. His research on NGOs and higher education in Sub-Saharan Africa has been published all over the world. Currently Dr. Banya is writing a book on NGOs and development in sub-Saharan Africa. Dr. Banya was a student of David Wilson in the early 1980s when David introduced him to the politics of development in Third World countries.
Correspondence: 5340 SW 139 Street, Miami, Florida, 33196, USA.
Email: banyak@fiu.edu, kingsley.banya@gmail.com

Paromita CHAKRAVARTI is Joint-Director, School of Women's Studies and Senior Lecturer, Department of English, Jadavpur University, Calcutta, India. She completed her doctoral studies in English at Oxford University, UK. Her work in the School of Women's Studies has focused on education and sexuality. She has coordinated national and international projects on gender representations in school textbooks, sexuality education, women's higher education, homeless women, as well as women and children and HIV/AIDS. She has worked with the state and central governments, the Women's Commission (national and state) and HIV control boards on educational policy related to education, health and trafficking in India.
Correspondence: 26 Townsend Road, Calcutta -700025, India.
Email: chakravarti6@gmail.com

Kelly CROWLEY-THOROGOOD is a doctoral student in comparative and international education at the Faculty of Education at the University of Western Ontario, Canada. She is currently working on completing her thesis on post-conflict education reform in Cambodia. Her interests include indigenous education, multi-national influence on education, post-conflict reform, globalization theory, and Southeast Asia. She has presented several papers on education reforms in Cambodia and indigenous education in Mexico and Canada.
Correspondence: Faculty of Education, The University of Western Ontario, 1137 Western Road, London, Ontario, N6G 1G7, Canada.
Email: kcrowley@uwo.ca

John FIEN is a Professor of Sustainability in the Innovation Leadership programme of Royal Melbourne Institute of Technology (RMIT) University in Australia, where he is responsible for supporting research on social, environmental, and economic sustainability across the Business and Design and Social Context Portfolios. His research focuses on social change processes for advancing sustainable development, particularly in the fields of organizational learning, public participation, youth culture and citizen science. He is also a specialist in teacher education and professional development, especially through action research, collaborative learning and multimedia approaches. He has worked extensively with UNESCO, and also OECD, the International Union for Conservation of Nature (IUCN) and the United Nations Environment Programme (UNEP) in the areas of education and sustainability.

Correspondence: Design and Social Context Office, RMIT University, GPO Box 2476, Melbourne, Victoria, 3001, Australia.

Macleans A. GEO-JAJA is Professor of Economics and Education at Brigham Young University. He spent many years as an Economics Professor at the University
of Port Harcourt in Nigeria. He has conducted research in the areas of Poverty, Economics of Education, and International Development Education. His works are widely published in international journals and in edited books. He has undertaken policy studies for a wide range of international organizations including theWorld Bank and UNDP. In 2007, he was appointed a member of The Nigerian National Think Tank. Since 2007, he has served as a Technical Expert to the Chinese Government on Sino-African Relations.

Correspondence: Professor of Economics and Education, David O. McKay School of Education, Brigham Young University, 306P MCKB, Provo, Utah 84602-5092, USA.
Email: geo-jaja@byu.edu

Ratna GHOSH is James McGill Professor and William C. Macdonald Professor of Education at McGill University in Montreal, Quebec where she was Dean of Education. Her research and teaching on women, education and development, and multicultural education reflect her research interest in issues related to diversity and discrimination. She is a Member of the Order of Canada, Officer of the Order of Quebec, and Fellow of the Royal Society of Canada. She was President of the Shastri Indo-Canadian Institute and is incoming CIES (US) President for 2011–12.

Correspondence: 3700 McTavish Street, McGill University, Montreal, Quebec, H3A 1Y2, Canada.
Email: ratna.ghosh@mcgill.ca

Louise GORMLEY, Ph.D., is an educational researcher who has both led and assisted with major research projects for two school boards, an elementary teachers' federation, a newcomer organization, and a non-governmental organization. Her doctoral research was a mixed methods case study of four public primary schools in northern Mexico that explored issues of success amidst conditions of poverty. Believing strongly that foreign language fluency is an integral component of comparative education research endeavours, she is a life-long learner, with varying

levels of success, of several languages including Spanish, French, Mandarin Chinese, Japanese, and Farsi.
Correspondence: 3377 Folkway Drive, Mississauga, Ontario, L5L 2E3, Canada.
Email: louise.gormley@gmail.com

Edward R. HOWE is an Assistant Professor in the Faculty of Education at Utsunomiya University. He has worked in Japanese universities since 2003. Prior to that, Edward was a high school science teacher in British Columbia, Canada. He obtained his M.A. from the University of British Columbia and Ph.D. from the Ontario Institute for Studies in Education of the University of Toronto. His main research interests are teacher education and comparative and international education. In particular, his focus is on the complex process of how one becomes a professional teacher through both the formal and informal mechanisms associated with teacher induction.
Correspondence: Assistant Professor, Faculty of Education, Utsunomiya University, 350 Mine-machi, Utsunomiya, Tochigi, 321-8505, Japan.
Email: ehowe@cc.utsunomiya-u.ac.jp

Yaacov IRAM is former Dean of the Faculty of Social Sciences (2007) and the Chairholder of the Josef Burg Chair in Education for Human Values, Tolerance and Peace-UNESCO Chair on Human Rights, Democracy, Peace and Tolerance. He is Professor of History and Comparative/International Education at the School of Education of Bar-Ilan University, Israel. His research interests, teaching and publications are in comparative education and social history of education affecting educational policy. He has published books, numerous articles in American and European journals, chapters in books and encyclopedias on educational policy in secondary education, universities, teacher training, colleges, multiculturalism and related social issues in Israel from comparative and historical perspectives.
Correspondence: School of Education, Bar-Ilan University, 52900 Ramat-Gan, Israel.
Email: Iram@mail.biu.ac.il

Ewa KOWALSKI is currently an independent researcher in Ontario, Canada. She obtained her Ph.D. degree in Comparative and International Education from the Ontario Institute for Studies in Education at the University of Toronto. She has worked on many research projects based in Poland and Canada, encompassing academic and policy-oriented research. Her previous experience also includes serving as a graduate research assistant for Dr. David N. Wilson and as a presenter during his last teaching project, *The Viet Nam Study Tours Program* in 2006.
Correspondence: 3147 Joel Kerbel Place, Mississauga, Ontario, L4Y 0B1, Canada.
Email: ekowalski@rogers.com

Rupert MACLEAN is currently Director of the Centre for Lifelong Learning Research and Development, and Chair Professor of International Education, at the Hong Kong Institute of Education. He is concurrently Senior Research Fellow, Dept. of Education, Oxford University; and Adjunct Professor of International Education at East China University, Shanghai, and at RMIT University, Melbourne. Professor Maclean was previously Director of the UNESCO-UNEVOC in Bonn, Germany; Director of Secondary Education in UNESCO Paris; Director ad interim of UNESCO Bangkok; and Chief Technical Advisor for a UNDP funded project to strengthen and upgrade teacher education throughout Myanmar. He worked very closely with David Wilson over several years as joint Editor-in-Chief of the recently published *International Handbook on Education for the Changing World of Work: Bridging Academic and Vocational Learning* (Springer, 2009).

Correspondence: Director, Centre for Lifelong Learning Research and Development; Chair Professor of International Education, Department of International Education and Lifelong Learning (IELL), The Hong Kong Institute of Education, 10 Lo Ping Road, Tai Po, New Territories, Hong Kong SAR, China.
Email: maclean@ied.edu.hk

Nava MASLOVATY (deceased) served in the Israel Defense Forces in the 1960s as a Hebrew teacher of immigrant soldiers and a teaching coordinator. In the 1970s she was the coordinator of the Committee for Educational Planning for Disadvantaged Students in the education system. She taught courses dealing with values, assessments, social and moral development, school environments and democratic attitudes. Her research fields included values citizenship education, the development of moral behavior, teacher ethics, and measurement and evaluation of educational achievements. She won competitive research grants awarded by the Ministry of Education and the Teachers' Union.

Correspondence: School of Education, Bar-Ilan University, 52900 Ramat-Gan, Israel. Regrettably, Dr Maslovaty suffered an untimely death on 11 October 2009.

Mina O'DOWD is Associate Professor at Lund University in Sweden. She was awarded her Ph.D. in International and Comparative Education by Stockholm University. O'Dowd has conducted both school-based and policy-oriented research. O'Dowd is President of the Nordic Comparative and International Education Society (NOCIES). She is a former member of the International Advisory Board of *Compare* and is currently a member of the International Advisory Board for *Research in Comparative and International Education.* O'Dowd's work is distinguished by its focus on the philosophy and sociology of education and a special interest in methodological and theoretical issues in education research.

Correspondence: Associate Professor, Department of Sociology, Lund University, Paradisgatan 5, Building G, Box 114, 22100 Lund, Sweden.
Email: Mina.O_Dowd@soc.lu.se

Eli SHITREET earned his Ph.D. at Bar Ilan University. He is the director of Children and Youth Village and was an instructor at Bar Ilan University. He studied the relationship between values and behaviour as well as acculturation processes and adaptation of adolescents of Ethiopian origin at youth village and models for immigrants' absorption in schools.
Correspondence: Talpiot, Children's Village, Hadera, Neve Haim, Israel.

Suwanda (H. J.) SUGUNASIRI is Founder of Nalanda College of Buddhist Studies, Toronto, and Adjunct Faculty at Trinity, University of Toronto. A former student of David Wilson, he is also Founding Editor of the *Canadian Journal of Buddhist Studies*. His latest publication is *Rebirth as Empirical Basis for the Buddha's Four Noble Truths* (The Sumeru Press, 2010). Author of three poetry collections, including *Obama Ji* (2009), he was featured in the Toronto Harbourfront Reading Series and on June Callwood's *National Treasures*, Vision TV. Past President of the Buddhist Council of Canada, and columnist in the *Toronto Star*, he has been advisor to governments on multiculturalism.
Correspondence: Trinity College, 6 Hoskin Avenue, Toronto, Ontario, M5S 1H8, Canada.
E-mail: suwanda.sugunasiri@utoronto.ca

Elizabeth Sherman SWING is Professor Emerita at Saint Joseph's University (USA) and an Honorary Fellow of the Comparative and International Education Society. Her research has focused on languages in conflict – and on minority and immigrant education in Europe and the United States. In 1990 she was named *Ridder in de Kroonorde* [Knight in the Order of the Crown] for her work on the Belgian language controversy. She served as Historian of the Comparative and International Education Society from 1999 to 2008, the first to hold this office.
Correspondence: 3500 West Chester Pike, J-303, Newtown Square, PA 19073, USA.
Email: eswing1@verizon.net

Norma TARROW is Professor Emeritus, California State University, Long Beach. She has been a Fulbright Scholar in Spain and Mexico and Director of California State University International Programs in Israel and Mexico. A Visiting Scholar at the Institut de Ciències de Educació, Universitat de Barcelona and at the Centre for Multicultural Education, University of London, she was elected Honorary Fellow of the Comparative and International Education Society in 2001. Her research interests include human rights and intercultural education. She has specialized in the education of indigenous minority groups, with publication of several books, chapters and articles in journals such as *Prospects, Educational Research Quarterly, International Journal of Early Childhood, Canadian and International Education, Compare,* and *Hagar.*

Correspondence: Professor Emeritus, California State University, Long Beach, USA. Israel: Hapalmach 23/10 Ramat Hasharon.
Email: ntarrow@csulb.edu

Carlos Alberto TORRES is Professor of Social Sciences and Comparative Education, and Director of the Paulo Freire Institute at the University of California, Los Angeles, USA. He is the Founding Director of the Paulo Freire Institute in São Paulo, Brazil (1991), Buenos Aires, Argentina (2003), and UCLA (2002), former Director of the Latin American Center at UCLA (1995–2005), Past President of the Comparative International Education Society (CIES), and Past President of the Research Committee of Sociology of Education, of the International Sociological Association. He is author, co-author or editor of more than 60 books and 250 research articles and chapters in books and encyclopedias.

Correspondence: Graduate School of Education and Information Studies, UCLA, 2018 Moore Hall. Box 951521. Los Angeles, California 90095-1521, USA.

David A. TURNER is Professor of Education at the University of Glamorgan, Wales, UK. He works in the Faculty of Humanities and Social Sciences where he has responsibility for promoting research in education. His research interests include the history of progressive education, policy, finance and governance of educational institutions, comparative education and theory in education studies. He has published widely on these topics, and has been a visiting lecturer in Japan, Mexico, Canada, and the USA. His books *Theory of Education* (Continuum, 2004) and *Theory and Practice of Education* (Continuum, 2007) have received very positive reviews. His latest book *Using the Medical Model in Education* (Continuum, 2009) was published in November 2009.

Correspondence: Professor of Education, Faculty of Humanities and Social Sciences, University of Glamorgan, Pontypridd, CF37 1DL, UK.
Email: dturner@glam.ac.uk

Derek A. URAM was a student of David N. Wilson in 2001. He completed his Master's degree in comparative, international and development education at the Ontario Institute for Studies in Education of the University of Toronto (OISE/UT) where he focused on educational policy in India, with specific focus on India's Scheduled Castes. Both before and after his time at graduate school, Derek traveled extensively throughout East Asia and the Indian subcontinent. He currently lives in Seoul, South Korea, and is further enhancing his international experience by teaching in an elementary school, which, without a doubt, has been his most challenging and rewarding job to date.

Correspondence: 609 Donam 2-Dong, Seongbuk-Gu, Seoul, 136-062, South Korea.
Email: derekuram@yahoo.com

M. Petronella VAN NIEKERK is currently an Associate Professor in the Department Educational Studies at the University of South Africa (Unisa). She is primarily involved in the teaching of Comparative and International Education in the B. Ed (Hons.) programme in distance education mode. She is also supervising Master's and Doctoral students, in the fields of Comparative Education, Philosophy of Education, and Education Management. Her current research interests and publications are to do with education provision in the developing world, the impact of values and ideologies on education, notions of indigenous knowledge systems, and postmodern theories of education.

Correspondence: Department of Educational Studies, AJH 6-119, Muckleneuk Campus, Preller Street, PO Box 392, Pretoria, 0003, Unisa, South Africa.
Email: vniekmp@unisa.ac.za

Anthony R. WELCH is Professor of Education, University of Sydney, and specialises in education policy, with particular interests in Australia, East Asia, and Southeast Asia. His current work focuses largely on higher education reforms, an area where he has consulted to governments and international agencies. A recent Fulbright *New Century Scholar*, he has also been Visiting Professor in Germany, USA, Japan, UK, Hong Kong, and France. Recent books include *The Professoriate* (2005), *Education, Change and Society* (2007), and *The Dragon and the Tiger Cubs* (on China-ASEAN relations) (2010). His next book is on South-East Asian higher Education. Professor Welch also directs the nationally-funded research project: *The Chinese Knowledge Diaspora*.

Correspondence: Professor of Education, Faculty of Education & Social Work (A.35), University of Sydney, New South Wales 2006, Australia.
Email: anthony.welch@sydney.edu.au

Melissa WHITE is a lecturer in the Centre for Labour Market Studies at the University of Leicester. Her primary research interests are adult education, the political economy of training, public policy, comparative education, post-industrialism, regional development, and globalization. She is currently working on a project on political leadership and economic development as well as writing in the area of online research methods. Melissa received her M.A. and Ph.D. in the Collaborative Programme in Comparative, International and Development Education, at the Ontario Institute for Studies in Education at the University of Toronto. She fondly remembers David Wilson as a supervisor, mentor, teacher and friend.

Correspondence: Lecturer, Centre for Labour Market Studies, University of Leicester, 7-9 Salisbury Road, Leicester, LE1 7QR, United Kingdom.
Email: melissa.white@le.ac.uk

Charl C. WOLHUTER studied at the Rand Afrikaans University, the University of Pretoria and the University of Stellenbosch, South Africa. He obtained a doctorate in Comparative Education at the University of Stellenbosch. He was a junior lecturer in History of Education and Comparative Education at the University of Pretoria and a senior lecturer in History of Education and Comparative

Education at the University of Zululand. Prof. Wolhuter is currently professor in Comparative Education at the Potchefstroom Campus of the North-West University, South Africa. He is the author of various books and articles on History of Education and Comparative Education.

Correspondence: Nagraadse Skool vir Opvoedkunde, Graduate School of Education, North West University, Potchefstroom Campus, South Africa.
Email: Charl.Wolhuter@nwu.ac.za

INDEX

general, 35, 37, 44, 45, 54, 63,
104, 119, 152, 180, 185,
214–218
health, 26, 147, 149, 167, 171, 194
missionary, xxii, 3–4
non-formal, 7, 25, 36, 68
peace, 42, 167
postsecondary, 60, 61
primary, 5, 9, 11, 25, 38, 80, 164,
165, 195, 230
private, 44, 60–61, 64, 227, 229
provision of, xxii, xxv, 4–6, 60,
145
public, 118, 166, 241, 249
quality of, 11, 70, 193, 201, 228,
241
reform, xxvii, 7, 52, 55–64, 207,
208, 213–218
secondary, 38, 45, 54, 55, 57,
146, 154
state, 115, 121–125, 132
system, 7, 8, 11, 17, 19, 20, 28, 33,
36, 38, 40, 43, 46, 47, 52–64, 117,
118, 120, 121, 123, 124, 126, 127,
132, 139, 148, 150, 155, 196, 213,
214, 217, 222, 223, 229
teacher, xx, 9, 99, 102, 106, 109,
110
technical, xviii, xix, xxiii, 18, 19,
23, 25, 35, 67, 69, 71, 72, 74, 77,
79, 223, 232, 233
tertiary, 5, 19, 20, 23, 24, 28, 38,
44, 52, 54, 56, 60, 61, 201
university, 201, 218, 222, 262–264
vocational, xix, xx–xxiii, xxvi,
17–20, 23, 25, 33–47, 52–64,
67–81, 129, 149, 163, 165, 167,
210, 221
educational
context, xxv, 139, 140
development, xxii, xxiv, xxv,
223, 228, 265
expansion, xxii, xxvii, 3–13, 37,
41, 54, 56, 60, 70–72, 77, 78,
148, 153, 223, 229, 241, 262

goals, xxiii, xxvi, 12, 41, 42, 52,
56, 57, 60, 61, 139, 163–166,
169–170, 174, 208–211, 216,
218, 219, 222–224, 228, 230, 234
inequalities, xxvii, 12, 67, 68, 72,
75–80, 192, 221, 241
institutions, xx, xxv, 13, 69, 71, 74,
193, 197, 202, 228, 233, 240, 245
markets, 192, 193, 202
quality, 5, 27, 38
research, xxiv, 100, 110–111,
245, 248–251, 255, 257
researcher, 256
education/educational
policies, xxiv, xxviii, 26, 54,
116–127, 132, 139, 152, 233
reform(s), xxvi, xxvii, 7, 21, 51,
52, 55–64, 117, 118, 207, 208,
213–218
Education for All (EFA), xxii, 43,
44, 166
Education for sustainable
development (ESD), xxv, xxvi,
xxviii, 163–175, 243
educators, xxvii, 88, 110, 111, 132,
152, 155, 157, 158, 160, 164,
171, 196, 239, 252
efficiency, 33, 38, 39, 46, 169, 192,
194–197, 202–203
Egypt, 93
employment, xxiii, xxvi, 8, 26, 34,
36, 37, 39, 40, 42–46, 54, 59, 60,
63, 67–75, 77, 78, 80, 81, 124,
146, 164, 169, 172, 178–182,
184–187, 216, 228, 230
England, 4, 89, 92, 96, 194, 196. *See
also* United Kingdom (UK)
London, 88, 262–264
Oxford, 265
Surrey, 102, 106
enrolments, 4–6, 9, 11, 12, 38, 40, 41,
45, 54, 58, 71, 79, 119, 135, 149,
195, 199, 200, 214, 218, 222, 230
equality
political, 130

Lightning Source UK Ltd.
Milton Keynes UK
09 June 2010

155341UK00001B/41/P

9 789460 912603